Dirty War is the first comprehensive look at Rho⟨ biological warfare (CBW) during their long coun⟨.._ nationalists. Having declared its Independence from Great Britain ... government – made up of European settlers and their descendants – almost immediately faced a growing threat from native African nationalists. In the midst of this long and terrible conflict, Rhodesia resorted to chemical and biological weapons against an elusive guerrilla adversary. A small team made up of a few scientists and students worked at a remote Rhodesian 'fort' to produce lethal agents for use. Cloaked in the strictest secrecy, these efforts were overseen by a battle-hardened and ruthless officer of Rhodesia's Special Branch and his select team of policemen.

Answerable only to the head of Rhodesian Intelligence and the Prime Minister, these men – working alongside Rhodesia's elite counterguerrilla military unit, the Selous Scouts – developed ingenious means to deploy their poisons against the insurgents. The effect of the poisons and disease agents devastated the insurgent groups both inside Rhodesia and at their base camps in neighboring countries. At times in the conflict, the Rhodesians thought that their poisons effort would bring the decisive blow against the guerrillas. For months at a time, the Rhodesian use of CBW accounted for higher casualty rates than conventional weapons. In the end, however, neither CBW use – nor conventional battlefield successes – could turn the tide. Lacking international political or economic support, Rhodesia's fate from the outset was doomed. Eventually, the conflict was settled by the ballot box and Rhodesia became independent Zimbabwe in April 1980.

Dirty War is the culmination of nearly two decades of painstaking research and interviews of dozens of former Rhodesian officers who either participated, or were knowledgeable about, the top-secret development and use of CBW. The book also draws on the handful of remaining classified Rhodesian documents to tell the story of the CBW program. *Dirty War* combines all of the available evidence to provide a compelling account of how a small group of men prepared and used CBW to devastating effect against a largely unprepared and unwitting enemy.

Looking at the use of CBW in the context of the Rhodesian conflict, *Dirty War* provides unique insights into the motivation behind CBW development and use by States – especially by States combating internal insurgencies. As the norms against CBW use have seemingly eroded with CW use evident in Iraq – and, most recently, in Syria – the lessons of the Rhodesian experience are all the more valid and timely.

Dr Glenn Cross currently works for the US Government, where he oversaw his department's biological weapons (BW) analysis. Since the early 1990s, he has worked on BW issues for several government agencies.

From September 2008 to October 2010, Dr Cross was the deputy national intelligence officer for WMD & Proliferation – responsible for biological weapons issues on the director of national intelligence's National Intelligence Council. He was also a post-doctoral fellow at Georgetown University, where he conducted an exhaustive study of the Rhodesian CBW program as an example of a CBW program that had slipped under the radar of most other nations.

Dr Cross has been quoted in books and periodicals on biological weapons and recently was acknowledged in a groundbreaking study on the Japanese CBW terrorist group, Aum Shinrikyo. Dr Cross received his AB from Columbia University in History and Political Science, an MA from King's College, London in War Studies, a second MA from George Mason University and a PhD in Biodefense from George Mason University.

DIRTY WAR

Rhodesia and Chemical Biological Warfare 1975-1980

Glenn Cross

Helion & Company

Helion & Company Limited
26 Willow Road
Solihull
West Midlands
B91 1UE
England
Tel. 0121 705 3393
Fax 0121 711 4075
Email: info@helion.co.uk
Website: www.helion.co.uk
Twitter: @helionbooks
Visit our blog at http://blog.helion.co.uk/

Published by Helion & Company 2017
Designed and typeset by Mach 3 Solutions Ltd (www.mach3solutions.co.uk
Cover designed by Paul Hewitt, Battlefield Design (www.battlefield-design.co.uk)
Printed by Lightning Source, Milton Keynes, Buckinghamshire

ISBN 978-1-911512-12-7

British Library Cataloguing-in-Publication Data.
A catalogue record for this book is available from the British Library.

For details of other military history titles published by Helion & Company
Limited, contact the above address, or visit our website: http://www.helion.co.uk

We always welcome receiving book proposals from prospective authors.

This work is dedicated to my beloved wife Elizabeth, without whose help, understanding and unfailing love, none of this would have been imaginable. She is my truest love and constant support, and her love and laughter are the balm that soothed me through often troubled times.

This book also is dedicated to my two extraordinary children, Rebecca and Kaitlyn – may they both share my unquenchable love of learning. *Intellectum valde amat et aude sapere.*

Contents

List of Figures

Credits for Figures

Photographs have been provided courtesy – and with the permission – of the late Peter Stiff (Peter Stiff collection), Dr J.C.A. Davies, William Higham, the collection of the late Dr Margaretha Issacson, Daniel Stannard and Dr James Watt. The copyright holders of some photographs are not acknowledged, although the author has made every effort to establish authorship. In some cases, authorship has been lost in the mists of time, or blown away by the winds of war and upheaval. The author will make every reasonable effort to amend or add credits in subsequent editions, and to make the necessary arrangements with those copyright holders unknown to him at the time of publication.

Preface

Rhodesia: Britain's last colony in Africa

Named after the 19th century British business magnate Cecil Rhodes, Rhodesia*
was the product of a royal charter – granted in 1889 – that allowed the British South
Africa Company (BSAC) to administer an area stretching from the Limpopo River
in the south to Lake Tanganyika in the north. The charter also allowed the BSAC to
trade and enter into agreements with the African kingdoms and to own, sell and trade
land. The charter only asked that the company develop the territory, respect existing
African laws, allow free trade and permit the free exercise of religion. In practice, the
BSAC – focused on mineral exploitation – used force to exert concessions from the
African rulers and compelled the local African population to provide cheap labor.

To enforce the company's domination of the native population, the BSAC created
a paramilitary, mounted police force: the British South Africa Police (BSAP). The
BSAP was instrumental in the settling of Rhodesia from the outset. In 1890, the
BSAP protected the Pioneer Column as it entered Matabeleland from the south and
moved to the site of Salisbury – raising the Union Jack there on 13 September 1890.
The BSAP also was critical to combating an African uprising† in 1896 that threatened
to eradicate the fledgling settlements. Failing to generate a profit, the BSAC negotiated in 1922 with South Africa to assume control of the territory. The Rhodesian
settlers scuppered those plans when they rejected union with South Africa in the
1922 referendum in favor of responsible government. With responsible government,
Rhodesia became a self-governing colony of Great Britain in 1923.

Geographically landlocked, Rhodesia (now Zimbabwe) is located in Southern
Africa and is bordered on the north and east by Mozambique (border length is
1,231km), the south by South Africa (border length is 225km) and Botswana (border
length is 813km), and the west by Zambia (border length is 797km).[1] The total area
of Rhodesia totaled 390,580km², or approximately the same size as the State of

---

*   For much of its colonial history, the territory was officially and legally known as Southern
Rhodesia. With the Independence of Northern Rhodesia (now Zambia) in 1964, Southern
Rhodesia was more commonly known as simply Rhodesia – a name the Salisbury Government
adopted and then formalized at the time of their Unilateral Declaration of Independence
(UDI) in 1965. British authorities insisted that the colony's legal name was Southern Rhodesia.
Zimbabwe-Rhodesia reverted briefly to the British nomenclature in late 1979 when British
governor Lord Soames arrived to oversee the transition to majority rule. For purposes here, the
name 'Rhodesia' will be used throughout.

†   That uprising is termed the 'First *Chimurenga*' (roughly translated from Shona as 'revolutionary struggle'), while the 1965 to 1980 insurgency is referred to as the 'Second *Chimurenga*'.

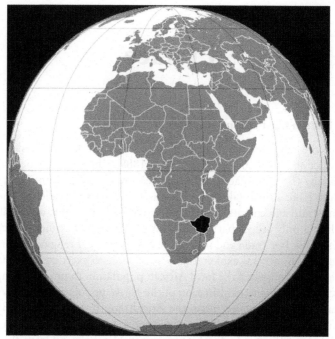

Figure 0.1 The location of Rhodesia (now Zimbabwe). (Source:
<www.wikipedia.org> CCL)

Montana (381,156km²), or slightly less than half the size of Turkey (780,580km²).
The topography is high plateau with a central plateau stretching from the south-west
to the north-north-east. The capital, Salisbury (now Harare), is located in the north-
central region. The Rhodesian climate is tropical, with a rainy season occurring from
November to March each year.[2]

Until Rhodesia became Zimbabwe in 1980, a small European minority – largely
of British origin – governed the colony. In the last official Rhodesian census (1969),
the population of Rhodesia numbered 228,296 Europeans, 15,153 Colored (mixed
race) and 8,965 Asians.[*] A separate African census conducted a month later counted
4,846,930 Blacks.[3] The ratio in 1969 of the black population to immigrant groups
was approximately 21:1. After the end of World War II, an influx of immigrants
(largely British) seeking the warmer climate, low unemployment, lower taxes and
higher standard of living afforded them in Rhodesia resulted in a jump in the colony's
European population. According to a now-declassified 1976 CIA economic assessment: 'Rhodesia's white 'European' population now totals 277,000 or roughly 5
percent of the African population'.

---

[*]   The 1969 census was the last official census in Rhodesia.

Almost 60 percent of the whites were immigrants – 'largely arriving from the UK and South Africa in the post-World War II period'.[4] As such, the small European population had few firm roots in Rhodesia and, as Godwin and Hancock argue, Rhodesians had no true sense of nationhood.[5]

The black African population of nearly five million people was divided roughly into two major cultural-linguistic groups: the majority Shona group* comprised approximately 80 percent of Rhodesia's African population, and the Ndebele (Matabele) group made up the remaining 20 percent. The Shona population inhabited the northern and eastern regions of Rhodesia, while the Ndebele inhabited the southern and western areas. The Shona are principally agriculturalists and pastoralists – living typically in small agricultural settlements called *kraals*. The Shona people had a long history in the region and are credited with the creation of the 'Great Zimbabwe' ruins (dating from circa 600 AD).

The Shona and Ndebele belief systems framed their reactions to poisoning incidents carried out by the Rhodesian Security Forces. These poisonings were linked to popular traditional beliefs in witchcraft, possession and the afterlife. Local shamans often attributed disease outbreaks to the ancestral spirits' displeasure that the people had abandoned their traditional lifestyles, mores and customs, and had embraced foreign (i.e. European) values. The traditional Shona belief system centers on the spirits of deceased ancestors as responsible for protecting the land and society. Good ancestor spirits communicate through spirit-mediums and represent the traditional morals and values of the culture. Although the good spirits are thought to protect the Shona people, the spirits' protection can be withdrawn if the living fail to adhere to the traditional practices. Bad spirits are associated with witchcraft. The Shona belief system framed their reaction to incidents of poisoning and disease – linking these incidents to witchcraft.

The Ndebele are an offshoot of the warrior Zulu nation of South Africa. In 1823, following a quarrel with the Zulu ruler Shaka, the Ndebele leader Mzilikazi – along with a number of his warrior followers – moved to the Transvaal province of South Africa, where they absorbed or destroyed tribes they encountered. Eventually, the Boers in 1837 forced the Ndebele northward out of the Transvaal. The Ndebele crossed the Limpopo River and established themselves in the southern areas of present-day Zimbabwe, where they assimilated the neighboring Shona tribes and subjugated the remaining Shona people under a military despotism.[6] For much of their early history in Rhodesia, the Ndebele sustained themselves by raiding Shona *kraals*. After their defeat by the BSAC in 1896 (the 'First *Chimurenga*'), the Ndebele became agriculturalists and herders. An antipathy between the Ndebele and Shona remains, and was a chief reason the insurgency divided into two factions: one Shona-dominated (the Zimbabwe African National Union, or ZANU) and one Ndebele-dominated (the Zimbabwe African Peoples Union, or ZAPU).

---

* Dating from around 1835, the word 'Shona' is a Ndebele term to describe a people belonging to a particular linguistic group.

In the 1962 census, 18 percent of the African population resided in urban areas, although the vast majority was born in the country's rural areas. Most urban black Africans were employed in the public service sector, industry and commerce, or domestic service. They resided in the outlying townships, although those working as domestic servants may have resided in servants' quarters provided by their employers. Until 1980, blacks in Rhodesia were forbidden to own property outside of the designated African Purchase Lands.[7] According to data from the 1962 census, 60 percent of the black populace in Rhodesia resided in the Tribal Trust Lands (TTLs), where they engaged in subsistence agriculture. Life in the TTLs was characterized by a cohesion that resulted from a very strong sense of tradition and a deeply engrained cultural identity. Lastly, a small number of black Rhodesians had qualified to purchase their own land in the Purchase Areas.[8]

Notes

1   Central Intelligence Agency, 'World Factbook 2005', entry for Zimbabwe: <http://www.cia.gov/cia/publications/factbook/geos/zi.html> (accessed on 6 August 2005).
2   ibid.
3   The terms used refer to the categories used in the 1969 census – see Peter Godwin and Ian Hancock, *Rhodesians Never Die: The Impact of War and Political Change on White Rhodesia, c. 1970-1980* (Harare, Zimbabwe: Baobab Books, 1997), p.16.
4   Central Intelligence Agency, 'Rhodesia: Economic Aspects of White Resettlement', dated 22 July 1976 (MORI DocID 1008808), p.1.
5   Godwin and Hancock, p.16.
6   <http://columbia.thefreedictionary.com/Ndebele> (accessed on 7 August 2005); <http://en.wikipedia.org/wiki/Matabele> (accessed on 7 August 2005).
7   Annette Seegers, an unpublished PhD dissertation written in 1983 for the Loyola University of Chicago, p.217.
8   ibid., p.220. Seegers states: '… given these conditions, it was clear that ZAPU and ZANU's efforts at mobilization would be difficult. Furthermore, their efforts would be subjected to government repression, which already had severely weakened the black organizations by arrests, detentions and the banning of organizations. These challenges from without could be complemented by any internal weaknesses (such as tribal squabbles and financial weaknesses) that ZAPU and ZANU developed…' See Seegers, pp.220-221.

Acknowledgments

This endeavor would not have been possible without the help of a great many people – including several key participants to the events as they unfolded. First and foremost, I need to recognize the role of the late Michael 'Mac' McGuinness, who shared his recollections of the Rhodesian chemical and biological weapons (CBW) program. As the head of Rhodesia's day-to-day CBW operations, 'Mac' not only shared his recollections, but much of his time, documents and books. He was able to meet with me on several occasions here and in South Africa. 'Mac' also helped me investigate links between the Rhodesian CBW efforts and South Africa's 'Project Coast'. Much of my research was done while I was a post-doctoral fellow at Georgetown University's Medical Center, and I greatly appreciate the support of Georgetown University and James Wilson MD.

Throughout this project, many former members of the Rhodesian Security Forces – including the BSAP's Special Branch and Selous Scouts – were very kind in sharing their time and energy in answering my often persistent questions. It was only with their help that I could understand the complexities of the Rhodesian conflict. Here I would like to recognize Timothy Bax, John Birch, David Blacker, Michael Borlace, Roger Capper, Henry 'Nobby' Clarke, John Cronin, David Cushworth, Michael Edden, Henrik Ellert, Andrew Field, Geraint Jones, Frank Mussel, James Parker, Peter Petter-Bowyer, Fred Punter, John Redfern, Dan Stannard, Peter Stanton, Peter Stiff, Tom Thomas, Norman Walsh, David Willis and J.R.T. Wood. Drs Stuart Hargreaves, Alan Mills, Richard Laing and John Goldsmid have been extraordinarily helpful as I attempted to navigate veterinary and medical issues in Rhodesia. A few individuals also made major contributions, but would prefer to remain anonymous. I have thanked them all privately.

The academic community interested in CBW issues is small, but I am fortunate to have been acquainted with many notable leaders in the field. Many of these experts have reviewed seemingly endless drafts of this book and have been very generous with their comments, advice and suggestions. They include Ken Alibek, Seth Carus, Richard Danzig, J.C.A. Davies, Chandré Gould, Martin Hugh-Jones, Arnold Kaufman, Gregory Koblentz, Milton Leitenberg, Caitriona McLeish, Susan Martin, Charles Melson, Julian Robinson, Andrew Shuttleworth, Nicholas Sims, Peter Turnbull, Kathleen Vogel and James Watt.

Most importantly, if anything good and worthwhile comes out of this effort at all, my wife, Elizabeth, rightly deserves all the credit. If it were not for her tolerance and forbearance, this work would never have begun, rather than ever been completed. For many years, she has endured tales of the Rhodesian War beyond her normal point of endurance.

Lastly, I alone am responsible for any errors or omissions.

List of Terms and Abbreviations

7 SAMS	7 Battalion, South African Medical Service
AAM	Anti-Apartheid Movement
ANC	African National Congress
APA	African Purchase Area
APU	Applied Chemistry Unit (South Africa)
AS	African Soldier
BSAC	British South Africa Company
BSAP	British South Africa Police (now the Zimbabwe Republic Police)
BWC	Biological Weapons Convention
C/Supt	Chief Superintendent (police rank)
CAF	Central African Federation (short-lived union of Northern Rhodesia, Southern Rhodesia and Nyasaland)
CBW	Chemical and Biological Warfare
CDU	Chemical Defense Unit (South Africa)
Chimurenga	War of liberation (Shona)
CID	Criminal Investigations Department
CIO	Central Intelligence Organization
CNS	Central Nervous System
COMOPS	Combined Operations
ComPol	Commissioner of Police
Cordon sanitaire	a mixed no-go area surrounding Rhodesia's northern and eastern borders
CPR	Chinese Peoples' Republic
CSI	Chief of Staff–Intelligence (SADF Military Intelligence)
CSIR	Council for Scientific and Industrial Research
CWC	Chemical Weapons Convention
DARE	ZANU's Supreme Council (i.e. *Chimurenga* –War Council)
DCC	N,N'dicyclohexyl carbodiimide
DFP	diisopropyl flurophosphate
DGS	*Direccao Genral de Suguranca* (General Security Directorate–Portugal)
DIN	Director-General (internal), Rhodesian Central Intelligence Organization
DMI	Director of Military Intelligence (army)
DMSO	dimethyl sulfoxide
DOD	Department of Defense (United States)
EMLC	*Elektroniks, Meganies, Landbou en Chemies* (South Africa)

EOKA	*Ethniki Organosis Kyprion Agoniston* (Greek for 'National Organisation of Cypriot Fighters')
FCA	DL-fluorocitric acid
FCO	Foreign and Commonwealth Office – Britain's foreign ministry
Fire Force	Rhodesian Army airborne and air-mobile reaction force – typically consisting of a group of helicopters with quick reaction troops supported by a K-car
FISB	Federal Intelligence and Security Bureau
FRELIMO	Front for the Liberation of Mozambique
FROLIZI	Front for the Liberation of Zimbabwe
Frontline States	Zambia, Botswana, Mozambique, Angola, Tanzania
GA	NATO designation for tabun (nerve agent)
GB	NATO designation for sarin (nerve agent)
GD	NATO designation for soman (nerve agent)
GCHQ	General Communications Headquarters (British), UK's SIGINT service
HAZMAT	hazardous material(s)
HUMINT	human intelligence
IIR	Information Intelligence Report (United States)
IMINT	imagery intelligence
Insp	Inspector (police rank)
Insurgents	Armed, trained members of either ZANLA or ZIPRA
INT	intelligence
Intaf	Internal Affairs
ISIL	Islamic State of Iraq and the Levant (also known as ISIS, Islamic State of Iraq and Syria)
JOC	Joint Operations Center
JPS	Joint Planning Staff
Kraal	African village
LD50	Lethal dose 50 – the amount of the substance required (usually per body weight) to kill 50 percent of the test population
MASINT	measurements and signatures intelligence
MFAA/FAA	monofluoroacetic acid/fluoroacetic acid
Mealie meal	corn meal – an African staple food
MI-6	popular term for the British Secret Intelligence Service (SIS)
MIC	methyl isocyanate
MNR	Mozambique National Resistance (Rhodesia/Mozambique)
MOD	Ministry of Defence (Britain)
Mujiba	Shona term for insurgent local youth supporters
NATJOC	National Joint Operational Centre [*sic*]
Nganga	witchdoctor, medicine man (Shona)
Ngozi	demon (Shona)
NIC	National Intelligence Council (United States)

NSO	ZIPRA intelligence
OAU	Organization of African Unity
OC	Officer Commanding
OCC	Operations Coordinating Committee
OP	organophophate
OPCW	Organization for the Prohibition of Chemical Weapons
OSINT	open-source intelligence
PACC	Psychological Action Coordinating Committee
PATU	Police Anti-Terrorist Unit
PBS	Public Broadcasting Service
PCC	People's Caretaker Council (formerly ZAPU)
PF	Patriotic Front – an alliance of convenience between ZAPU and ZANU
PIDE	*Policia Internacional e de Defesa do Estado* (International Police for the Defense of the State), Portuguese Security Police – subsequently the DGS
POU	Psychological Operation Unit
ppm	parts per million
PSBO	Provincial Special Branch Officer (BSAP)
PSYAC	Psychological Action (Unit)
Psyops	Psychological Operations
Psywar Committee	Psychological Warfare Committee
PV	Protected Village
RAR	Rhodesia African Rifles
RBC	Rhodesian Broadcasting Corporation
RF	Rhodesia Front (ruling Rhodesian political party)
RhSAS	Rhodesian Special Air Service
RhSigs	Rhodesian Corps of Signals
Rh$	Rhodesian dollar
RhAF	Rhodesian Air Force
Rhodesia	Zimbabwe (name used for the period up to 1 June 1979)
Rhodesian Front	Rhodesian Front Party (now the Republican Front Party)
RIC	Rhodesian Intelligence Corps
RLI	Rhodesian Light Infantry
RP	Rhodesia Party
RRAF	Royal Rhodesian Air Force
RSA	Republic of South Africa
SA	South Africa
SAANC	South Africa African National Congress
SADF	South African Defense Force
SAHA	South African History Archive
SAPS	South African Police Service
SAS	Special Air Service

SASS	South African Secret Service (formerly the Bureau of State Security (BOSS), but now a division of the State Security Agency (South Africa))
SB	Special Branch (BSAP)
Security Forces	Rhodesian/Zimbabwe-Rhodesian Army, Air Force, BSAP, Guard Force, Security Force Auxiliaries and paramilitary Internal Affairs forces
Sellout	traitor (usually a term applied to Black Rhodesians working for the Rhodesian Security Forces)
SF	Security Force
SFA	Security Force Auxiliary
SIGINT	signals intelligence
SIS	Secret Intelligence Service (Britain) – also known popularly as MI-6
SOC	Special Operations Committee
SOE	Special Operations Executive
SOP	Standard Operating Procedures
Supt	Superintendent (police rank)
SWAPO	South West African People's Organization
TIC	Toxic Industrial Chemical(s)
TTL	Tribal Trust Land(s)
TRC	Truth and Reconciliation Commission (South Africa)
UANC	United African National Council
UDI	Unilateral Declaration of Independence
UK	United Kingdom
USAMRIID	US Army Medical Research Institute of Infectious Diseases
VAG	Vital Asset Ground
VCU	Vermin Control Unit (Rhodesia)
WHO	World Health Organization
WMD	Weapon(s) of Mass Destruction
ZANLA	Zimbabwe African National Liberation Army
ZANU	Zimbabwe Africa National Union
ZANU(PF)	Present name of ZANU; 'PF' refers to the Zimbabwe Patriotic Front (now known as the Patriotic Front)
ZAPU	Zimbabwe African People's Union
Zimbabwe-Rhodesia	Zimbabwe (refers to the period 1 June 1979 to April 1980)
ZIPRA	Zimbabwe People's Revolutionary Army
ZPRA	Zimbabwe People's Revolutionary Army (also known as ZIPRA)

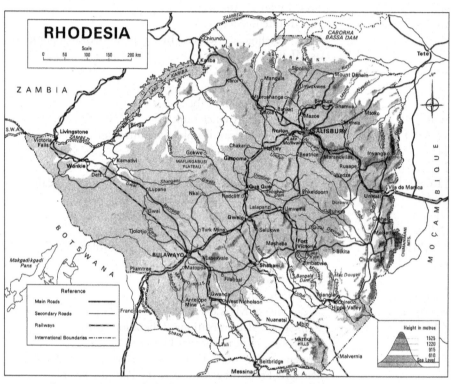

Figure 0.2 A map of Rhodesia. (Source: courtesy of Colin Weyer, accessed at
<www.rhodesia.me.uk>)

Introduction

'There's a Truth that Lives and a Truth that Dies'.[1]

Why a book on the Rhodesian use of chemical or biological warfare (CBW) agents in their counterinsurgency operations? After all, few people probably can even recall a nation named Rhodesia – much less locate it on a map or identify the continent on which it was located. Even the most highly educated of readers may puzzle over a CBW history involving a country that disappeared 37 years ago in such a remote and often forgotten land. Some might describe the history of Rhodesia's CBW efforts as a footnote to a footnote in the history of warfare. Others have described Rhodesia's CBW efforts as a 'sideshow or distraction from the course of the Rhodesian war and its story'.[2] They see the CBW experience in Rhodesia as a minor and unimportant aspect of the story, where the focus should highlight the counterinsurgency strategy, tactics and operations of Rhodesia's conventional military and paramilitary forces.[3]

The relevance today of a book on Rhodesia's CBW effort is many-fold. First, the Rhodesian example sheds light on perhaps the only example of BW use by a nation since the end of World War II. As that unique example, the Rhodesian story allows us to examine the rationale behind a decision not only to develop, but also to use, BW agents. In analyzing the Rhodesian CBW case study, light also is shed on other post World War-II CW uses, such as the Iraqi use – particularly against their Kurdish population – and the recent well-publicized Syrian use since 2013 against civilians. The conclusion drawn from these examples is that regimes* in extremis, where the battle is for their very survival, seem to have little compunction about resorting to CBW use. The much-heralded international norms and conventions prohibiting and condemning CBW development and use go out the window when a regime's survival is at stake. In academic and policy circles, the norms against CBW development and use seem almost sacrosanct, inviolable.[4] The Rhodesian case dispels the myth and leads to a more nuanced understanding of the role the norms play and the circumstances in which those norms are abandoned.

The historical context underlying the Rhodesian conflict is crucial to explaining the origins of the Rhodesian CBW effort. The context also demonstrates a number of possible preconditions that could predispose State or non-State actors to develop

---

*   'Regime' here is defined as an oligarchical governing elite (socio-economic, ethnic, religious or political) which has national economic, political, military, judicial and law enforcement powers, as well as having a major influence over public opinion. These elites often seek to preserve their position and prerogatives even if contrary to national interests.

chemical or biological weapons. In the Rhodesian case, factors that led to the decision to establish a CBW effort included: (a) scarce resources (especially manpower) against a numerically superior opponent; (b) perception of an asymmetrical threat or change in the strategic military balance; (c) status as a pariah State or rogue nation – outside international law, conventions or regimes; (d) dehumanized or demonized adversaries; (e) regime survival at stake (race, values, religion, political/economic power at risk); and (f) available materials, know-how and infrastructure.

The Rhodesian case demonstrates how a small, internationally isolated regime can develop effective CBW agents undetected and use those agents with lethal effect against both internal and external guerrilla threats. Rhodesia covertly developed a rudimentary, small-scale CBW program by using materials, equipment and techniques that were readily available. With scant material resources, the project employed relative novices (at least uninitiated in the arcane science of CBW development and weaponization) in basic facilities to produce significant amounts of lethal material in a short period of time. The Rhodesian CBW effort also demonstrates that the use of readily available toxic agricultural and industrial chemicals as CW agents is easily accomplished by States, groups or individuals lacking funds or sophisticated equipment. By minimizing reliance on foreign sources of materials and limiting personnel to only a small, tightly knit group, nations and non-State actors can reduce the likelihood of discovery by foreign intelligence services.

Theoretical models exist that offer frameworks for better understanding weapons of mass destruction (WMD) proliferation, and some of these may provide insights into why the Rhodesians turned to CBW agents in their counterinsurgency struggle. None of these models is wholly satisfactory. In examining the pursuit of WMD, the academic and policy focus is on the acquisition of nuclear weapons. Chemical and biological weapons are seen as 'substitutes' (i.e. 'poor man's atomic bombs') or complements to nuclear weapons. In some nations, such as Syria, Iran, Pakistan or North Korea – which are facing nuclear-armed external adversaries – the substitution argument possesses some persuasive power in explaining each nation's decision to adopt CBW weapons as they strive to develop nuclear arsenals;[5] yet in countries fighting for their regime survival against internal threats (i.e. insurgency), neither of these explanations seems relevant. Developing a framework to understand a nation's decision-making path to CBW development and use is critical, given that most examples of CBW use outside World Wars I and II took place in the context of counterinsurgencies. These examples include Iraq (1988), Italy (1935-1936), Rhodesia (mid-late 1970s), South Africa (1980s), Spain (1921-1927), Iraq (1988), Syria (2013) and Yemen (1963-1967).[*]

A new paradigm – or at least a corollary to the existing paradigms on WMD proliferation – needs to be explored to adequately explain CBW use in the counterinsurgency context. One recent contribution to the field by Gregory Koblentz has

---

[*]   This list excludes use in World War I, World War II (Japan) and the Iran-Iraq War. In all these cases, except for Japan in World War II, CW and not BW was used. The list also excludes cases in which CBW agents (mostly toxins) were used in covert assassination operations.

introduced the concept of regime security to the academic study of WMD prolif-eration.[6] While the conventional academic frameworks[7] fail to explain the acquisi-tion and use of CBW in counterinsurgencies, Koblentz's argument comes closest to describing the general incentives behind regimes' quest to develop CBW. This neo-realist rationale is rooted in a fundamental need to defend the regime (i.e. a socio-economic political ruling elite) from an internal threat to the regime's dominance and survival.

Rhodesia also illustrates the difficulty faced by intelligence agencies in detecting the existence of CBW programs and the challenges they face in accurately attributing CBW use to a particular actor. The Rhodesian CBW effort operated for several years and went undetected by the West until long after Zimbabwean Independence in 1980. Apart from the information the Rhodesians shared with South Africa about their CBW efforts, almost certainly no other nation had knowledge that a Rhodesian CBW effort even existed, much less was contemplated or planned. The first revela-tions about a Rhodesian CBW effort came soon after the war had ended in a ZANU-sponsored history of the conflict, *The Struggle for Zimbabwe*, by former journalist David Martin and his partner, Phyllis Johnson.

In their book, Martin and Johnson stated that:

> Poisons were often introduced by enemy agents into both refugee and military caps, and many people died from a poison soaked into jeans and T-shirts which caused bleeding from the nose, mouth, and ears. It was later discovered that there was a unit in Salisbury experimenting with poison and that tests had been conducted on captured guerrillas at Mount Darwin and elsewhere, with an unknown number of casualties.[8]

Martin and Johnson's mention passed into obscurity with no further discussion. The issue seemed forgotten until the Rhodesian Intelligence chief Ken Flower recalled it in his 1987 autobiography. The first clandestinely acquired information reported to US Intelligence did not take place until 1990.[9] A fuller, but still far from complete, account of the Rhodesian CBW story emerged only with the revelations of South Africa's CBW program: 'Project Coast'. As South African researchers delved into the tale of 'Project Coast', tidbits of the Rhodesian story emerged almost as a prologue. The point remains that the Rhodesian use of CBW is one of the strongest examples of how a small-scale CBW program can operate effectively for an extended time without detection. The ease by which a small-scale CBW effort can operate undetected is a lesson that intelligence services around the world need to keep in mind when attempting to ferret out State and non-State (i.e. terrorist) CBW efforts. Rhodesia's CBW program further illustrates the utility of CBW in counterinsurgency opera-tions. In the Rhodesian example, a small-scale CBW program using readily available materials and a small team with only basic training produced agents effective against an unprepared insurgent force. The Rhodesian example is an important case study in how some nations and non-State actors might view the utility of CBW in 21st century counterinsurgency warfare. As the battlefield utility of CBW has virtually disappeared, few observers now expect CBW in force-on-force engagements between modern militaries. The utility of CBW lays in the Rhodesian experience – focusing counterinsurgency or counterterrorism operations in a regime survival context.

Examining the Rhodesian CBW program also provides a means to understanding the factors that incentivize a nation to abandon the norms against CBW use. The Rhodesian example demonstrates not only how, but why a small, economically and diplomatically isolated nation faced with the threats to regime survival turned to develop and use CBW agents. In counterinsurgency conflicts, the strength of prohibitive norms seems easily eroded, as evident in Algeria, Kenya, Malaysia, Vietnam, Rhodesia and in Syria today. The lessons of Syria's Assad Government and its use of chemical agents reinforces that regimes are much more likely to use these agents against internal opposition than against foreign State adversaries. The study of the Rhodesian CBW example also provides a window into the determinant factors that would influence any rogue nation or group when selecting CBW agents, production pathways, choices in dissemination methods and scientific and technical expertise. The Rhodesian model for the development of its CBW program also is useful in understanding the factors involved in South Africa's decision to develop its own CBW capability.

Lastly, Rhodesia is a perfect practical lesson in the challenges of CBW attribution. We now know that chemical agents ('poisons') were used extensively, but in small quantities, using rudimentary dissemination techniques. This use of chemicals was detected by doctors at Harari Hospital in Salisbury, but never overtly connected to the Security Forces. Similarly, hospital staff outside Bulawayo detected the intentional thallium contamination of canned beef, but no investigation was ever conducted. Lastly, in this brief list of examples, an American doctor in Mozambique was inundated late in the war with a flood of young, otherwise fit, black Rhodesians. He initially suspected a hemorrhagic fever (such as Ebola or Marburg), only to find that these men – guerrilla fighters at a nearby Zimbabwe African National Liberation Army (ZANLA) base – had been poisoned with the blood thinner sodium coumadin (warfarin). In none of these examples was any effort made to attribute these clearly intentional acts to a specific actor. Even if an effort had been made, attribution probably would have been very difficult, given the Rhodesian Government's control over information and the Rhodesian press' habitual self-censorship.

The most difficult attribution case – that of the 1978-1980 anthrax outbreak – remains highly controversial today and highlights the limits of technical or scientific information when attempting to attribute the cause of a disease outbreak as intentional. As we will examine in detail later, by 1978 the Rhodesian security situation had eroded considerably. Travel to – or through – large areas of the country was safe only during daylight and in the company of armed guards. In that environment, much, if not most, of the rural veterinary services had collapsed. A massive anthrax epidemic swept through the livestock herds of the rural black population. The total loss to the communal herd due to anthrax may never be known fully. The human toll was high: more than 182 black Rhodesians died of anthrax in the epidemic, and nearly 11,000 were ill from the disease. Those figures are based on known cases recorded in hospitals and clinics; the true toll lost to history, with many of the afflicted ill or dying in their villages. Yet despite the cost to human life, no scientifically sound study has been done to explain the outbreak. One American clinician has concluded that the epidemic was man-made – an intentional attack by the Rhodesian Security Forces. Her argument is frequently rebutted by similarly qualified scientists who argue that the disease exploded out of control due to the collapse of the country's veterinary service. The lesson is that, like in many jury trials, either side of a case can find scientists to support its claims. Truly definitive attribution of CBW use – more important for BW attribution[*] – is to have evidence linking human action (intention, plans, preparation and execution) to the outbreak.

Rhodesia's CBW effort: a snapshot

Although some nations have developed or acquired chemical or biological agents, few have ever used these weapons against their adversaries.[†] One of the few countries ever thought to have used chemical or biological agents was Rhodesia[‡] – a small, landlocked breakaway British colony[§] in Southern Africa – which used chemical and biological agents during its protracted struggle against an increasingly numerous African nationalist insurgency in the years following Rhodesia's UDI in November 1965. The genesis of the Rhodesian CBW effort was be found in the deteriorating security situation that developed following Mozambique's Independence from Portuguese colonial rule following the 25 April military *coup d'état* in Lisbon

---

[*] BW attribution is more difficult for the simple reason that BW agents (likely pathogens) are naturally occurring, living organisms. They often are found naturally in the ecology of the locale in which an attack might be suspected – therefore, differentiating organisms in nature from those introduced there by man is difficult. The exception are those biological agents genetically engineered for increased transmissibility, virulence, pathogenicity etc. Chemical agents are synthetic chemical compounds, and – apart from toxins – they are never found in nature. Detection of chemical warfare agents or their degradation chemicals is highly indicative of CW use.

[†] The countries believed to have used chemical and/or biological weapons against adversaries include France, Germany, Iraq, Italy, Japan, Rhodesia, South Africa and the United Kingdom. French, German and British use of chemical weapons occurred during World War I.

[‡] The name 'Rhodesia' is used throughout this book to refer to the present-day Zimbabwe. The British colony was formally known as Southern Rhodesia until Northern Rhodesia (now Zambia) received its Independence in 1964. Thereafter, Southern Rhodesia was mostly commonly known simply as Rhodesia until its formal Independence from Great Britain in 1980, when the country's name was changed to Zimbabwe.

[§] As a British colony, Rhodesia was a rarity. From its creation in 1896 until 1923, Rhodesia was operated by the British South Africa Company. Although Britain oversaw the colony's defense and foreign policies, Rhodesia was, essentially, self-governing and self-financing. In 1923, following a referendum in which only property-owning white males out of a total white settler population of 35,000 voted, the United Kingdom took responsibility for the colony, but continued to allow Rhodesian self-rule. Although never formally granted Dominion status within the British Commonwealth, the Rhodesian Prime Minister was allowed to attend meetings of the Dominion prime ministers. On 11 November 1965, the Rhodesian Cabinet voted to adopt a UDI – severing the colony's constitutional links with Great Britain.

and the subsequent 'Carnation' revolution. The rise of the *Frente de Libertação de Moçambique* (FRELIMO) in Mozambique effectively forced the overstretched and under-resourced Rhodesians to defend a second front.

During the Rhodesian War, Rhodesian Security Forces were far better trained and equipped than their guerrilla adversaries. In a pitched battle between the Rhodesian Security Forces and guerrillas, the guerrillas usually lost. For that reason, guerrillas typically avoided contact with Rhodesia military or police units – seeking instead to ambush soft, largely civilian targets (i.e. isolated farmhouses, rural schools, district commissioners, veterinary workers and civilians traveling on the roads). Later in the struggle, the Rhodesians (facing severe manpower and materiel shortages) adopted unconventional tactics or techniques against a foe that fled rather than fight – including the use of recruited agents to insert CBW-contaminated food, beverages, medicines and clothing into guerrilla supplies. Some of these supplies were provided to guerrilla groups inside Rhodesia, and some were transported to guerrilla camps in Mozambique. In all, deaths attributed to CBW agents often exceeded the monthly guerrilla body count claimed by conventional Rhodesian military units – demonstrating the utility of CBW agents in a counterinsurgency campaign against an elusive enemy.

Former guerrilla intelligence agent Jeremy Brickhill argues that the Rhodesian CBW program was meant to instill fear.[10] JoAnn McGregor, a professor at the University of Reading in the United Kingdom, posits that the use of CBW was a tactic designed to disrupt relations between guerrilla bands and the rural villagers providing them with food and clothing.[11] The most likely explanation, however, is that the Central Intelligence Organization (CIO) and Special Branch resorted to CBW agents when they realized that Rhodesia's reliance on conventional military force alone could not eliminate the swelling ranks of guerrilla fighters who were taught to live among the rural population.[12] Any disruption in the villagers' support for the guerrillas almost certainly was a second-order effect.

This rag-tag band of amateurs – working with makeshift equipment and readily available commercial materials – developed the means to inflict casualties on insurgent forces beyond the capabilities of Rhodesia's professional conventional military. The chemical and biological agents developed by this small, rudimentary program were based almost exclusively on readily available toxic agricultural and industrial chemicals – including warfarin (rodenticide), thallium (rodenticide), methyl parathion (an active ingredient in several organophosphate pesticides used in Rhodesia), *Vibrio cholera* (the causative agent of cholera), *Bacillus anthracis* (the causative agent of anthrax) and botulinum toxin. The Rhodesians also may have experimented with several other agents – including ricin,[13] abrin, amanita toxin, 2,4-dichlorophenoxyacetic acid (2,4-D), sodium fluoroacetate (compound 1080), cyanide, arsenic and tetra colchicine [*sic*][14] – but information on those experimental agents has proven hard to substantiate.

Of those knowledgeable insiders willing to talk, all share a consistent story about Rhodesia's development and use of chemical and biological agents during the Bush War; they even chillingly admit that chemical and biological agents were used in experiments on captured insurgents. In short, the story centers on an element of the BSAP Special Branch* (attached to the Rhodesian Army's Selous Scouts), which implemented and oversaw the Rhodesian CBW effort from mid-to-late 1976 until late 1979. The daily operation of this limited effort fell to a small Special Branch counter-terrorist unit (sometimes referred to as 'Z Desk'[15] or 'Counterterrorist Operations') under the command of Chief Superintendent Michael 'Mac' McGuinness.[16] The Rhodesian CBW program was staffed with a small number of scientists and techni-cians working as 'consultants' to the Special Branch and co-located at the Special Branch/Selous Scout 'fort' outside Bindura (80 km north of Salisbury). The descrip-tion of these insiders is instructive; it is one of a small band of scientists and students who served their 'call-ups' (often as long as three months) at the Bindura 'fort'.

What can we reasonably know about the Rhodesian CBW effort?

The literature on the Rhodesian CBW program is sparse at best – consisting of a few articles and references in a handful of books. No systematic study of the program exists. Apart from Ken Flower's short account published more than two decades ago, some additional information on the Rhodesian CBW program has emerged from academic and media interest in the South African program.† Although lacking specific details, the new information has allowed the general outline and extent of the Rhodesian program to emerge.

No doubt can exist that Rhodesia developed and used CBW agents during its counterinsurgency in the late 1970s. Key participants admitted this fact as early as 1987, when CIO Director-General Ken Flower published his autobiography, *Serving Secretly: An Intelligence Chief on the Record*; yet anyone exploring the topic of Rhodesia's use of CBW agents during its civil war enters a dark and murky world – one filled with intentional misdirection and deception. Only a handful of contem-porary documents survive – forcing researchers to rely on the recollections of the very few participants willing to recount their experiences. Almost all of the relevant documents were destroyed in bonfires on the eve of Zimbabwe's Independence, while others were taken secretly to South Africa. Just how many papers taken to South Africa survived a second wholesale purge of documents at the end of the apartheid era is unknown. What remains often are shadows – vague, often deliberately distorted recollections of events now over 30 years past. Even these recollections more often than not are remembrances of rumor and speculation. Almost no direct participants involved in the Rhodesian program remain, and few knowledgeable security officials

---

* The BSAP Special Branch served two masters: as Branch I–Internal (domestic intelligence), the Special Branch reported to Rhodesia's CIO. The Special Branch also reported to the Police Commissioner. The Special Branch liaison officers also provided intelligence support to the army's Selous Scout special operations unit.

† The South African media reported extensively on South Africa's 'Project Coast' in the press coverage of the Truth and Reconciliation Commission's investigation – and subsequent public hearings – on 'Project Coast', as well as during the trial of 'Project Coast' head Dr Wouter Basson.

are willing to discuss what they know about Rhodesia's CBW efforts. Most seem genuinely horrified that anyone is interested in dredging up this dreadful issue. Their few comments on the subject often are intentionally vague, or self-serving; others are dismayed that anyone would waste time exploring what they consider to be a footnote to a footnote in history. Now years later, the Rhodesian War is remembered only by a rapidly shrinking diaspora of Rhodesian émigrés, with little or no interest in this unseemly, ungentlemanly footnote. They rather glorify the past as the realm of heroes.

With their numbers having shrunk dramatically in the past couple of years, almost no direct participants with first-hand knowledge about the Rhodesian CBW program are still alive – and none of the living are willing to discuss the program and their role in it in any meaningful way. This research built on the contribution of dozens of individuals deemed knowledgeable about the Rhodesian CBW efforts, including former high-ranking BSAP officials, Special Branch officers and Selous Scout members – chiefly the senior Special Branch officer who oversaw the CBW work, Michael J.P. McGuinness. 'Mac' elaborated on the tale of the CBW effort that he had previously told other researchers – notably Chandré Gould.

Given McGuinness' prominence in this story, he deserves more of an introduction here. Michael John Peter 'Mac' McGuinness was born on 5 August 1932 in Orpington, UK – a suburb of London. Raised in an Irish family and proud of his Irish roots, 'Mac' was the son of a police officer turned publican. At the age of 18, McGuinness enlisted in the Royal Air Force and served as a military policeman for nearly four years. On 3 January 1954, he joined the BSAP and rose through the ranks to become a highly decorated officer before retiring on 30 April 1980. On retiring, McGuinness moved to South Africa, where he maintained close ties with both South African Intelligence,[*] as well as Mugabe's Central Intelligence Organization.[17] McGuinness' ties to Zimbabwe's CIO remained close until the day he was brutally murdered in his home on 4 July 2011 by the son of his former batman.[†] As the chief of the Special Branch contingent assigned to the Selous Scouts, 'Mac' was instrumental in the creation of the Selous Scouts and was responsible for the their intelligence

---

[*] In fact, following his retirement from the BSAP, McGuinness was a serving officer in the South African Defense Forces' (SADF) Chief of Staff-Intelligence (CSI) – the military intelligence arm of the South African armed forces – probably for nearly a decade. All the while, 'Mac' also provided intelligence to Zimbabwe's CIO under a personal contract between himself and Robert Mugabe.

[†] McGuinness' Gift Takpas – the son of his long-time 'batman' (servant), Silva. 'Mac' supposedly had brought Silva and his family to South Africa, when 'Mac' moved there in 1980. Silva died within the past couple of years and Gift's behavior had become intolerable, so 'Mac' threw him out of the house. Gift's wife, Bridget, and their three-year old daughter remained and helped 'Mac' with housekeeping chores. On Saturday, 4 July, 'Mac' remained home while Bridget and the little girl went shopping. On returning, Gift attacked Bridget with an axe. The daughter attempted to defend her mother and both were wounded. Gift then entered the house, where he mortally wounded 'Mac'.

efforts. In that role, he earned the undying loyalty of many Special Branch officers and Selous Scout operators throughout the war and afterward.

As an operator, 'Mac' was often personally involved in Special Branch activities as part of the Selous Scouts. Rarely seen in uniform, 'Mac' typically was seen dressed in a T-shirt, *veldskoens* (hiking boots), shorts and a full beard. By conventional standards a maverick, he self-confessedly was responsible for possibly hundreds of 'non-judicial killings'.[18] According to a former BSAP officer, 'he [McGuinness] had good intelligence and acted on it. His sources were superb, as they were throughout the war. From an intelligence point of view, Mac was the ace leader and the core player. It is my opinion that throughout the conflict no member of Special Branch or the CIO came anywhere close to him'.[19]

McGuinness also took credit for uncovering a plot by former members of the Rhodesian Security Forces to detonate shrapnel bombs along the parade route on Zimbabwe's Independence Day.[20] The plotters were part of Operation 'Barnacle' – an element of the South African Defense Forces aimed at destabilizing Zimbabwe. Among the arsenal of sophisticated explosives were two surface-to-air missiles, traffic-light roadside maintenance containers and photographic light beacons – all filled with explosives, remote-controlled devices and other materiel. If this plot had succeeded, it would have possibly killed scores of people – including Prince Charles, Robert Mugabe and the British Governor Lord Soames. In addition, a probable blood-bath would have ensued, as the African population sought retribution against the remaining Europeans. On hearing of the plot, McGuinness alerted his close friend and *protégé* Daniel Stannard, who would remain with the Zimbabwe Republic Police (successor to the BSAP) and later rise to become the Director Internal (DIN) of the Zimbabwean Central Intelligence Organization. 'Mac' only asked that Stannard hold off on raiding plotters' homes until the next morning, a Monday. That Sunday afternoon, at least one plotter – Peter Stanton – was at McGuinness' home enjoying a traditional South African *braai* and sundowners when McGuinness called Stanton into the house and told him that the plot was foiled and that Stanton needed to get himself and his family out of the country before morning. According to 'Mac', Stanton broke down and wept like a child before 'Mac' had to 'grab him by his balls' and throw him into a taxi. The next day, BSAP officers led by Stannard raided the deserted homes and found the bombs – claymore-like devices disguised as traffic-light control boxes and electrical transformers. For his part disrupting this 'Barnacle' operation, Dan Stannard received the Gold Cross of Zimbabwe from Mugabe in 1990. Stannard recounts that at the award ceremony, he whispered to then-Justice Minister Emmerson M'nangagwa that 'Mac' deserved the medal. In the aftermath of the assassination plot, 'Mac' retired from the BSAP, but remained on good terms with Mugabe and his then-Minister for State Security M'nangagwa to the point that they even kept 'Mac' on contract to liaison between Zimbabwean Intelligence and the South Africans. The goal of this liaison was to limit the South African efforts to destabilize the new regime in Zimbabwe.

As the song goes, 'There's a Truth that Lives, and a Truth that Dies'. This statement was never truer than in the case of the Rhodesian CBW effort, where insiders on both sides of the conflict earnestly endeavor to starve the truth, or at least the whole truth, that it might die. Most steadfastly refused to believe that the Rhodesian Security Forces would have ever countenanced the use of chemical or biological agents during the war. For example, senior Rhodesian military officers – including Rhodesian Air Force chiefs Frank Mussel and Norman Walsh, army commander John Hickman, and Rhodesian Special Air Service (SAS) commanders Garth Barrett and Brian Robinson – all claimed that they had no direct knowledge of any Rhodesian CBW efforts. These statements are incredulous in the case of Mussel, Walsh and Hickman, who as among the most senior military leaders in Rhodesia, had been briefed at least once on the CBW effort. In addition to the carefully controlled message coming out of the Selous Scout Association, one also needs to be very circumspect about the large mass of rumor and innuendo that has taken on a life of its own after more than 30 years of rum-soaked retelling around the bars and clubs frequented by ex-Rhodesians.

Given his official position, access to information and role as ultimate manager of the CBW program, former Rhodesian CIO Director-General Ken Flower – in his autobiography, *Serving Secretly* – provided the seemingly most authoritative first-hand account that explicitly mentions the CBW program.[21] Unfortunately, Flower's description of the Rhodesian CBW program is both brief (less than one page) and misleading. In *Serving Secretly*, Flower describes how the CIO recruited The Reverend Kanodareka and his followers in Muzorewa's United African National Council (UANC) to supply poisoned clothing to guerrillas.[22] According to Flower, the Rhodesian poisoning program resulted in the deaths of many hundreds of guerrillas. Flower left his readers to assume that the program ended with Kanodareka's assassination in 1978 at the hands of the CIO. We will deal more with this topic later.

Evidence to substantiate Flower's claim is sketchy. From the documents, we can confirm that the Rhodesians contaminated clothing with lethal chemicals to kill guerrilla recruits and that several hundred died that way. No confirmation exists regarding The Rev Kanodareka's involvement, however; in fact, a senior BSAP officer has refuted the allegations about Kanodareka. Bill Crabtree – Flower's Special Branch deputy until 1970 – in his autobiography, *Came the Fourth Flag*, repeats Flower's admission without any elaboration except that he attributes the poisoning mentioned in Flower's book to a CIO 'dirty tricks' branch, and he thought the poisoning program was out of character for the introverted Flower.[23] Crabtree, for his part, had limited access to the inner workings of the CIO once he was assigned in 1970 to serve as the CIO liaison in Athens. Although he reportedly enjoyed a close relationship with – and respect for – Flower, Crabtree's autobiography does not shed any further light on the Rhodesian program. The one question raised by Crabtree's inclusion of any mention about the program was why he mentioned it at all. Crabtree almost certainly had no involvement in the program and probably no direct knowledge of it. In Crabtree's book, the reference to the Rhodesian CBW program seems out of context.

In dealing with Flower's veracity, many former Rhodesians hold to the opinion that Flower pandered to the opinions and prejudices of his new masters in Zimbabwe and put forth these claims to whitewash his own involvement in Rhodesia's 'dirty tricks' against the African nationalists. Although Flower had served at the helm of an organization that waged a ruthless secret war against the African nationalist leaders, the new government asked that he continue serving as Zimbabwe's intelligence chief for nearly two years after Independence in 1980. Flower's association with Mugabe and the Zimbabwean Government has tarnished his reputation, along with long-standing rumors that Flower was an agent of the British Secret Intelligence Service (MI-6). Even today, veteran Rhodesian Intelligence officers speculate about the identities of the 'traitors' who betrayed Rhodesia by providing the plans of Rhodesian Intelligence, the Selous Scouts and the SAS to British Intelligence.[24] Given the common acceptance of these rumors among former Rhodesians, I posed the question of Flower's possible relationship with British Intelligence to both Lord David Owen (British Foreign and Commonwealth Minister at the time) and Lord Robin Renwick (then-head of Britain's Foreign and Commonwealth Office's Rhodesia Office). As Lord Renwick stated, 'Ken Flower kept in touch with various intelligence agencies, but never worked for any of them except his own'.[25] These denials of a relationship between Flower and British Intelligence were cast into doubt with the broadcast of a BBC documentary program, '*Document*', on 8 January 2011.[26]

Putting aside allegations of Flower's duplicity, we need to apply Luise White's questions when examining Flower's statements. Flower, after all, was the first Rhodesian official to openly describe their CBW effort. He characterized that effort as a morally reprehensible activity and blamed it on a dead man who, as a UANC official, had no discernible ties to either ZAPU or ZANU. Flower's revelation about the CBW program also did not come as a surprise to the Zimbabwean Government, which had information about the program stretching back almost to its inception.

Often quoted in the secondary literature, Henrik Ellert's book *Rhodesian Front War*,[27] published in Zimbabwe in 1989, is a revealing account of the 'dirty tricks' perpetrated by the Rhodesian Special Branch and the Selous Scouts from the viewpoint of a BSAP Special Branch officer assigned to counterintelligence duties at Special Branch Headquarters in Salisbury. Ellert had no direct access to information on the Rhodesian CBW effort, however. His duties consisted of monitoring the foreign European presence and Europeans suspected of subversion – including left-wing intellectuals, radicals at the university, religious organizations, trade unions and the media. Ellert is familiar with many of the individuals and locations involved in the CBW program, but his understanding of the program is based on second-hand information and hearsay.[28] After contacting Ellert about my research for this book, he said that he did not believe there was much of a story beyond what he had written in his book.

Former BSAP members and soldiers serving with the Selous Scouts have written several books detailing aspects of Rhodesia's CBW use. *Assignment Selous Scouts: The Inside Story of a Rhodesian Special Branch Officer* by Jim Parker is the controversial autobiographical account of a Rhodesian BSAP member who quit the force for family reasons to become a farmer near Fort Victoria in South-Eastern Rhodesia. At the height of the war, he rejoined the BSAP as a police 'A' reservist.[29] Typically, 'A' reservists are uniformed BSAP members assigned to support duties at a BSAP post (i.e. taking calls, answering inquiries from the public and performing clerical functions).

Given the general manpower shortage, Parker claims that he became embroiled in the activities of the Special Branch liaison assigned to the local Selous Scout fort at

Chiredzi. Like all participant recollections of events in the Rhodesian War, Parker's account is interesting, but largely anecdotal, and many of his claims remain uncorroborated; however, in his book, Parker published the documents from a BSAP file on the use of chemical agents and included new material from his interviews with McGuinness.[30] Several former Special Branch members and former Selous Scouts have angrily denounced Parker's book as fiction and derided his role as a police reservist. They asserted that as a civilian, Parker was not in a position to know about extremely sensitive Special Branch activities or Selous Scout operations. On the other hand, as the war intensified, manpower shortages were acute and any willing and able-bodied man – especially one already versed in BSAP procedures – likely would have been used. We cannot completely discount Parker's accounts out of hand as so many of his detractors would have us do, yet I have not been able to independently confirm all of what Parker describes in his book.

Analyses to date of the Rhodesian CBW program

To date, only two journal articles, chapters in two books, two *exposés*, one website[31] and a few PhD dissertations have looked at the Rhodesian CBW program. The academic articles – one by former CIA analyst Ian Martinez in the *Third World Journal* and another by Professor Luise White in *OSIRIS* – examined the publicly available information. No new information is uncovered in either. A summation of the secondary literature, Martinez's article contributes little original thought or perspective, and his article is replete with factual errors. White adds additional insight to the question based on her years of field research as an oral historian in Zimbabwe. In particular, White contributes a detailed understanding of traditional African belief systems and the impact of poisonings on relations between guerrillas and their rural supporters. White also makes some insightful observations about the spirit mediums and their explanation of the 1979-1980 anthrax outbreak.

Tom Mangold's book, *Plague Wars*,[32] includes a chapter on the Rhodesian CBW program in which he largely repeats material found in other publications. Because Mangold was able to interview several of the participants, his book chapter adds some additional details not found in other publications. Unfortunately, Mangold's work is unreliable because the chapter is sensationalistic – failing to fully describe the program or place it in its historical context. Although focused on South Africa's CBW program, Chandré Gould – in the book *Project Coast: Apartheid's Chemical and Biological Warfare Programme*,[33] co-authored with Peter Folb – provided one of the first accurate, but brief, descriptions of the Rhodesian CBW effort. She went on to use much of the material in later articles and in her PhD dissertation. Her corpus of work on the South African CBW program contains enough material on the Rhodesian effort to form a useful foundation for later researchers. Chandré Gould's dissertation (August 2005),[34] which is largely derived from her earlier published work previously mentioned in this chapter, focuses on the South African development and use of CBW – and she treats the Rhodesian CBW effort as a prologue to the South African case.

The two *exposé* articles – both by Jeremy Brickhill, who is a former Zimbabwe People's Revolutionary Army (ZIPRA) intelligence officer and anti-apartheid activist – offer nothing new, are politically charged and inaccurate. Interestingly, Brickhill points to Henrik Ellert's book – *Rhodesian Front War* – as 'the only reliable published evidence' concerning the Rhodesian CBW program.[35] Brickhill's articles contain a rehash of old facts mixed with some questionable assertions and, again, factual errors. For example, Brickhill claims that Dave Anderton (Detective Inspector on the Terrorist Desk at Special Branch Headquarters in Salisbury) was a key participant in the CBW program. In attempting to validate Brickhill's statement, no link can be found tying Anderton to chemical or biological warfare agents.[36] A close friend and colleague of Anderton's commented that Anderton was never involved in the CBW effort. The subject never came up in conversation, although Anderton recounted several war stories involving unorthodox operations.[37] Readers should treat Brickhill's claims with skepticism.

Despite the passage of time since the events unfolded in Rhodesia, one indisputable fact has emerged: without any doubt, the Rhodesian Security Forces – with the approval and support of the country's political leadership – did develop and use CBW agents against guerrilla forces with remarkable effectiveness. Also remarkable is that this effort remained secret and undetected by Western Intelligence until public revelations emerged as part of the South African Truth and Reconciliation Commission's investigation into that country's apartheid-era CBW program, codenamed 'Project Coast'. Lastly, the demonstrated effectiveness of CBW in Rhodesia's counterinsurgency efforts should alert everyone to the potential utility of CBW in modern counterinsurgencies. We need to be mindful that although some nations may no longer perceive CBW as having the same utility it did during the 1950s and 1960s as a battlefield weapon against opposing armies, some countries may perceive use of CBW by Special Forces or in counterinsurgencies as a valuable addition to their arsenal.

Notes

1   'Nevermind' – a poem by Leonard Cohen (2005); song (2014).

2   Comment by Marine Corps historian Charles Melson in a literature review he prepared on the Rhodesian use of CBW, dated 9 August 2005 (author's collection).

3   This view is perhaps best exemplified in J.R.T. Wood's *Counter-Strike from the Sky: The Rhodesian All-Arms Fireforce in the War in the Bush 1974-1980* and in a plethora of articles that attempt to make the case Western counterinsurgency operations should examine the Rhodesian Fireforce as a possible model (for example, see books and article by former Selous Scout officer Timothy Bax).

4   See Leonard Cole, 'The Poison Weapons Taboo: Biology, Culture, and Politics', *Politics and the Life Sciences*, vol.27, no.2 (September 1998), pp.119-132.

5   Here, Susan Martin rightly argues that BW is a poor counterforce weapon and that nations seeking BW do so as a strategic deterrent due to absent nuclear arsenals of their own. In this context, BW is a temporary 'poor man's' substitute for nuclear weapons; her argument fails to explain CBW development and use for much of the historical record. See Susan Martin, 'The

Role of Biological Weapons in International Politics: The Real Military Revolution', *Journal of Strategic Studies,* vol.25, no.1 (2002), pp.63-98.

6   See Gregory D. Koblentz, 'Regime Security: A New Theory for Understanding the Proliferation of Chemical and Biological Weapons', *Contemporary Security Policy,* vol.34, no.3 (2013), pp.501-525.

7   Loosely described as models in Scott D. Sagan's seminal article, 'Why Do States Build Nuclear Weapons? Three Models in Search of a Bomb', *International Security 21* (Winter 1996-1997), pp.54-86.

8   David Martin and Phyllis Johnson, *The Struggle for Zimbabwe* (London: Faber & Faber Ltd., 1981), pp.276-277.

9   See Thomas Mangold and Jeff Goldberg, *Plague Wars: The Terrifying Reality of Biological Warfare* (New York: St. Martin's Press, 2001), p.218. Also see op. cit. footnotes 8 and 9 on p.418.

10   Jeremy Brickhill, 'Zimbabwe's Poisoned Legacy: Secret War in Southern Africa', *Covert Action Quarterly 43* (Winter 1992-1993), p.9.

11   JoAnn McGregor, 'Containing Violence: Poisoning and Guerrilla/Civilian Relations in the Memories of Zimbabwe's Liberation War' in K.L. Rogers, S. Leysesdorff and G. Dawson (eds.) *Trauma and Life Stories: An International Perspective* (London: Routledge, 1999), p.131. The disruption of relations between guerrillas and village supporters was a second-order effect, and may not have been intended or anticipated by the Rhodesian Security Forces. Regardless of whether the Rhodesians planned for this rupture in relations, they almost certainly welcomed it.

12   See Ken Flower, *Serving Secretly: An Intelligence Chief on the Record,* (London: John Murray Ltd., 1987), p.137; Bill Crabtree, *Came the Fourth Flag,* (Lancaster, UK: Scotforth Books, 2002), p.251; and T. J. Byron, *Elimination Theory: The Secret Covert Networks of Project Coast,* (Baltimore: PublishAmerica, 2004), p.21.

13   Ricin is mentioned in Peter Stiff's book *See You in November* as an assassination weapon considered for use by the Rhodesian CIO in a planned operation against ZANU leader Robert Mugabe (later President of Zimbabwe following Independence) during the 1979 Lancaster House talks on a negotiated peace settlement.

14   McGuinness, personal communication, September 2006. Most of the experimental agents were provided to the Rhodesians by South Africa.

15   Henrik Ellert, 'The Rhodesian Security and Intelligence Community, 1960-1980: A Brief Overview of the Structure and Operational Role of the Military, Civilian, and Police Security and Intelligence Organizations which Served the Rhodesian Government during the Zimbabwean Liberation War' in N. Bhebe and T. Ranger (eds.), *Soldiers in Zimbabwe's Liberation War,* (London: James Currey Ltd., 1995), p.100: 'The planning and intelligence aspects of the Selous Scouts were coordinated at Salisbury Headquarters level under Department "Z" while field operations HQ was located first at Bindura and then at Inkomo Barracks. Provincial and district "forts" were established adjacent to Joint Operational Command posts (JOCs)'.

16   McGuinness also is referred to as having the higher rank of Assistant Commissioner. See Henrik Ellert, *The Rhodesian Front War: Counter-Insurgency and Guerilla War in Rhodesia, 1962-1980,* (Gweru, Zimbabwe: Mambo Press, 1989), p.102. He was never promoted to that rank.

17   Heidi Holland, *Dinner with Mugabe: The Untold Story of a Freedom Fighter Who Became a Tyrant* (Johannesburg, South Africa: Penguin Books, 2008), p.36.

18   According to Wikipedia: '... an extrajudicial killing is the killing of a person by governmental authorities without the sanction of any judicial proceeding or legal process. Extrajudicial

punishments are by their nature unlawful, since they bypass the due process of the legal jurisdiction in which they occur. Extrajudicial killings often target leading political, trade union, dissident, religious, and social figures and may be carried out by the state government or other state authorities like the armed forces and police...' See <http://en.wikipedia.org/wiki/Extra-judicial_killing> retrieved on 28 July 2011.

19   Personal communication from BSAP/2, dated 3 March 2005.

20   Heidi Holland, *Dinner with Mugabe: The Untold Story of a Freedom Fighter Who Became a Tyrant* (Johannesburg, South Africa: Penguin Books, 2008), pp.35-36 and ft.1; similar stories told to author by both McGuinness and Stannard.

21   Flower (1987), p.137.

22   ibid.

23   Bill Crabtree, *Came the Fourth Flag* (Lancaster, UK: Scotforth Books, 2002), p.252.

24   Ken Flower and Derrick Robinson (the Director-General and Deputy Director-General/Internal of the CIO respectively) are among the two names most often mentioned as possible British spies. According to McGuinness (a close associate of Flower and Robinson), he believes that Flower and Robinson both maintained close ties with Britain's MI5 and MI6 – including information exchanges – but neither man would have betrayed Rhodesia or acted against Rhodesia's best interests (personal communication, dated 24 April 2006). Suspicion of Flower and Robinson's ties to MI-6 was reiterated by another senior CIO officer (personal communication from CIO/3, dated 18 May 2007).

25   Personal communication, dated 14 December 2011.

26   BBC documentary, '*Document*' <http://www.bbc.co.uk/programmes/b012wf3s> (accessed on 15 November 2016).

27   Henrik Ellert, *The Rhodesian Front War: Counter-Insurgency and Guerilla War in Rhodesia, 1962-1980* (Gweru, Zimbabwe: Mambo Press, 1989).

28   BSAP/15, personal communication, n.d.

29   Among the BSAP Regimental Association, some members have raised concerns that Parker has inflated his role in the Rhodesian War. One former Special Branch member who was assigned to the same area as Parker has stated: 'Jim Parker certainly was present, as a Police "A" Reservist, and very much involved with the activities of the Selous Scouts at the Chiredzi Fort during my frequent visits there. He was a close colleague with the SB [Special Branch] and military commanders at that fort, all, who I might add were Umtali boys'. (Andrew Field, personal communication, dated 7 June 2006).

30   In a letter to the editor of *The Sunday Times* (Johannesburg), former C/Supt McGuinness wrote: '... regarding 'South Africa's plot to kill Prince Charles' (May 7), and the status of Jim Parker, author of *Assignment Selous Scouts*. As the officer commanding Special Operations CIO Headquarters, I categorically state that Parker was never an attested member of the BSAP Rhodesian Special Branch, or the Selous Scouts Regiment. At no time during his service as a police reservist was he authorised by a competent authority to direct, brief or command personnel in the field...' – *The Sunday Times* (Johannesburg), 28 May 2006. <http://www.sundaytimes.co.za/PrintMail/FinishPrint.aspx?ID=ST6A187090> (accessed on 8 June 2006). In response, Peter Stiff – publisher of Jim Parker's book – wrote to the same newspaper, saying: 'I have the utmost respect for McGuinness, a former colleague from my Rhodesian BSA Police days. I have listened to several hours of taped interviews that Parker conducted with McGuinness while researching his book. Much of what he wrote emanated from McGuinness, including the plot to assassinate Prince Charles. Surely he wouldn't have been so revealing if he hadn't accepted Parker's *bona fides* as a former subordinate – albeit a 'lowly' reservist and not a regular policeman? Particularly as he also acknowledged Parker as 'his man' in the tapes' – *The Sunday Times* (Johannesburg), 4 June 2006. <http://www.

sundaytimes.co.za/PrintMail/FinishPrint.aspx?ID=ST6A188354> (accessed on 8 June 2006).

31   <http://www.nti.org/e_research/profiles/SAfrica/Chemical/> (accessed on 10 August 2005).

32   Tom Mangold and Jeff Goldberg, *Plague Wars* (New York: St. Martin's Griffin, 1999).

33   Chandré Gould and Peter Folb, *Project Coast: Apartheid's Chemical and Biological Warfare Programme* (Geneva: United Nations Institute for Disarmament Research, 2002).

34   Chandré Gould (2006) *South Africa's Chemical and Biological Warfare Programme 1981-1995* (PhD thesis, Rhodes University).

35   Jeremy Brickhill, 'Zimbabwe's Poisoned Legacy: Secret War in Southern Africa', *Covert Action Quarterly* 43 (Winter 1992-1993), p.7.

36   Brickhill's claims regarding Anderton's involvement almost certainly can be traced back to Ellert. Colleagues close to Anderton (who committed suicide several years ago) have stated that he never spoke to them of any involvement in the Rhodesian CBW effort. The PSBO for Mashonaland and Salisbury was the leading distributor of poisoned clothing, food, beverages and medicines to guerrillas; however, Anderton was not the PSBO for Mashonaland and Salisbury at the time of the Rhodesian CBW effort. Alan Best was PSBO in Mashonaland and Salisbury until October 1976, when he was replaced by Michael Edden. When Edden moved to a position on COMOPS in May 1977, he was replaced by Gordon Waugh as PSBO.

37   Email from BSAP/2. The email also went on to state that given Anderton's ease in relating stories of his activities, BSAP/2 is convinced that Anderton would have told him about any role he may have had in the CBW program.

1

Rhodesia's Deteriorating Security Environment

'The more we killed, the happier we were. We were fighting terrorists'.[1]

Ian Smith, Rhodesian Prime Minister

Given the exhaustive treatment of the Rhodesian War elsewhere, this chapter is meant only to convey a broad understanding of Rhodesia's deteriorating strategic situation as a backdrop to the Rhodesian CBW program. The rationale for Rhodesia's adoption of chemical and biological weapons lies in the regime's inability to defeat decisively a growing guerrilla insurgency through conventional arms alone. Although the Rhodesian Security Forces were able to dominate the conventional battlefield, the guerrilla forces continued to grow in size and capabilities. Other factors increased the stresses on the Rhodesian Security Forces as the conflict progressed: demands on the small European-origin population in Rhodesia for manpower and resources, and the economic constraints of internationally imposed sanctions, sapped the will of the white Rhodesians – leading to a net exodus from the country in the late 1970s. In early 1979, with the creation of Zimbabwe-Rhodesia – led ostensibly by Bishop Abel Muzorewa – the political consensus underpinning the legitimacy of Rhodesian rule began to unravel. Furthermore, international pressure for a settlement was mounting.

Following the collapse of Portuguese colonial rule in Mozambique, ZANLA established safe havens there – effectively opening a second front along Mozambique's 1,200km-long border with Rhodesia.* These guerrilla safe havens in Mozambique outstretched the limited ability of Rhodesia's small Security Forces to cope with the increasing threat, so the Rhodesians turned to unconventional techniques to combat the expanding threat. To understand the changing strategic environment facing the Rhodesian leadership, we need to briefly explore the evolution of the Rhodesian conflict.

---

*   The Chinese-backed – largely Shona-dominated – ZANLA safe havens were located largely in Mozambique, while the Soviet and Cuban-backed – Ndebele-dominated – ZIPRA was located chiefly in Zambia. ZANLA was the military wing of ZANU and ZIPRA was the military wing of ZAPU. The differences between ZANU and ZAPU lay in the ethnic division in Zimbabwe between the majority Shona people and the minority Ndebele people.

The origins of the Rhodesian conflict

The origins of the Rhodesian conflict must be viewed in the overall context of British decolonization of Africa. World War II had been an enormous drain on Britain's financial, material and manpower resources – making the post-war burden of maintaining its far-flung empire overwhelming and, ultimately, unsustainable. In 1960, the British Government adopted a policy of decolonization, as announced by British Prime Minister Macmillan in his 'Wind of Change' speech to the South African Parliament.[2] By the mid-1960s, the British had granted Independence to most of their colonial possessions in Africa – including Ghana (1957), Guinea (1958), Nigeria (1960), Sierra Leone (1961), Tanganyika (1961, later Tanzania), Uganda (1962), Kenya (1963), Zambia (1964), Malawi (1964), The Gambia (1965), Botswana (1966) and Swaziland (1968).

At the time of Macmillan's 'Wind of Change' speech, Southern Rhodesia was part of the Federation of Rhodesia and Nyasaland, which was created on 1 August 1953. The federation united the British protectorates of Northern Rhodesia (now Zambia), Nyasaland (now Malawi) and the self-governing colony of Southern Rhodesia (now Zimbabwe). In creating the federation, the United Kingdom sought to create an economically viable country resistant to socialist political influences, and yet capable of transitioning to eventual majority rule. Most of the political and economic power in the federation rested in the hands of Europeans living in Southern Rhodesia. Although the white settlers in Southern Rhodesia had pushed for an amalgamation of the three territories, the British Government would only agree to a federation under a UK-appointed colonial governor responsible for external relations, defense, the currency and intra-territorial issues. A federal prime minister governed the policies of the federation, but the territorial governments ruled each territory separately. Growing African resentment over the dominance of European politicians ruling from the federal capital at Salisbury fueled an emerging African nationalism that forced the dissolution of the Central African Federation (CAF) on 31 December 1963.

With the dissolution of the federation, the United Kingdom granted Independence under majority rule to Zambia and Malawi, but denied Rhodesia Independence until agreement on a mechanism for eventual majority rule was reached. Even after the collapse of the CAF, Rhodesian politicians claimed that the United Kingdom had promised Independence to Rhodesia in exchange for Salisbury's acquiescence to the dissolution of the federation. They labeled Britain's refusal to grant Rhodesian Independence as a betrayal of the purported promise – and as unjust in the face of Zambian and Malawian Independence. When British officials countered that majority rule was a prerequisite for Independence, Rhodesians argued that, as a self-governing and self-financing colony, London had no right to dictate the terms of Independence to Rhodesia.

Rhodesia's failure to gain a negotiated Independence from Great Britain led to increasing domestic pressures for the Unilateral Declaration of Independence (UDI). Although London and Salisbury continued to negotiate about Rhodesia's Independence, neither side could find an acceptable middle ground. The British position was that Independence was contingent on agreement regarding a process that would move Rhodesia to majority rule; the Rhodesian position was that Britain should grant Independence based on Rhodesia's 1961 constitution, which guaranteed a privileged position for the European minority for the foreseeable future. With both sides firmly entrenched – and no compromise in sight – the Rhodesian Cabinet signed the UDI on 11 November 1965. Britain immediately declared Rhodesia's UDI illegal; London announced that the colony was in rebellion and presented its case to the United Nations Security Council, which also condemned the Rhodesian action. Later, after declaring Rhodesia's UDI to be a threat to international peace, the United Nations announced international sanctions against Rhodesia. Over the next decade, the sanctions themselves were largely ineffectual as long as Mozambique and South Africa continued to trade with Rhodesia. Rhodesia also mounted highly successful (albeit costly) sanctions-busting operations. Through most of the period from 1965 to the mid-1970s, the Rhodesian economy prospered and productivity grew, as did personal incomes (for at least the European population). Until the late 1970s, taxes remained low and the standard of living for the European population remained relatively high, despite shortages of some imported luxury goods. The global recession that hit the world economy in the late 1970s; the closure of the Mozambique border to trade after the Portuguese withdrawal in 1974; and South African manipulation of Rhodesian trade all combined to have a more serious impact on the Rhodesian economy and warfighting abilities than did the UN sanctions.

Before Rhodesia's Declaration of Independence, the African nationalist leaders in Rhodesian detention met with British Prime Minister Harold Wilson in 1965. At that meeting, Wilson responded negatively when African leaders asked if London was prepared to use military force to retain its control of Rhodesia. Failing to garner any assurances from Wilson, the African nationalist leadership was convinced about the inevitability of the UDI.[3] Wilson reportedly offered the nationalist leaders a gradual transition to majority rule, which was unacceptable in light of the African leaders' demands that Britain immediately – and unconditionally – impose majority rule in Rhodesia by force if necessary.[4]

The first phase of the conflict (1965 to 1969)

Unable to organize any effective resistance, the immediate reaction of the African nationalist parties* to the UDI was muted.[5] The African uprising in Rhodesia – anticipated by the nationalist leaders in response to the UDI – did not materialize.[6] According to the BSAP history:

> whilst there was no reaction initially, nationalist violence flared up in different parts of the country after a few days and ineffectual attempts were made to promote a 'general strike.' The situation quickly returned to normal due to the

---

*   At the time of Rhodesia's UDI, the major African nationalist parties included ZAPU – led by Joshua Nkomo since its foundation in 1961 – and ZANU, which The Reverend Ndabaningi Sithole and lawyer Herbert Chitepo founded in 1963.

lack of organisation amongst the nationalists at large in Rhodesia, their poor
lines of communication with the 'north' and the general lack of 'second string'
leaders.[7]

Despite their opposition to the UDI, the nationalist leadership faced limited options.[8]
The first strategy adopted by the nationalist leaders was to employ cadres trained
overseas[9] to conduct operations aimed at disrupting law and order in Rhodesia; to
terrify the white population; and to ignite a 'wave of civil disorder by the Blacks'.[10]
The purpose behind these attacks was to demonstrate to London and Salisbury that
the Rhodesian authorities were incapable of protecting the populace from these
terrorist tactics – thereby forcing Britain to retake control of the colony and grant
immediate majority rule.

Early in the conflict, the nationalists grossly underestimated the capabilities of
the BSAP to respond to the small numbers of guerrillas sent on sabotage and terror
missions inside Rhodesia. In 1965, the BSAP successfully dismantled the ZANU
network tasked with launching a large-scale terrorist campaign targeted mainly
against Rhodesia's urban centers.

The Rhodesians had effectively emasculated guerrilla capabilities inside Rhodesia,
as described in a BSAP chronology:

> In May 1965, pre-emptive arrests of most of the 38 Z.A.N.U. terrorists, trained
> in Ghana and returning to Rhodesia by legitimate means via various ports,
> forestalled a plan by Ndabaningi Sithole to bring about wide-scale terrorism and
> sabotage in Rhodesia with special emphasis on the urban areas. The arrest of
> Russian trained Z.A.P.U. intelligence agent and leading party member Edward
> Bhebe, in Bulawayo in July 1965, led to the further arrest of 18 Z.A.P.U. sabo-
> teurs who had successfully infiltrated the country by various means.[11]

Based on their previous experiences, the Rhodesians expected that the African
nationalist strategy would remain focused on disrupting law and order – a strategy
that the Rhodesian authorities were well equipped to combat. The Rhodesians accurately perceived that the African nationalists were unprepared to conduct a general
insurgency at this stage:

> The Africans were not organized for serious insurrection, having depended on
> world opinion, British intercession, and the winds of change … If the national-
> ists had switched tracks to immediate and widespread terror, assassination, and
> orchestrated chaos, perhaps the Europeans might have given way or the timid
> fled or the British been forced to intervene, albeit reluctantly. The nationalists,
> however, were not organized for such an effort, did not at first perceive the
> necessity, and instead followed an ultimately self-defeating source of moderate
> disorder that could be repressed and that led to even greater African frustration.[12]

By 1966, the nationalists concluded that the British would not forcibly wrestle control
of the colony from the Rhodesian authorities. This realization led the nationalists to

adopt a new strategy,[13] which was based on the belief that the nationalists would have to seize control of Rhodesia if they wanted to transform the country into an Independent Zimbabwe. The first guerrilla action took place on 28 April 1966 when one of three groups of ZIPRA* guerrilla infiltrators fought a BSAP detachment near Sinoia (100km north-west of Salisbury). This first encounter ended in the complete elimination of the guerrilla group. The Rhodesians also eliminated the other two groups – charged with attacking power lines and isolated European farmsteads – after a short period. Of the 14 guerrillas composing these three groups, 13 were killed or captured within days.[14]

ZIPRA's lack of success – and its strategy of limited incursions – did not appreciably change for the remainder of the 1960s.[15] Sizable bands of two dozen or more guerrillas would infiltrate across the Zambian-Rhodesian border into a sparsely populated, generally inhospitable terrain. Under these conditions, and given the local villagers' suspicion of the guerrillas, the Rhodesian Police (i.e. the BSAP) were able to locate and eliminate these guerrilla groups quickly and effectively. The Rhodesian CIO and the BSAP also reportedly had penetrated all levels of ZAPU and ZANU and were able to alert the Rhodesian Security Forces to the operational plans of the nationalist groups.[16]

A declassified US National Intelligence Estimate sums up the security threat to Rhodesia in 1967 as follows:

> With the help of black informers, urban as well as rural, Rhodesia's security forces have proved highly effective in ferreting out dissidents and combating guerrilla infiltrators. These forces include 6,000 police, an army of 3,000, and trained reserves of 30,000. Blacks make up most of the police force and have served with distinction in occasional combat against liberation groups. So far, neither the security forces nor the white civilian population has suffered many casualties at the hands of insurgents. The cost of preserving supremacy must of course also include the economic losses brought about by the sanctions instituted against the regime, first by the UK and then by the UN. A sharp decline of exports has somewhat depressed the general level of economic activity. But the white community has suffered no privation and its political support for the Smith regime has, if anything, increased.[17]

Losses to ZIPRA, which made up the bulk of the guerrilla groups then fighting in Rhodesia, were substantial and unsustainable without a change in strategy. To compensate for their losses, both ZIPRA and ZANLA† coerced Zimbabwean refugees to join the guerrilla groups, as Cilliers describes:

> It also was apparent that if Rhodesia was to become Zimbabwe, Zimbabweans themselves would have to take up arms and fight for it. While the leaders of

---

*   ZIPRA was the military arm of the Soviet-backed ZAPU.
†   ZANLA was the military arm of the Chinese-supported ZANU.

ZANLA and ZIPRA were convinced of this, Black Rhodesians as yet were not. Rhodesian citizens resident in Zambia and Tanzania were thus forcibly recruited to swell ZANLA and ZIPRA ranks until the trickle of refugees and recruits turned into a flood.[18]

Among the first major supporters to provide aid to ZIPRA was the African National Congress (ANC) in South Africa. On 15 August 1967, ANC Acting President Oliver Tambo and ZAPU Vice-President James Chikerema announced a military alliance.[19] The same month, a joint ZIPRA-ANC guerrilla force of between 70 and 80 men[20] entered Rhodesia across the Zambezi River – upstream from Victoria Falls – and proceeded toward the Wankie Game Reserve. Although the Rhodesian Security Forces were surprised by the size of the ZIPRA-ANC force, the guerrillas proved to be ineffective against the better trained, better equipped and more mobile Rhodesian units. News of the ZIPRA-ANC military alliance and the ANC's participation in combat inside Rhodesia resulted in South Africa's active involvement in the Rhodesian conflict on the side of the Rhodesian Security Forces. South Africa soon began supplying men (South African Riot Police, helicopter pilots, mechanics and later, Special Forces troops), helicopters and materiel on the side of the Rhodesian Security Forces.[21] Trained as an urban unit, the South African Riot Police had limited military capability to fight effectively in a bush war. Other later South African units – including those from the South African Security Police – deployed to Rhodesia as part of training and orientation courses. Some South African Special Forces ('Recce') elements were wholly integrated into the Rhodesian Special Air Service (RhSAS) as 'D' Squadron – wearing Rhodesian uniforms, insignia and carrying Rhodesian weapons and equipment.

Incursions continued through 1968, and ZIPRA was even able to establish a string of six bases inside Rhodesia that remained undetected for three months before being destroyed by Rhodesian forces in March 1968. In addition, Rhodesian forces pursued 125 guerrillas in a running battle during Operation 'Cauldron'.[22] Overall, the guerrilla strategy failed disastrously – precipitating wholesale revisions of insurgents' strategies and tactics. By 1969, most of the guerrillas had been either killed or captured, and the limited raids to date had failed to incite an African uprising. Support among the African population appeared to be steadfastly behind the Rhodesian Government, as demonstrated by ZIPRA and ZANLA's continued reliance on kidnapping and coercion to fill their decimated ranks of guerrilla fighters.[23]

The lull (late 1969 to late 1972)

In this period, the leaderships of ZIPRA and ZANLA paused their guerrilla incursions into Rhodesia and re-evaluated their strategies. In early 1969, ZIPRA attempted to establish a foothold in Rhodesia across the Zambezi River from ZIPRA's bases in Zambia.

As the BSAP chronology describes, those efforts failed – and ZIPRA limited its military activities inside Rhodesia:

Z.A.P.U. [ZIPRA] once more attempted to establish itself by infiltrating groups across the Zambia border at various vantage points, at the same time undertaking hit-and-run attacks. By April these tactics had also failed to achieve significant results … Following the failure of the January/February 1970 offensive, Z.A.P.U. terrorists restricted their activities to reconnaissance and hit-and-run tactics along the southern border.[24]

For four years prior, ZANLA and ZIPRA suffered defeat after defeat – leaving them demoralized and exhausted in terms of men and materiel.[25] According to Rhodesian Intelligence chief Ken Flower, 'although CIO did not fully appreciate it at the time, the nationalists' morale had been shattered by the Security Forces' successes: the extent of this defeat was such that the war virtually stopped for four years'.[26] Although the Rhodesian Security Forces may have succeeded in eliminating the earlier guerrilla incursions with relative ease, Ken Flower later in his autobiography described a gap in the CIO's intelligence collection during this time: '… a few minor incursions occurred during the lull in fighting. CIO was never fully certain at this time what ZAPU and ZANU were up to – regrouping, licking their wounds, or just lying low…'[27] The lack of intelligence on ZAPU, in particular, probably was due to a lack of African nationalist activity ('laying low') rather than a lack of CIO intelligence collection capabilities.

During this period, the Chinese-supported ZANU leadership also re-evaluated its strategy in light of Mao Zedong's revolutionary theories. The evolution in ZANLA strategy was to combine guerrilla war with a new emphasis on politicization of the peasantry. Whereas ZAPU and ZANU previously had believed that the Zimbabwean peasantry would instinctively rise up and support the guerrilla fighters whenever they appeared, the nationalist leaders had underestimated the innate conservatism of peasant communities. To win the support of the rural African population in Rhodesia, the African nationalists would require intensive political indoctrination rather than a mere show of force. Cilliers quotes a paper written in 1974 by Wellington Nyangoni, in which Nyangoni states: '… by 1971, ZANU's emphasis was on the political education of the Zimbabwe workers and peasants. The purpose of this was to elicit support from the masses and to recruit more people for guerrilla warfare training…'[28] Regardless of their plans for mass subversion of the peasant consciousness, coercion and intimidation remained at the core of the African nationalist strategy. Although the peasantry in subverted areas could be counted on to provide passive support to guerrillas operating nearby, active support often only came following threatened or actual violence to terrorize the indecisive.

As part of its new strategy, ZANU focused on developing a support base among the rural African population living in the TTLs along Rhodesia's north-eastern border with Mozambique's Teté Province.[29] CIO chief Ken Flower described the intelligence available to the CIO:

> The lull in the war showed signs of being over in the latter half of 1971 when Intelligence reports coming in from the north-eastern districts indicated a guerrilla presence in the border regions and fleeting contact was made with columns

of porters passing southwards through the Mazarabani and surrounding areas. The guerrilla presence and activity were not defined clearly enough for the Security Forces to react militarily, but the consistency of the reports was such that it seemed that guerrillas were now living among the population.[30]

Mozambique's Portuguese colonial rulers had been fighting an African nationalist insurgency of their own since 1964. The Mozambique guerrilla war was dominated by a Marxist-oriented guerrilla organization named the *Frente de Libertação de Moçambique* (FRELIMO). Beginning in March 1968, FRELIMO intensified operations in Mozambique's Teté Province – and by November 1970, it had crossed the Zambezi River to operate in that portion of Teté Province on the Rhodesian border.[31] FRELIMO originally offered to house ZIPRA bases in FRELIMO-controlled areas of Teté, but ZIPRA declined the offer – preferring to conduct its conventional military strategy from bases in Zambia. ZANLA, however, accepted the offer and began operating out of Mozambique in 1971. At the same time, ZANLA operatives crossed the border and began indoctrinating the rural populations inhabiting the TTLs across the border in North-Eastern Rhodesia. Guerrilla cadres enlisted porters to bring weapons and supplies from the camps in Mozambique to stock caches in North-Eastern Rhodesia – and the shared ethnic identity of the Korekore people living on both sides of the border in this region aided ZANLA's mission immensely.*

By focusing on mobilizing support among the rural population – and avoiding contact with the Rhodesian Security Forces or the European population – ZANLA was able to establish a relatively secure base of operations in Rhodesia and maintain a reliable supply line back to camps in Teté, as described in the official BSAP account:

> During 1971, ZANU established a protocol with FRELIMO (both parties then Chinese Peoples Republic (CPR) orientated) as well as capitalizing on the tribal affinity, which existed across the international border of North-Eastern Rhodesia with Teté Province, Mozambique. This resulted in the establishment of a supply and communications route from Zambia through the Teté Province to North-Eastern Rhodesia where ZANU also commenced establishing bases, arms caches and contacts within Rhodesia from where recruits were also removed for military training. By the end of 1972, this led to a situation where ZANU was in a position to launch a terrorist offensive in the North East of Rhodesia, having completed the basic precepts to wage guerrilla warfare in the classical Chinese Communist style.[32]

---

*   The border area of North-Eastern Rhodesia consisted of a 241 km long frontier with Mozambique's Teté Province and a 64 km wide group of TTLs – inhabited largely by the Korekore Shona sub-tribe. The Korekore had a long history of animosity to European rule; the region was largely undeveloped and featured a rugged terrain offering cover for guerrilla movement.

According to Annette Seegers, the successful ZANLA mobilization of the popu-lace in the region did not lead to the creation of a 'liberated zone' with ZANU-run political committees or institutions. Despite the support of many (if not most) of the local inhabitants, ZANLA control of the area was far from complete. As Seegers points out, the Rhodesian Security Forces still had the ability to locate and attack any detected guerrilla activity.[33]

The Rhodesian CIO was not completely ignorant of guerrilla activities in the Rhodesian regions bordering Teté,[34] but a general complacency worked to mute any Rhodesian reaction. One possible explanation is that the CIO may have believed that they had successfully contained the threat within Teté. The Rhodesian CIO had been monitoring FRELIMO's gradual progress over several years from camps in Tanzania through Northern Teté toward the Rhodesian border.[35] To monitor FRELIMO's progress, the CIO obtained a 'gentlemen's agreement' from the Portuguese colo-nial authorities to operate a clandestine intelligence collection unit made up of Mozambicans in Teté.[36] As described in his autobiography, Flower states: '... the situation convinced CIO of the need to carry out our own intelligence pursuits in Teté province for which we had the blessing of the DGS [the Portuguese *Direccao Genral de Suguranca* – aka the General Security Directorate]; our probing led to the discovery of a significant ZANLA presence in Teté'.[37] That agreement almost certainly was worked out in the context of Exercise 'Alcora'[38] – a then-top-secret agreement covering military and intelligence cooperation among Rhodesia, South Africa and Portugal.* The Rhodesian response to the intensified FRELIMO/ZANLA activity in Teté was to deploy the Rhodesian SAS and the 1st Battalion, Rhodesian Light Infantry into Teté on an almost-continuous basis. At the same time, the total strength of Rhodesian forces deployed on the Rhodesian side of the border equaled the equivalent of one infantry company.[39]

Despite the CIO's intelligence of a 'significant ZANLA presence in Teté', the Rhodesian Security Forces seemed surprisingly unaware of the ZANLA infiltration of the Rhodesian north-eastern border region. The Rhodesians also had little under-standing that ZANLA was successfully employing its mass indoctrination strategy to subvert the local population – many of whom were enlisted as porters to ferry arms and equipment from camps in Mozambique to caches in Rhodesia. The Rhodesian Intelligence failure to detect ZANLA's covert presence in the bordering Rhodesian territory largely was due to ZANLA's dismantlement of the government's 'Ground Coverage'[†] capabilities there. ZANLA was able to dismantle the 'Ground Coverage' network in the north-east due to the BSAP's sparse presence there and relative neglect.[40] With the loss of its 'eyes and ears' on the ground, the Rhodesian Security Forces were blinded to developments that led to Phase 2 in the conflict.

---

*   Exercise 'Alcora' often is mistakenly linked to the Rhodesian CBW effort in postings on the internet. 'Alcora' ended with the 'Carnation Revolution' in 1974, before the Rhodesian CBW effort began.

†   'Ground Coverage': a network of information sources and informers.

To sum up the situation at the end of Phase 1 of the war, the Rhodesian Security Forces had managed to successfully isolate and eliminate all the guerrilla incursions into the country with significant losses to the insurgents. At the same time, the guerrillas had failed to establish any permanent military presence in Rhodesia, except for a nascent ZANLA foothold in the country's north-eastern region bordering Mozambique's Teté Province. Losses to the Rhodesian Security Forces during this phase had been modest; guerrilla loses, on the other hand, had been much higher – and these losses had failed to achieve any meaningful objective. Given their successes in countering guerrilla incursions, the Rhodesian strategy remained unchanged throughout Phase 1. The strategy focused on treating the guerrilla threat as a law-and-order problem requiring a police response. Rhodesia's small regular military was seen as an adjunct to the police effort.

The second phase of the conflict (late 1972 to early 1975)

The second phase of the Rhodesian conflict began on 21 December 1972 with a ZANLA attack on Marc de Borchgrave's Altena Farm in Rhodesia's Centenary District. The attack on this isolated farmstead rang alarm bells throughout Rhodesia – alerting the country to the extent of the guerrilla presence in that region and signaling to the majority of Rhodesians that the nearly four-year lull in the insurgency had ended. A crucial difference that marked the second and third phases of the conflict was the guerrillas' emphasis on winning at least the passive (if not active) cooperation of the rural African population. The guerrillas also successfully managed to dismantle the BSAP Intelligence networks in the region – effectively blinding the Rhodesians to guerrilla build-up in the north-east. By late January 1974, guerrilla infiltration in the north-east shut down the Rhodesian Intelligence system of informers and co-optees, and ground intelligence could not be resurrected despite the BSAP's efforts.[41] The tempo of the conflict also had changed: after the Altena Farm attack, guerrilla operations in North-Eastern Rhodesia were continual, as opposed to the previous sporadic guerrilla hit-and-run raids.

The Rhodesian response

The dramatic transformation in the guerrilla threat was not lost on the Rhodesians. On 18 January 1973, Rhodesian Prime Minister Ian Smith described the nature of the new threat to the nation in a radio broadcast. In his speech, Smith said:

> The terrorist incursion in the northeast of our country has developed in a manner that we had not previously experienced and as a result we have to face up to a number of serious problems. In the first place, for some months now these terrorists have been operating in this area, quietly and methodically undermining the local population. They have done this in a number of ways. Firstly, through intimidation at the point of a gun; secondly they have found a few witchdoctors of doubtful character and of little substance, and succeeded in bribing them to their side.[42]

In line with the Rhodesian Army's emphasis on a counterguerrilla strategy (as opposed to counterinsurgency), the overt reaction of the Rhodesian authorities to the increased guerrilla threat was to extend the call-up period for men of military age, allocate more money for defense spending and establish the *cordon sanitaire* and Protected Village (PV) programs.

With the attack on Altena Farm, the Rhodesian Security Forces established the first of several Joint Operations Centers (JOC) to coordinate operations in an area with an active guerrilla presence. Located at Centenary and later moved to Bindura, the first JOC (codenamed 'Hurricane') covered the north-eastern region. Given that guerrilla activity seemed limited to the 'Hurricane' region, almost all the resources of the Rhodesian Security Forces were focused there. The Rhodesian strategy was twofold:

Figure 1.1 Rhodesian Prime Minister Ian Smith. (© unknown – suspected to be in the public domain)

first, to prevent guerrilla infiltration from Mozambique into Rhodesia; and second, to separate the guerrillas from their rural African supporters. To accomplish the first element of the strategy, the Rhodesian Security Forces increased their presence in the country's north-eastern districts and created a *cordon sanitaire* along the border with Mozambique. The *cordon sanitaire* included fences and minefields, as well as a 'no-go area' along the border in which the Security Forces could operate without restriction. The second element was to relocate the population into the PVs.

Modeled after the camps created during the Malaysian Emergency to prevent Chinese guerrilla intimidation of Malay peasants in the 1950s, the creation of PVs was the means adopted by the Rhodesians to separate the guerrillas from possible supporters in rural villages. By isolating the guerrillas from the local population, the Security Forces believed they could identify, track and eliminate guerrilla fighters operating inside Rhodesia – much as the Rhodesians had been able to do when ZAPU guerrillas infiltrated across the Zambian border in the 1960s. The PVs also were intended to separate the guerillas from their village supporters, who often were the guerrillas' primary sources of food and supplies. As the PVs reduced the amount of food available to guerrillas from their rural supporters, the guerrillas increasingly turned to thefts from rural shops and farm stores.

One senior BSAP officer commented that:

> The idea behind the PV programme was sound and it had worked in Malaya but, while recognising that it would not be popular the question remained – "how else could the SF [Security Forces] reduce the contact between the rural population and the CTs [Communist Terrorists]?" The armchair pundits who have

criticised this programme have never come up with a better idea, so the problem remained until the end of the war. However, that was one of the reasons why the CBW programme was introduced; once these stores were closed to the public the goods therein should have remained safe but, when they became targets for thieves and CTs to break in and steal, then the penalties of such behaviour were that the incidence would be seriously reduced in the future once it became known and the stores hopefully would be left alone.[43]

Limitations in manpower and materiel did not allow Rhodesian authorities to fully implement either element of their strategy. The *cordon sanitaire* was largely ineffective, and the PV program only further served to alienate the rural African population. Announced in late 1973, the PV concept forced the peasants off their traditional lands and relocated them in government-established camps[44] – often several kilometers from their fields and pastures. Because of insufficient government resources, many of the PVs lacked the most basic amenities, which only served to stoke the peasants' increasing ire. The Guard Force, made up of locally recruited Africans, was intended to protect the PVs; yet the Guard Force – largely undisciplined and untrained – often exploited and mistreated the PV inhabitants. As a result, the forcible relocation of tens of thousands of rural peasants into PVs only exacerbated their mistrust and anger at the Rhodesian Government and fueled the refugee exodus that, in part, led young men to flood into the guerrilla training camps.

The increase in resources devoted to 'Hurricane' seemed to have contained the guerrilla threat for the moment. By the end of 1973, only approximately 145 guerrillas remained in the 'Hurricane' region, and guerrilla losses totaled 179. Losses among the Rhodesian Security Forces included 44 dead; 12 European civilians also were killed that year.[45] By the end of 1974, the Rhodesian Security Forces estimated that only approximately 70 ZANLA guerrillas remained in Rhodesia's north-east.[46] The advantage held by the Rhodesian Security Forces was that they could focus all their resources against guerrillas in a relatively small, confined region.

A BSAP appraisal of the situation describes it as:

> By November 1974, Z.A.N.L.A., whose operations were still confined to the 'Hurricane' theatre, was sustaining heavy casualties and was beginning to suffer reversals. It was further weakened by upheavals in the High Command, which came to a head that month. Opposition to Karanga domination led to open revolt by field commanders, such as Thomas Nhari and Dakarai Badza. The incident was officially known as the 'Nhari Rebellion'.[47]

The Nhari Rebellion had been instigated by the Rhodesian Special Branch to sow dissension among ZANLA. The Special Branch had obtained intelligence that ZANLA commanders were disgruntled about the worsening conditions in the field, while senior commanders reportedly enjoyed more comfortable lives and various perks at the base camps. Instigated by the Rhodesian Special Branch, these junior field commanders focused their resentment on the senior leadership. Ken Flower had high hopes for cultivating Nhari and his followers.

Acting on this Intelligence, we had met some of ZANLA's junior commanders in the field. From these meetings it was clear that there was dissension within their ranks which we could turn to our advantage. Among those contacted were Thomas Nhari, ZANLA commander of the Nehanda Sector, and Dakari Badza, commander of the Chaminuka Sector... To sow further dissension we had ready tools in Nhari and his companions, who became willing conspirators. Nhari seized command of ZANLA's Chifomo base on the Mozambique/ Zambia border, indulging in random killings as he did so ... With every day that passed, CIO was gaining ground within ZANLA. But Tongogara then began to recover something of his command and re-entered Chifombo with the co-operation of FRELIMO. Nhari, his principals and some fifty of his followers were executed, and in the ensuing purge within ZANLA forces in Zambia about 150 more guerrillas were killed.[48]

The Nhari Rebellion had long-lasting repercussions for ZANU and ZANLA – including (most significantly) the subordination of ZANLA to ZANU. The trial[49] of Nhari and his cohort was conducted and presided over by Herbert Chitepo, who ZANLA believed to have sympathized with Nhari.[50] Chitepo condemned the rebels and ordered they be turned over to the Mozambique authorities for punishment. According to Fay Chung, a mid-level ZANU official at the time:

> The military leaders under Tongogara, while satisfied with the conduct of the trials, were not satisfied with the punishments meted out. They believed that Chitepo had shown extreme leniency, considering that the rebels had actually disrupted the armed struggle and killed some of their own colleagues. Soon after the trial, the military leaders executed the rebels secretly, without the consent of the political leadership. These extra-judicial executions were to cause further internal conflict within ZANU, with the political leaders dividing against the military leaders.[51]

The sentences imposed by the ZANU court on the rebels angered Tongogara (ZANLA's military commander), particularly because he and his family had been rebel targets. After the ZANU tribunal granted lenient treatment to the rebels, Tongogara ordered their secret executions. Tongogara's unilateral rejection of the leadership's decision regarding Nhari created a breach between the political leadership in ZANU and the military command in ZANLA.

In addition to their overt strategy to combat the insurgency, the CIO and BSAP Special Branch pressed for the creation of a joint Special Branch-Army covert intelligence collection unit (the Selous Scouts) to compensate for the loss of vital intelligence networks.* The formation of the Selous Scouts transitioned Rhodesian intelligence gathering from a strictly police function into a major role for the army's

---

* The Selous Scouts grew out of an earlier failed attempt to form a joint Army-BSAP tracking unit. That effort collapsed due to interservice rivalry over resources and command authority.

Special Forces – and the Selous Scouts became one of the most significant intelligence producers,[52] as well as the covert action arm, of Rhodesian Intelligence. In creating the Selous Scouts, Rhodesia sought to resurrect its earlier attempts to form 'pseudo gangs' based on the British experience in Kenya.

In discussing the impetus for the creation of the Selous Scouts, the unit commander – Ron Reid-Daly – stated:

> While nothing much was gained from the point of view of killing (the original concept), a substantial amount of information became available to the security forces. CIO, Special Branch, and the army realizing that they had something that might well be an effective substitute for the gap in Special Branch intelligence took the idea to Ian Smith, who gave it his warm blessing.[53]

The CIO turned to the Rhodesian Army for manpower and logistics to form the Selous Scouts, but mandated that the Special Branch be responsible for all intelligence collected by the unit. To ensure Special Branch control of the intelligence, Special Branch members were assigned to the Selous Scouts and commanded by a Special Branch chief superintendent.* Although these liaison officers never numbered more than about 12 men at any one time, they played a pivotal role in ensuring the success of Selous Scouts' operations.[54]

Impact of Portuguese withdrawal from Mozambique (1974)

A key turning point in the Rhodesian conflict occurred on 25 April 1974 when a military *coup d'état* in Lisbon overthrew President Caetano and replaced him with Army General Antonio de Spinola. Within a month of the *coup* – and the resulting 'Carnation Revolution' – the new Portuguese Government ended its counterinsurgency cooperation with Rhodesia and requested that the Rhodesian Security Forces refrain from any cross-border operations.[55] A vocal opponent of Portugal's efforts to maintain control over its African colonies, de Spinola on 27 July 1974 announced the right of Angola, Portuguese Guinea and Mozambique to Independence.

The ultimate impact of Portugal's withdrawal from Mozambique was to create a power vacuum that allowed FRELIMO to seize control of the government. With a FRELIMO Government in power in Mozambique, ZANLA was allowed by 1975 to establish bases all along that country's 1,231-km border with Rhodesia – effectively forcing the Rhodesian Security Forces to defend along a second front.[56] Whereas the Rhodesians had managed to contain the insurgency to the country's north-eastern areas, despite complaints about manpower and materiel shortages, the liberation of Mozambique allowed ZANLA to open a second front that eventually would stretch Rhodesia's limited resources beyond the breaking point.

---

* Chief Superintendent Michael J.P. 'Mac' McGuinness led the Selous Scout intelligence effort for the conflict's duration.

Replacement of the friendly Portuguese colonial administration by an African nationalist party also meant a serious reduction – then elimination – of Rhodesian imports and exports passing through the Mozambican port of Beira. While in friendly hands, Mozambique (like South Africa) had lent a blind eye to Rhodesian sanctions-busting activity; the FRELIMO Government was not so inclined. Lastly, the Portuguese abandonment of Mozambique encouraged the African population living in Rhodesia about the possibility that one day, European domination of Rhodesia might end. With this encouragement, the exodus of Rhodesian refugees grew – and many of them found their way to ZANLA guerrilla training camps that had been newly established in Mozambique.[57]

Based largely in Zambia, ZIPRA activities were much more modest – focused more on reconnaissance, intelligence gathering and the formation of undercover cells of supporters. ZIPRA's goals were to prepare for a conventional invasion of Rhodesia along a Soviet-inspired model, and not the model of mass indoctrination and intimidation employed by ZANLA.

In 1974, ZIPRA's achievements included the following:

> During the year 1974 Z.P.R.A. [ZIPRA] had commenced building up logistics along the northern border, improving its waterborne capabilities on Kariba and the Zambesi, reconnoitering the Rhodesian bank at suitable points and establishing food and war material caches inland, generally taking a leaf from Z.A.N.L.A.'s book by preparing the ground before major infiltration. During this period weapons from the U.S.S.R. were being channeled to Z.A.P.U. ... By late 1974, Z.P.R.A. had programmed Batonka tribespeople and established a network of caches in the Omay T.T.L.[58]

South African-brokered *détente* (late 1974 to late 1975)

Realizing that the Portuguese withdrawal from Mozambique and Angola signaled a sea change in the balance of power in Southern Africa in favor of African nationalist governments, South African Prime Minister John Vorster in a 23 October 1974 speech before the South African Senate called for a *détente* with Africa. President Kenneth Kaunda of Zambia responded a few days later – saying that Vorster's speech was 'the voice of reason for which Africa and the world have been waiting'. Kaunda also forced the Zimbabwean nationalist leadership to unite under the UANC banner of Bishop Abel Muzorewa to represent the African nationalists in negotiations with the Smith Government to end the conflict.*

Under South African pressure to support the *détente* process, Rhodesians agreed to participate in the *détente* on 11 December 1974;[59] shortly thereafter, Rhodesian Prime Minister Smith ordered the release of the African nationalist leaders, who by

---

*   Bishop Muzorewa's UANC was the only legally recognized black-led nationalist party in Rhodesia. The UANC was allowed to operate legally inside Rhodesia because of its commitment to non-violence. Both ZAPU and ZANU were banned inside the country.

that time had been in Rhodesian detention for more than a decade. Both Vorster and Smith believed that the guerrilla groups would respect the *détente* and cease offensive operations. ZANU leader Robert Mugabe was one of those leaders released in the *détente*, and he fled across the Rhodesian border to Mozambique soon after. Despite a short-lived lull in guerrilla attacks, the tempo of guerrilla operations increased – and by 10 January 1975, the Rhodesian authorities ceased releasing detained nationalists because the nationalists were not observing the ceasefire.[60] Prime Minister Smith balked at concessions aimed at moving forward to a constitutional conference. Smith's intransigence led the South Africans in August 1975 to withdraw the 2,000 police officers stationed in Rhodesia, but many of the helicopters and their ground crews remained, as did many South Africans, who were integrated into Rhodesian forces.

Although Security Force operations in 1973 and early 1974 had eliminated all but approximately 70 ZANLA guerrillas in the north-east, the guerrilla groups used the *détente* throughout 1975 to reinforce their depleted numbers, to re-arm and to resupply in preparation for the stepped-up attacks in Northern and Eastern Rhodesia.[61] Although the guerrillas benefited from the *détente*, other factors reduced their effectiveness – including: (a) the losses experienced during 1973 and 1974; (b) the assassination of ZANU leader-in-exile Herbert Chitepo;* and (c) the factional infighting (the Nhari Rebellion) that left many senior ZANLA field commanders dead among the ZANU/ZANLA leadership.

Following Chitepo's assassination, Zambian authorities launched an investigation that resulted in the arrest and detention of most of ZANLA's leadership for more than a year. The Chitepo assassination, as well as the increasing disaffection of the frontline governments for the bickering Rhodesian nationalists, culminated in the restriction of thousands of guerrillas to their base camps.[62]

The decimation of the experienced ZANLA operational commanders – through death or detention – left a void that was difficult to fill. The impact of this loss was that relatively junior, inexperienced guerrilla commanders were tasked to lead men against battle-hardened Rhodesian troops. Under these conditions, the Rhodesian units dominated the engagements – and with predictable consequences for the guerrilla bands, as described by CIO chief Ken Flower:

> ZANLA's war was brought to a standstill. The detention and flight of the leaders had a serious effect on morale and ZANLA's casualty rate grew catastrophically as less experienced commanders and their men fell victim to Rhodesian Security Forces. By December 1975 only a handful were still operating within Rhodesia. Superficially, it appeared that Rhodesia was once again on top of the situation, which encouraged Ian Smith to begin his talks with Nkomo.[63]

---

*   Herbert Chitepo died on 18 March 1975 when a car bomb denotated underneath his vehicle outside his home in Lusaka, Zambia.

According to Martin and Johnson:

> By late 1975 the *détente* exercise had brought the guerrilla war to a virtual stand-still, as Smith had hoped it would, and the Rhodesians estimated that there were only three guerrilla groups with about ten men each inside the country. Guerrilla commanders say that the figure was slightly higher but admit that, of a force of more than 400 early in the year, about half had been killed and most of the remainder had retreated to Mozambique.[64]

As well as losses in leadership and manpower, ZANLA also experienced serious resupply problems. Supplied by China, ZANLA's access to arms and munitions was much more precarious than that experienced by Soviet-supplied ZIPRA. In comparison to ZANLA, ZIPRA was equipped with more, better and heavier weapons. In addition to a lack of supplies, all of ZANLA's weapons, ammunition and equipment had to be carried by porters from bases in Mozambique to camps in Rhodesia. The large influx of guerrilla recruits compounded the supply problems at the camps; food, clothing, blankets and medicines were in short supply.

According to Fay Chung's description:

> One of my most vivid memories of Pungwe III guerrilla military base in Mozambique was the severe shortage of food. Long lines of freedom fighters would queue up to receive a handful of *mangai*, dried grains of maize that had been boiled. In addition, each one received a bit of salt, literally in their hands, as there was a shortage of plates ... One of the major problems besides the lack of food and clothing was illness, in particular dysentery and malaria. These were both killer diseases that took as many lives as the enemy bullets.[65]

For food and clothing, the guerrilla fighters in Rhodesia were largely left to depend on their supporters in the villages and on thefts from stores.

Decisive turning point

By the mid-1970s, Rhodesia confronted the very real likelihood that it would soon be unable to counter increases in both guerrilla recruitment and the number of guerrilla infiltrations. With the collapse of the Portuguese colonial regime in Mozambique, the Rhodesian Security Forces were stretched extremely thin in the face of an insurgency that was becoming more numerous and better equipped than ever before. The collapse of Portuguese colonial rule in 1974 also allowed the Rhodesian insurgents to open a second front from bases in Mozambique. The insurgents also benefited by Zambia's release of leaders detained following Chitepo's assassination. Although largely driven out of Rhodesia, the guerrilla forces amassed a relatively large force of recruits – undergoing training in Mozambique, Zambia and Tanzania. According to Seegers: 'By the end of 1975 there were between 5,000 and 10,000 guerrillas of ZANLA gathered in Mozambican camps, as well as a much smaller ZIPRA contingent, and in January 1976 infiltrations began again. Unlike their earlier efforts, the guerrillas now had few recruitment problems and could infiltrate Zimbabwe at more points'.

On 6 February 1976, Prime Minister Ian Smith announced in a nationwide radio broadcast that Rhodesians should prepare for a renewed guerrilla offensive. Smith's speech reflected official concerns based on intelligence assessments of possible increased guerrilla infiltrations. Selous Scout commander Lieutenant Colonel Ron Reid-Daly told army commander Lieutenant General Peter Walls* that the military's attempts to eliminate the guerrilla presence in Rhodesia were akin to emptying a bathtub with a teacup while both taps were running.[66] From the ZANU perspective, Fay Chung describes the situation as 'the Rhodesian regime was clearly losing the battle for hearts and minds, with the guerrilla army swelling from just over 3,000 before *détente* began in 1974 to potentially tens of thousands at the end of *détente* in mid-1976, as hundreds of thousands of refugees flooded into neighboring countries'.[67]

The final phase of the conflict (1976 to late 1979)

The third and final phase of the war began on 18 January 1976 when 60 ZIPRA guerrillas infiltrated into Rhodesia, and the threat of guerrilla incursions all along the border with Mozambique became a reality. From January to April 1976, three waves of guerrilla forces entered Rhodesia;[68] on 6 February 1976, Smith told the nation that Rhodesia faced the most serious guerrilla threat since 1972. With ZANLA's move into Southern Mozambique,[69] the guerrillas were stretching Rhodesia's limited military thinner and thinner as the Security Forces attempted to defend an increasingly vulnerable border.† Despite rhetoric about the need to win the hearts and minds of the rural black peasants, the prevalent Rhodesian attitude was to exterminate the terrorist threat.

To organize a coordinated response to the guerrilla incursions, Rhodesian authorities established JOC 'Thrasher' (Operation 'Thrasher') in February 1976 and JOC 'Repulse' (Operation 'Repulse') in May 1976. To counter the increased ZIPRA threat, JOC 'Tangent' (Operation 'Tangent') was established in August 1976. By the beginning of the rainy season in the fall of 1976, an estimated 1,200 guerillas were operating in Rhodesia, and another estimated 6,000 were preparing to enter the country.[70] By the middle of 1977, guerrilla activity had spread across the whole of Rhodesia.[71]

The Rhodesia Security Forces understood that one of the guerrillas' greatest vulnerabilities was their dependence on food, clothing and medical supplies from

---

*   Reid-Daly and Walls were old friends and comrades, and served together in the Malayan Emergency – and later, in the Rhodesian Light Infantry. Walls was an officer and Reid-Daly was a non-commissioned officer.

†   One reason that Rhodesian resources were stretched as thinly as they were was because of the government's lack of political will to open the army to greater numbers of black recruits. The decision constrained the size of the Rhodesian Army and placed a heavy burden on the small European population, which constituted the majority of the country's skilled labor.

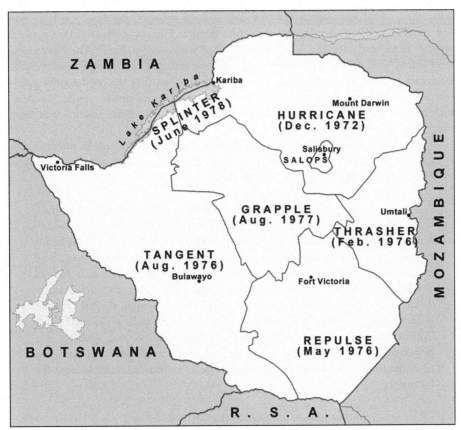

Figure 1.2 Rhodesian Security Forces' operating areas. (Source: <www.wikipedia.org> CCL)[72]

their local supporters inside Rhodesia. The PV strategy – instituted in the early 1970s – aimed to prevent villagers from supplying guerrillas in their areas; this vulnerability was becoming acute by 1976. According to Cilliers: 'During 1976, intelligence reports indicated that ZANLA forces in the Hurricane operational area were increasingly able to obtain food from labour compounds on white commercial farms. Both the movement of the local population into Protected Villages and the general drought had reduced the available food within the Tribal Trust Lands'.[73]

Operation 'Turkey'

In January 1977, the Rhodesian Government enacted an amendment to its emergency powers legislation – empowering far more stringent food security measures. Known as Operation 'Turkey', these steps consisted of white farmers rationing food on a day-to-day basis to their farm workers – allowing the laborers only that food sufficient to feed themselves for one day and no more. Operation 'Turkey' was dependent on the cooperation of the white farmers and, as such, could be applied only to European farming areas where it had wide acceptance.[74] The operations were introduced first in the Mtepatepa farming area, between the Chiweshe and Madziwa TTLs.[75] Although relatively successful in limiting the food supply available in European farming areas, Operation 'Turkey' could not be applied consistently in the TTLs. The most notable region where Operation 'Turkey' was least effective was Ndebele land.

The lack of means to control the movement of people also limited the effectiveness of Operation 'Turkey', as food was transported from areas of relative lax control to areas under stringent controls, as Cilliers points out:

> As the war progressed, reports received from Selous Scout pseudo teams indicated that the limited results initially obtained were diminishing. At a later stage attempts were made to enforce food control within the Tribal Trust Lands themselves by placing legal limitations on the amount of foodstuffs being held in stock by stores, as well as on the amounts sold. Ration cards were printed and issued. Store-owners had to apply for permits from District Commissioners to buy food supplies in bulk. These measures would theoretically have further reduced the availability of food supplies for insurgent forces in the rural areas. To institute and effectively enforce such measures, however, total control over population movement was needed to prevent members of the local population from obtaining food from the nearest village or town if unavailable from the local store.[76]

A 1979 report by the Catholic Commission for Justice and Peace (CCJP) claimed that 'according to government regulation, rural Blacks are not allowed to own or carry food beyond the immediate requirements of their families. Quantities of food have been confiscated from granaries and from people traveling so that the overall food shortage in the tribal areas has been made even more acute'.[77] As Rhodesian Security Forces attempted to limit the available food surplus in the TTLs, they instituted punitive measures against villages suspected of supporting guerrillas – including the destruction of granaries, grinding mills and cattle. Efforts also were instituted to hinder the transportation of food between regions; for examples, buses often were searched for contraband food.

According to Danaher:

> I talked with several rural people who reported that the buses on which they were traveling had been stopped by military personnel, who then proceeded to check the amount of food being carried by each person. 'They let us keep a few kilos each and then what we couldn't eat on the spot was destroyed,' one elderly woman told me.[78]

Clearly, rural blacks frequently transported foodstuffs and other supplies from areas with surpluses to areas experiencing shortages.

War intensifies, cracks appear

In a 12 January 1977 meeting with Ian Smith, Rhodesian Intelligence chief Ken Flower argued that the conflict could not be won by military means; the military situation would only deteriorate further. After discussing the issue at length, Smith seemed begrudgingly to agree – and two days later, the military situation was raised at a War Council meeting. There, the War Council was informed that 'action would be required very soon, as the Security Forces would be unable to hold the position indefinitely'. Smith stated at the meeting: '… there… would be no end of the war until a political solution was achieved. It was vital, however, that Rhodesia remain in a strong position militarily in order to enable the Prime Minister to negotiate from a position of strength…'[79] As of March 1977, the Rhodesian Government realized that it faced a full-blown insurgency and, on 23 March, established the Combined Operations (COMOPS) – placing the military in control of counterinsurgency operations.[80] The head of COMOPS was Lieutenant General Peter Walls – a 50-year old, Rhodesian-born graduate of Sandhurst. A veteran of World War II – having served in the famous Black Watch Regiment – Walls also had counterinsurgency experience from his time serving as an officer in 'C' Squadron (Rhodesia), SAS during the Malayan Emergency.

The insurgency was intensifying and expanding nationwide. By mid-1977, attacks were occurring in every Rhodesian province – including the European farming enclaves. By November 1977, the total guerrilla strength inside Rhodesia was more than 5,200 men – and attacks averaged around 500 a month.[81] For the remainder of the war, insurgent numbers both inside and outside Rhodesia continued to grow.[82] Although the Security Forces inflicted greater numbers of casualties than ever before, the increased guerrilla recruitment more than made up for the losses. A dramatic increase in Soviet Bloc aid in 1977 fueled the guerrilla escalation – and according to a declassified April 1978 CIA assessment: 'In 1977, total Soviet military shipments reaching Zimbabwe rebel groups were triple the 1976 level. For the first time Moscow furnished them a small number of up-to-date heavy artillery pieces and armored vehicles in addition to traditional small arms, machineguns, and small-caliber mortars. This escalation was in direct response to insurgent appeals following Rhodesia's late-1976 cross-border raids'.[83]

The effectiveness of the greatly expanded guerrilla forces has been widely debated. ZIPRA cadres often

Figure 1.3 Lieutenant General Peter Walls.
(Source: public domain)

are described as better trained and disciplined than their ZANLA counterparts, but by this stage in the conflict, relatively few ZIPRA guerrillas were actively operating against Rhodesian forces. ZAPU head Joshua Nkomo – in a 1977 meeting with Soviet leaders – had decided on a strategy that emphasized ZIPRA development of a large conventional military force with only a small effort aimed at guerrilla activities.[84] Nkomo's goal was to build a military capable of a conventional invasion of Rhodesia from Zambia – complete with armored units and fighter aircraft. The Soviet role in 'Zero Hour' remains uncertain, but at least some Soviet military advisors were advocating Nkomo concentrate his forces for 'decisive blows'.[85]

A declassified March 1978 CIA assessment of ZIPRA's performance stated that:

> ZAPU guerrillas usually have fared poorly against Rhodesian Security Forces. If the guerrillas should surprise and isolate a small Rhodesian unit, however, they could achieve a limited tactical success they could label a significant military victory. ZAPU leaders apparently believe they need such a victory to boost deteriorating morale and offset this week's successful Rhodesian raid near Feira during which at least 80 guerrillas were killed and large amounts of equipment and weapons – including SA-7 surface-to-air missiles – were destroyed.[86]

Most accounts claim that ZANLA forces (making up the majority of guerrillas operating inside Rhodesia) were poorly trained, ill-equipped and undisciplined. In accounts of firefights with Rhodesian Security Forces, the guerrillas are described as having poor fire discipline, inaccurate marksmanship and a tendency to flee at the first opportunity. ZANLA seems to have been ill-prepared to rapidly train and equip the large influx of recruits to take on the Security Forces – and ZANLA's strategy was not to confront the Security Forces in firefights; instead, ZANLA sought to stretch the Rhodesian Security Forces to their breaking point by flooding the country with guerrillas, who would conduct hit-and-run attacks on soft (undefended or lightly defended) targets. In this role, the ZANLA guerrillas were adequately equipped.

ZANLA's military strategy was to overextend the Rhodesian Security Forces, which never amounted to more than 4,400 full-time, professional soldiers who were supplemented with part-time army and BSAP reservists. European manpower was at a premium, and extending the call-up period for men serving in reserve units meant that skilled labor was moved from productive industrial and commercial application to military service. The loss of skilled labor had economic consequences for Rhodesia: coupled with a global economic recession, a rapidly rising defense budget and international sanctions, the loss of skilled labor (both through call-ups and emigration) exacted a heavy toll on Rhodesia's economic and financial well-being.

Aiming at the most vulnerable targets, ZANLA also began a campaign of attacks on European farms in the nation's Eastern Highlands – one of Rhodesia's agricultural heartlands.[87] The attacks aimed at damaging European morale and forcing a white flight from the farms that produced a significant proportion of the agricultural product exported by Rhodesia. In addition, guerrilla attacks on the government infrastructure in rural Rhodesia resulted in an almost complete collapse of medical, veterinary, education and transportation services in the TTLs. During this period at its bases in Zambia and Angola, ZIPRA was preparing to launch a conventional military invasion of Rhodesia using Soviet-supplied armored vehicles and artillery. ZIPRA's guerrilla activities were minimal and the BSAP did not see ZIPRA as a significant threat.

Rhodesian Fireforce tactics could not cope with the growing numbers of guerrillas operating in Rhodesia, and the effective dispersal – and frequent relocation – of guerrilla camps in Mozambique had reduced the number of high-value targets that the Rhodesians could strike. According to a declassified 1977 CIA intelligence assessment of the Rhodesian situation:

> Rhodesian Security Forces do not have the capabilities, especially the manpower, to wage a prolonged counterinsurgency struggle; they would be stretched very thin to defend against the expanded insurgent effort that we foresee as likely by the end of the period of this paper. Rhodesian leaders are aware both of this and of the economic strains that a prolonged war would entail. They, therefore, will attempt to continue to use their technological superiority and aggressive tactics based on this superiority rather than engage in purely defensive operations that would necessitate large numbers of men. Nevertheless, a gradual increase in guerrilla capabilities and especially the improvement in the defense of the Mozambican border area through the use of more sophisticated weapons will in time force the Rhodesians to adopt a more defensive strategy.[88]

To combat the guerrilla threat, the Rhodesians resorted to intensified external raids against ZANLA camps in Mozambique and ZIPRA bases in Zambia.

Rhodesian decision-making

Ian Smith's efforts to preserve his own personal prerogatives and political position were manifest in his refusal to delegate authority to subordinates – including the commander of COMOPS. The hypercentralization of authority in the Prime Minister's office fostered the formation of factions, interservice rivalries and personal feuds. The factionalism and rivalries crippled decisive Rhodesian decision-making on defense policy, war aims, resource allocation, division of responsibility, proper accountability and intelligence sharing.

Given the emergence of personal fiefdoms – responsive only to the Prime Minister – departmental bureaucracies became compartmentalized and formal interagency cooperation and coordination collapsed except at the senior-most levels. Rival organizations created units to pursue identical missions, and ad-hoc groups were improvised to meet needs at local levels. The breakdown of bureaucratic control in the Rhodesian security apparatus created a vacuum filled by informal networks. As a rule, informal networks are created when the existing bureaucratic institutions are weak and ineffective. These informal networks were the product of personal networks of like-minded individuals often sharing common outlooks, backgrounds, educations and experiences – providing members with mutual support, patronage, protection from political/bureaucratic rivals and alternate communication paths. Informal networks also

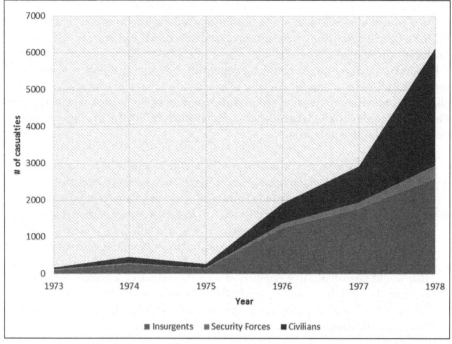

Figure 1.4 Escalating casualties in the Rhodesian War. (Source: the author, based on data provided by the Trevor Dupuy Institute, with permission of the Trevor Dupuy Institute)

damaged organizational effectiveness because they fostered factionalism, obstructed effective management and oversight, hampered communication flow and cooperation between government offices, weakened accountability, allocated resources inefficiently and promoted corruption.

The personal networks magnified the information asymmetries – thereby accentuating the problems with accountability. Responsibility and authority devolved to the lowest common denominator, as many Rhodesian security personnel sought to develop innovative, field-expedient solutions to immediate problems. Extant Rhodesian documents indicate that at least two private individuals separately suggested adapting the use of chemical agents to combat the guerrilla insurgency. In the first case, a proposal in 1973 to use sulphur mustard to reinforce the *cordon sanitaire* was never adopted; in the second case, Symington's proposal in 1976 to set up a poisoned clothing, food and beverage program was accepted.

The system of informal, personal networks created bureaucratic vacuums – pockets in which actors operated with little-to-no oversight or accountability. Chief Superintendent McGuinness operated in just such a vacuum, in which he could choose to 'work' or 'shirk' for either one or both of two highly competitive bureaucracies (the CIO on one hand and the BSAP on the other). Having split or divided loyalties allowed subordinates to balance competing loyalties (and, in the Principal-Actor paradigm, chose whom the CBW effort 'worked' for and whom it 'shirked'). The subordinates responsible for the CBW effort could balance loyalties to differing bureaucratic organizations to earn the greatest rewards while minimizing oversight and accountability. They did this largely by working through the CIO chain of command when it suited them – and they received CIO monies to fund activities that the BSAP was unwilling to provide. The CIO funds allowed them to engage in activities and hire supernumeraries not approved or sanctioned by the BSAP's leadership.

As the war intensified, the Rhodesian SAS and the Selous Scouts both competed for high-profile external missions. The army commander General John Hickman – resentful about his loss of control over Rhodesian Special Forces units – tapped the Selous Scout commander's phone so Hickman could get access to intelligence being shared with the COMOPS commander. The Selous Scout commander undertook risky operational missions without CIO knowledge, concurrence or support – preferring to rely on his own assets. Rivalries between the Selous Scout commander at Chiredzi and the Rhodesian Air Force commander at nearby Buffalo Range led to a collapse in air force support to the Scouts – a unit dependent on air transport.

Distrust among agencies resulted in a failure to share intelligence. The lack of sharing led the military to duplicate the function of Rhodesian Intelligence organizations and to compete for information from sources inside and outside Rhodesia.

Internal settlement

The deteriorating security situation – and realization that no military solution existed – led the Rhodesian political leadership to accept an interim political solution, which was largely a half-measure. This half-measure was termed the 'Internal Settlement', in which Rhodesia would hold national elections with universal suffrage, and include UANC participation. On 3 March 1978, the Rhodesian Government – along with nationalist leaders Abel Muzorewa, Ndabaningi Sithole and Cherimish Chirau – signed the 'Internal Settlement Agreement', which resulted in the setting-up of a transitional government. The 'Internal Settlement' established the framework that would govern the country until majority rule (with extensive protections for the European population) would take place on 31 December 1978. Elections were scheduled for April 1979: UANC was on the ballot, but ZANU and ZAPU were banned and their leaders boycotted the voting. In the end, the UANC won the election and Zimbabwe-Rhodesia was born, with Abel Muzorewa as its first and only Prime Minister; however, the European elite maintained control over the Security Forces.

One of Smith's hopes was that the apparent progress toward majority rule would cause the international community to lift the economic sanctions and diplomatic isolation imposed on Rhodesia, but that hope was ill-founded: the United Nations condemned the internal settlement,* no sanctions were lifted and no other nation recognized the new Zimbabwe-Rhodesian Government. In the end, the 'Internal

---

*   United Nations Security Council Resolution 423, adopted on 14 March 1978.

Settlement' and the birth of Zimbabwe-Rhodesia had no meaningful effect on the course of the war.

Coming out of the 'Internal Settlement' and Muzorewa's election, the government believed that fractures among the insurgent groups would widen and insurgents would defect to Zimbabwe-Rhodesia and the UANC. Many did abandon ZANU, but not enough to make a meaningful difference. Defectors often enlisted in the government's Security Force Auxiliary (SFA) – established by the BSAP's Special Branch as part of Operation 'Favour'.

The beginning of the end

During this same period, the global economic recession was being felt in Rhodesia, as real wages and the standard of living fell. The economic problems, the onerous military requirements, the decline in the living standard and the dramatic increase in guerrilla violence throughout Rhodesia fueled the steady growth in European emigration out of Rhodesia. With native-born Rhodesians making up only one-third of the European population, a lack of connection or nationalism was lacking in the Rhodesian polity. The majority of European Rhodesians had other places they had called – or could call – home, and home they went.

A declassified April 1979 CIA assessment stated that:

> The economic decline is closely related to the protracted guerrilla fighting. Mounting diversion of resources into defense since 1975 has directly undercut economic growth since Rhodesia buys most of its military equipment and supplies abroad, except for small arms and ammunition. Military, police, and internal security outlays in the 1978/1979 fiscal year rose to nearly one-third of the budget compared to only 17 percent in the early 1970s. Although actual casualties and physical damage by the guerrillas have been relatively low, the accelerating war effort has sharply undermined white morale, further dampening business and consumer confidence.[89]

The psyche of the white Rhodesians was changing; now growing ever more evident was a war-weariness, uncertainty about the future and perhaps a fatalistic resignation about the eventual outcome. Godwin and Hancock described it as 'exhausted by war and ready of peace at (almost) any price, Rhodesian society in 1979 exhibited unmistakable signs of military failure, moral decline, and political disintegration'.[90]

In 1979, the mounting pressure on the increasingly scarce resources forced a number of Rhodesian military officers to advocate a war strategy based on area defense. The country was surveyed and the Military Intelligence Directorate placed areas of the country in one of three categories: (1) 'Vital Assets/Ground', (2) 'Ground of Tactical Importance' and (3) 'Other Ground'.[91] Largely abandoned by the Rhodesian Security Forces, the 'Other Ground' consisted largely of areas of TTLs not adjoining white-held lands.

The Rhodesian military also was determined to put increased pressure on neighboring Zambia and Mozambique to weaken their support for the insurgents; this pressure took the form of escalatory external raids. From a military perspective, the external raids also forced the guerrillas to locate their bases further from the Rhodesian border – lengthening their transit and resupply times.

To combat the large number of guerrilla forces before they entered Rhodesia,[92] the Rhodesian Security Forces began to conduct external raids on ZANLA and ZIPRA camps in Mozambique and Zambia respectively, despite South African concerns about escalating the war. The Selous Scouts conducted the first external raid on 8 August 1976 against the ZANLA training camp at Nyadzonia, Mozambique. A now-declassified 1979 internal CIA military analysis of Rhodesian tactics states: '... During this period, the Rhodesians have developed successful tactics for inflicting heavy personnel and equipment losses on the insurgents .... The vigorous campaign of cross-border raids has kept the increasing level of guerrilla activity inside Rhodesia within manageable bounds...'[93]

Raids by the RhSAS not only targeted insurgent base camps, but also attacked Zambia and Mozambique's road and rail infrastructure. The goal of the RhSAS attacks on Zambia road and rail bridges was to impede the movement of ZIPRA conventional units to the Rhodesian border, as well as to damage the Zambian economy, which depended on its rail links for the movement of its exports to ports in Tanzania.

According to Kevin Danaher:

> On October 12, Rhodesian commandos demolished three bridges, among them the Chambeshi river bridge of the Tazara railway linking Zambia to Dar-es Salaam. This railroad is the main artery for Zambia's crucial copper exports as well as general imports, including food. During the month of November, a total of ten more bridges were either destroyed or severely damaged. This not only crippled the imports and exports of other neighboring countries to and from Zambia, it also left the Zambians with only one source of vital maize imports, namely the 150 tons being transported daily through Rhodesia and across the Victoria Falls railway bridge. The Muzorewa government finally halted this traffic completely.[94]

The mounting economic damage inflicted by the Rhodesian Security Forces in the destruction of vital Zambian and Mozambican road and rail links almost certainly was a key factor that led the frontline presidents (Kaunda, Machel and Nyerere) to push ZAPU and ZANU to talks with the Rhodesians at Lancaster House in 1979.

According to a March 1979 CIA intelligence assessment:

> The security forces are conducting a vigorous campaign of cross-border raids to strike at most guerrilla concentrations ... By forcing the guerrillas to relo-cate to their camps, command centers, and supply structures farther from the border, the Rhodesians are trying to lengthen guerrilla communication links and supply lines. This would decrease the ability of guerrilla leaders to issue timely commands and would weaken their control over units in Rhodesia. It would also delay or reduce logistical support for guerrillas in the field, forcing

them to be more dependent on local sources, which would make them easier targets for the security forces.[95]

The demise of Rhodesia

The Rhodesian conflict ended when the Rhodesian Government returned control of the colony to Great Britain as part of the Lancaster House Accords signed in late 1979. Facing intense international pressure for a political settlement – and convinced that this was possible only while the Security Forces still had some teeth – the Rhodesian Government agreed to relinquish control to Britain as a prelude to rule by a popularly elected Parliament under majority rule.

The African nationalist groups were in no better position than the Rhodesians. Although outnumbered, the Rhodesian Security Forces still dominated the battlefield – besting the guerrillas in every encounter. The April 1979 elections demonstrated that – when mobilized – the Security Forces still retained control of the country. Rhodesia's external raids were inflicting enormous damage on the infrastructure of Zambia and Mozambique; landlocked Zambia was dependent on Rhodesia for passage of its exports to South African seaports. Following Portugal's abandonment of Mozambique, the ruling FRELIMO party struggled to combat the Rhodesian-sponsored *Resistência Nacional Moçambicana* (RENAMO) insurgency within Mozambique and was unable to continue supplying ZANLA with arms and ammunition. According to Rhodesian Air Force Group commander Peter Petter-Bowyer, a senior ZANLA commander stated after the Lancaster House Accords that ZANLA had no reserves in Mozambique – and had the conflict continued, ZANLA's operations would have 'collapsed around mid-1980'.[96] Both Kaunda (Zambia) and Machel (Mozambique) were eager for a peaceful agreement: each told ZIPRA and ZANLA respectively that aid to the insurgency would end, and basing privileges would cease if a political settlement was not concluded.

As agreed to in the Lancaster House Accords, the Rhodesian Government turned control of the colony over to Great Britain – represented by the transitional governor, Lord Soames. Soames oversaw the preparations for free elections with universal suffrage, and the return of Rhodesian refugees – including a large number of armed guerrillas. Returning guerrillas moved into camps – protected by a Commonwealth Monitoring Force to ensure that violence was avoided. Elections took place in March 1980 and saw the election of Robert Mugabe to be Prime Minister of a new Zimbabwe. Mugabe pledged that Zimbabwe would be inclusive of all ethnic groups and races – and he even retained senior members of the security apparatus (such as Ken Flower) in key positions; however, many die-hards in the Rhodesian military and BSAP promptly left the country. Many emigrated to South Africa, some returned to Britain and others moved to Australia, Canada or the United States. Perhaps in spite, Mugabe did disband the Selous Scouts. Many of the black members of the Scouts who remained in Zimbabwe were hunted down and murdered – and many others joined the newly formed 5 South African Reconnaissance ('5 Recce') unit modeled on the Selous Scouts.

Notes

1   Comment made in a debate before the Oxford Union, October 2000; online at <www. guardian.co.uk/Archive/Article/0,4273,4083111,00.html> (accessed on 19 September 2006).

2   Martin and Johnson (1981), p.60. Macmillian's 'Wind of Change' speech was given on 3 February 1960 before the South African Parliament in Cape Town. The speech is notable in that it recognized the existence of black nationalism as a political reality and clearly signaled Britain's intent to grant Independence to its African colonies. The speech also announced a shift in British attitudes to South Africa's apartheid laws and policies – leading to Pretoria's withdrawal from the Commonwealth the following year.

3   'Rebellion!', episode 1 (mark 24 minutes, 17 seconds).

4   ibid., (mark 24 minutes, 48 seconds to 25 minutes, 55 seconds).

5   Flower (1987), p.104.

6   Anthony Wilkenson, 'Insurgency in Rhodesia, 1957-1973', Adelphi Paper No. 100 (London: International Institute for Strategic Studies, 1973); online at <home.wanadoo.nl/rhodesia/ wilkinson.html> (accessed on 8 August 2005).

7   'History of Nationalism', p.9.

8   In Bowyer Bell's description of the situation at UDI, 'by the time of the break with Britain, Ian Smith's government had largely wiped out internal opposition, forcing the nationalists to pursue the war of liberation from exile bases... After November 1965, the focus of the conflict shifted from the repression of internal subversion, still a clear if not quite present danger, to repelling guerrilla intrusions'. See J. Bowyer Bell, 'The Frustration of Insurgency: The Rhodesian Example of the Sixties', Military Affairs (February 1971), p.1.

9   Martin and Johnson (1981), p.11: 'ZANU's first group of guerrillas had gone to China for training on 22 September 1963. This group was led by Emerson M'nangagwa and included John Shioniwa, Eddison Shirihuru, Jameson Mudavanhu, and Lawrence Swoswe'. A second group began its training in Ghana and received its advanced instructor training in China in 1965. In 1966, a third group – led by Josiah Tongogara – trained in mass mobilization, strategy and tactics at China's Nanjing Academy, according to Martin and Johnson. According to the BSAP chronology: 'During the same year, 1965, Z.A.P.U. was offered and accepted training facilities in Algeria. Basic training was given to a large contingent at Boghari and, for selected cadres more advanced courses were provided at Cherchell and Skikda'. (See 'Growth ...', p.7.)

10   Martin and Johnson (1981), p.11.

11   'Growth ...', p.7.

12   Bowyer Bell (1971), p.1.

13   Jakkie Cilliers, Counter-Insurgency in Rhodesia (London: Croom Helm, 1985), p.6. Also see 'Growth ...', p.7: '... that year, 1966, saw a slight change of tactics by both Z.A.P.U. and Z.A.N.U. from a military viewpoint. While Z.A.P.U. continued with a campaign of urban terrorism, in Salisbury largely, aided by White lecturers at the University College, both organizations sought to commence rural guerrilla operations, using small bands of terrorists who, as time passed, were issued with more and more sophisticated Communist weapons...'

14   ibid., p.7.

15   See ibid. (pp.7-8) for statistics on the rate of infiltrations and guerrilla casualties. According to Flower: 'During this period 1964 to 1966 over a hundred ZANLA and ZIPRA guerrillas were known to have been killed; the Rhodesian Security Forces suffered no losses but CIO lost a number of men'. (Flower (1987), p.107.)

16   Flower (1987), p.107: 'CIO's penetration of the guerrilla organizations from the pre-UDI days until the early 1970s was as complete as it could have been. There was virtually nothing we did not know of their inner workings at all levels, for our informers served us no less

faithfully than they served their nationalist leaders'. Also see Bill Crabtree, *Came the Fourth Flag* (Lancaster, UK: Scotforth Books, 2002), p.241.

17   Central Intelligence Agency, *The Liberation Movements of Southern Africa*, National Intelligence Estimate 70-1-64, dated 24 November 1967, p.7.

18   Cilliers (1985), p.6.

19   Martin and Johnson (1981), p.10.

20   Martin and Johnson claim the ZIPRA-ANC force consisted of 70 guerrillas. Flower states that 80 guerrillas were involved (p.107) and Cilliers numbers the guerrillas at 90 men (p.7).

21   Flower's comments on the South African aid are telling of the ambivalent reaction of the Rhodesian leadership toward South African support. According to Flower: 'South African aid, whether 'police,' or 'military' proved to be a mixed blessing ... On the military front, the South African units were a liability initially ... Ultimately, the involvement of South African units in Rhodesia's war was of more use to South Africa than to Rhodesia in that South Africa used Rhodesia as a training ground, withdrawing men as they became trained and replacing them with untrained ones'. (Flower (1987), p.108.)

22   Cilliers (1985), p.7 and Flower (1987), p.109. Operation 'Cauldron' was the last operation in which ZAPU and South Africa's ANC operated jointly.

23   'In desperation, ZAPU resorted to press-ganging Zimbabweans living in Zambia. Many of those who were press-ganged escaped at the first opportunity; a number proved unreliable in other respects'. See Flower (1987), p.110.

24   'Growth ...', p.7.

25   'History of Nationalism', p.9.

26   Flower (1987), p.110.

27   ibid., p.114.

28   Wellington Nyangoni, 'Revolutionary Strategies for National Liberation in Zimbabwe' (paper presented at the African Studies Association conference in Chicago, 31 October-3 November 1974), p.10, as quoted in Cilliers (1985), p.10.

29   'Z.A.N.U. saw the Teté Province as an ideal launching pad for operations into the north-east of Rhodesia and in early 1971 deployed 45 terrorists from Tanzania to F.R.E.L.I.M.O.'s Chifonbo base on Zambian soil, close to the Mocambique border. The terrorists were split into two detachments known as the Takawira and Ntini squads, and initially their role was to porter arms and equipment south. They learnt a considerable amount during those months that they lived and worked with F.R.E.L.I.M.O.'. See 'Growth ...', p.9.

30   Flower (1987), p.115.

31   Martin and Johnson (1981), p.14.

32   'History of Nationalism', p.10.

33   Seegers (1983), p.258.

34   Neither was the Rhodesian Army. According to Ronald Reid-Daly: '... two years before the Altena farm attack was launched, things had begun to happen in Rhodesia's north-eastern border area as FRELIMO advanced south across the Zambezi River, and the Mozambique war started to spill over into Rhodesia. It showed all the signs too of being difficult to contain as tribal affinities and loyalties straddled the borderlands...' See Ron Reid-Daly (as told to Peter Stiff), *Selous Scouts: Top Secret War* (Alberton, South Africa: Galago Publishing, 1982), p.20. 'In March 1972, a [*sic*] SAS team led by Lieutenant Bert Sachse attacked FRELIMO's Matimbe base in Mozambique, killing many guerrillas and capturing a mass of documentation. When analysed by Special Branch, it was discovered that ZANLA and FRELIMO were operating jointly from FRELIMO bases'. See Peter Stiff, *The Silent War: South African Recce Operations, 1969-1994* (Johannesburg, South Africa: Galago Press, 1999), p.88.

35   Interview with Ken Flower, chapter two (produced by 'Memories of Rhodesia', DVD format).

36   ibid.

37   Flower (1987), p.116. The CIO initiative led to the creation of RENAMO (aka Mozambique National Resistance [MNR]).

38   'Alcora' may be an acronym for *Aliança Contra as Rebeliões em Africa* – a Portuguese phrase meaning 'Alliance against the rebellions in Africa'. The 'alliance' operated from 1970 to 1974. In some published accounts, Alcora is confused with the Rhodesian CBW effort; no connection exists. For more information on Alcora, see Filipe Ribeiro de Meneses and Robert McNamara, 'Parallel Diplomacy, Parallel War: The PIDE/DGS's Dealings with Rhodesia and South Africa, 1961–74', *Journal of Contemporary History* (2014), 49 (2), pp.366–389.

39   Cilliers (1985), p.14.

40   Bruce Hoffman, Jennifer M. Taw and David Arnold, *Lessons for Contemporary Counterinsurgencies: The Rhodesian Experience* (Washington, DC: The Rand Corporation, 1991), p.30.

41   Crabtree (2002), p.242.

42   Ian Smith quoted in Martin and Johnson (1981), p.74.

43   BSAP/10 in email to the author, dated 15 March 2011.

44   op. cit., p.14. According to Cilliers (1985), a total of 750,000 rural Africans had been relocated in about 200 PVs when all was said and done.

45   Cilliers (1985), p.18.

46   R.E.H. Lockley, 'A Brief Operational History of the Campaign in Rhodesia from 1964 to 1978'; online at <www. rhodesianforces.org/Pages/General/A_Brief_Operational_History. html> (accessed on 9 August 2005), p.5.

47   'Growth …', p.11.

48   Flower (1987), pp.145-146.

49   The term 'trial' may be inappropriate, because whatever inquiry was conducted almost certainly would have had little resemblance to a legal proceeding in the Western sense. A BSAP report described it as 'in keeping with the counter-strategy for dealing with the 'rebellion,' evolved by the DARE [Dare re Chimurenga – the ZANU War Council], an ad hoc committee was set up in order to investigate the occurrence. The Committee of Three, as it later became known, included Herbert Chitepo, Rugare Gumbo, and Kumbirai Kangai. Whilst a number of interviews were conducted, the committee never concluded its proceedings and no report of its findings was forthcoming'. See 'Zimbabwe African National Union (ZANU): Zimbabwe African National Liberation Army (ZANLA): Analysis of Internal Dissension', BSAP File No. XYO 2500/24, dated 9 January 1980, p.6.

50   'Growth …', p.12: 'At a meeting of the 'Chimurenga General Council' on 22 January 1975, Tongogara, who emerged stronger than ever from the Nhari rebellion, accused Chitepo, Noel Mukono, and John Mataure of conspiracy with the rebels. At that time, Karanga elements were pursuing a blood purge and Chitepo's days were numbered'.

51   Fay Chung, *Re-Living the Second Chimurenga: Memories from Zimbabwe's Liberation Struggle* (Stockholm: The Nordic Africa Institute, 2006), p.95. Chung's detailed description of the Nhari Rebellion and its long-lasting impact on ZANU and ZANLA can be found on pp.90-95.

52   'The truth was the Special Branch members assigned to the Selous Scouts were thin on the ground and could hardly cope with their ever-increasing workload. What's more, it was quite apparent that the Police Commissioner P.K. Allum was hardly sympathetic as far as their needs were concerned, and had refused to sanction staff increases'. See Reid-Daly (1999), p.304.

53   R.F. Reid-Daly, 'War in Rhodesia: Cross-Border Operations' in A.J. Venter (ed.), *Challenge* (Gibraltar: Ashanti Publications, 1989), p.165.

54   Peter Stiff, *Selous Scouts: Rhodesian War – A Pictorial Account* (Alberton, South Africa: Galago Publishing, 1984), pp.59-61. The number of Special Branch men assigned as liaison officers never exceeded about 12 men – including European officers and ranks, and African constables – at any one time. P.K. Allum refused to authorize any manpower increase for McGuinness' mission. McGuinness, however, had access to sufficient funds that allowed him to hire supernumeraries to supplement his teams; for example, according to Parker (p.249), Dave Broom 'has been taken on by Mac as a supernumerary. He was not attested as a police officer, but was paid from special funds held by McGuinness. By this stage in the war, many supernumeraries were employed by Special Branch Selous Scouts to bolster manpower'.

55   Cilliers (1985), p.19.

56   'Growth …', p.11: 'In mid-year 1974, F.R.E.L.I.M.O. agreed to hand over military bases in Mocambique to Z.A.N.U. once it became Government. It was also arranged that Z.A.N.U. would establish a central command base at Chimoio (Vila Pery)'.

57   ibid., p.20.

58   ibid., p.12.

59   Lockley, p.5.

60   Cilliers (1985), p.24.

61   'Rhodesia – Mzilikaze to Smith', *Africa Institute Bulletin*, vol.15 (1977); online at <home. wanadoo.nl/rhodesia/mztosm.html> (accessed on 9 August 2005).

62   Chung (2006), p.104: 'Ian Smith had managed to disarm the majority of guerrillas through the *détente* exercise. With over 1,000 being held at Mboroma in Zambia, several hundred more immobilized in military camps in Tanzania, and a few hundred more immobilized in Mozambique, Smith now saw the wiping out of the remaining 300 guerrillas within the country as a fairly easy task'.

63   Flower (1987), p.148. In Chung's description, 'President Kaunda's decision to imprison the old leadership as well as more than 1,000 of the veteran freedom fighters left a vacuum in the leadership of the liberation movement that was soon filled by young men and women who had recently left the classrooms of high schools and universities'. See Chung, p.171.

64   Martin and Johnson (1981), p.215.

65   Chung (2006), pp.194-195. Also see Chung, p.213, in which she states: '… food shortages and unbalanced diets led to night blindness, a problem that could become chronic. Constant attacks of malaria led to many people involved in the struggle developing diabetes, apparently a side effect either of malaria or of the chloroquine that was used to cure it…'.

66   'Memories of Rhodesia', 'Selous Scouts' (interview with Ron Reid-Daly).

67   Chung (2006), p.153.

68   Cilliers (1985), p.27.

69   'Growth …', p.14: '27 January 1976 saw the arrival of the first 147 Z.P.A. terrorists at Mapai in Gaza Province of Mozambique. They were reinforced and the first Z.P.A. incursions took place at Sangwe, Matibi 2 and Sengwe T.T.L.s in the Lowveld in February/March. Contact with the terrorists first occurred in the Sangwe T.T.L. on 17 February 1976'.

70   Cilliers (1985), p.31. A BSAP document described the situation at the end of 1976 in the following terms: 'By the end of 1976, Z.A.N.L.A. had made significant territorial gains in the eastern half of Rhodesia and stepped up its recruiting, training, and logistical support with the aid of the O.A.U. Liberation Committee'. See 'Growth …', p.14.

71   ibid., p.42.

72   <https://en.wikipedia.org/wiki/Rhodesian_Bush_War#/media/File:Rhodesian_Security_ Forces _operational_areas.png> created on 19 October 2011, CC BY-SA 3.0 (accessed on 16 August 2015).

73   Cilliers (1985), p.158.

74   ibid., p.32.

75   ibid.

76   ibid., p.159.

77   Quoted in Kevin Danaher, 'The Political Economy of Hunger in Rhodesia and Zimbabwe', *Issue: A Quarterly Journal of Africanist Opinion*, 11 (Fall/Winter 1981), p.33.

78   ibid., p.34.

79   Flower (1987), p.177.

80   Cilliers (1985), p.39.

81   ibid., p.42.

82   ibid., p.53. In December 1978, the number of insurgents in Rhodesia was estimated at 8,952 (7,256 ZANLA and 1,696 ZIPRA). By January 1979, the number had increased to 11,183 (9,277 ZANLA and 1,906 ZIPRA).

83   Central Intelligence Agency, 'Communist Military Support for the Rhodesian Insurgency' (ER-78-10190), dated April 1978 (declassified as of 20 April 2008, NLC-31-75-5-7-3), p.1.

84   Thabo Kunene, 'How Rhodesians forced Zapu to abandon its 'Operation Zero Hour'', *Bulawayo 24 News* (15 January 2015); online at < bulawayo24.com/index-id-opinion-sc-columnist-byo-60889.html> (accessed on 16 August 2015).

85   Vladimir Shubin, *The Hot "Cold War": The USSR in Southern Africa* (London: Pluto Press, 2008), p.174.

86   Central Intelligence Agency, *Rhodesia: ZAPU Military Plans*, dated 11 March 1978 (MORI DocID: 123228).

87   ibid., p.30.

88   Central Intelligence Agency, *Special National Intelligence Estimate: Rhodesia – Looking Ahead*, SNIE 72.1-1-77, dated 28 January 1977 (MORI DocID: 121413), p.12.

89   Central Intelligence Agency, *Rhodesia: The Economy, Sanctions, and the War Effort*, dated 17 April 1979 (MORI DocID: 177388), p.1.

90   Godwin and Hancock (1993), p.245.

91   Cilliers (1985), p.250.

92   ibid., p.53. By 1979, the number of ZIPRA insurgents outside Rhodesia was estimated at between 2,500 and 3,000, and the number of ZANLA insurgents outside Rhodesia was between 10,000 and 11,000.

93   Central Intelligence Agency, 'Rhodesia: Cross-Border Raids', *Military Weekly Review*, dated 12 January 1979 (MORI DocID: 105953), p.4 and p.6.

94   Danaher (1981), p.34.

95   Central Intelligence Agency, 'Rhodesia: Military Preparations for Election', *Africa Review*, dated 23 March 1979 (MORI DocID: 105954), p.4.

96   P.J.H. Petter-Bowyer, *Winds of Destruction* (Victoria, Canada: Trafford Publishing, 2003), p.582. According to a former senior BSAP officer, ZANU chief Robert Mugabe confided after the conflict's end that they could have only continued fighting for about three more months. This statement contrasts with other reported statements by Mugabe in which he expresses his resentment that the Lancaster House Accords denied him the military victory he sought over the Rhodesians.

2

The Rhodesian CBW Effort

'It was war, and in war all things are allowed'.[1]
Ken Flower, Director-General, CIO

Although few details are known about Rhodesia's clandestine CBW efforts, a broad-brush picture is clear. The project was born out of desperation as the conflict intensified in the mid-1970s, and was the brainchild of a professor – Robert Symington – at the University of Rhodesia's medical school. He reportedly put forward the idea to the then-Minister of Defense, who advocated it to the Prime Minister. The Prime Minister – almost certainly in consultation with his War Cabinet – delegated responsibility to the CIO, and implementation was assigned to the Special Branch liaison component in the Selous Scouts.[2] Although they were aware of the CBW program's existence, the full extent to which the Rhodesian political and military leadership was involved in the effort is obscure due to the lack of documentary material or living witnesses. Prime Minister Ian Smith publicly denied any knowledge of the program,[3] but almost certainly approved the program's creation, even if he was not aware of the details of its daily operations.[4] In December 1998, a Zimbabwe newspaper quoted Ian Smith as saying: 'It's a lot of rubbish. I know nothing about [such germ warfare]. They [the Rhodesian Security Forces] could have done so without my knowledge... Those saying that are giving us credit for being more creative and brilliant than what we were'.[5]

CIO chief Ken Flower was very aware of the CBW activities – having received bi-weekly status reports on the effort from McGuinness. BSAP commissioners – first Sherren, and later, Allum – were briefed on the CBW efforts, and at least Sherren took steps to ensure that the program remained concealed. In 1977, McGuinness briefed the COMOPS – headed by Lieutenant General Peter Walls[6] – about the CBW effort. Selous Scout commander Lieutenant Colonel Reid-Daly also knew of the CBW effort – once commenting to an interviewer that the program was a CIO operation run out of a derelict facility.[7] Most readily available information about the program is based on the half-truths, rumors, conjectures, anecdotes and myths that circulated around the officers' messes and pubs frequented by members of the Rhodesian Security Forces.

The genesis

The consensus is that the CBW idea originated with the aforementioned Robert Symington – a professor of anatomy at the Godfrey Huggins School of Medicine, the University of Rhodesia. Symington supposedly put the proposal to the then-Defense Minister – P.K. van der Byl[8] – and an unnamed senior army officer.[9] With van der Byl's approval, the plan was passed to Prime Minister Ian Smith,[10] who authorized CIO Director-General Ken Flower[11] to implement the plan.

In one of McGuinness' interviews with FBI special agents investigating the 2001 anthrax letter attacks (AMERITHRAX), he told the agents that:

> Symington was responsible for coming up with the ideas that were disseminated by [Victor] Nobel's team. Symington, a right-wing racist, was close to P.K. van der Byl. Van der Byl was the Minister of Defense in Rhodesia and also a right-wing racist. Symington and van der Byl came up with the idea of using poisons on the terrorists. McGuinness believes that any plans to use poisons had to be approved by Peter Walls prior to being implemented in the field. McGuinness is not aware of any attempts to tinker with the poisons to make them more effective. He thought that the poisoned clothes operation began in late 1977 and ended in 1979.[12]

Jim Parker described the implementation of Symington's proposal as beginning with Flower's meeting with McGuinness:

> Flower called Chief Superintendent McGuinness to his office and told him that the Prime Minister had given him and the service chiefs the go-ahead for a top-secret operation under the wing of the Selous Scouts in which poisons would be used to kill the enemy. Flower ordered McGuinness to organize the exercise from the Bindura Fort. He said it wouldn't be a good idea to establish the project at the Selous Scouts' Inkomo Barracks because there were many people other than regular soldiers coming and going there.[13]

Several senior BSAP officers have talked about the origins of the CBW program; all describe it as a Rhodesian-born concept. According to a former senior BSAP officer:

> The Rhodesian CBW effort was born of desperation. The CBW program was amateurish. The most competent scientist involved was Symington, and he was a tinker. No real sophistication or thought was involved, and the materials used were entirely off-the-shelf. The concept and choice of agents/materials rested with the Rhodesians. McGuinness placed the burden for creation of the CBW program on Rhodesian shoulders – including Ron Reid-Daly (deceased), Symington (deceased), and P.K. van der Byl (deceased).[14]

According to a separate former senior BSAP officer:

I suspect that Rhodesia came up with the idea of CBW before RSA [Republic of South Africa]. My reasoning is based on the fact that CT [communist terrorist] gangs were breaking into stores in the TTLs to steal food and clothing from their fellow Africans. McGuinness told me privately in 1976 of the experiments in the Bindura Fort to use poison to contaminate underwear that were then placed in those stores, which were closed to the general public but open to criminal acts by the CTs. Thereafter, it was a closed book as far as the JOC was concerned and was limited to the Special Branch operations out of Fort Bindura. Obviously, if successful, it was disseminated through CIO links to other members of the team but was not generally circulated throughout the SF (Security Forces). I subsequently learned, privately, that the programme was used to contaminate food and liquids. I seem to remember that the SAS contaminated food supplies at Chimoio after the raid.[15]

Dating the start of the CBW effort

Given Defense Minister P.K. van der Byl's key role in the CBW initiative, Rhodesia's CBW efforts almost certainly began before van der Byl was removed from his defense portfolio on 9 September 1976 at the insistence of the South African leadership. Symington's proposal for a chemical and biological weapons program then probably dates from mid-to-late 1975[16] to early-to-mid 1976,[17] but the exact date for the begin-ning of the CBW effort cannot be determined. Once authorized, Rhodesian CBW experiments at Bindura date from sometime in 1976, and operations almost certainly began by late 1976. According to Jeremy Brickhill, the Special Branch and Selous Scouts disseminated chemical and biological agents against target areas in 1976.[18] By late 1976, Symington had recruited a number of volunteers from the University of Rhodesia to work on the project.[19] According to members of the Rhodesian CBW team, they began to poison clothing in April 1977 and contaminate food, beverages and medicines in May/June 1977. They also stated that the project did not end until late 1979.[20]

Flower's account diverges: the role of The Rev Arthur Kanodareka

Ken Flower's description of the Rhodesian CBW effort is noteworthy for several reasons: first, his 1987 account is the first description made public about the Rhodesian CBW effort. Secondly, his account differs significantly from others' recol-lections of the CBW program in that it focuses on the role of the Methodist minister and UANC activist The Rev Arthur Kanodareka;[21] lastly, Flower's description also remains among the oft-quoted accounts repeated in the media and on the internet.

For his part, Ken Flower briefly described the CBW effort in his autobiography *Serving Secretly: An Intelligence Chief on the Record*, in which he puts the Rhodesian CBW program in the context of ZANLA's first efforts to mobilize the masses inside Rhodesia. Flower quotes a statement by Herbert Chitepo in 1973 about the need to emphasize 'political matters' over 'military activity'. In this context, Flower claims

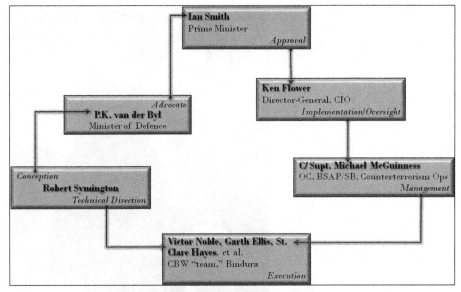

Figure 2.1 A diagram showing the approval chain to establish the CBW effort.
(Source: the author's work)

Figure 2.2 CIO Director-General Ken Flower. (Source: *Evening News*, London – reprinted in *Serving Secretly*; permssion requested)

Figure 2.3 Selous Scout Commander Lieutenant Colonel Ron Reid-Daly. (Source: public domain)

Figure 2.4 Defense Minister P.K. van der Byl. (© William Higham, with permission of William Higham)

that the conflict at this time had none of the characteristics of a war. The guerrilla groups avoided contact with the Rhodesian military and focused their attacks on 'soft targets' instead. According to Flower: 'CIO changed tack accordingly and tried to match the guerrilla tactics by using pseudos and paid agents to operate against similarly chosen soft targets'.[22]

In his description of the CBW effort, Flower identified Kanodareka as one of those CIO-paid agents. He stated:

> For more years than I would like to tell, young men were recruited for the guerrilla cause under the aegis of the CIO and with the willing cooperation of Kanodareka and his helpers who supplied them [young men] with poisoned uniforms. The men would be sent on their way to the guerrilla training camps, but before reaching their destination would die a slow death in the African bush. Many hundreds of recruits became victims of this operation. It became so diabolically successful that exposure seemed inevitable, and so the principal perpetrators had to be eliminated – rather as a hunter will finish off a wounded animal to stop further suffering.[23]

Figure 2.5 The Rev Arthur Kanodareka.
(Source: CAUX-Initiatives of Change
Foundation, with permission)[24]

Figure 2.6 Another photo of Kanodareka.
(Source: <www.colonialrelic.com>
© unknown)[25]

From Flower's statements, one can infer that the Rhodesian CBW program probably began no earlier than 1975 and certainly no later than 1977. He implies that the CBW program began at approximately the same time as the Selous Scout pseudo operations, which was around 1974.[26] In Flower's account, the purpose of the program was to eliminate recruits identified by the CIO and in transit from Rhodesia to guerrilla training camps in neighboring countries (probably Zambia and Mozambique). He implies that the program was ended to prevent its exposure; Kanodareka's death at the hands of the CIO was part of that cover-up.

According to McGuinness:

> He (Flower) knew about the use of stuff contaminated with poisons, and he also knew the role that Bob Symington had played in it. Ken wrote in his book about the Rev Kanodareka [sic] helping to supply terrorist recruits with poison-impregnated uniforms. He told me that the only thing he felt guilty about was ordering that the Rev be knocked off to stop the story getting out! It's possible that he couldn't recall who had started it, but he obviously knew about it, so who started it is irrelevant. He was obviously kept fully informed.[27]

All the published references to Kanodareka repeat Flower's description of the man and his role in the poisoning program. The most detailed account is in Henrik Ellert's book, *The Rhodesian Front War: Counter-Insurgency and Guerilla War in Rhodesia, 1962-1980.* Ellert describes Kanodareka's involvement as stemming from his role in providing beaconed radios to guerrillas operating in the TTL near Mount Darwin:

> Kanodareka was in regular communication with ZANLA units and before long he, too, started receiving letters asking for supplies. The Special Branch examined these notes and started making up parcels of food and drink which Kanodareka sent out together with gifts of cash. Kanodareka told his Special Branch controllers that he would make arrangements for guerrillas to come to Salisbury and meet him at his church near the Mbare hostels. The night vigils at the church came to naught, and the Special Branch started to suspect that their man was playing a double game.[28]

In a book by Peter Godwin and Ian Hancock, Kanodareka is depicted as:

> the real villain in 'a most sordid tale of treachery and betrayal.' ... When Kanodareka was murdered near Salisbury in late 1978 a number of prominent Whites attended the funeral of this presumed victim of nationalist faction-fighting. They did not know that CIO had ordered the assassination because the scheme was 'so diabolically successful' that Kanodareka had to be eliminated to avoid an inevitable exposure ... So the reverend gentleman was the truly guilty one, and his removal – forced on the CIO because his controller reported that he had become greedy and ill-disciplined – became morally justified.[29]

No independent evidence exists to support Ken Flower's claims regarding Kanodareka's involvement in the Rhodesian CBW program, or Flower's supposed remorse over his role in Kanodareka's death.

As Kanodareka's handler, McGuinness' account of him differs significantly from Flower's.[30] According to McGuinness, Kanodareka was a highly placed Special Branch source within Muzorewa's UANC and he provided valuable intelligence on terrorist plans and intentions;[31] however, his undoing was not greed or ill-discipline, as Flower would have many believe. Some senior Rhodesian officials considered Kanodareka to be a serious contender for the UANC presidency, which was occupied by Bishop Abel Muzorewa. Kanodareka, along with The Rev Max Chigwida and Byron Hove, joined forces to 'form a militant group within the UANC opposed to the Bishop (Muzorewa). On 12 September 1978 the Bishop expelled the militants from his party; shortly thereafter, Kanodareka disappeared from public view'.[32] Kanodareka's elimination fits more neatly in the battle for control of the UANC than in the CBW story.

Behind the scenes, Rhodesian backers of Muzorewa – concerned that Kanodareka threatened Muzorewa's leadership position – sought to eliminate him as a contender. Shortly after Peter K. Allum[33] became BSAP Commissioner (February 1978), Ian Smith held a meeting in his office to discuss the Kanodareka question. A Muzorewa supporter, Commissioner Allum argued for Kanodareka's elimination. Smith was non-committal, and Flower and McGuinness backed Kanodareka because of his long, distinguished service to the CIO and his popularity in the UANC. Flower and McGuinness reportedly argued that Muzorewa had no credibility in nationalist circles because he had never spoken out publicly against the Rhodesian Government. In the end, Allum won Smith's acquiescence and Flower backed down – commenting to McGuinness that one day they might need Allum. McGuinness then tasked his team to eliminate Kanodareka.[34] He had last been seen on the morning of Monday, 4 December 1978 leaving his Methodist church in Harari – a township outside Salisbury. Later that day, he was found mortally wounded inside his bullet-riddled

car on a road 29 kilometers outside the capital. The press report stated that Kanodareka had been expelled from the UANC three months previously because of 'political ineptitude'.[35] A brief news bulletin announced that The Rev Arthur Kanodareka was slain in an ambush. The common assumption following his assassination was that he was killed by rivals in the Black Liberation Movement.

In the final assessment, Kanodareka's complete role in supporting the Rhodesian CBW efforts may never be fully understood. One thing that does seem clear is that Kanodareka had only a fleeting involvement with the CBW program, if any at all. His more important contribution to the Rhodesian cause was in the prevention of a nationalist urban bombing campaign. Within the Rhodesian mindset, his death can be explained as a matter of political expediency, as the Rhodesian leadership sought to find any acceptable African face for the transition to majority rule.

Figure 2.7 BSAP Commissioner P.K. Allum.
(Source: <www.bsap.org> © unknown)

The program

Participants in the Rhodesian CBW program have confirmed that a small-scale, rudimentary program did exist,[36] although many details probably will never be fully disclosed. The facilities used in the CBW program almost certainly consisted of a Special Branch-funded laboratory at Professor Robert Symington's Borrowdale residence,[37] and facilities at the Selous Scout 'fort' in Bindura were likely used, as were similar facilities at the Selous Scout 'fort' outside Mount Darwin. Starting from sometime in 1978, some of the more sensitive CBW-related activities – including experimentation on humans – almost certainly took place at the Mount Darwin site, which was more remotely located than Bindura. The later presence of large numbers of former insurgents undergoing training to serve as Rhodesian auxiliaries almost certainly would have compromised the CBW-related activities at the Bindura 'fort'. The CBW team also may have found that Bindura was too big a town to keep their more sensitive operations, such as experimentation and BW production, closely held.

Selection of agents

The Rhodesian rationale for selecting chemical and biological agents for use is unclear. One document is extant that sheds some light on the characteristics the Rhodesians sought in their selection process. That document – undated and with no attribution – is a list of toxic chemicals along with their effects, prices and possible suppliers. The assumption is that the document may be part of a proposal written by Robert Symington. Described in greater detail in the appendix, the materials described in the Rhodesian document included the following:

Powdered solids such as
- 1,5-bis-(4-Allyldimethyl-Ammoniumphenyl) Pentane-3-One Dibromide
- N,N'-Dicyclohexyl Carbodiimide (DCC) ($C_{13}H_{22}N_2$)
- DL-Fluorocitric Acid (FCA)
- Monofluoroacetic Acid (MFAA or FAA)

Liquids
- Diethyl-P-Nitrophenyl Phosphate (aka paraoxon – a metabolite of parathion)
- (The Rhodesians adopted this chemical in its commercial form (the readily available pesticide parathion) for use in the country's CBW program.)
- Diisopropyl Flurophosphate ($C_6H_{14}FO_3P$)
  (This chemical was highlighted, and its dermal absorption was underlined.)
- Methyl Fluorosulfonate

Toxins
- Aflatoxin
- Phalloidin
- Alpha-Amanitin or α-amanitin
- Tetrodotoxin

Alloxan ($C_4H_4N_2O_2$)
Venoms

Other chemicals used or considered for use, but not included in the 'founding' document, included telodrin and warfarin. South African-provided materials (used experimentally) included colchicine, ricin, amanita extract, 2,4-dichlorophenoxyacetic acid, sodium fluoroacetate (aka compound 1080), cyanide, arsenic and warfarin.[38]

In general, the 'founding' document demonstrates a dilettante's level of understanding regarding toxic chemicals and toxins. Most of the chemicals listed are not highly toxic or the most useful, and the list is reminiscent of a catalog shopper (in this case, the catalog was Sigma's*) perusing the pages searching for attractive items. Some choices (i.e. alloxan, methyl fluorosulfonate and N,N'-dicyclohexyl carbodiimide) confound logic. Of the items toxic and useful enough to be reasonable choices, the predilection seems to be for chemicals suitable for assassinations and small-scale attacks. Even so, the author of the list suggests the purchase from an overseas supplier of snake and scorpion venoms that could be extracted from local animals.[39]

The chemicals most used in the Rhodesian program were parathion (an organophosphate insecticide) and thallium (a heavy metal commonly found in rodenticide), probably because these compounds were readily available in Rhodesia at the time and were relatively inexpensive. In selecting suitable poisons for use in food, Symington accessed that diet and defecation frequency were key factors in a CBW agent's effectiveness. Defecation that is more frequent meant that poisons were more quickly eliminated from the body; less frequent defecation allowed more time for poisons to act. Symington judged that Africans defecated twice as often in a day than did Europeans because of differences in their diets.[40] Symington held that mealie (corn meal, which was the dietary staple of rural Africans) increased the frequency of defecation, while European diets high in refined and bleached grains lowered the defecation rate[41] – therefore the higher defecation rate in the black African population needed to be taken into account when choosing an effective agent and the required dosage.

Among the biological agents the Rhodesians selected for use included *Vibrio cholerae* (the causative agent of cholera) and possibly *Bacillus anthracis* (the causative agent of anthrax). They also looked at using *Rickettsia prowazekii* (the causative agent of epidemic typhus) and *Salmonella typhi* (the causative agent of typhoid fever), and toxins such as ricin and botulinum toxin.[†] According to an unidentified FBI informant, the 'Dirty Trick Squad' dealt with biological weapons, such as cholera and anthrax.[42]

Purpose

Although little specific information remains available about the Rhodesian CBW effort, what is indisputable is that its primary purpose was to kill guerrillas – whether they were recruits transiting to camps in Mozambique,[43] or guerrillas operating inside Rhodesia. The CBW effort took on the guerrilla threat from three fronts: first, the effort aimed to eliminate guerrillas operating inside Rhodesia through contaminated supplies either provided by contact men, recovered from hidden caches or stolen from rural stores; a second-order effect was to disrupt the relations between village supporters and the guerrillas. Secondly, the effort worked to contaminate water supplies along guerrilla infiltration routes into Rhodesia – forcing the guerrillas either to travel through arid regions to carry more water and less ammunition, or travel

---

*   Sigma was a major international chemical producer and supplier, which is now known as Sigma-Aldrich.

†   'Toxins' are defined as chemical compounds derived from living organisms.

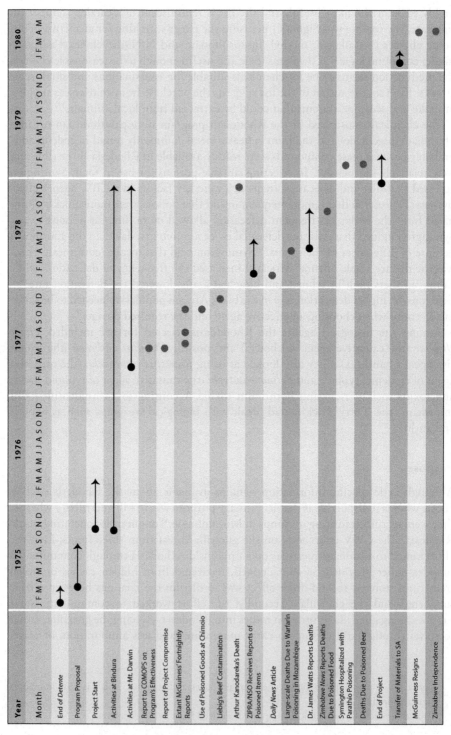

Figure 2.8 The Rhodesian CBW chronology. (Source: the author's work)

through areas patrolled by the Security Forces; finally, the Rhodesians sought to hit the guerrillas in their safe havens by poisoning food, beverages and medicines.

Facing growing numbers of elusive guerrillas operating from safe havens in Mozambique, the Special Branch sought to kill as many insurgents as possible by poisoning supplies provided by Special Branch-controlled contact men,* or by poisoning supplies left in food caches or in rural stores vulnerable to theft. Guerrillas operating in Rhodesia relied almost exclusively on local supporters, theft from farm or rural stores and coercion of the rural population to satisfy their supply needs: clothing, food, beverages and medicines. The only equipment supplied to the guerrillas operating in Rhodesia consisted of weapons and ammunition. In using 'contact men' to provide tainted food, beverages, medicines and clothing to guerrillas, the Rhodesian Security Forces exploited the guerrillas' reliance on their supporters.

In those cases when the villagers wittingly or unwittingly provided poisoned materials to the guerrillas, the guerrillas often would hold 'witch hunts' to identify the perpetrators. Guerrilla-orchestrated witch hunts targeted adult females in the village and subjected the suspects to interrogation, torture and eventual execution; guerrilla deaths by poisoning made the guerrillas suspicious of the villagers.[44] The violence and intimidation exercised by the guerrillas during the witch hunts made the villagers much less willing to provide supplies to guerrilla bands. Whether the schisms between village supporters and insurgents was intended, or merely an unanticipated second-order consequence, is unknown, but some former members of the Rhodesian Security Forces assert that the Rhodesians were certainly aware of traditional superstitions surrounding the use of poisons. The use of CBW to deny food supplies to the guerrillas also was consistent and supportive of the Rhodesian Government's Operation 'Turkey', which sought to limit the food supplies in the rural areas of Rhodesia that might be available to guerrillas. Operation 'Turkey' sought to restrict the amount of food available in rural Rhodesia to a level needed to sustain the local population, and eliminate the likelihood that food surpluses would be given to feed guerrillas; excess food was either confiscated or destroyed on the spot. Operation 'Turkey' increased hunger and malnutrition in rural populations – especially among children. It also led to widespread smuggling and black marketeering in foodstuffs; one possible explanation for the scale and extent of the anthrax epizootic in 1978 is the black market beef trade.

By contaminating boreholes supplying water – especially in Mozambique's arid Gaza Province – and poisoning food, the Rhodesian Security Forces attempted to funnel the insurgents to killing zones where the undermanned Rhodesian military

---

* The term 'contact men' refers to members of the insurgents' clandestine logistical and support network inside Rhodesia. Contact men typically were villagers or local African townspeople with access to food, clothing and other supplies, who provided these materials to insurgents. The Rhodesian Special Branch successfully recruited several contact men as a means to funnel tampered equipment – such as beaconed radios – poisoned food or contaminated clothing into the insurgent resupply network.

could concentrate its firepower.* The tactic of poisoning certain water supplies while leaving others untouched was an effective force multiplier – causing guerrillas to choose between carrying ammunition or water for the trip to Rhodesia. If they chose to carry ammunition rather than water, they could replenish water supplies from untainted boreholes, but their route would lead them into a Rhodesian killing zone. If they chose to avoid Rhodesian forces, they would have to carry more water and less ammunition – leaving them undersupplied for operations in Rhodesia.

The Rhodesians also attempted when possible to poison food and medical supplies destined for guerrilla camps. In the first instance, the Special Branch recruited contact men who supplied guerrillas operating in Rhodesia. The contact men often received lists of supplies sought by the guerrillas, and the Special Branch team at Bindura would gather the goods on the list and poison them. The contact men then would deliver the goods to the guerrillas, or deposit the items in a cache for the guerrillas to retrieve later. As the war progressed, African villagers were relocated to PVs and the areas were 'frozen' – meaning that movement in the region was forbidden. The Special Branch also stocked contaminated goods in rural general stores in the frozen areas – knowing that guerrilla groups likely would raid these stores. During Rhodesian external operations, Rhodesian forces often would add contaminated food and medical supplies to those discovered in those guerrilla camps overrun by Rhodesian troops; similarly, guerrilla caches in the bush were replaced with contaminated supplies.

A less discussed goal was the development of toxins as assassination tools – and the Rhodesian 'founding' document describes several toxins as suitable for assassinations.[45] Peter Stiff's account in *See You in November* and statements by former senior BSAP Special Branch officers all indicate that the Rhodesians at least explored the use of toxins for assassinations. In *See You in November*, Stiff describes Sam Roberts (a pseudonym for Robert Symington) and an exchange he had with Rhodesian assassin Alan 'Taffy' Brice.[46] The CIO tasked Brice to assassinate then-ZANU leader Robert Mugabe during the 1979 Lancaster House talks. Brice's CIO handler, Ricky May, instructed Brice to approach Robert Symington about possible poisons for use in the assassination.

In an interview with British journalist Tom Mangold, Brice stated:

> The toxins we used came under three headings. One of them was ricin, which comes from the castor bean and has to enter the body intravenously. The second one is a heavy metal called thallium, which has to enter the body orally and kills like ricin in a matter of three days. There was a third one, researched and used by Symington, which was called Parathion that was something I had never heard of before. It enters the body through the hair follicles.[47]

---

* As the conflict intensified, the Rhodesian Government sought a number of strategies to prevent the insurgents from operating freely in the country's rural areas. These strategies included establishing 'Protected Villages', which involved the forcible removal of tens of thousands of African peasants to government-constructed camps – restricting the movement and possession of food, and the poisoning of water (and possibly animals).

Figure 2.9 ZANU leader Robert
Mugabe. (Source: public domain)

Symington reportedly suggested the use
of a ricin-tipped bullet. In Mangold's
account, Symington (here described
as an 'enterprising Welshman') modified a rifle round by moving the tip
and creating a cavity in the lead to
hold ricin. 'Taffy' reportedly tested the
rounds by firing them into stray dogs
from the local humane society. The
dogs took three days to die, according
to Mangold.[48] A former BSAP officer
recounted: 'Ricky May did ask Brice to
approach Symington for a poison to use
in assassinating Bob [Mugabe]. I know
the man involved in procuring the castor beans for use in producing the ricin. The
problem was that Symington ran into difficulties achieving the purity of ricin he
needed to poison Bob'.[49] A ricin-tipped bullet seems to be a far-fetched, implausible
plot; the intended victim is more likely to die of the wound from a high-velocity rifle
round than from ricin poisoning.

Organization, command and control

The organization of the CBW program was extremely simple. Chief Superintendent
McGuinness was in overall command of day-to-day operations, and he reported
directly to CIO chief Ken Flower. In bi-weekly reports (marked 'XYS 8777/7' for
the Special Branch filing nomenclature),* McGuinness communicated the status
of CBW efforts to Flower and the Officer Commanding (OC) Special Branch.
From the few reports that remain, the focus was on the number and types of
goods distributed, and the reported deaths. After discovery of some disclosures
about covert Selous Scout operations involving poisons, McGuinness in late 1977
changed his reporting format – dropping the Special Branch file number and
carrying the more restrictive 'For Sight and Destruction' marking.[50] McGuinness
delivered the bi-weekly reports personally to Flower, who reportedly never made
any comment.[51] Although the Special Branch OC also received the reports until
at least post-February 1978, no record exists of any Special Branch role in what

---

*   See appendix for reproductions of the few XYS 8777/7 reports that are extant.

had become an exclusively CIO-controlled operation after P.K. Allum became the Commissioner of Police in February 1978.

At the Special Branch-controlled Selous Scout fort outside Bindura – 88 kilometers north of Salisbury – McGuinness oversaw a group of three to four technicians who were nominally supernumeraries to his unit. All were placed on the pay rolls of the Selous Scouts, and Selous Scout commander Reid-Daly allowed all but one to become 'Territorial' members of the Scouts, but none were 'badged'. McGuinness' oversight responsibility focused on funding, supply and distribution of the contaminated goods. Symington would have overseen technical and scientific issues – including any field trials that may have been done.

Figure 2.10 depicts a notional command and control schematic of the formal command structure and an informal command structure. A key takeaway from this diagram is that command and control of largely covert Rhodesian operations – including those of the Selous Scouts, their Special Branch liaison and the Rhodesian CBW effort – were highly personality-driven. Selous Scout commander Lieutenant Colonel Reid-Daly often chose to bypass the military chain of command and seek operational approval from Lieutenant General Walls. Reid-Daly's slighting of the formal military command structure – and his often-impetuous decisions – gave him a reputation as a 'cowboy'. His relationship with his commander, Lieutenant General John Hickman, worsened over time and led to a very public falling out that resulted in Reid-Daly's court martial and subsequent resignation.

McGuinness was a chief superintendent in the BSAP's Special Branch, yet his ties to his formal command structure in the BSAP were strained when P.K. Allum became BSAP Commissioner. Allum was an old-school policeman with a long history of working criminal matters – and he had little-to-no experience or affinity

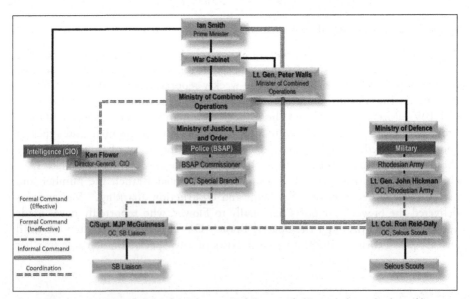

Figure 2.10 Formal and informal command & control. (Source: the author's work)

with the secretive work of the Special Branch. Allum and McGuinness also may have shared a personal animosity for each other. In part, this tension may be due to Allum's rise through the BSAP's Criminal Investigation Department (CID), which as the name implies, focused on criminal – not national security – issues. Given his CID background, Special Branch activities probably were alien to Allum. As Commissioner of Police, Allum – a devout Roman Catholic with suspected ties to the CCJP – quickly attempted to assert his authority to prevent what he saw were abuses by the Special Branch. Allum was deeply suspicious of the Special Branch's ties to the CIO – especially the role McGuinness' Special Branch liaison officers had with the Selous Scouts.[52] Almost immediately on taking over as BSAP Commissioner, Allum requested McGuinness prepare a top-secret memorandum on the Selous Scouts and their function.[53] This request may have stemmed from a desire by Allum to reign in what he saw as rogue elements inside the BSAP. McGuinness' ties to Flower strengthened, as he sought to avoid Allum's scrutiny.

Regardless of the reason, McGuinness would bypass the formal chain of command within the BSAP and seek authorization and approval for his activities from CIO chief Ken Flower. In Moorcraft and McLaughlin's history, they claim 'Chief Superintendent 'Mac' McGuinness ran the Special Branch element of the Selous Scouts and kept a lot of information close to his chest. Information was also compartmentalized because of the unadulterated mutual loathing of BSAP Commissioner Peter Allum and CIO boss Ken Flower'.[54] Peter Godwin and Ian Hancock wrote that '… They [Flower and Allum] utterly detested each other and could not have worked together for any reputable or disreputable purpose. Relations between them had long been tense, probably because of the ambiguous status of Special Branch, which Flower controlled for some operations but which remained the responsibility of the Police Commissioner…'[55] Flower, in his autobiographical account of his time as CIO head, revealed that Allum had gone to Mugabe after Independence – accusing Flower of plotting Mugabe's assassination. Flower, at the time, feared for his life until Mugabe assured Flower that he put no stock in the claims of a 'police informer'.[56]

Although a serving senior officer in the BSAP, McGuinness was able to bypass the formal police chain of command because of the Special Branch's subordination to two masters. The Special Branch was created as the internal security arm of the BSAP on the model adopted by many, if not most, British colonial police services; however, with the dissolution of the Central African Federation (to which Rhodesia belonged) and its security and intelligence agency, the Federal Intelligence and Security Bureau (FISB), Rhodesia sought to create its own intelligence service. Rhodesia's CIO was born out of the Rhodesian remnants of the FISB, plus the BSAP Special Branch Headquarters. Within the CIO, Special Branch Headquarters' function was to ensure intelligence on internal security threats (African nationalism, terrorism, sabotage, subversion, counterespionage and communist party and trade union activities) reached the CIO. The CIO acted to coordinate intelligence activities, set national-level priorities and disseminate intelligence to Rhodesian policy-makers. All Special Branch members were BSAP policemen, and the BSAP controlled Special Branch pay, promotion and assignments, as well as Special Branch operations at the provincial and district levels.

Figure 2.11 Rhodesian CIO Headquarters ('Red Bricks'). (Source: © Chris Cocks, with permission of Chris Cocks)

In this bifurcated authority structure, Allum had a great deal of control over McGuinness in administrative terms, but McGuinness had the latitude to ignore Allum, which McGuinness did with alacrity. Two notable examples include Allum's order to terminate the CBW effort and his push to reassign McGuinness to criminal investigations. McGuinness' latitude was a product of several factors: (a) the dual leadership structure; (b) the rivalry and animosity between Allum and Flower; (c) Flower's confidence in McGuinness; (d) the intense secrecy shrouding his operations;[57] (e) information asymmetry under wartime conditions;[57] (f) a network of close personal friends in influential positions – notably CIO deputy Derrick Robinson; and (g) an exceptionally strong unit cohesion involving McGuinness and his subordinates. Of these factors, the dual leadership structure involving Special Branch, McGuiness' monopoly on information (information asymmetry) and the intense secrecy surrounding his counterterrorism operations were key to his ability to maneuver bureaucratically.

Regarding whether the senior Rhodesian leadership was knowledgeable about the Rhodesian CBW effort, COMOPS was informed about the program's effectiveness. One document exists indicating that McGuinness reported an estimate of CBW-related casualties to COMOPS in 1977. The report to COMOPS reveals that the Rhodesian military leadership[60] also was aware of the covert CBW program. According to Brickhill, his interviews with senior Rhodesian military officers revealed that the service chiefs all were knowledgeable about the poisons program.[61]

Labeling the Rhodesian CBW program as a rogue operation by a covert unit unaccountable to any higher authorities would be a mistake. The program was authorized at the highest levels of the Rhodesian Government, whose leadership was fully cognizant of the program's purpose. The senior leadership also received at least one briefing on the results to date of the program. A system of official accountability

Figure 2.12 Michael J.P. McGuinness. (Source: the author's collection)[58]

existed with both the CIO chief and OC Special Branch receiving bi-weekly reports on the effort. Although the program became more compartmented later following security breaches, the program continued with the approval of the senior leadership. Although the responsible leadership chose not to actively exercise its oversight role to scrutinize the CBW program's activities, these activities went forward with official sanction. In the one case involving Allum's attempt to shut down CBW-related operations at Bindura, the program continued to function probably without Allum's knowledge. This situation illustrates one of the dangers in operating a highly secretive program with dual controls.

The Rhodesian CBW program was conceived as a CIO/Special Branch effort. Control of the program nominally passed in parallel through CIO and BSAP chains of command, with the CIO as the major partner. This arrangement undercut the BSAP Commissioner's authority over McGuinness' activities. When confronted by

Figure 2.13 Special Branch officers at a Selous Scout parade, February 1979.
(Source: © Peter Stiff collection, with permission of Peter Stiff)[59]

Allum's insistence to terminate the CBW effort, McGuinness exercised the authority he received from CIO chief Flower to maintain the CBW activities. Allum's protestations would have been feckless, given the secrecy surrounding the effort and McGuinness' bifurcated chain of command.

Facilities

Work for the Special Branch program was performed at two known locations:[62] the Special Branch-controlled 'fort' at Bindura (approximately 89 kilometers north of Salisbury) and the Mount Darwin 'fort' (19 kilometers north of Bindura).

The first Selous Scout 'fort' was built at Mount Darwin. According to author and former BSAP Chief Superintendent Peter Stiff, the Mount Darwin 'fort':

> was surrounded by corrugated iron walls, five meters high, without any windows or means of looking in. In the interior, facing inwards and following along the walls, were long prefabricated blocks which were divided up into rooms and offices as were necessary. The Bindura Fort and the Bulawayo Fort had operating theaters added to the basic design, because there was often a need to treat wounded terrorists in a secure area.[63]

The 'fort' was located along the Mtepatepa Road (approximately 2km west of the town center).[64] According to participants, the 'fort' was used to prepare botulinum toxin in water bowsers filled with rotten meat and water.[65] One participant claimed that the Rhodesian CBW team conducted animal tests (probably a euphemism for human experimentation) at Mount Darwin. Participants also describe Mount Darwin as a primary storage and distribution location for the CBW program. McGuinness dates the CBW team's use of the 'fort' to around February 1978, but one CBW team member claims that they began to use Mount Darwin around June 1977.

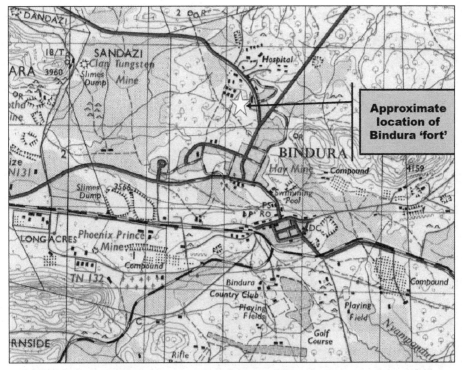

Figure 2.14 A map of Bindura showing the location of the police station and the airfield.
(Source: the author's work)

A small town in the center of an agricultural region growing mostly wheat and corn,[66] Bindura was home to JOC 'Hurricane' and one of the first locations for a Selous Scout 'fort'. Dating from 1974, the Bindura 'fort' was one of the original Selous Scout installations and, like its sister at Mount Darwin, was constructed of corrugated metal perimeter walls approximately 13 to 16 feet high and wooden frame structures sheathed in corrugated metal. The inner courtyard was designed to serve as a discreet helicopter landing pad.* The 'fort' was located just south and across the road from the hospital, and near the BSAP station and police soccer field. The Bindura 'fort' was equipped with facilities (including an operating room) for a physician assigned to the Selous Scouts. The 'fort' did not have an x-ray machine or laboratory equipment for medical testing.

As with all Selous Scout forts, Bindura did not have a permanent Selous Scout garrison assigned there. The Scouts used the Bindura 'fort' (when needed) to support operations. When operations were not under way, the Scout presence would have

---

* The idea of landing helicopters at the pad inside Bindura 'fort' was abandoned after the first helicopter landing blew the metal sheeting off the sides of the buildings at the 'fort'. Helicopters were forced to land on the adjoining police camp's soccer field instead.

Figure 2.15 Mount Darwin. (Source: the author's collection and © Peter Stiff collection, with permission of Peter Stiff)

been minimal, if any were there at all. The only permanent presence at Bindura consisted of Special Branch officers.

According to Ellert's description of the Bindura 'fort':

> The Bindura fort was the most sophisticated and in addition to standard communications also had direct telex links with CIO headquarters in Salisbury, the South African Police security branch in Pretoria and the South African Directorate of Military Intelligence. Bindura functioned as the security and intelligence headquarters for all Selous Scouts field operations under the command of assistant commissioner [*sic*] Mac McGuinness.[67]

By the time the CBW team began operations in late 1976, the Selous Scout presence at the 'fort' probably was minimal. The Special Branch – and by extension, the CBW team – would have had free run of the facility. Although not used by the Selous Scouts on a daily basis, the small 'fort' almost certainly would not have been considered 'derelict'.[68] Facilities at Bindura 'fort', however, would be considered rudimentary at best. No laboratory existed, and the CBW effort was confined to one room at the fort.[69]

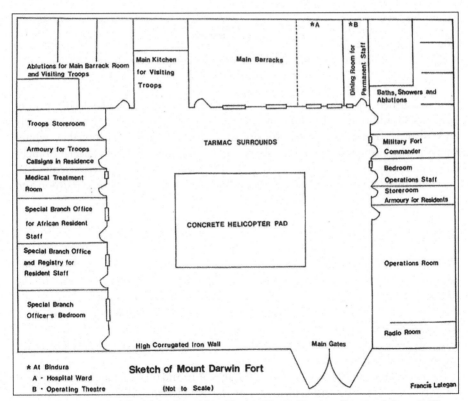

Figure 2.16 A sketch of the Selous Scout 'fort' at Mount Darwin. (Source: © Peter Stiff collection, with permission of Peter Stiff)[70]

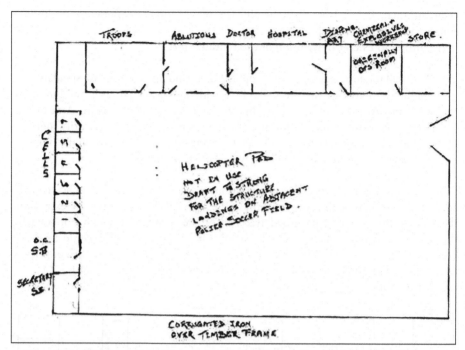

Figure 2.17 A diagram of the Selous Scout 'fort' at Bindura. (Source: Michael McGuinness, in the author's collection)[73]

Unconfirmed reports claim that the CBW team may have operated out of other locations in addition to Bindura and Mount Darwin. In one published (similarly unconfirmed) account, Symington's home in Borrowdale – a fashionable, white-dominated suburb of the capital Salisbury – was described as having a Special Branch-built laboratory for conducting CBW-related research.[71] Symington reportedly used the laboratory to develop several types of poison – including thallium, parathion and ricin.[72]

Personnel

The CBW team[74] was almost exclusively drawn from the University of Rhodesia. Several sources have pointed to Robert Symington as the scientific head of the Rhodesian CBW program. He personally selected several individuals – typically medical or veterinary students[75] – to become involved in the CBW effort. Symington occasionally assisted in the production of materials, but most of the day-to-day processing was performed by two individuals – occasionally aided by Special Branch members and their wives.[76]

Because all men in Rhodesia between the ages of 16 and 60 were required to perform military service as reservists, members of the Rhodesian CBW team periodically reported to Bindura for call-ups. In Symington's case, he was assigned as *a reservist to the Rhodesian Intelligence Corps and seconded to the Special Branch as a super-numerary.[77] The other individuals almost certainly were required to perform reserve duties with any one of the Rhodesian Security Force units, but they were seconded from those units to the Special Branch at Bindura at Symington's request. Although his unit of Special Branch liaison officers (on the nominal roll) never amounted to more than a dozen men at any one time, Chief Superintendent McGuinness had the latitude to add anyone to his unit as a supernumerary.[78] McGuinness supplemented the team's regular reservist pay with funds from his CIO account – and he told FBI investigators that he paid each member of the CBW team $900 a month.[79] From what information can be pieced together, the Rhodesian CBW team consisted of the following individuals:[80]

Professor Robert Burns Symington: Symington was born in 1925 in Edinburgh, Scotland and educated there in agricultural chemistry. After emigrating to Rhodesia, Symington rose to become an anatomy professor at the Godfrey Huggins School of Medicine, the University of Rhodesia.[81] He died in 1982[82] (aged 57) reportedly of a heart attack after having moved to Cape Town, South Africa in 1981. Symington – on sabbatical from the University of Zimbabwe – had joined the faculty at the University of Cape Town, and he reportedly never intended to return to Zimbabwe.[83] According to one of his medical students, Symington was a charismatic individual with an excellent sense of humor, and he often developed close friendships with his students. He was an excellent neuroanatomist, but he had little understanding of other aspects of anatomy when the departure of a colleague elevated him to head of anatomy. The former student also recounted that Symington's chief research interest was in the role of the pineal gland in controlling cyclical hormonal activities.[84] Others have described Symington less charitably as a 'hateful man' and as a 'racist'. As previously described, Symington was the originator of the CBW effort – and he continued to provide technical direction to the team. He also selected all of the individuals who made up the CBW team; lastly, Symington often consulted and shared CBW-related data with his South African colleagues.

Peter Stiff describes Symington (aka Sam Roberts) as

> a born Scotsman, was an elderly man with grey hair and bushy eyebrows... Sam was kindly, concerned, and always prepared to listen to people's problems... except when he was busy with his hobby – his all-consuming passion. He was an agricultural chemist by profession and spent his days analyzing soils and looking to the nutritional needs of plants. At weekends he spent most of his time at that hobby of his, which was researching for and distilling rare poisons... From

---

*   According to McGuinness, former Rhodesian Intelligence Corps (RIC) Major Ian King recounted hearsay that Symington had been given the honorary rank or either major or lieu-tenant colonel in the RIC. According to Colonel John Redfern – commanding officer of the RIC – Symington was never a member of the RIC.

the privacy of a remarkably sophisticated and well-equipped laboratory at the rear of his Borrowdale residence, he had produced large numbers of intriguing poisons, many of them forgotten since the Middle Ages.[85]

According to a former BSAP officer, Symington experimented extensively ('tinkered') with poisons and toxins and had nearly died once as a result of a laboratory accident involving a poison.[86] Stiff's account also mentions that Symington admitted once to nearly dying after accidentally ingesting a minute amount of thallium. The officer further stated that Symington's death in South Africa was due to another laboratory accident involving poisons. Symington was not a stranger to accidental poisoning: he may have experienced an accidental chemical exposure in January 1979 – and according to one source, his death was due to a second accidental poisoning.[87]

Descriptions of his work at both the Special Branch-constructed home laboratory and at the Selous Scout 'fort' at Bindura further demonstrates that Symington was involved in the Rhodesian CBW effort – including the production of poisons for assassinations.[88] The most tangible indications of Symington's involvement are references to his development of poisons for use in the CIO's attempted assassination of Mugabe during the 1979 Lancaster House talks in London. Drawing from his interview with 'Taffy' Brice, British journalist Tom Mangold described Symington as an anatomy professor at the University of Salisbury who emigrated to South Africa to take a position at the University of Cape Town[89] shortly after Rhodesia's black-majority government took power in 1980. Brice reportedly told Mangold that Symington had been 'producing and testing and using toxins to supplement the war effort for the Rhodesian forces'.[90]

Victor Noble: Victor Noble (deceased) worked at the University of Rhodesia, where he supposedly was Professor Symington's laboratory assistant. He volunteered to

Figure 2.18 Alan 'Taffy' Brice, circa 1990. (Source: © Peter Stiff collection, with permission of Peter Stiff)[91]

assist Symington in the CBW work at Bindura, where he probably headed the small team responsible for chemical and biological agent production. Noble described his training as consisting of a diploma in Medical Technology from the Witwatersrand Technical College and a partially completed BSc (Hons) in Biochemistry from the University of the Witwatersrand – having failed one subject in his third year.[92] As Noble described it, he jumped at the chance to serve with the Rhodesian Intelligence Corps – having no hope of playing a part in any really physically active unit because his heart had been weakened by a childhood bout of rheumatic fever.

According to Noble:

> … when the opportunity arose to play a really meaningful role in the war effort as a member of the Selous Scouts, I was more than willing to accept their offer and joined Mr. Mac's unit. Everything I did was highly classified and I … have always simply maintained that I was a very small cog in a large organization and had nothing of real import to tell them…

Noble, along with St Clair Hayes, were the principal producers of poisoned materials.[93] Noble resided in South Africa until his death and despite one brief moment of conscience when he appeared willing to discuss his role in the CBW effort, he was resistant to describing his role in the Rhodesian efforts – saying that he was only a Territorial (military reservist) in the Selous Scouts. Noble claimed that what he did was 'top secret' and was done for the purest of patriotic motives; he referred any questions about the Rhodesian CBW effort to the 'big fish'. In reply to a detailed list of questions, Noble answered that McGuinness should have been able to answer all of the queries and refused to elaborate.

At the end of his life, Noble was completely disillusioned and disappointed. In addition to his heart problems, he lost both his legs as a direct result – he was convinced – of what he did in the war.[94] The inference to be drawn from his statement is that he lost his legs because of his exposure to chemicals he was handling during his time in Bindura. Noble died in Cape Town, South Africa on 8 December 2011 after a long illness.

St Clair Hayes: Hayes – then a student at the University of Rhodesia – was 'called up' in late March 1977 to serve 18 months of military service in the Rhodesian Security Forces. Given his academic credentials, he was inducted into the BSAP and sent to the police training school. While still in training, he was informed that he was being transferred to the army and ordered to report to Selous Scout commander Reid-Daly. Reid-Daly reportedly informed Hayes that Symington had selected him to work on a top-secret project involving poisons; he then was instructed to report to Chief Superintendent McGuinness at Bindura. Hayes continued his national service at Bindura until late 1978/early 1979, when he began his studies at the University of Pretoria's Onderstepoort Veterinary Institute in South Africa. He, however, continued until war's end to do his periodic call-ups at Bindura, where he and Vic Noble were the major producers of CBW agents.

Hayes was the first-year veterinary student described in an incident at Bindura involving a botched attempt to castrate a monkey belonging to the commander of the 'fort' at Bindura. Supposedly, Hayes and another man then doing call-ups at Bindura – annoyed by the monkey's very public and frequent displays of self-gratification – endeavored to end the monkey's 'reign of terror'. Unfortunately, Hayes chose to use the only tranquilizer available: one used on elephants. The monkey reportedly died, and our two intrepid heroes drove around all night searching for a means to dispose of the monkey and avoid having to admit their involvement to the commander. Hayes continued his veterinary studies at Onderstepoort – graduating in 1982.

Garth Ellis: Little is known about Ellis, except that he was a weaponeer who specialized in the construction of explosive devices – notably letter bombs and 'roadrunner' radios at the Bindura 'fort'. Letter bombs were designed to assassinate key opposition figures – often in exile in Mozambique; 'roadrunner' devices were modified commercial radios fitted with homing beacons or explosive devices – and once tuned on, the hidden device (either a homing beacon or the explosive device) was activated. A Rhodesian Fireforce (helicopter-borne assault troops) would respond to a 'roadrunner' activation, or an airstrike would be conducted. An explosives-fitted 'roadrunner' would have a pre-set timer delay, but later versions became more sophisticated. The Rhodesian expectation was that most of the insurgent band would have gathered around the radio when the device detonated.[95] On one occasion, Ellis suffered severe shrapnel wounds when an explosive device being constructed by BSAP weapons expert David Perkins prematurely detonated – killing Perkins.

One additional person could be added to the list, though he probably was not a member of the 'team' as such, but rather aided their efforts as needed. Henry Wolhuter was one of McGuinness' Special Branch members assigned as liaison to the Selous Scouts at Bindura. Wolhuter – aided on occasion by his wife – prepared chemicals used to contaminate clothing and foodstuffs. They both emigrated to South Africa once Rhodesia became Zimbabwe – and Wolhuter's wife died of a cancer she believed was due to her handling of chemicals in Rhodesia; Wolhuter died of a similar cancer soon after. Before his death, Wolhuter passed on documents related to the Rhodesian CBW effort to Peter Stiff.

Supplies

The source of materials – both the chemicals and the biological pathogens – remains cloaked in secrecy. Information indicates that the parathion was obtained from local retailers.[96] When McGuinness interviewed Victor Noble, Noble claimed that the anthrax was stolen by he and Symington from the University of Rhodesia's microbiology laboratory. The amount stolen was small and used for experimental contamination of cigarettes and food. Another source claims that the anthrax seed stock at Bindura originated from South Africa. Symington reportedly never contacted colleagues at the university for bacterial cultures or for help regarding microbiology.[97]

One BSAP document suggests that at least some materials were South African in origin; this document explains that one reason for a lower death rate during the reporting period was due to 'the shortage of necessary ingredients which are to be obtained from South Africa within the next two weeks'.[98] One Rhodesian CBW participant claimed that South African Police Service (SAPS) Colonel J.J. Viktor – based for a time at Bindura – provided the Rhodesians with any materials that Symington or Noble required from South Africa.

According to former BSAP reservist Jim Parker, Symington or his lab assistant (probably Noble) selected the types of chemicals the project would use, and Chief Superintendent McGuinness arranged:

> ... for the collection of substances from the South African Special Forces' Detachment Medical Special Operations (later known as 7 South Africa Medical Service)* in Pretoria. The substances were couriered to Bindura by a particular Special Branch officer attached to the Selous Scouts [and working for McGuinness]...[99]

What materials were needed from South Africa remains unclear – and why the Rhodesians were dependent on the South Africans to supply the Rhodesian CBW effort also remains a question. One document indicates that the South African-supplied materials included colchicine, ricin, amanita toxin, 2,4-dichlorophenoxy-acetic acid, compound 1080, cyanide, arsenic and warfarin.[100] This list largely mirrors the Rhodesian 'founding' document except for colchicine (a gout medicine that mimics arsenic toxicity if one is overdosed), cyanide, arsenic and warfarin – items not included on the 'founding' document.

Most, if not all, of the materials the CBW team needed could be readily found among the agricultural and industrial chemicals used in Rhodesia – including pesticides and cattle dip solutions such as Supermix DFF (a commercial organophosphate cattle dip). Telodrin used by the CBW team was obtained from the Rhodesian Department of Wildlife and National Parks.[101]

The clothing, food and beverages to be poisoned were purchased from a retailer, Madziwa Trading, which was based in Bindura and owned by a Greek Cypriot named Maki Christou. A Salisbury manufacturing firm owned by Maki Tselentis produced many of the clothing items Christou sold to the CBW team at Bindura. In some cases, Rhodesian labels were removed from clothing items and replaced with South African-origin labels.[102]

According to a separate source, Christou had been:

> an active member of Ethniki Organosis Kyprion Agoniston (EOKA)† before leaving for Rhodesia, and had owned several general dealers stores throughout

---

* Detachment Medical Special Operations (aka 7 SAMS) was assigned to support South African Special Forces (i.e. Reconnaissance Commandos, or 'Recces') and later to support 32 Battalion as well.

† A Greek Cypriot organization that during the 1950s, fought against British colonial rule – and for the unification of Cyprus with Greece.

Bindura and Mount Darwin districts. His main store, Madziwa Trading, was based in Bindura where he lived with his wife in a house adjacent to the store. His stores had virtually everything for sale; tins of food, tinned meat, corned beef, jams, dairy products, soft drinks, dried fish, mealie meal (staple diet and most popular with the local Africans), cigarettes, tobacco, clothing (shirts, shorts, trousers, underwear), footwear, and socks – everything an ordinary supermarket would stock. He used to supply his chain of stores throughout the district from his Bindura base. He did extremely well businesswise when he was contracted to supply McGuiness and his team together with the Selous Scouts.

In 2006, Christou reportedly died in Cyprus of leukemia.[103]

Funding

Clearly, McGuinness had substantial sources of funding that he used to support the counterterrorism activities of his unit, the Selous Scouts in general and the CBW team in particular. The actual source of those funds is obscure, but South Africa was at least the conduit for the funds, if not the actual source.[104] South African Intelligence regularly supplied the Rhodesian CIO with significant funding; a senior CIO operative reportedly couriered $750,000 to $800,000 a month from South Africa to Chief Superintendent McGuinness for his operations.[105] The amount may have been as large a US$1 million a month, but the CIO is thought to have diverted as much as US$250,000 off the top each month.[106] The funds are believed to have originated from Saudi Arabia, with the United Arab Emirates as a possible contributor. No rationale has been offered to explain why the Saudis were interested in funding the Rhodesian War to the tune of several million dollars a year.[107] The funds were used to pay supernumerary salaries; to purchase CBW-related materials (including goods to be contaminated) and raw materials from South Africa; and to pay death bonuses to contact men. Death bonuses alone were Rh$1,000 per guerrilla death. The Special Branch also used the funds to entertain Selous Scouts, hold dances and *braais* for the local populace at Bindura, and sponsor Bindura's local soccer team in matches throughout Rhodesia. These types of expenditures were approved by CIO chief Flower.[108]

In a heavily redacted FBI interview report, a former Rhodesian Special Branch officer claimed that:

> (redacted) would travel from Rhodesia to South Africa up to eight times per month to brief (redacted), to pass on and receive intelligence as well as to collect money to bring back to (redacted). (redacted) would bring back varying amounts of United States currency to (redacted) ranging from $100,000 to $500,000 per trip. The money was used to pay the salaries of the (redacted). (redacted) said that (redacted) would often have access to as much as $8,000,000 in US currency. The money was provided to (redacted) by the Saudi Government, according to (redacted).[109]

According to former Special Branch officer Henrik Ellert, the CIO station in Pretoria, South Africa was an important conduit of funds from South African Intelligence to the Selous Scouts. Members of the Scouts regularly couriered large amounts of South African currency to the Rhodesian Reserve Bank; there the money was converted to Rhodesian dollars and deposited in the secret intelligence vote supplementary account controlled by the Prime Minister's office.[110]

According to a former senior BSAP officer:

> Mac (C/Supt. McGuinness) and the Scouts were the catalysts and implementers for all unconventional warfare. The South Africans became intensely interested in their success rates. They were initially and politely rebuffed, but mounting political pressure led to them being taken into Mac's confidence. General Magnus Malan, the SA [South African] Minister of Defence, came up with the novel idea of paying for the information. The offer was gratefully accepted and members of SA's Recce Units were thereafter trained alongside Scouts who had been selected for the programme's "dark side." It can be said that SA bankrolled the Scouts and their associated SB intelligence effort. Without those funds there would have been a far lower level of achievement.[111]

The South Africans also funded Rhodesian Special Branch covert actions against South African ANC targets in Mozambique.[112]

CBW testing and experimentation

Evidence of Rhodesian CBW testing or experimentation is scant, but what little information exists suggests that some experimentation was conducted. Testing is a critical component of a CBW program in order to determine the effectiveness of the agent or pathogen, and of the delivery system (whether it be poisoned food and beverages, or contaminated clothing). A possible reason for the lack of chemical or biological testing typical of State-sponsored CBW programs was the Rhodesian reliance on trial and error to determine the lethal dose $(LD_{50})^*$ of its agents or the efficiency of its delivery mechanisms.[113]

Most published accounts suggest that the scientists at Bindura recognized the need for testing and, for some unknown reason (possibly the ready availability of captured terrorists), chose to conduct testing on human subjects. One document states: 'There was no testing or trials of CBW experiments [sic] in the Bindura fort, but once Mount Darwin fort was closed for operational purposes, Noble and Hart used same [the Mount Darwin 'fort'] for their own private experiments'.[114] The reliance on the Mount Darwin 'fort' as the scene of CBW experimentation is borne out by statements from another CBW participant – and the same participant emphasized the use of trial and error to determine dosages for lethal effect.[115] According to Ellert, the scientific team attached to the Special Branch at Bindura recommended

---

*   LD50 refers to the lethal dose for 50 percent of a population.

testing the effectiveness of poisoned clothing. Although Ellert admits that he has no evidence that any tests were conducted, he suggests an incident in 1975 may be linked to human experimentation related to the CW program. In that incident, a number of Shona-speaking individuals (referred to by Ellert as 'political dissidents') were arrested in Salisbury and turned over to the Selous Scouts, who allegedly took them to the Mount Darwin 'fort'. The rumor among Special Branch officers at the time was that the Scouts and a team of doctors used the prisoners as 'human guinea pigs'. Soon afterward, the Scouts borrowed a Special Branch Land Rover and dumped the bodies in the nearby mine. Ellert's suspicions were further raised when the Scouts refused to allow the BSAP member who normally conducted the 'Mashfords' runs to be involved in the disposal.[116] In mid-2004, Zimbabwean authorities announced the discovery of an estimated 5,000 bodies in a disused mineshaft (28km from Mount Darwin) and in nearby mass graves dating from the time when the Rhodesian Special Forces controlled the area. The newspaper account of the discovery claimed that many of the dead probably had been poisoned during the war.[117]

Jeremy Brickhill alleges that by 1975, Rhodesia had begun human experimentation using chemical agents on captured insurgents. The purpose of these experiments was to determine the LD_{50} for each agent and the effectiveness of different dissemination techniques. According to Brickhill, the Special Branch provided 'guinea pigs' from various Special Branch detention centers and disposed of the bodies down mineshafts.[118] Brickhill's information almost certainly comes from Ellert, and therefore cannot be seen as confirmation.

In *Secrets and Lies*, Chandré Gould recounts from Wouter Basson's trial testimony that a Rhodesian in 1979 delivered to Jan Coetzee a report detailing the effects of organophosphates on humans. Testing involved application of the chemicals to different human body parts and through different types of contaminated clothing.[119] Because Rhodesian observation of poisoned guerrillas in the bush was not possible, the data almost certainly was derived from experimentation on captured guerrillas.[120] When Coetzee asked McGuinness about the source of the report, McGuinness replied that it came from a professor at the University of Rhodesia. Other information exists that lends credence to the likelihood that the Rhodesians maintained records detailing which chemical agents were used and their lethality; these records reportedly included human LD_{50} data.[121]

In a somewhat bizarre, but not entirely far-fetched account, a South African policeman (probably Eugene de Kock) – assigned to 'PATU 7' operating in the Mtoko District along the Mazoe River – recounted that his unit had instructions on discovery of a guerrilla camp to collect samples of defecated fecal matter for 'analysis in Pretoria'. The South African commented that this exercise probably was conducted to determine whether the guerrilla group had been poisoned and update the guerrilla casualty list.[122]

Supposedly, their analysis had one finding:

> I found this man's [Rhodesian Special Branch officer] recollection of the tests very interesting. According to him, they established by means of tests and examinations that a Black man evacuate[d] the bowels twice a day and not once

a day like Europeans. These tests brought about [*sic*] that the dosage of thallium had to be doubled since they came to the conclusion that a Black man's metabolism is double the speed of that of a European.[123]

Chemical agent production

By all accounts, the clandestine Rhodesian CBW program was small-scale and rudimentary. The program had no laboratory facilities at Bindura[124] and limited protective clothing (apart from gloves, masks and aprons).[125] According to McGuinness' statement to the FBI investigators, 'several different poisons made by (redacted) were used during the war'. This included drying pesticides on corrugated tin (to remove any chemical odors) and placing it on clothing to be given to terrorists, placing heavy metals (thallium, for example) in various types of foods to be distributed to terrorists, and using pure alcohol to poison liquors that were then given to terrorists. McGuinness thought (redacted) operation at JOC Bindura crude and described it as 'low tech' and 'very rudimentary'.[126]

The methods used were primitive – consisting largely of sun-drying liquid pesticides to a powder and brushing them onto clothing. Warfarin was mixed with corn meal and other foods, while thallium was injected into canned foods and beverages using a micro-needle.[127] Medicines probably were treated with poisons using a similar method; cigarette tips were poisoned with a mixture of telodrin and potassium chloride. No information exists to suggest how the CBW technicians avoided the inhalational hazard posed by solid pesticide that was powdered to the consistency of talc.

In his 2013 autobiography, former Selous Scout Major John Cronin recounted that while serving as an officer in the Rhodesian Light Infantry (RLI), he saw a Special Branch officer in Mount Darwin wearing gloves while arranging stacks of shirts and trousers into separate piles:

> I reached down to pick up a pair of new denims when the man told me sternly that I didn't want to do that. I looked up at him, curious about why he would object to this innocent gesture, but the gloves should have tipped me off.
>
> What's the problem? I asked.
>
> —That'll kill you. Just take my word for it, mate. It'll kill you.
>
> I don't understand.
>
> —We've sewn some things into the linings of this stuff.
>
> What kind of things?
>
> —Powders.
>
> What kind of powders?
>
> —Various crystallized pesticides.
>
> Why?
>
> —Because we're going to send all of this out to the TTLs where the terrs'll get them eventually.
>
> How will they do that?
>
> —Through the stores out there.
>
> This clothing goes into public stores?

—Yes.

That raised an obvious question. But how can you be sure that the terrs and not some other African civilians will get these things?

He smiled indulgently. You're new here, aren't you?[128]

The Rhodesian program manufactured none of the chemicals they used; instead, the Rhodesians processed readily available agricultural pesticides and toxic industrial chemicals – adapting them for use in the conflict. The processing involved converting the chemicals into forms that were easily absorbed into the body through the skin, and that resulted in death as quickly as possible.[129] One process that allegedly increased the lethality of pesticides used to contaminate clothing was the addition of dimethyl sulfoxide (DMSO) as a skin penetrant to aid in the body's rapid absorption of the pesticide; the South African CBW program would adopt the use of DMSO later. The specific types of clothing (underpants and T-shirts) were chosen to ensure the greatest dermal penetration – and the groin and underarms were target areas because the skin at those locations more easily absorbed the chemicals from the clothing.

No evidence exists in the available literature to suggest that the Rhodesian CBW program was geared for large-scale use against insurgents. Rhodesian production and dissemination of chemical agents seems confined to targeting specific insurgent groups identified by the Special Branch. All of the chemical materials reportedly used by the Rhodesians as part of their chemical agent production were used in Rhodesian agriculture or by industrial firms. The clothing – and presumably the consumable items destined for contamination – were purchased from Rhodesian suppliers.[130]

Production was tailored to meet the needs of provincial Special Branch members (or Special Branch's Project Section) for very specific types and quantities of goods sought by guerrillas. In some cases, guerrillas provided contact men with a list of needed supplies. Those lists went to Bindura, and the requested materials (poisoned, of course) were supplied to the contact men for distribution to the guerrillas. Although demand generally set the production rates, the team at Bindura probably had some latitude in producing goods that would be placed on rural store shelves or in guerrilla caches; some common or much-sought-after products may have been stockpiled in anticipation of demand.

According to an often-quoted description of the Rhodesian process:

> ... M.J. McGuinness, the man who facilitated the chemical programme at the Bindura Fort, as it was called, and the most senior Special Branch Officer seconded to the Central Intelligence Organisation and afforded the title Officer Commanding Counter Terrorist Operations said that about a dozen times during 1977, 25-gallon drums of foul smelling liquid were delivered to the officer in charge at the Fort. The chemicals were poured onto large sheets of tin and dried in the sun. When the liquid had dried, the resulting flakes were scooped up and pounded in a mortar with a pestle. That powder was then brushed onto clothes and also mixed into processed meat such as bully beef, and then repacked into new tins. The poison was injected using a micro needle into bottles, most of them containing alcoholic drinks...[131]

The reported purpose of drying the pesticide to a powder before applying it to the clothing was to eliminate the chemical odor.[132] A member of the Rhodesian CBW team directly involved in processing the pesticide indicates that the clothing was dipped in a solution of parathion and methanol (as a solvent) and then dried.[133] According to 'Mac', he estimated that approximately 2,500 pairs of contaminated underwear and a like number of T-shirts were processed and distributed to the field. As previously mentioned, underwear and T-shirts were considered the most effective articles of clothing for dissemination of poison because they had direct contact with vulnerable skin regions (e.g. the groin, armpits etc.). 'Mac' went on to claim that several hundred sets of poisoned socks, shirts and jackets also were produced, but these clothing articles were not generally effective and were merely used to cloak the more dangerous items as they entered the distribution system.[134]

According to one senior BSAP officer:

> Mac told me that the clothing was coated with a chemical formula at its natural perspiration points that took "forever" to dry. It was spread out in the sunlight for this purpose, as opposed to accelerated drying by other means. The effect was deadly. The chemical formula passed into the wearer's body and he succumbed to its effects… I recall hearing on one occasion of a "double hit." An exiting (into Moçambique) group was supplied with the clothing. When they arrived at their base the older hands pulled rank and took the clothing to wear themselves![135]

According to Ellert, the process involved soaking clothing in stainless steel vats containing a solution of odorless and colorless poisons.[136]

In a reported discussion between Symington and CIO assassin 'Taffy' Brice, Symington described how he contaminated clothing destined for guerrillas:

> Special Branch once brought me several hundred pairs of underwear and T-shirts. I soaked them in a solution of parathion and allowed them to dry. Afterwards, they put them in bundles and deposited them at a number of stores anticipated as future terrorist targets. The owners were not put in the picture, but were told to place the bundles on high shelves in their stores … and not to sell the stuff under any circumstances.
>
> A number of these stores were subsequently raided by terrorists and put to the torch. The gangs took their loot, including the doctored underclothing and T-shirts, back to their bases, and [they] later put them on. Parathion is a poison that works its way into the human system through hair follicles.[138]

The production was sporadic: all of the team members were reservists assigned to Bindura during their 'call-ups'. Initially, they worked full-time producing materials that could be stockpiled and distributed as needed; later, they worked only during their 'call-ups' to replenish the stocks of contaminated goods at Bindura.[139]

The quantity of contaminated food and clothing was largely dependent on supplies of raw materials – at least some of which were imported from South Africa. This dependency is illustrated in a top-secret Special Branch report dated 25 August 1977 that stated:

> It will be noted that there is a considerable decrease in the quantity of materials directed into the field during the fortnight under review. This being due to (a) staff shortage in the field and subsequent inability to recruit contact men, and (b) the shortage of necessary ingredients which are to be obtained from South Africa within the next two weeks [see appendix].

When supplies were available, production of contaminated items was substantial. In a two-week period in late November 1977, over 365 pieces of clothing and 85 cans of 'tinned' meat were contaminated along with a wide assortment of sundry other items – including canned peas, toothpaste, cookies, jam, brandy, medicines, vitamins and cigarettes. The number of guerrilla dead due to poisoning during this same period was 79 (see appendix).

Chemical use

Parathion: The liquid chemical prepared at the Selous Scout 'fort' near Bindura almost certainly was parathion[*] – and it would have been a potent nerve agent that could be used to contaminate clothing.[†] When poisoned clothing was worn by insurgents, the agent would have been easily absorbed into the body through soft tissues in the groin and armpits. Untreated, the victim of organophosphate poisoning would probably experience the onset of symptoms in six to 12 hours depending on dosage and metabolic rate. Death could be expected within a few hours after the onset of symptoms.

At roughly the same time as the start of the Rhodesians' CBW use of parathion to poison clothing, hospitals in a Salisbury township (Harari) and Bindura reported an over-threefold increase in the number of parathion poisonings.[‡] Investigations by attending physicians ultimately determined that many of the cases resulted from poisoned clothing, but the doctors could not determine the cause of the contamina-

---

[*]   Parathion is not odorless or colorless; instead – depending on purity – its color can range from yellowish to brown, and it has the faint odor of garlic. Depending on its purity and formulation, a parathion-based pesticide could exhibit the 'foul' odor characteristic of the material reportedly processed at the Bindura 'fort'.

[†]   The parathion may have been mixed with DMSO (a skin penetrant) to speed absorption of the poison through the skin. BSAP/4 stated that after the initial attempts to poison guerrillas failed because the chemical was not readily absorbed by the body, he suggested that the pesticide be mixed with DMSO. The team adopted his suggestion and the new mixture was very effective. BSAP/4 stated that he came up with the idea of mixing the pesticide with DMSO after recalling experiments in the US to develop ways to deliver drugs to patients without using needles.

[‡]   Harari was a predominantly black township on the outskirts of the Rhodesian capital, Salisbury – and all of the patients with OP exposure were black.

tion. One woman who purchased clothing for her family stated that she obtained the trousers from a local vendor. According to the attending physicians:

> Poisoning with organophosphate compounds was a comparatively rare clinical event until a few years ago. However, over the last two years and in particular the last 12 months, the number of cases of organophosphate poisoning at Harari Hospital has increased remarkably. Indeed, organophosphate compounds were implicated in the majority of patients with poisoning seen at the hospital in the last year.[140]

The attending physicians were at a loss to explain this sudden increase in organo-phosphate poisoning (OP) cases. As they admitted, 'the source of the poison in these cases is open to debate'.[141] The study found a distinct male preponderance among the victims – and although the age ranged from 11 to over 40 years of age, the vast majority of cases were between 11 and 30 years old. Rhodesian physicians classified most OP poisoning cases as suicide attempts until 1977, when the number of cases with unknown causes jumped dramatically – and the number of accidental inges-tions also doubled. 'Accidental ingestion' was defined as eating contaminated food or

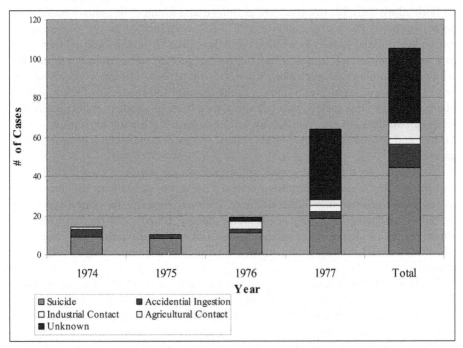

Figure 2.19 Sources of poisoning in patients at Harari Hospital, 1974-1979. (Source: the author's work – based on data from M.M. Hayes, N.G. van der Westhuizen and M. Gelfand, 'Organophosphate Poisoning in Rhodesia: A Study of the Clinical Features and Management of 105 Patients', *South Africa Medical Journal* 55 (5 August 1978), pp.230-234)

beverages (typically home-brewed beer). The authors of the article also ascribed most of the unknown cases to accidental consumption of contaminated food or beverages in the rural districts.

Of the 105 patients treated at Harari Hospital, 89 survived and 16 died of OP poisoning. Of the 89 survivors, 13 relapsed – including two patients who were each readmitted three times because of a reoccurrence of symptoms.[142] Relapses were not uncommon when the patient's clothing had been contaminated with OP pesticides. Upon release from the hospital, the patient often donned the same contaminated clothes he wore to the hospital and unintentionally caused a re-poisoning.

While serving as the Government Medical Officer at Bindura General Hospital, Dr R.O. Laing observed a case in which three family members experienced OP poisoning. Laing learned that the only wage-earning member of the family bought sets of clothing from an itinerant vendor. Unknown to the family member, all the clothes she purchased for the family contained large amounts of parathion. Laing speculated that the vendor must have unknowingly wrapped the clothing in material containing parathion.[143]

In the first case that was presented to Bindura General Hospital, a 19-year-old man (Case 1) was admitted because of OP poisoning. He was released, but readmitted 10 days later with a severe case of poisoning. Because he was wearing the same clothes on both admissions, his trousers were examined and found to be contaminated with 5g of parathion. The young man's uncle (Case 2) was admitted for OP poisoning; he responded to therapy and was released three days later. He was readmitted that night in a serious condition – having relapsed; his trousers were found to be contaminated with 'large amounts' of parathion. Case 3 – the nephew of Case 2 (and younger brother of Case 1) – also was admitted to the hospital and treated for OP poisoning. He responded to therapy and was released after a week in another set of trousers. He relapsed two days later – experiencing OP poisoning. Both pairs of trousers – from his first and second admissions – were tested, and each contained a large quantity of parathion.

The sudden, inexplicable increase of OP-related admissions at Harari Hospital – and the similar relapses at Bindura General Hospital – all point to the intentional use of parathion to contaminate clothing. Such use confirms the statements made by numerous former members of the BSAP Special Branch and the Selous Scouts about the use of chemical agents as poisons. These clinical reports from the hospitals at Harari and Bindura also confirm the efficacy of contaminating clothing with parathion.

The Rhodesian program reduced (if not outright abandoned) its usage of parathion after Symington was hospitalized with parathion poisoning in January 1979. Following Symington's hospital stay, the CBW effort instituted protective measures – including the use of surgical masks, rubber aprons and rubber gloves. Symington's accidental parathion poisoning also may have forced the Rhodesians to adopt telodrin as their CW agent of choice.

Telodrin: The Rhodesian CBW team adopted telodrin (isobenzan) in late 1979/ early 1980[144] because it was 'found to be an excellent poison, completely odourless, tasteless, and very quick working… towards the end of the war, telodrin was the favourite poison, produced by Shell Chemical for the extermination of baboons'.[145] The team concluded that 80mg of telodrin crystallized in potassium chloride and placed on the end of a cigarette would kill a man before he had finished smoking. The team believed that a death due to telodrin poison could easily be attributed to anthrax 'poisoning', because telodrin produced identical symptoms. The comparison of telodrin intoxication with anthrax is, frankly, absurd. As an organochloride pesticide, symptoms of telodrin intoxication will include convulsions, seizures, coma and respiratory depression.

Thallium: Where parathion and telodrin were used to contaminate clothing, thallium was used to poison food – largely beverages and canned meats; for example, in one small area of Rhodesia, 11 out of 34 insurgents reportedly died as the result of food poisoning.[146] The clandestine distribution of canned beef contaminated (the Liebig's beef case) with thallium reportedly resulted in the deaths of numerous civilians in the Arcturus District*, as well as insurgents – prompting an investigation by the unsuspecting manufacturers and the Rhodesian Ministry of Health.[147] The possible contamination of foodstuffs did not escape the attention of the African population, which believed that the Rhodesians had poisoned cans of Leox-brand (Liebig's) canned meat.[148] Thallium also was used to poison mealie meal – and the use of thallium sulfate as a poison would have readily occurred to Rhodesians, as the country had a relatively long history of using thallium in its efforts to eradicate baboons (a persistent pest – raiding farms and preying on sheep and goats).

In an account describing the effects of poisoned medicines on guerrillas, Special Branch member Ed Bird wrote that:

> The terrorists, still numbering thirty, had remained at the beer drink until early on the Monday morning when, as a group, they headed south into the Mtetengwe TTL. Presumably after the weekend beer drink, most were hungover and to remedy this they dug into the vitamin pills, the Dr. Strong 500 capsules, and the Eno's liver salts. The group stayed together for the next forty-eight hours when two of their number started complaining of severe toothache and headaches before being treated by the section medical officer. The condition of the two rapidly deteriorated with their vision becoming impaired (they were starting to become blind, their hair falling out in tufts and their feet developing suppurating sores which necessitated the two having to be carried). They both died during the night. The next morning, with other members of the group complaining of the same symptoms, it was decided to obtain the services of a witch doctor in the Mtetengwe TTL.[149]

---

* · The Arcturus District is located approximately 30km east of Salisbury (now Harare).

According to Bird, diaries recovered later by the Rhodesians paint a picture of desperation as more and more of the guerrilla section fell ill with the same symptoms and succumbed to the poisons, which Bird describes as a 'mercury-based poison which caused a terrible and painful death'.[150] On the basis of Bird's description, the lethal poison probably was thallium.

Warfarin: Despite denials by the Rhodesian CBW team that they used warfarin,[151] Dr Paul Epstein's account of an incident at the Central Hospital in Beira, Mozambique during the late 1970s indicates otherwise:[152] Epstein – an American physician working in Beira – recounted that on 28 April 1978, the first five ZANLA insurgents arrived at the hospital with nosebleeds. One died in the emergency room, another died while being moved to the ward and a third was in shock. Within the next two weeks, 15 men hemorrhaged to death out of 35 admitted to the hospital. Approximately 200 men in total from an insurgent camp at Chibawawa – in Mozambique's Sofala Province – were suffering from the mysterious hemorrhage.

In the course of six to seven days, the ailment typically progressed from headaches around the eyes to nosebleeds often accompanied by fever. In its advanced stages, the patients experienced more severe hemorrhagic symptoms – including vomiting blood, bleeding gums, bloody urine, blood under the whites of their eyes and blood in their lungs. After a week, the symptoms stopped for a day or two and then began again. In the two weeks after the first admission, the first three patients died, along with 10 others; the last two died shortly thereafter, as their lungs filled with blood.[153] The medical team treating the ZANLA members at first considered that they were suffering from sepsis resulting from a bacterial infection. On ruling out a bacterial infection, the doctors considered whether the patients were suffering from a viral hemorrhagic fever. The first outbreak of Ebola Zaire had taken place in 1976 with very similar symptoms, except for the absence of tremors or convulsions in the Mozambique patients. None of the medical staff became ill – ruling out the possibility that the causative agent was a communicable disease. Dr Epstein considered whether the patients may have contracted cholera, but he ruled that out after examining their diet, which had consisted of only rice and milk. In the end, testing of abdominal wall fat from one deceased patient indicated warfarin was present.[154] The poisoning of 200 insurgents at Chibawawa in April 1978 followed a similar poisoning during November 1977 that affected several hundred individuals at another insurgent camp in Mozambique. These poisonings most likely were the result of warfarin mixed with a food staple such as mealie meal, rice or canned beef.[155]

Biological agent production

Given the size and limited capacity of Rhodesia's rudimentary CBW facilities, the program almost certainly was restricted to batch-type production of *Vibrio cholerae*, *Clostridium botulinum* and possibly *Bacillus anthracis*. The Rhodesians considered, but rejected the idea of, producing *Rickettsia prowazekii* and *Salmonella typhi*. We have no description of how the Rhodesian CBW program acquired its bacterial cultures, or how or where they were cultivated, except for a description of how the Rhodesians produced botulinum toxin by heating water bowsers filled with water, corn, rotted meat and *C. botulinum*.[*][156] No evidence exists to suggest that the Rhodesians ever attempted to isolate, culture or cultivate *B. anthracis*.

Rhodesian production of biological pathogens and toxins probably began in early 1979 after Victor Noble returned from South Africa with South African *Elektroniks, Meganies, Landbou en Chemies* (EMLC)[†] head Dr Jan Coetzee.[157] Noble and Coetzee brought a tiny vial of *C. botulinum* and a sample of *B. anthracis*.[158] Production and use of *V. cholerae* almost certainly predated the Special Branch's CBW effort, given that *V. cholerae* was widely disseminated in Mozambique by Rhodesian and Portuguese troops as early as 1973.

The Rhodesian Army medical laboratories did not possess the capability to produce biological pathogens in militarily significant quantities.[159] The SAP Forensic Laboratory also lacked the ability to develop, test or produce chemical or biological agents.[160] Three possibilities (in order of greatest likelihood) exist for the production for BW agents – and they are: (1) South Africa provided bacterial cultures for use in the Rhodesian program and may have provided 'finished' BW agents; (2) the Rhodesians isolated the organisms (*V. cholerae, C. botulinum* and possibly *B. anthracis*) from the environment; or (3) the Rhodesian BW production was housed in a location equipped to produce BW agents, not Bindura.[161]

Biological agent use

Interviews of former Rhodesian Special Branch officers and Selous Scouts, as well as published accounts, indicated that *V. cholerae* was widely used against guerrilla water supplies – almost exclusively in Mozambique. Botulinum toxin probably was used and *B. anthracis* was used in experiments (and was considered for use in assassinations). No conclusive link can yet be found to tie the Rhodesian experimentation with anthrax to the large-scale 1978 anthrax epizootic that ravaged large parts of Rhodesia. The allegations of a causal connection between the Rhodesian Security Forces and the unusually large anthrax epizootic (1978 to 1982) will be explored in the next chapter.

***Vibrio cholerae* (cholera):** The Rhodesian military's use of *V. cholerae* needs to be distinguished from the Special Branch's CBW effort.[162] The Rhodesian Army – notably the RLI – had used *V. cholerae* to contaminate wells and other water sources in Mozambique since probably the early 1970s.[163] [164] Targeted water sources were largely located in Mozambique's Gaza and Teté Provinces along Rhodesia's border,

---

* Not an effective method for cultivating *C. botulinum*, which is an anaerobic bacterium requiring oxygen-free conditions for growth. *C. botulinum* produces botulinum toxin, which is considered the most deadly toxin found in nature.

† *Elektroniks, Meganies, Landbou en Chemies* (EMLC) was a front company attached to SADF Special Forces. 'EMLC' was an Afrikaans acronym that in English translated to 'Electronics, Mechanics, Agriculture and Chemistry'.

where potable water was scarce. The Rhodesian goal – especially in the arid regions of Mozambique's Gaza Province on Rhodesia's south-eastern border – was to force guerrillas transiting to Rhodesia to make a trade-off between ammunition and water. Where watering holes and pans along selected infiltration routes were contaminated with *V. cholerae*, guerrillas traveling along these routes would have to carry their own water supplies – meaning that they had to carry less ammunition.

In a study by a Zimbabwean academic – Mediel Hove – he has estimated that poisoned water supplies in South-Eastern Rhodesia resulted in the deaths of up to 200 guerrillas (largely in the Chilohlela and Masukwe communal areas and the Gonarezhou National Park). [165] A declassified CIA report from April 1979 described Robert Mugabe's disclosure that cholera was spreading through the refugee camps – resulting in about 20 deaths per day.[166]

In *The Saints*, former members of the RLI described the use of *V. cholerae*. Marshall Ross recounted that in 1973, when his RLI unit was patrolling an arid region of Teté Province, they sought out a waterhole and filled their water bottles. Within 15 minutes of drinking their water, the entire RLI troop was doubled over in agonizing stomach cramps and had to be evacuated by helicopter. Later, they discovered that the RhSAS had contaminated that water source with *V. cholerae*.[167] In another account found in *The Saints*, an RLI section introduced *V. cholerae* into the water source supplying the FRELIMO garrison at Malvernia, Mozambique, when they were surprised by an approaching FRELIMO water detail with drum-laden donkeys.[168] The Selous Scouts also were involved in using cholera to contaminate the water supply serving a FRELIMO garrison in Mozambique,[169] which also housed a ZANLA insurgent unit. According to Ellert, the Scouts contaminated the reservoir – and CIO intercepts of radio communications indicated that approximately 200 people died from the disease.[170] [171] In another example, a localized cholera epidemic forced the evacuation of a guerrilla base at Caponda, Mozambique in March 1975.[172]

Despite restrictions against the use of *V. cholerae* inside Rhodesia, two published accounts mention dissemination of *V. cholerae* domestically. In one account, McGuinness described a Rhodesian Army attempt to contaminate a portion of the Ruya River with *V. cholerae*. The targeted location on the Ruya River* was a sheltered area of relatively calm water used as a bathing site by guerrillas from a nearby base. Despite two attempts to contaminate the site, the dilution of *V. cholera* – and that the bathers probably did not swallow sufficient amounts river water there – likely reduced their exposure to the pathogen. In the end, no cholera cases resulted from that contamination attempt.[173]

In Ellert's account, he claims that the use of *V. cholerae* took place in 1976 when Selous Scouts operating in the Ruya wildlife sanctuary near the Mozambique border introduced bacterial pathogens into the Ruya River at several points. This intentional contamination allegedly coincided with a cholera outbreak among villagers living

---

* Originating in Rhodesia (north-north-west of Salisbury), the Ruya River – a tributary of the Zambezi River – flows north-easterly into Mozambique's Teté Province. The Ruya runs a few kilometers north of Mount Darwin.

along the river. In a separate account of cholera dissemination, an unidentified FBI informant told investigators that:

> (redacted) talked (redacted) had taken a plastic bag full of cholera to poison the last watering hole in Mozambique. This watering hole was significant to the rebels because it was their last staging area prior to engaging the Rhodesians. (redacted) ordered (redacted) to take the bag of cholera to the watering hole, and stab the bag with a knife, and toss both the bag and the knife into the water. (redacted) said the cholera killed "hundreds" of people and animals. (redacted) said that the rebels eventually caught on and would not drink the water.[174]

The RLI and the Selous Scouts maintained maps of contaminated wells and water sources; other Rhodesian units were warned about the danger of drinking water found in certain, identified locations. Lionel Dyck, former Officer Commanding the Rhodesian African Rifles, said in an interview that he – along with other commanding officers – were routinely briefed on areas in which well water had been contaminated. He claimed that 'there were places where we were told categorically that the waters had been salted [sic] with cholera and we would have to be careful'.[175]

Botulinum toxin reportedly also was used to contaminate water sources. The Rhodesians produced the toxin at the Mount Darwin 'fort', probably beginning in 1979, when the South Africans supplied a vial of C. botulinum. The toxin supposedly was used in attacks on ZANLA camps in Mozambique – resulting in 'many deaths'.[176] No confirmation exists to substantiate this claim, which on its face, seems unbelievable.

Dissemination methods

Dissemination of poisoned materials was handled by Special Branch at the provincial level. In each Rhodesian province existed a provincial Special Branch office, which was commanded by the Provincial Special Branch Officer (PSBO), with a 'Projects Section' under him. The 'Projects Section' in each province was responsible for the dissemination of poisoned items – using a network of co-opted contact men who were recruited to provide doctored food and clothing to guerrillas or otherwise into the insurgent supply system.[177, 178]

Typically, the contacts would receive lists of needed supplies from guerrilla groups operating or transiting through their region. The contacts would provide the lists to the provincial 'Projects Section', which – with their respective PSBO's approval – would request that the team at Bindura produce contaminated supplies to meet the guerrillas' requests. 'Projects Section' members would then arrive at Bindura, pick up the tailored package for the specific guerrilla group, sign for all the materials (everything was strictly accounted for) and provide the items to their contacts in the province. The provincial 'Projects Section' was responsible for accounting for their receipt of the materials at Bindura and on delivery to the contact – returning any unused material to Bindura. The contact man also was required to account for what materials he delivered and to report whether any were refused or returned.[179]

The PSBO for Mashonaland and Salisbury was the largest distributor of poisoned materials:

> The Provincial Special Branch Officer (PSBO) Mashonaland was the most frequent recipient of both contaminated food and clothing. It may be estimated that in the region of 2,500 pairs of underpants and a similar number of vests or "T" shirts were issued, these being the most effective carrier of parathion to sensitive parts of the wearer's body. In addition, several hundred socks, shirts, and jackets were issued, but they were not effective and were merely used to cloak the more dangerous items as they entered the field.[180]

Given that contact men could receive Rh$1,000 per guerrilla death, a system was instituted to account for each guerrilla death resulting from the poisoning program – and Chief Superintendent McGuinness was responsible for allocating the death bonuses. He reportedly would review the contact man's claim, look at the amount of materials provided to the guerrillas, examine any reports of guerrilla deaths in the area – especially if bodies could be linked to the targeted guerrilla group – and attempt to confirm through intelligence any other reports of guerrilla losses attributable to poisoning. Based on the contact man's claims and all the other available intelligence, McGuinness would pay the bonus based on his assessment of the likely number of deaths due to poisoning; no firm figures were ever available. The estimate had a ceiling based on the amount of tainted materials provided and a basement of zero. According to Gould and Folb: 'There was no way McGuinness could verify the kill claims, and in some instances he believed that one of the Special Branch men was falsifying deaths'.[181]

In addition to using contact men to distribute tainted goods to guerrilla groups operating in Rhodesia, the Special Branch also would use co-opted storeowners to stock contaminated goods on store shelves in expectation that guerrillas would ransack the store for supplies. Storeowners also could be used to deliver goods to guerrilla bands in Rhodesia, or to insurgent camps in Mozambique.

Cronin recounts learning from a Special Branch member in Mount Darwin that:

> We have some of the store owners working for us, and they make sure that the right people get these things (poisoned clothing). I see. And what happens then? After they begin wearing them? Takes awhile, but in four to five days it begins with the headaches and fevers and shakes, and before long they're bleeding uncontrollably out of every hole in their bodies. Even their eyes and ears. Tongues swell up and they can't drink anything, and when they can't walk any more, their own people take their weapon and leave them out in the bush alone like that until they just roll over and die.[182]

In his recent memoir of the Rhodesian Bush War, Special Branch officer Ed Bird offers a lengthy description of how in September 1977 he provided poisoned medicines

– including Dr Strong 500 capsules (a brand promoting sexual prowess), Endo liver salts (to treat hangovers), tins of bully beef, underpants and T-shirts. To summarize Bird's account, he was aware that a supermarket owner in his region weekly provided supplies to a local mine. The supermarket employees making the supply run were known or suspected of providing items to guerrillas as a form of protection. Bird contacted McGuinness, who dispatched Henry Wolhuter to Bird's office with a consignment of contaminated goods, as well as some unsullied Coca-Cola and bread. As suspected, the supply run was intercepted by the guerrillas – demanding goods in exchange for protection. The grocery employees willingly, but unwittingly, provided the contaminated material to the guerrillas. Of the guerrillas, three reportedly died, as did two local village women cohabiting with the guerrilla band. The incident led the guerrillas to suspect poisoning, and they sought retribution against the supermarket employees – capturing them on their next mine supply run and killing four of the five men.[183]

A senior BSAP officer recalled:

> I first encountered the impregnated clothing concept at Buffalo Range (Rhodesian Lowveld between Triangle & Chiredzi) in 1976 when a CID Officer suggested I use it and a "road runner" (radio complete with transmitter) to slip into supplies, provided to ZANLA by a "turned" store owner. While I was allowed to make the arrangements, the Scouts and one of Mac's SB staff from Bindura carried out the very act of supply. I was kept well away from it, presumably to maintain the concept's secrecy.[184]

The Selous Scouts may have used all-black pseudo call signs to deliver materials to contact men in some instances, but it is unlikely that operational Selous Scout groups were involved in disseminating items on a regular basis. In some external (outside Rhodesian borders) operations, Selous Scout call signs did support Special Branch members with inserting poisoned medicines into guerrilla caches;* for example, a BSAP Intelligence report (dated 22 May 1978) stated:

> after the raid† a number of people died from poisoned medicine and food stuffs stored in the National Stores complex. Because of this a large amount of their supplies were thrown away. He [Rex Nhongo] was unable to explain how the food had come to be poisoned.[185]

The Selous Scouts may have played a role in disseminating materials to Special Branch 'turned' storeowners and contact men. According to a former BSAP officer, former RLI/Selous Scout officer John Cronin recalled that in the immediate aftermath of the Operation 'Dingo' assault on Chimoio, members of his assault group

---

* The Selous Scout role almost certainly was limited to transport and security.

† The reference is to the 23-27 November 1977 Rhodesian assault on the ZANLA base at Chimoio – aka Operation 'Dingo'.

who were suffering from severe headaches broke into the camp hospital's supplies and swallowed aspirins found there. A Special Branch officer assigned to them came running up and asked what they had just done. When they explained that they had taken some aspirins, the officer informed them that some of the left-behind supplies contained poisoned medications. Special Branch had left the poisoned medications in the belief that guerrillas would return and retrieve any remaining materiel after the Rhodesian forces had left. The officer also explained that if they inadvertently had swallowed any of the tainted medicine, they would be dead in 15 minutes.[186] Cronin retells this encounter with the Special Branch in his recent memoir, *The Bleed*.[187] In *The Bleed*, Cronin also recounts how the Special Branch specifically targeted the medicines at Chimoio because they expected those supplies would be used by the guerrillas to treat possibly thousands of wounded following the Rhodesian attack.[188]

Some contamination of food and beverages was intended to debilitate or incapacitate guerrillas – typically by adding high-proof alcohol to beer or spirits. According to one BSAP officer:

> I recall an incident in Manicaland in about 1977/8 when SB Umtali (at the time commanded by the PSBO/PCIO Manicaland, Bill Essler) captured a virtually entire ZANLA Detachment command structure (I think the total was 12) by "doctoring" bottles of brandy with a powerful sedative, introduced into one of their command meetings within the Manica TTL by an SB resource. The idea wasn't new. It was copied from Malaya where a similar ploy had been successful.[189]

Effectiveness

The effectiveness of the Rhodesian poisons effort was constrained by its limited scope and application; the nature of the raw materials employed; and the crude dissemination methods. Nevertheless, participants in the poisons program saw it as hugely successful – at least early on. As mentioned earlier, CIO Director-General Ken Flower claimed in his autobiography that many hundreds of guerrillas were killed as a result of the poisons program; also mentioned earlier, the leadership saw the CBW effort – at least in its early days – as more effective than the conventional military. Symington echoed that sentiment. South African policeman Eugene de Kock stated: 'This [fact] confirmed that they [killed] a lot more of the enemy by means of the food and the clothing, than what they did in [daily] operations'.[190]

Jeremy Brickhill wrote from the perspective of a guerrilla intelligence officer, when he stated that:

> The research ... also included interviews with ZIPRA Field Commanders concerning the extent and impact of CBW use in Rhodesia, in particular the possibility that large numbers of civilians died as a result the use of CBW and that the cause of their deaths was not understood and reported at the time or indeed subsequently ...The information obtained after the war enabled more

sense to be made of the reports ZIPRA High Command and NSO had received concerning mysterious illness and death during the war. Analysing this material subsequently, we concluded that several hundred deaths were likely to have been caused by CBW in ZIPRA operational areas. We also noted that the CBW programme had caused a significant, though not decisive, disruption in civilian/ guerilla relations in the affected areas causing increasing accusations of collaboration and witchcraf.[191]

Most importantly, the 1977 Special Branch briefing to COMOPS opened by stating: '... The true extent of our success may never be known...' The report went on to claim 809 guerrilla deaths due to poisoning.

The most serious detriment to the project's continuing success was the guerrillas' eventual discovery of the program's activities, which made dissemination of poisoned items more difficult, as guerrillas became less trusting. Although the Special Branch continually devised new dissemination techniques, the growing guerrilla awareness of the poisoning effort did reduce the program's effectiveness. On this subject, the 28 June report stated: 'Our methods of operations are changing continually in order to keep the enemy guessing and (illegible) improved methods have recently come to light that bode well for the future [see Appendix]'.

According to Symington in Peter Stiff's account (*See You in November*), the Rhodesian poisoning program was very successful – resulting during some months

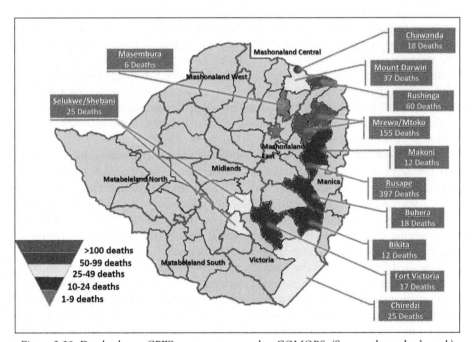

Figure 2.20 Deaths due to CBW agents, as reported to COMOPS. (Source: the author's work)

in a greater number of guerrilla fatalities than the conventional military operations of the RLI.[192] This claim is plausible, given the reluctance of most guerrilla groups to engage conventional Rhodesian Security Forces in head-on battle; guerrilla bands preferred hit-and-run tactics against soft targets. The only official Rhodesian assessment of the program's effectiveness is the estimate prepared for COMOPS – and that paper estimates that as of 28 June 1977, the poisoning program had resulted in the deaths of 809 individuals.[193] Parker states that: 'At this time the initial stage of the poison programme and with operations escalating all the time, the extrapolated figure of the next two and a half years could have well been in the thousands. Within SB circles at the time, it was widely believed that more guerrillas were dying from poison than from conventional Fireforce contacts'.[194] Uncertainly remains whether the numbers briefed to COMOPS included estimates of deaths due to cholera; if not, the total for the CBW effort (including use of cholera) could be doubled. Paul Moorcraft and Peter McLaughlin – in their history of the Rhodesian War – state that the death toll from CBW used in the conflict was 'perhaps thousands of guerrillas'.[195]

Several approaches can be used to estimate deaths associated with CBW use: the conservative estimate would accept Flower's account of 'several hundred', which is in line with the 1977 COMOPS briefing stating 809 deaths. To establish a baseline range for the Rhodesian CBW program, we will produce a low, mid and high baseline. The high number is derived from the 1977 COMOPS briefing and assumed that 809 deaths occurred for each of the three years the program was active. The midpoint estimate takes the 809 figure for 1977 and reduces it by 30 percent compounded for each subsequent year – assuming a steady decline in effectiveness due to increased guerrilla awareness and improved countermeasures. The low estimate assumes problems with fraud and poor reporting have inflated the initial 809 figure by 30 percent, and reduces each subsequent year by 30 percent compounded due to increased guerrilla awareness and improved countermeasures. Using the low estimate (the greatest number of assumptions), the total insurgent dead due to CBW is 1,239 and the highest is 2,427. These figures form the ballpark baseline derived from the reported COMOPS figures – modified with specific sets of assumptions. These estimates do not include deaths due to cholera. If we were to include estimated deaths due to intentional use of *V. cholerae*, the number would increase by hundreds at least.

Another approach would attempt to estimate the quantity of contaminated materials produced and apply a casualty rate to determine total deaths. If Rhodesian production of poisoned underwear and T-shirts amounted to approximately 5,000 items – with a fatal exposure rate ranging from 5 percent to 15 percent – guerilla casualities due to parathion poisoning would be from 250 to 750 people. Without any scientific data on variables, such as actual dose or toxicity of the material as disseminated per exposure, estimating the effective dermal absorption of the poisoned clothing is difficult. Given the amounts of material produced, we can reasonably assume that deaths due to the poisoned clothing – along with the contamination of food, medicine and beverages – well could have exceeded 1,000 people during the entire operational period of the program.

In terms of the CBW deaths as a percentage of total casualties inflicted on insurgents, the CBW program probably accounted for a greater percentage than did CW use in World War I. Realistically – taking the conservative number of Rhodesian CBW deaths and the conservative estimate of insurgent losses – the percentage of insurgent CBW-related deaths would be about 15 percent. That rate of loss due to CBW use would be unprecedented in the history of warfare.

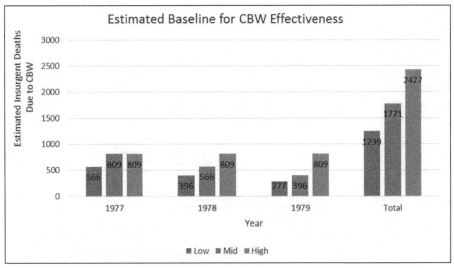

Figure 2.21 Estimated baseline for CBW effectiveness. (Source: the author's work)

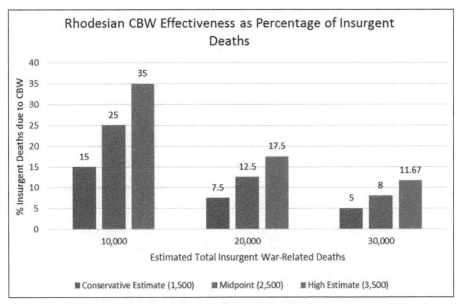

Figure 2.22 Rhodesian CBW effectiveness as a percentage of insurgent deaths.
(Source: the author's work)

The ultimate test of effectiveness is whether the CBW effort contributed to national goals (i.e. the end of the insurgency and the preservation of political, economic and military power in the hands of the European elites). The answer is clearly yes, although the Rhodesian CBW effort was not decisive in ending the insurgency favorably for the governing elite, despite the body count. Although the use of CBW agents at times inflicted more casualties on the insurgents than were caused by conventional means, the rate of guerrilla attrition attributable to CBW always was much smaller than the rate of guerrilla recruitment. Also, as a covert program hidden in the highly secretive Special Branch and Selous Scouts, the CBW effort was politically toothless. Secret CBW programs have little-to-no political value – they are useless as deterrents, given that the adversary is unaware of the program, and they cannot be used as bargaining chips for the same reason. Even insurgent efforts to make political hay by revealing glimpses of the Rhodesian CBW effort failed to garner public interest or scrutiny.

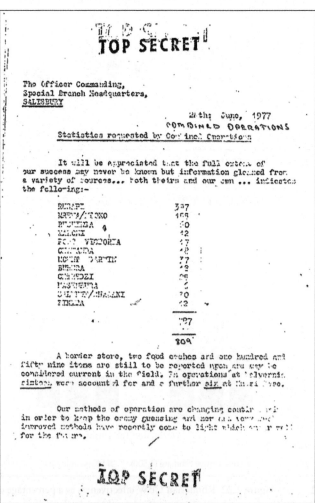

Figure 2.23 A facsimile of a COMOPS report. (Source: © Peter Stiff collection, with permission of Peter Stiff)

Ken Flower, in his autobiography, claimed that the program had caused the deaths of many hundreds of guerrilla recruits.[196] McGuinness stated that the use of organophosphate pesticides on clothing was far more effective than the use of thallium and warfarin to contaminate food, beverages or medicines.[197]

Although the poisoning program continued until late 1979, it almost certainly became less and less effective with the passage of time and a growing guerrilla understanding of the program and its dissemination methods.

A panel of former CBW participants concluded in 2006 that:

> As to whether or not the CBW programme achieved its objective, it is difficult to say but if reports emanating from the field were at least 80% correct, then it was certainly worthwhile. A calculated guess would put the ZANLA losses due to the programme in excess of 600. It was a cheap and relatively risk-free way of either killing or incapacitating the enemy and, according to captures, had a demoralizing effect on their forces. In effect, those who engaged in the operation believe that it played its part in hitting at the enemy.[198]

According to a former Selous Scout officer, at its outset the poisoning program was seen as very successful – and some reportedly in the Special Branch and the Selous Scouts were so impressed by the initial successes of the program that they considered it as a decisive tool in defeating the guerrillas. The former Selous Scout officer also remarked that the program had achieved two or three enormous successes by eliminating entire guerrilla camps. The officer estimated that the program began during the *détente* period[*] and ran for one and a half to two years before it ended. In his opinion, the program was terminated because the guerrillas became suspicious about poisoned supplies. As a result, they vetted their suppliers more closely and took steps to avoid goods they considered possibly tainted.[199] The guerrilla statements support the contention that the poisoning program was remarkably effective.[200]

The guerrilla accounts of the Rhodesian CBW program

Few published non-fiction accounts by guerrilla fighters about the Rhodesian conflict exist. Although relatively educated – compared to their comrades from Mozambique or Angola – the majority of Zimbabwean 'war veterans' have remained apathetic about sharing their experiences of the conflict.[201]

Despite the apparent reluctance of ZIPRA and ZANLA veterans to commit their stories to paper, some field researchers have been able to elicit statements from at least a few who observed the impact of the Rhodesian CBW program. While conducting field research with her colleagues in Zimbabwe's Lupane District (Ndebele land), JoAnn McGregor and her team gathered perhaps the most detailed and cogent description by a guerrilla field commander of the Rhodesians' CBW use.[202] McGregor, along

---

[*]   Rhodesia's aborted *détente* with the African nationalist movements lasted from 11 December 1974 to February/March 1976.

with Jocelyn Alexander, interviewed Nicholas Nkomo – a ZIPRA commander in the Lupane District. In his unpublished autobiography, *Between the Hammer and the Anvil* – and in his interviews with Alexander and McGregor – Nkomo laid out a vivid depiction of a ZIPRA commander's struggle to cope with fighters dying as a result of Rhodesian poisons, and the survivors' violent backlash against the villagers who supplied them. According to McGregor et al.: 'ZIPRA commanders claimed that the 'Rhodesian poisoning was the most effective' strategy used against them: Nicholas Nkomo claimed that more guerrillas died in ZIPRA's Northern Front 2 (NF2) through poisoning than in battle'.[203] Nkomo asserted that the poisoning program also led to a complete cessation of guerrilla operations in NF2.[204] The poisonings resulted in a violent reprisal, with the guerrillas launching a witch hunt to identify and punish whoever could be culpable in the poisoning of their comrades.

JoAnn McGregor detailed the witch hunt and its outcome in a book chapter[205] and places it in the sociological context of the peasantry for that region. Professor McGregor argues that the Rhodesian poisoning tactic was a deliberate attempt to exploit the popular association between poisoning and witchcraft, and to break the relationship between guerrillas and civilians, on which successful guerrilla warfare depended.[206] Her claim is not supported factually, however. The statement begs an unanswered question about whether the Rhodesians realized that the CBW program would result in these tensions between the guerrillas and their supporters. Was this tension an intentional consequence of the poisonings? At what point did the Rhodesians become aware of this consequence, and did they then attempt to exploit it?

Professor McGregor believes that the Rhodesian poisoning program 'was a deliberate attempt to exploit the popular association between poisoning and witchcraft and to break the relationship between ZIPRA guerrillas and village supporters on which successful guerrilla warfare depended'.[207] She asserts that the Rhodesians deliberately set out to disrupt relations between ZIPRA fighters and their rural supporters. Unfortunately, she makes the faulty assumption that the Rhodesians deliberately intended the effect with forethought. According to Rhodesian participants in the program – including a senior BSAP officer – the Rhodesian CBW effort did not target ZIPRA forces, and the Special Branch and Selous Scouts had only a minimal effort directed against ZIPRA in Matabeleland (Southern and South-Western Rhodesia). The Rhodesian statements are substantiated by the few extant documents linked to the program (see appendix), which list the guerrilla casualties in regions targeted by the program; for example, the 25 June 1977 Special Branch report to COMOPS states that the known guerrilla deaths took place in North-Eastern, Eastern and South-Eastern Rhodesia – not in Western Rhodesia. Given that the PSBO for Mashonaland and Salisbury (Northern Rhodesia) was the largest distributor, it only makes sense that the bulk of poisoned items would be found in Mashonaland, and not Matabeleland – an assessment supported by the available documents and participant statements. In several conversations with Rhodesian CBW participants, all have stated emphatically that the CBW effort targeted ZANLA forces.

Although no information is extant in the Rhodesian record to confirm McGregor's belief that the Rhodesians consciously designed the CBW program to exploit the superstitions of the rural population, the Special Branch and Selous Scouts did understand the importance of traditional beliefs. The 1974 BSAP publication 'The African Way of Life' described the traditional belief systems of the Shona and Ndebele. The Selous Scouts, for example, would enter *kraals* under the cover of darkness and deposit hyena carcasses on the doorsteps of targeted villagers, as the association of hyenas with witchcraft sent a powerful message to traditional believers. In at least one case, a Selous Scout had trained a hyena from a pup to follow him and obey commands – and the sight of a hyena following this man through rural villages led superstitious observers to conclude that the man possessed a powerful spiritual magic; yet the Rhodesians probably did not plan for the CBW effort to cause guerrilla violence against their village supporters. To the extent that it benefited the Rhodesian war effort, the violence was an unintended second-order effect.

The Rhodesians claim that guerrilla retaliation against villagers because of suspected poisonings was very rare. According to Rhodesian participants in the CBW program:

> Retaliation by section commanders on villagers who were suspected of poisoning groups who passed through their areas was not a common occurrence. Initially this was seen in the Rusape [Manica Province] area where, following the death or sickness of many cadres passing through the area, section commanders murdered and or mutilated many tribesmen and women, causing a once friendly populace to become anti the cause and report on sight any movement of ZANLA forces in the area. In a very short space of time, an instruction was circulated forbidding the indiscriminate murder of tribesmen and women unless there existed positive proof of their connivance with the enemy.[208]

McGuinness reported the fact that ZANLA guerrillas were massacring villagers who the guerrillas thought were responsible for the poisonings. In his report to the Officer Commanding Special Branch and to the Director-General CIO, it stated: '... nineteen African civilians in the Beit Bridge area[209] have been murdered by terrorists who believed that they were responsible for giving them poisoned food...'[210]

One small anecdote suggests that the Rhodesian CBW program intended to incite this violence. In John Cronin's recollection of his discussion with a Special Branch officer in Mount Darwin, the officer stated:

> It makes them go after the very people who've been helping them. They've never once in all the time we've been doing this put the clothing together with their illness, so that's always covered the store owners, and we've never lost one of them yet, but as soon as they start dropping like flies after visiting a village or two, suddenly they're thinking everyone out there is a witch, and I'm not pulling your piss. They really believe in witchcraft. Soon they're slotting (killing) all kinds of people who never did a thing to them, and before you know it, the survivors, or what's left of them, are staying away from the villages altogether and the locals aren't doing anything to help 'em. Buggers don't even take the time to think this through, the stupid sots.[211]

The reasonable conclusion is that the violence between villagers and guerrilla bands was not an anticipated consequence of the CBW effort, but the Rhodesians would have welcomed the violence and the resulting rift between guerrillas and their rural supporters.

Poisons and witchcraft in Rhodesia

The Rhodesian use of chemical agents (and less so, biological pathogens) had a powerful psychological effect on the guerrilla groups experiencing casualties from contaminated food or clothing. The use of poisons is very significant to the culture of the rural Rhodesian black population, and is closely tied to their belief in witches and witchcraft.

At the center of the traditional black Rhodesian belief system is the belief that ancestor spirits (*midzimu*) are responsible for caring for their families just as the living do. According to traditional beliefs, the protection of their descendants becomes the spirits' sole concern, as long as the family does not neglect or forget them.[212] After death, the spirits of the ancestors acquire extraordinary powers, such as the ability to predict the future, cure illness and be omnipresent. As David Lan described it: '... human life is enriched by the ending of it...'[213] Just as familial ancestors look after the living family members, the deceased kings (*mhondoro*) continue to care for and protect the country.

Admission to the ranks of the ancestor spirits, or the *mhondoro*, is not automatic; elaborate rituals must be observed on the first anniversary of the individual's death to ensure that the spirit is led from the bush back to the village. Without the proper burial of the body and the ceremony on the first anniversary, the spirit becomes a *ngozi*, who wanders the land lost. Other types of *ngozi* include a childless person, a murder victim or anyone who has died unjustly. In all cases, the *ngozi* is a restless, malevolent entity which, as David Lan describes, 'wanders through the villages angry and malicious, bringing harm and destruction for no other reason than its unquenchable fury and spite'.[214]

In the traditional culture, witches (*muroyi*) are feared; they kill people, consume the flesh of the human dead and commit incest and adultery. They also can transform themselves into hyenas, crocodiles and snakes at will. According to Lan, people become witches in two ways:

> They may become involuntarily possessed by the *shave*, or non-human spirit, of a hyena, an animal that hunts by night and eats dead animals found in the bush. Once a hyena *shave* has control of a woman or man, the *shave* of witchcraft is handed down from generation to generation, from mother to daughter, from father to son. Alternatively, people may become witches of free choice by apprenticing themselves to a practicing witch and eating certain medicines. Once they have achieved witch status, they carry out their murders either by magical acts that is in ways non-witches know nothing about, or by the use of poisons.

Traditional mediums embody the spirit of the ancestor and communicate the messages of the ancestor spirit to the living. Although mediums convey the best intentions of the spirits for the benefit of the living, witches in the traditional belief system operate clandestinely to harm the living. Witches act out of malice or a sense of revenge. Their actions are conducted secretly and they hide their identities as witches from the community. [215]

The Rhodesian authorities had a keen appreciation of the power of traditional beliefs over much of the rural inhabitants. A 1974 BSAP publication, 'The African Way of Life' summed up the traditional view of witches as follows:

The Shona term is muroyi, the Ndebele equivalent being umthakati. The use of these words conjures up in the mind of the Africa the most dangerous individual in their society. Africans sincerely believe that such people exist and that their familiars are hyenas, baboons and owls. Practising at night sometimes in invisible form, male or female, they are certain killers. Numerous recorded cases in the High Court of Rhodesia testify to the confession of witches and wizards in crimes of murder of innocent men, women, and children.[216]

Realizing the value of traditional healers and mediums, the Rhodesians sought to recruit them to the government's cause. In most cases, the government was failed; the majority of healers and mediums covertly, if not openly, sided with the insurgents. A Zimbabwean physician has written about the war's impact on the health of female ZANLA members. In a book that relies heavily on oral histories, she has written that:

As the war progressed, the use of poisons was employed by the colonial Government [sic] in order to implicate and discredit the spirit mediums. To this extent, a "spirit index" was drawn up that aimed to include every priest and medium in Zimbabwe and to note which ones were supporting the "terrorists" … when the guerrillas died from wearing poisoned clothes and eating poisoned food, both the spirit mediums (who guided the war) and the civilians who supplied these were either killed or beaten badly by the surviving guerillas.[217]

The association of poisons with witchcraft carries a very powerful connotation in the traditional culture. Mysterious deaths are seen as poisonings and attributed to the work of witches. The traditional witches are believed to have mastered an extensive traditional pharmacopeias of effective poisons and toxins.

Guerrilla use of poisons

Not all reports of poisons use can be attributed to the Rhodesian Security Forces; the rural populations of Rhodesia possessed a long history of using poisons to eliminate rivals, exact revenge and kill their enemies. As previously described, poisons have a prominent place in the rich cultural heritage of the Shona. Unexplained or mysterious deaths – possibly the results of poisoning – continue to occur in Zimbabwe long after the conflict's conclusion. These deaths, then and now, are frequently described as *muti** deaths. In the cases of *muti* deaths in Rhodesia, the typical scenario was that a gang of guerrillas would enter a village and extort supplies from the villagers. After their arrival, several of the guerrillas would die mysteriously. A Rhodesian pathologist often would be called to examine the bodies and he would be unable to find any identifiable cause of death. According to a Rhodesian pathologist who handled many of these cases, the rural Rhodesian population possessed an extensive knowledge of poisons and toxins available from nature, and the Rhodesian understanding of this traditional pharmacopoeia was extremely limited.[218]

The use of poisons was not confined to Rhodesia's rural populations; rivals within the nationalist leadership also used poisons in assassination attempts. Fay Chung recounted a conversation she had with Sally Mugabe (Robert Mugabe's first wife):

> One day when we were together in Dar-es Salaam, she recounted to me an incident when one of the top ZANU leaders who was later to oppose Mugabe openly, had come to give Mugabe a present of a tube of toothpaste. She said the bottom of the toothpaste roll had been opened, and a poison had been inserted into it so that when Mugabe used it to brush his teeth, he would also be poisoned. She was quite convinced about this. I tried my best to reassure her that it was quite impossible that a top ZANU leader would try to poison a close colleague. However, I was unable to persuade her.

Whether Mrs Mugabe's concern was borne out of the traditional fears of poisoning by rivals, or whether she could base her suspicions on more substantial information, is unknown. We do know that not all guerrilla deaths due to poisoning can be attributed to the Rhodesian Security Forces; many may have resulted from the rivalries and internecine struggles within the nationalist movements. Even the poisoning of guerrillas by villagers inside Rhodesia may not all have been instigated by the Security Forces. In an unknown number of cases, villagers extorted to provide supplies to a transiting group of guerrillas may have poisoned them to prevent the continued extortion of money or supplies; the forcible recruitment ('press-ganging') of young men to fill guerrilla ranks; and the sexual abuse of young women and girls. According to one BSAP intelligence report: '... locals poisoned three sections (approximately 24 to 30 men) from the Bikita 'A' detachment along with their commanders ('Double Killer,' Taurayi Zvakanaka, and Mavungiedza Mahunu)...'[219] In one reported instance early in the war, the guerrillas planned to use arsenic to contaminate a water supply used by Europeans.[220] In a journal article by the University of Zimbabwe academic Mediel Hove, he asserts that ZANLA also engaged in targeting water points in South-Eastern Rhodesia that resulted in the deaths of hundreds of Rhodesian troops.[221] No evidence is available to substantiate Hove's claim.

---

* '*Muti*' is the Shona word for 'medicine'.

In describing Rhodesian concerns about guerrilla use of poisons, Dr John Goldsmid
– a former professor at the University of Rhodesia, and now a distinguished professor
at the University of Tasmania's school of tropical medicine – writes:

> [T]he army were [*sic*] concerned that the terrorists might poison water supplies.
> To that end a colleague of mine was involved in developing a rapid test for pesti-
> cides/poison in water for the troops to use in the field. Whether one can believe
> terrorist claims that they were deliberately poisoned, I take leave to doubt! In
> this respect you might be interested in the contents of a letter, a copy of which
> I have, from Major Morton to the Medical Directorate at Rhodesian Army
> Headquarters dated Feb 3rd, 1977. This letter was a recommendation for awards
> for myself and John Gooch, for meritorious service rendered to the army, I quote
> the relevant part:
>
> L/Cpl J.A.A. Gooch, as you are aware of Sir, was given a task to detect orga-
> no-phosphate poisons in water supplies. No simple and compact methods are
> known to the world, yet after many months of research (in his own time) devel-
> oped a simple and compact method. A world invention. The successful results
> and breakthrough of his untiring research can only be of immense benefit to the
> safety of all members of the Security Forces, and to the security of the country
> as a whole.[222]

Interestingly, the Rhodesian work on a detection capability aimed at identifying
organophosphates in drinking water may be the result of 'mirror-imaging', or just as
likely the result of a practical need for troops to identify which water sources other
units may have poisoned. If the latter explains the need for a water test for these
chemicals, it would confirm Parker's claims that Rhodesian forces used Supermix
DFF in wells – a claim previously unconfirmed.

Exposure

Inevitably, the Special Branch could not keep their program entirely secret. Guerrilla
concerns about the Rhodesian use of chemical agents began as early as late 1970,
when both ZANU and ZAPU Headquarters in Zambia alleged that Rhodesian
Security Forces had contaminated tributaries of the Zambezi River with poison in
the belief that these tributaries were essential guerrilla water sources.[223] Soon after
the Rhodesian CBW efforts began in earnest in the mid-1970s, guerrillas became
suspicious about mysterious deaths that, in some cases, decimated their ranks. Given
their cultural proclivities, many guerrillas blamed untimely, unusual or unexpected
illnesses or deaths on peasant supporters – and witch hunts began to root out those
responsible for the poisoning. In other cases, the guerrillas realized that the Rhodesian
Security Forces were responsible for the poisoning deaths and warned others away
from accepting offered supplies from suspect contact men.

In an early incident of poisoning that captured the attention of the press, UANC
Publicity Secretary Edson Sithole claimed in July 1975 that Rhodesian agents
had poisoned him on a flight to Zambia for talks there. Suspicions about possible

Rhodesian involvement heightened when one of Sithole's colleagues, Enos Nkala (who was traveling on the same plane with Sithole), also fell ill.[224] The incident led Zambian President Kenneth Kaunda to allege that the Rhodesians had poisoned Sithole's tea in the airport lounge – resulting in a severe stomachache that required hospitalization. According to Kaunda, the poisoning was part of a plot designed to embarrass Zambia.[225]

According to P.K. van der Byl's biographer:

> P. K. refuted Sithole's claims of having only tea and biscuits before the flight. "My information is that he had large quantities of beer and baked beans for lunch followed by brandy on the plane." One can only assume that he was being less than sincere when he warned that "baked beans can sometimes produce regrettable symptoms, although they are seldom serious. Furthermore, he (Sithole) has an extremely complicated private life and one of his lovers has let on that she sometimes spikes his food with a 'love potion' in order to get hold of him and this might account for his occasional bowel discomfort.[226]

Although Rhodesian agents may have poisoned the Zambezi tributaries in 1970 and doctored Edson Sithole's food prior to his flight, these incidents both predate the timeline postulated for the start of the Rhodesian CBW program. More likely, both incidents have other explanations, but made useful fodder for African propagandists. Concrete examples of Rhodesian CBW use did not come to insurgents' attention until much later (i.e. 1977-1978).

Figure 2.24 Edson Sithole. (© unknown)*

Figure 2.25 Another photo of Edson Sithole. (Source: <www.colonialrelic.com> © unknown)

---

* Edson Sithole was later assassinated – along with his secretary – by a Special Branch-Selous Scout team.

The first solid evidence that the Rhodesian CBW activities had been compromised was in a top-secret circular dated 29 June 1977 sent from the acting Officer in Command of the Special Branch to all the Provincial Special Branch Officers. The circular stated:

> Recent references have been made to certain clandestine activities of the Selous Scouts in secret reports and captured documents which are sent to CIO Headquarters. These concern allegations of the use of poison allegedly introduced into (illegible) food and clothing. Addressees are to ensure that this is no longer done and that any captured documents containing allegations of this nature are destroyed after being made the subject of a Top Secret report to this Headquarters and Supt. McGuinness only [see appendix].

We know from documents dated months later that Rhodesia's CBW activities did not halt, but gathered steam.

By 1978, ZIPRA Intelligence reportedly was aware of the Rhodesian CBW effort and its impact on ZIPRA forces. According to Jeremy Brickhill, a former ZIPRA Intelligence officer:

> In 1978 ZIPRA High Command and NSO (ZIPRA Intelligence) began receiving reports from Field Commanders concerning the increasing incidence of mysterious illnesses and deaths amongst both ZIPRA forces and civilians in the liberated/semi-liberated areas of Tjolotjo, Lupane, and Nkai. Initially the wide range of the field reports was not correlated; and only after some further assessment and the emergence of information about an anthrax outbreak from the same areas was the conclusion reached that the systematic launch of CBW by the Rhodesian regime was likely to be responsible for these incidents. This conclusion was subsequently confirmed by NSO intelligence assets.[227]

In his PhD dissertation, Clapperton Mavhunga cites several examples that illustrate the awareness of nationalist groups concerning Rhodesian use of poisons. On 11 January 1978, the pro-nationalist Tanzanian paper *The Daily News* carried three news items suggesting that Rhodesia's poison warfare had switched into a new gear, according to Mavhunga. He also reports that:

> four months earlier, 12 schoolchildren had died in the Shabani area of south-central Rhodesia after eating poisoned wild fruits called *matohwe* that the RSF [Rhodesian Security Forces] had laced with poison for guerrillas. In the same month, four schoolchildren died in Selukwe after eating poisoned tinned foods that they had picked by the roadside on the way home from school. On 29 December 1977, the *Voice of Zimbabwe* reported that African civilians – most of them children – died, and 17 others were admitted in hospital after eating poisoned tinned food set as bait for guerrillas just outside the northern town of Shamva.[228]

ZANU Secretary for Health Dr Herbert Ushewokunze – a medical doctor by training and the future Zimbabwe Home Affairs Minister – reported on the Rhodesian use of chemical agents on ZANLA and its civilian sympathizers to an audience in Durham, North Carolina on 25 June 1978. He stated that:

> The most important department in our situation is the department of war medicine to treat gunshot wounds, punctures, shrapnel in wrists, napalm burns, and poisoning. Imagine the poisoning. In the classical clinical case, we have the patient go into epileptic fits and die within thirty minutes. There is also a sub-department of germ warfare, the enemy pollutes the wells and water supplies with cholera and typhoid. He then rushes back to vaccinate the whites in case the thing boomerangs. Fourteen days ago typhoid fever came from such a poisoning and claimed seven lives. At that time I didn't even have a single capsule of the drug for treatment of typhoid.[229]

Ushewokunze then showed pictures of a truck of poisoned beans – adding that:

> This van is carrying a load of beans, one of the most important kinds of relish in our camps. This van was attacked by the enemy. They only destroyed the engine section. This load of beans had been poisoned. How did I discover that? Life around was dying, the pigeons, the ducks. The monkey population in the area is quite big, so I grabbed one little monkey and threw it on to the back of the van. It nibbled a few of the bean seeds. Within ten minutes it developed a fit and died.[230]

The account of the poisoned beans is reminiscent of Edson Sithole's flight to Zambia several years earlier.

Rhodesia's medical practitioners also became aware of suspicious poisonings in the course of treating many of the civilian victims. Dr James Watt – a Canadian physician who, from 1970 to 1984, was the Medical Superintendent of the Salvation Army's Howard Hospital in the Chiweshe Tribal Trust Land (north of Salisbury) – was one such witness to the effects of the Rhodesian CBW effort. On the subject of the Rhodesian use of contaminated clothing and food, Dr Watt has written that:

> In late 1978 (September-October), we had a sudden influx of patients brought to our emergency department by cars and trucks with signs of organophosphate poisoning. We normally had a few poisonings a year, usually attempted suicides from swallowing a commercial insecticide, usually in coma with pin-point pupils and sweating, and often recoverable with gastric lavage and atropine injections. These cases, however, were much more serious. Several were convulsing, some in respiratory arrest, all sweating and salivating profusely and all with pin-point pupils. Gastric lavage was not an option, as none had swallowed anything. The common history was of putting on underwear that had been found in plastic bags in the hills. Some had become immediately ill and removed the clothing, washed it repeatedly and sold it – and still it was toxic. One woman was killed

by a bra, a man by a pair of shorts that had been repeatedly washed. My first thought was that the clothing had been contaminated with commercial insecticides from some large local farm and improperly disposed of, but we had never seen commercial products cause such severe disease. Farm workers commonly mixed commercial pesticides with their bare hands, and their clothing was often contaminated, without symptoms. We were not familiar with this product.

Howard Hospital is linked with the University of Zimbabwe, training medical students in Community Medicine. The lecturer at that time, Dr. Eileen MacIntosh, collected medical records from us and from surrounding hospitals that had similar cases, especially Glendale, Concession, and Harare. She also collected material for toxicology, pulling it all together in an article for the South African Journal of Medicine, "The Strange Case of the Poisoned Underwear." The article was never published, by order of the Central Intelligence Organization (CIO), who ordered silence on the subject and took all records and notes, presumably to be destroyed. The obvious implication was that the outbreak was no accident, and that the contaminated clothing had been planted, as we thought, to target guerillas and had embarrassingly killed civilians instead.[231]

Watt noted in a letter home dated 14 August 1978 that:

Just had a group of 8 brought in with poisoning from up the reserve – someone mixed DDT in the sadza by mistake. There have been a lot of cases nearer town and in other areas of parathion poisoning (another insecticide, very potent), oddly enough, in discarded clothes that people find, put on, then die. Dr. MacIntosh has been working up a paper on the subject, but not allowed to publish as yet. Unfortunately, this sort of thing is common up here ... Actually, police being very evasive about these poisonings which come from all parts of the north-east – there is a suggestion that the clothes might be planted where guerillas would find and wear them!![232]

In his email in 2009, Dr Watt went on to elaborate that:

The 'group of 8' with two deaths were [sic] a separate poisoning of food, from a village (Nzvimbo) next to the police base (Chombira). It also appeared to be deliberate, and organo-phosphate rather than DDT. In retrospect, four deaths I was not allowed to attend to in 1973 which resulted in excruciating abdominal pain and bleeding from all orifices may have been an early trial of poison.[233]

Having seen to the medical needs of both the African and European communities in Rhodesia for 14 years, Dr Watt eventually returned to his native Calgary. In the last years of the conflict, he began to experience several symptoms (hair loss, dark hair roots, weakness, peripheral numbness) which are associated with thallium poisoning. He did not make the connection at the time, but years later, an African youth working at the mission admitted to having witnessed the deliberate contamination of Dr Watt's food on several occasions.[234]

Figure 2.26 Howard Hospital, circa 1979. (Source: © Dr J.A. Watt, with permission of Dr J.A. Watt)

Another doctor, Alan Mills (who worked at Mpilo Hospital in Bulawayo), reports this:

> anecdotal recollection of thallium poisoning. After diagnosing our first case, we planned to present it at a weekly case discussion meeting … The patient was positive. The Secretary for Health, Dr. Eric Burnett-Smith, got wind of this, and banned us from discussing the case. I think we blamed contamination with thallium on 'Jection' pills. Jection was a popular laxative made in Bulawayo by Stern's pharmacy.* Further cases were associated with contamination of cans of bully beef. These were made by the Liebig's Company. However, we were uncertain whether these originated in Liebig's factories either in West Nicholson, Rhodesia, or from Dar es Salaam, Tanzania.[235]

The Liebig's Beef incident began following a security breach in December 1977, in which a Special Branch-recruited contact man sold thallium-tainted Liebig's canned beef to a civilian store – resulting in the death of nearly a dozen people.

At least two cases of suspected poisoning involved Liebig's tinned beef. In the aforementioned case, McGuinness had a case of Liebig's beef contaminated with thallium – and contents from that case either were unwittingly sold to customers at a

---

*   Jection pills were rectal suppositories used to treat constipation. Thallium poisoning cases among rural blacks in Rhodesia often were ascribed to oral ingestion of Jection pills.

store, or found abandoned by children. In addition, Ed Bird reports that unhygienic conditions at the Liebig processing plant in West Nicholson, Rhodesia may have resulted in the large number of deaths:

> In 1977, fourteen locals had died in the Shamwa area after eating contaminated bully beef which had been canned at the Liebig's factory. Accusations were leveled that the bully beef had been intentionally contaminated by agents of the Rhodesian government, a fact that was vehemently denied. Tests were carried out by government scientists on the unopened tins, and traces of bubonic plague bacteria were detected in some. The British management of Liebig's decided to send a team out from the UK to investigate. The team carried out tests and inspections at the canning factory, which led to over one hundred employees being fired for unhygienic work practices as traces of bubonic plague were discovered at the factory. One case of bully beef had in fact been 'treated' by Mac's staff but, as the inspection finding indicated otherwise, the matter was dropped.[236]

A potential source of the factory contamination likely would have been *C. botulinum* rather than plague (*Yersinia pestis*). This possibly accidental contamination of Liebig's products is separate from the intentional use of thallium to poison cans of Liebig's beef product.

On 27 October 1978, the ZANU-controlled *Zimbabwe News* reported that:

> [i]n Madziwa Village, Chibi District, ZANU patriotic youths arrested an African member of the notorious BSAP. He had been trapped by a female comrade from the area's militia, who had pretended to be falling in love with him. In the process, the enemy dog revealed that he had poison to put in the food destined for guerrillas, and a radio communication set he could use in emergency cases. When he was brought before the people's court, he recounted his mission and admitted having taken part in the Gutu massacre earlier this year at which 105 African civilians were brutally murdered. He was sentenced to death. The poison was sent to our health department for analysis so as to be able to provide medicine to the people to counter it.[237]

In January 1979, the British Anti-Apartheid Movement (AAM) published a book entitled *Fireforce Exposed*,[238] which detailed many of the guerrilla claims about the Rhodesian program. The description in *Fireforce Exposed* of Rhodesia's CBW use duplicated material in an earlier publication, *FOCUS*, which was a news magazine published in November 1978 by the International Defence and Aid Fund. In *Fireforce Exposed*, ZANU's chief medical officer – Dr Herbert Ushewokunze – stated that his doctors regularly dealt with cases of poisoning and the use of cholera and typhus to contaminate wells and water sources.[239] The book went on to cite Zambian and Mozambican press claims from 1976 and 1977 that the Rhodesian Security Forces were poisoning the water sources in South-Eastern Rhodesia.[240] In one cited account, 115 Africans had died after drinking tainted water in South-East Rhodesia.[241]

Fireforce Exposed also references incidents in which civilians ate thallium-tainted canned beef made by Liebig's. In the AAM account, 11 Rhodesian agricultural workers from a farm near Shamva[242] died – and another six became ill in December 1977 after eating the canned beef. The manufacturer reportedly conducted an investigation and warned the public about consuming any of their product found in the bush. Liebig's claimed that the farm workers had eaten cans of beef they found laying in the bush. The cans reportedly had been in the bush for an indeterminate time and had spoiled – building up lethal amounts of botulinum toxin. ZANU-Patriotic Front (PF) responded by claiming that the Rhodesian Security Forces had placed the canned meat in the bush 16 kilometers from Shamva in an attempt to poison ZIPRA guerrillas operating in the area. ZANU (PF) also claimed that in the previous three months, 73 Africans had died after eating poisoned foods.[243]

ZANU and ZAPU both issued repeated warnings about the threat of poisoned clothing, food and beverages. On 7 October 1978, the nationalist publication *Zimbabwe People's Voice* stated that the Rhodesian Security Forces had provided innocent people in many areas of the country with poison to give to guerrillas, and that shopkeepers had been provided with poisoned clothes and foodstuffs to sell to guerrillas.[244] ZANU (PF), in February 1979, submitted its evidence about Rhodesia's CBW efforts to the first session of the International Commission of Inquiry into the Crimes of the Racist and Apartheid Regimes in Southern Africa meeting in Brussels, Belgium. The ZANU (PF)-provided evidence included claims that Rhodesian agents had infiltrated into Mozambique to poison the food supplies at guerrilla camps, distributed poisoned aspirins to African villagers and poisoned wild fruit in the bush.[245] Including the poisoning of wild fruits is unusual, as it is not mentioned by any of the Rhodesian participants, or referenced in any of the literature.

Other ZANU (PF) claims of poisoning included:

- Thirty people died and many were hospitalized on 27 January 1979 after drinking homemade beer mixed with poisoned clear beer in the Midlands. The Rhodesian Security Forces reportedly were responsible.[246]
- On 31 March 1979 many Black peasants died after 40 of them were forced to drink water that had been sprayed with an acid in the Fort Victoria area.[247]

Dismantlement

Although no information exists as to the exact date that the program was dismantled, the poisoning program almost certainly ceased operations by late 1979 – and the materials and records at both the Bindura and Mount Darwin 'forts' were transferred to South Africa by February-March 1980.[248]

Ellert claims [249] that BSAP Commissioner Allum ended the poisoning program in early 1978, following the revelations about the contaminated Liebig beef cans. [250]

According to Parker:

In February 1978 Peter K. Allum was appointed Commissioner of the British South Africa Police. He gave the OC Special Branch a direct order to halt the covert poisoning operations. Despite this, the SB, and the Selous Scouts continued to distribute poisoned items without his [Allum's] knowledge. The manufacture and deployment of poisoned articles and food from Bindura and Mount Darwin forts continued until mid-1979.[251]

Although Allum attempted to shut the CBW effort down, he was unable to do so because the CBW effort fell under the CIO's operational control and had Ken Flower's support.

The Rhodesian CBW effort probably continued operations until the war came to a close in late 1979, when all parties met to negotiate a settlement at Lancaster House, and certainly by the time that the rebellious Rhodesian Government returned control of the colony to British authorities. According to Rhodesian participants, the Special Branch courier (and liaison to the South African Security Police and Special Forces) transported a large quantity of CBW-related materials and sundry other equipment to EMLC and Vlakplaas.* This explanation does not address which specific materials were transferred to South Africa, and how the South Africans may have used those materials.

Conclusion

That Rhodesia used chemical and biological weapons for years against guerrillas in the latter days of the war is an inescapable conclusion; the documentary evidence and testimony of key participants erases any doubt possible in even the most skeptical minds – and these facts are undeniable. The Rhodesian CBW efforts began at a critical time in the country's counterinsurgency. The security leadership concluded by early 1977 that conventional military methods would be wholly inadequate to stem the increasing numbers joining the guerrilla ranks and the guerrillas' hit-and-run tactics. In addition, the Rhodesians needed to ensure the relative safety of their sanctuaries in neighboring countries. The Rhodesian solution was to take an asymmetrical approach to the security dilemma facing them. That solution – the use of CBW agents – would prove effective against those guerrillas hiding in the bush and in funneling guerrillas into areas more easily and frequently patrolled by the Rhodesian Security Forces. Despite the lack of any sophistication in development, production, testing or dissemination, the effort resulted in at least several hundred deaths. The Rhodesian CBW effort demonstrated the effectiveness of CBW use against guerrillas and as an assassination tool.

The program operated under the aegis of Rhodesia's CIO and was fed and cared for by the top-secret element of Rhodesia's secretive Special Branch, which was commanded by a legendary figure: Chief Superintendent Michael 'Mac' McGuinness. This secret CBW effort was concealed within another highly clandestine organization

---

* The Rhodesian material sent to South Africa was to assist in the creation of the SAP Security Police's C1 unit at Vlakplaas, and Koevoet ('Crowbar') – the SAPS's special counterinsurgency unit (based on the Selous Scout concept) – operating in Namibia.

– the Special Branch liaison to the Selous Scouts – and located at the Selous Scout 'forts' of Bindura and Mount Darwin well away from prying eyes. Clandestine and virtually unaccountable, the program went on unhampered by bureaucratic threats or political necessities.

Although the preparation of CBW materials was rudimentary, 'low tech' and somewhat amateurish, the use and dissemination of these materials in everyday objects much in demand by guerrilla bands was ingenious, as was the secondary effect in driving a wedge between guerrillas dependent on local support and the villagers supplying them. The Special Branch officers involved in the CBW effort also proved highly capable of inventing new dissemination techniques to keep ahead of guerrilla suspicions. Although the poisons effort ultimately was not decisive in bringing about victory for Ian Smith's government, it was effective. The use of poisoned clothes, food and medicines had devastating effects on guerrilla bands; casualties in some guerrilla groups ranged from 30 to 100 percent.

The program, with only a very small team of technicians, was rudimentary and lacked the backing of scientific testing or analysis; to quote one participant, the Rhodesian CBW effort was a 'back street' operation.[252] Using basic techniques to process agricultural and industrial chemicals in primitive facilities, technicians with basic laboratory bench skills poisoned batches of clothing, food, beverages and medicines for dissemination to ZANLA guerrillas; the targets were small groups of guerrillas operating inside Rhodesian territory. As an adjunct to major external raids, contaminated food, beverages and medicines were added to guerrilla warehouses.

Agents were chosen for their availability and low cost – and they were adopted following trial-and-error field testing on animals and humans. The primary focus was on contamination of clothing with a pesticide containing parathion; of food; and of beverages, with a rodenticide containing thallium. Warfarin most likely was used to poison bulk foods, such as the staple mealie meal; *V. cholerae* was used as an area denial weapon through the selective contamination of guerrilla water supplies; botulinum toxin was experimented with, but little evidence exists that it was used; *B. anthracis* was used in experiments. Other chemical and biological agents were considered and debated; however, at least one agent – *B. anthracis* – was rejected at the senior most level. From those experiments, *B. anthracis* most likely was intended as an assassination tool. The extent to which the Rhodesians experimented with, or used, other agents probably will never be known; that information probably is lost forever.

Another lesson is that the Rhodesian CBW effort operated in the dark until the very end of the war without Foreign Intelligence – at least Western Intelligence – even suspecting its existence. The first word of the Rhodesian CBW effort emerged only with the publication of Ken Flower's book in 1987. The takeaway here is that a small-scale, relatively unsophisticated CBW production effort – using readily available agricultural and industrial chemicals – can operate undetected even by some of the world's largest, most capable intelligence organizations; yet for all the effort and reputed success, the Rhodesian use of CBW agents could not produce a decisive victory and probably had no effect on the war's ultimate outcome. In the end, the insurgency ended only with the transition of political power through a political process mediated and overseen by Britain and the Commonwealth. Rhodesian military power – conventional and unconventional – in the end was used in the hope of negotiating a political agreement from strength, and may have succeeded in pressuring the frontline States (chiefly Zambia and Mozambique) to bring ZANU (PF) and ZAPU to the table at Lancaster House.

Notes

1   See Barbara Cole, *The Elite: The Story of the Rhodesian Special Air Service.* (Durban, South Africa: Three Knights Publishing, 1984), p.242.

2   ibid.: 'The line of command in the poison operation is unclear. Lt. Col. Reid Daly surmised that CIO Director-General Ken Flower was in charge of the operation'.

3   Jeremy Brickhill, 'Zimbabwe's Poisoned Legacy: Secret War in Southern Africa', *Covert Action Quarterly* 43 (Winter 1992-1993), p.9.

4   We have a document briefing COMOPS on the progress of the program. Former senior Rhodesian members of the Security Forces claim that if COMOPS was briefed on the program, so was the Prime Minister.

5   'Probe launched into Rhodesian forces' use of biological warfare', *Financial Gazette* (Harare) internet edition, 10-11 December 1998 via FBIS-AFR-98-345. Reuters reported Smith's comments as: '… It's a lot of rubbish … I know nothing about germ warfare. They (Rhodesian forces) have done so without my knowledge … listen it's a long time ago, I can't remember anything'. Reuters, 'Zimbabwe probing warfare germ use by colonial govt', 10 December 1998.

6   In an interview with journalist Peta Thornycroft, Lieutenant General Peter Walls reportedly 'said he had no idea that either chemical or biological warfare agents had been used in 1977. Walls said that he could not recall any of what Thornycroft had told him about the project, but said he was worried that he may no longer have full control of his memory'. See Gould and Folb (2002), p.29.

7   Whether informed by Symington early on, by van der Byl or by McGuinness later, Reid-Daly was aware of the poisoning program. He stated in an interview with David Cushworth for 'Memories of Rhodesia' that he was aware that the poisoning effort was a CIO operation using a 'derelict' fort. (See 'Memories of Rhodesia', 'Selous Scouts'.) In earlier comments made to Chandré Gould, Reid-Daly 'surmised' that CIO Director-General Ken Flower was in charge of the operation. Reid-Daly describes the Selous Scouts as a bifurcated organization. He dealt with military operations and Chief Superintendent McGuinness handled intelligence activities and covert operations (i.e. 'funnies', probably better described as 'dirty tricks'). (See 'Memories of Rhodesia', 'Selous Scouts'.) See Gould and Folb (2002), p.28. In actuality, Reid-Daly almost certainly had a solid understanding of the program; he also reportedly participated in discussions regarding the program and the proposed Rhodesian use of anthrax.

8   Commonly referred to as P.K. van der Byl, his full name was Pieter Kenyon Fleming-Voltelyn van der Byl (11 November 1923–15 November 1999). Van der Byl was appointed Rhodesian Minister of Defence on 2 August 1974 – a post he held until a sudden Cabinet shuffle on 9 September 1976 removed him from office. In Ian Smith's autobiography, he stated that: '… Vorster found it difficult to accept P.K. van der Byl as our Minister of Defence, dealing with such highly confidential and sensitive matters. However, I was assured that if we wished to maintain our favourable relations and the smooth supply of our requirements it would be advisable to heed the warning. Clearly, I had no option, and on 9 September, in a cabinet reshuffle, I gave Reginald Cowper Defence, but kept P.K. as my Foreign Minister'. (Ian

Smith, *The Great Betrayal: The Memoirs of Ian Douglas Smith* (London: Blake Publishing, 1997), p.197.) In a differing account, van der Byl's removal reportedly came because he was increasingly at odds with Lieutenant General Walls over prosecution of the war: 'Van der Byl, because of his hardline attitude, also is said to be unpopular with the Rhodesian army commander, Gen. Peter Walls. 'He tries to tell the General how to run the war,' said a senior army officer'. See Reg Shay, 'Rhodesia Names New War Council', *Washington Post*, 10 September 1976, p.A16.

9   Parker, p.157. BSAP/10 believes that Symington approached van der Byl and Lieutenant Colonel Ron Reid-Daly with the poisons proposal. (See personal communication, dated 14 November 2005.) Doc/1 claims that the un-named officer probably was Lieutenant General Peter Walls. Walls' involvement is more likely, given that he reported to van der Byl. Walls may have communicated the proposal to Reid-Daly, but Reid-Daly was not in a position to approve it.

10   Brickhill, 'Zimbabwe's Poisoned Legacy Secret War in Southern Africa', p.9. In an August 1991 interview with Jeremy Brickhill, Brickhill asked Ian Smith about whether he was aware of the Rhodesian development and use of CBW agents, to which Smith replied: 'This is the first I've ever heard about it'. Given that the CIO was a department in the Prime Minister's office, any direction would have had to come from the Prime Minister, and not the Defense Minister or the service chiefs.

11   One unlikely alternate theory is that the concept of a CBW effort originated from South Africa. According to a Selous Scout officer not directly involved in the Rhodesian CBW effort, the concept for the CBW program probably originated in a conversation between Ken Flower and South African BOSS chief General Hendrik van den Bergh. Although the Rhodesian approach to the war was purely reactive, the officer believed that the South Africans had a greater proclivity for unconventional solutions to security problems. According to the Selous Scout officer, the CIO probably assessed that unconventional means were needed to reverse the deteriorating security situation and the military's inability to cope with the growing guerrilla presence in Rhodesia. The Selous Scout officer opined that van den Bergh probably suggested the use of chemicals against the guerrillas. Flower would then have identified the Selous Scouts as the unit best able to undertake the CBW mission based on the following rationale: the poisoning program would have had to have been a CIO/Special Branch operation, with significant support from the Rhodesian Army; the Special Branch and army already had built a unit in which both worked together (i.e. the Selous Scouts); the South Africans then dispatched scientists (probably seconded from the Council for Scientific and Industrial Research, or CSIR – a division of ARMSCOR) to Bindura to work with McGuinness. McGuinness would have had daily oversight of the program – providing administrative support, manpower and funding (out of the Selous Scout slush fund).

12   FBI interview with Michael McGuinness (Case 279A-WF-222936), London, UK, dated 19 October 2002; redacted version released under FOIA, dated 5 December 2011.

13   Parker, pp.157-158. McGuinness almost certainly was Parker's source for this information, so this quotation is useful to compare with McGuinness' other statements.

14   Notes of conversation with BSAP/14, dated 14 November 2005.

15   BSAP/10, email to the author, dated 15 March 2011.

16   Although some accounts date the program back as early as 1973 – see Chandré Gould and Peter Folb, *Project Coast: Apartheid's Chemical and Biological Warfare Programme* (Geneva: United Nations Institute for Disarmament Research, 2002), p.26 – the program almost certainly began in early to mid-1976, with initial deployments of materials in the late 1976 or early 1977 timeframe. If the Rhodesians had used poisons any earlier, the numbers of guerrillas in Rhodesia would not have presented a significant enough target to warrant the

use of CBW. As guerrilla deployments inside Rhodesia grew dramatically – beginning in late 1977 – CBW use becomes a more effective option to counter the growing disparity between guerrilla and Rhodesian force levels.

17   Doc/1 states the Rhodesian CBW program began in late 1976; we have no information on when Symington first proposed the concept to P.K. van der Byl. Selous Scout/2 dated the beginning of the CBW effort at around the time of the Rhodesian Government's *détente* with the nationalists. The *détente* is generally accepted to have begun when South Africa forced Rhodesia into accepting a ceasefire on 11 December 1974 and lasted until December 1975 or February-March 1976.

18   Quoted in Mangold, p.223.

19   Doc/1, personal communication, dated 19 July 2006. Also see Thomas Mangold and Jeff Goldberg, *Plague Wars*, (New York, St Martin's Griffin, 1999), p.222.

20   Doc/2 (Annex).

21   ibid. Also see 'History of Nationalism', BSAP File # XYS 533/1, dated 1 November 1978, p.16. The file states that the ANC (Muzorewa) became the UANC on 1 March 1977, with The Rev A.T. Kanodareka as the UANC's Treasurer-General.

22   Flower, p.137. In Flower's description of Kanodareka's activities, he may be conflating the CBW effort with a Special Branch operation that recruited Rhodesian African young men to join the guerrilla forces – and the similarity bears mentioning: Special Branch-recruited contact men would enlist these villagers to the guerrillas' cause and arrange transport for them to the promised training camps in either Zambia or Mozambique. *En route* to the camps, these guerrilla recruits were ambushed by Special Branch and slaughtered, according to McGuinness. Given that the CBW effort targeted trained, armed guerrilla groups operating inside Rhodesia or the camps in Mozambique, Flower's account more closely resembles this Special Branch operation against recruits in transit.

23   ibid.

24   Online at <www.caux.iofc.org/en/healing-wounds-of-history#zimbabwe> (accessed on 23 February 2011).

25   Online at <www.colonialrelic.com/brief-career-details-of-office-holders-in-the-nationalist-movement/attachment/kanodareka/> (accessed on 9 August 2015).

26   This timeframe is consistent with the date (late 1976) found in Doc/1 for the start of CBW operations. According to Ron Reid-Daly, he received the first call from General Walls to create the Selous Scouts in November 1973, and initial Selous Scout operations began in April 1974.

27   BSAP/14, email to the author, dated 28 September 2009.

28   Henrik Ellert, *The Rhodesian Front War: Counter-Insurgency and Guerrilla War in Rhodesia, 1962-1980* (Gweru, Zimbabwe: Mambo Press, 1989), p.145.

29   Godwin and Hancock (1997), p.285.

30   The Special Branch account is confirmed by a separate – very senior – source, CIO/3, who has stated that: '… The Rev. Arthur Kunodareka [*sic*] was a Methodist Minister in the same ministry as Bishop Abel Muzorewa. For some reason the commissioner of Police, P.K. Allum and the CIO DG Ken Flower perceived him as a threat to Muzorewa (that) may split the UANC party and take away support from Muzorewa. He was a very good source, apparently, and was responsible for the discovery of several 'bombs' and helped pre-empt several bombing incidents. I cannot for the life of me understand why this was done. He was ambushed by a (Selous) Scout call sign disguised as a ZANLA group and shot to death. Ken Flower's version in his book is totally incorrect and I felt very sorry for Kunodareka's widow and children having to live with that story…'

31   McGuinness credited Kanodareka with providing valuable, actionable intelligence – allowing the Rhodesians to disrupt guerrilla efforts to take their terrorist campaign to Rhodesia's urban centers. According to McGuinness, the bombing of the Woolworths in Harari Township on 6 August 1977 was allowed so that growing terrorist suspicions about Kanodareka's *bona fides* would lessen. Kanodareka supposedly had provided intelligence that allowed the Rhodesians to prevent similar bombings, and Kanodareka was feeling the heat among terrorist circles. As a result, the Rhodesians allowed the Woolworths bombing to maintain Kanodareka's credibility. The bombing resulted in the deaths of 11 people and the wounding of 76 others.

32   Ellert (1982), p.145. Ellert mistakenly claims that Kanodareka's '… bullet-riddled body was found several days later…' Kanodareka's assassination did not take place until 4 December 1978.

33   Peter Kevin (P.K.) Allum was born on 12 June 1926 in Isleworth, UK and educated at Gunnersby Catholic Grammar School. Allum served in the Fleet Air Arm before attesting into the BSAP as a trooper on 28 April 1946. Allum served almost his entire career within the CID at Beitbridge (Immigration), Umtali, Salisbury, Bulawayo and Gwelo Stations. He was commissioned in 1960 and was appointed Provincial Commander (PCIO) CID Midlands Province in 1963 and the Salisbury and Mashonaland Province in 1967. On 1 October 1970, Allum became Officer Commanding CID and was promoted to Deputy Commissioner (Crime and Security) on 7 February 1974. He became BSAP Commissioner in February 1978 and served through the transition to retire as the Commissioner of the Zimbabwe Republic Police in 1982. Allum died in South Africa on 17 April 2015, aged 88. (See <www.bsap.org> retrieved on 22 August 2015.) Critics point to the fact that Allum rose from inside the CID (Criminal Investigations Department) and that the secret work of Special Branch was not only alien to him, but an anathema.

34   McGuinness, personal communication, dated 23 April 2006.

35   Associated Press, dated 9 December 1978.

36   Chandré Gould and Peter Folb (2002), pp.26-30, which recounts statements from a number of senior Rhodesian officers about the CBW program.

37   For a description of Robert Symington (aka Sam Roberts), his laboratory and his involvement in the Rhodesian CBW program, see Peter Stiff, *See You in November* (Johannesburg, South Africa: Galago Publishing, 1985), pp.307-310.

38   Doc/2, dated 23 September 2006, p.2.

39   I want here to thank Dr Benjamin Garrett for providing a scientific review of all the chemicals listed on the 'founding' document.

40   In an account by Peter Stiff, Symington states: 'Africans need twice as much to constitute a fatal dose than does a white. A white man moves his bowels only twice a day, while an African goes three or four times. The material lingers longer in a white man's body'. Stiff, *See You in November*, p.308; supported by statements from BSAP/4.

41   See BSAP/4 personal communication, dated 1998.

42   FBI interview with undisclosed informant (Case 279A-WF-222936, serial 508), dated 19 November 2002; redacted version released under FOIA, dated 5 December 2011.

43   Selous Scout/3, personal communication, dated 24 April 2006.

44   Selous Scout/2, personal communication, dated 30 October 2005. In at least one case, villagers warned a Selous Scout pseudo call sign to avoid a specific store, because that store was supplying poisoned goods to guerrilla groups. Obviously, the security of the Rhodesian distribution of CBW had been compromised, given that local supporters had identified sources of poisoned materials and were informing guerrillas to avoid those sources.

45   'Founding' document, ns, nd (Peter Stiff Collection).

46   Alan 'Taffy' Brice died of cancer in March 2006. Brice also was interviewed by journalist
      Tom Mangold about the same events, which Brice confirmed. See Mangold and Goldberg,
      Plague Wars: The Terrifying Reality of Biological Warfare (New York: St Martin's Griffin:
      1999), pp.224-227. Brice also has been implicated in other high-profile Rhodesian assassina-
      tions – including that of ZANU leader Herbert Chitepo (car bombing) in 1975 and ZAPU
      deputy leader Jason Moyo (parcel bombing) in 1977. (See Morris Mkwate, 'Hired Killer
      Targeted President Mugabe', *The Sunday Times* (Zimbabwe), dated 22 March 2015; online at
      <www.sundaymail.co.zw/?p=28736> (accessed on 27 August 2015). Article cites Peter Stiff as
      its source.
47   Mangold (1999), p.226.
48   ibid.
49   BSAP/14, personal communication, dated 27 December 2006.
50   See facsimiles of documents in Appendix D.
51   McGuinness, personal communication, dated 25 April 2006.
52   According to McGuinness, Allum also may have harbored a personal animosity toward him
      based on a long-standing rivalry. Allum almost certainly saw McGuinness as an unconven-
      tional officer, despite McGuinness' own exemplary early career as a CID investigator.
53   See memorandum from M.J.P. McGuinness to P.K. Allum, dated 3 February 1978 (author's
      collection).
54   Paul Moorcraft and Peter McLaughlin, *The Rhodesian War: A Military History* (Barnsley,
      South Yorkshire: Pen & Sword Military, 2008), p.174.
55   Godwin and Hancock (1997), p.274.
56   Flower (1987), p.2.
57   A rich literature on information asymmetry in the principal-agent problem (agency dilemma)
      exists. Clearly from all accounts, McGuinness possessed a virtual monopoly on intelligence
      derived from the covert operations of his SB liaison team, and from what they obtained
      through the Selous Scouts. Possession of that information – and his ability to act or not act on
      it – created a strong information asymmetry and the conditions for moral hazard. Examples
      of this literature include Nico Groenenduk's 'A Principal-Agent Model of Corruption' in
      Crime, Law, & Social Change 27 (1997) and Thomas S. Sowers' 'Beyond the Soldier and the
      State: Contemporary Operations and Variance in Principal-Agent Relationships' in *Armed
      Forces & Society* 31 (Spring 2005).
58   Photographs are sourced to: photograph of McGuinness in uniform (1975) top-left was
      retrieved from the BSAP regimental website (<www.bsap.org>) on 23 July 2011; three
      photographs of 'Mac' on vacation are in the author's possession; and the top-right photo was
      retrieved from the BSAP regimental website on 23 July 2011.
59   Used with permission of Peter Stiff from the Peter Stiff collection, published in Stiff, *Selous
      Scouts: A Pictorial Account*, p.152.
60   COMOPS consisted of the Commander, Combined Operations; the Army Commander;
      the Air Force Commander; the Commissioner of Police; the CIO Director-General; and
      a Special Branch representative. COMOPS also had a relatively large staff – giving rise to
      allegations that many people without a clear need-to-know had access to sensitive opera-
      tional details. This situation at COMOPS led to allegations that leaks from within COMOPS
      compromised many RhSAS and Selous Scout missions.
61   Brickhill, 'Zimbabwe's Poisoned Legacy Secret War in Southern Africa'.
62   Ellert (p.110) claims that a team of three 'medical men' was assigned to the Selous Scouts and
      operated a secret laboratory at the Andrie Rabie Barracks (formerly Inkomo Barracks) near
      Salisbury. According to BSAP/12, the Special Branch's CBW team was located at Bindura
      'fort', where most operations took place. Unbeknownst to McGuinness, some members of the

CBW team also used the 'fort' at Mount Darwin for some CBW-related activities. Inkomo Barracks was never used because the barracks was frequented by too many personnel and visitors without a need-to-know. McGuinness, personal communication, dated 15 November 2005.

63   Stiff, *Selous Scouts: A Pictorial Account*, p.80.

64   BSAP/1, personal communication, dated 13 November 2006.

65   Doc/2, dated 15 August 2006.

66   In the late 1970s, Bindura boasted a population of approximately 1,200 Europeans and an estimated 5,000 African inhabitants. See Peter McAleese, *No Mean Soldier: The Story of the Ultimate Professional Soldier in the SAS and Other Forces* (London: Orion, 1993), pp.160-161.

67   Ellert, p.102. To clarify matters, Michael J.P. McGuinness retired from the BSAP in April 1980 with the rank of Chief Superintendent, although he had been offered a promotion to Assistant Commissioner – commanding the CID – by BSAP Commissioner P.K. Allum. By offering to promote McGuinness, Allum was hoping to dismantle the Special Branch ties to the Selous Scouts.

68   See 'Memories of Rhodesia', 'Selous Scout' (interview with Ron Reid-Daly).

69   Online at <www.colonialrelic.com/brief-career-details-of-office-holders-in-the-nationalist-movement/attachment/kanodareka/> (accessed on 9 August 2015).

70   Schematic taken from Stiff, *Selous Scouts: A Pictorial Account*, p.80.

71   Stiff, *See You in November*, p.307-308.

72   ibid., pp.308-310.

73   Drawn by Michael McGuinness, personal communication, dated 24 April 2006.

74   In the wake of the 2001 anthrax mail attacks in the US, some commentators alleged that Steven Hatfill may have played a role in the Rhodesian CBW effort (see Marlene Burger, 'Murky past of a US bio-warrior', *The Johannesburg Mail & Guardian*, dated 16 August 2002; and Nicholas Stix, 'Scientist with Rhodesian past still centre of media crosshairs', *Insight on the News*, Volume 18, Issue 36, dated 30 September 2002). I posed the question to McGuinness, who admitted that (a) he knew Hatfill and (b) he had 'hired' Hatfill at Bindura, at the insistence of Symington. Hatfill was paid out of Selous Scout funds, but was not a member of the Selous Scouts or the BSAP Special Branch, according to McGuinness. McGuinness stated that Hatfill did not have access to any sensitive areas or operations at Bindura, given that he was a US citizen and deemed a possible security risk. McGuinness went on to say that Hatfill's duties at Bindura included driving a truck on a regular supply run between Bindura and the 'fort' at Mount Darwin.

Based on Peter McAleese's autobiography (*No Mean Soldier*), Hatfill may have associated with at least one member of the Rhodesian CBW team at Bindura – and possibly more. By virtue of his plausible access to members of the CBW team, Hatfill may have been familiar with aspects of the Rhodesian CBW effort learned from his acquaintants. Hatfill himself claims to have worked as a medic attached to the Selous Scouts while he was attending medical school in Rhodesia (see David Freed's article 'The Wrong Man' in *The Atlantic Monthly* (May 2010); online at <http://www.theatlantic.com/magazine/archive/2010/05/the-wrong-man/308019/2/> (accessed on 30 December 2012)). Hatfill also identified himself as a 'member of the Selous Scouts/Special Branch' in an article he co-authored with former Selous Scout officer Timothy Bax (see 'Securing and Holding Rural Territory', *Small Wars Journal*, 12 August 2011; online at <smallwarsjournal.com/jrnl/art/securing-and-holding-rural-territory> (accessed on 30 December 2011)).

75   Martin (1993), p.6.

76   Doc/1, private communication in the author's hands, dated 19 July 2006, p.1.

77   RIC/2, personal communication, dated 16 November 2005.

78   Stiff, *Selous Scouts: A Pictorial Account*, p.56.

79   FBI interview with Michael McGuinness (Case 279A-WF-222396), London, UK, dated 19 October 2002; redacted version released under FOIA, dated 5 December 2011.

80   According to Jim Parker, the team consisted of Symington; a laboratory technician referred to as 'VN'; another technician referred to as 'GE'; and a veterinary student referred to as 'SH' (Parker (2006), p.158). The veterinary student on Symington's team also featured in another vignette involving – along with an American friend – the botched castration of a pet monkey belonging to the 'fort' commander at Bindura. See private communication (1998); for a description of the monkey's fatal operation, see McAleese, pp.165-166.

81   Symington has been identified as either an agricultural chemist (Stiff (1985), p.307), or as the head of the medical faculty at the University of Salisbury (see David Martin, 'The Use of Poison and Biological Weapons in the Rhodesian War: Lecture for the University of Zimbabwe War and Strategic Studies Seminar Series' (University of Zimbabwe, 7 July 1993), p.6). Most accounts agree that Symington held a faculty position at the Godfrey Huggins School of Medicine, the University of Rhodesia.

82   Symington died of a heart attack in 1982 while swimming in the pool at the University of Cape Town. For more on Symington's possible involvement, see Simon Cooper, 'How One Man Lied His Way Into the Most Dangerous Lab in America', *SEED Magazine* (May/June 2003); online at <www.angelfire .com/ex/projecthatfill/ seed.html> (accessed on 21 May 2006).

83   Cooper (2003).

84   UR/2, personal communication, dated 13 November 2006. Part of the endocrine system, the pineal gland is responsible for the secretion of melatonin, which controls the circadian rhythm. A review of PubMed identified several articles authored or co-authored by Symington up until 1976 (when the CBW program was established). The majority of the articles focused on the mammalian endocrine system – most notably the pineal gland.

85   Stiff (1985), pp.307-308.

86   Doc/3 indicates that in January 1979, Symington was hospitalized and nearly died following an accidental exposure to parathion.

87   Comments by BSAP/4, nd.

88   Private communication (nd). According to an admitted participant in the Rhodesian CBW program, Symington provided both scientific oversight and hands-on development of several poisons for the Rhodesian Special Branch. Experimentation with various poisons amounted to one of Symington's passions. He allegedly died as the result of a botched experiment with a poison.

89   Martin, p.8.

90   Mangold, p.226.

91   Peter Stiff collection; online at <www.galago.co.za/CAT1_034_b.html> (accessed on 25 April 2012).

92   Email to the author, dated 5 August 2011.

93   Doc/1, p.1.

94   Email to the author, dated 5 August 2011.

95   For an explanation of the 'roadrunner' devices, see J.R.T. Wood's *Counter-Strike from the Sky: The Rhodesian All-Arms Fireforce in the War in the Bush 1974-1980* (Johannesburg, South Africa: 30° South Publishers, 2009), pp.96-97.

96   Doc/1, private communication, dated 19 July 2006, p.4. In Doc/1, the CBW participants express some uncertainty about the source of the materials – claiming that as best, they can recall the parathion was obtained locally.

97   UR/1, personal communication, dated 1 October 2005.

98   BSAP document dated 25 August 1977; reprinted in Parker, p.164.

99   Parker, p.159. Although Parker's statement may be accurate, the weight of evidence suggests that EMLC (working for South African Special Forces HQ in Pretoria) and the SAP Forensic Laboratory provided materials for the Rhodesians.

100   Document/4.

101   ibid.

102   Document dated 16 July 2006.

103   CIO/3, communication dated 9 November 2007. EOKA is an acronym for *Ethniki Organosis Kyprion Agoniston* (Greek for 'National Organisation of Cypriot Fighters') – a Greek Cypriot nationalist organization that fought for the end of British rule of Cyprus, as well as for self-determination and for union with Greece.

104   On 3 February 1998, Colonel Craig Williamson told the South African Truth and Reconciliation Commission that the South African Security Branch funded the Selous Scouts out of its secret account. See 'The State Outside South Africa between 1960 and 1990', *Truth and Reconciliation Final Report*, volume 2, chapter 2, paragraph 165; online at < www. news24.com/Content_Display/TRC_Report/2chap2.html> (accessed on 13 June 2006).

105   Doc/1, private communication, dated 19 July 2006, p.3: 'The amount allocated by CIO to run the entire budget of the Scouts was US$750,000 per month equal to Rh$375,000. All monies were provided to C/Superintendent McGuinness and a monthly audit was carried out. All receipts were destroyed after inspection ... the deputy chief finance officer for CIO ... advised that all the monies supplied to McGuinness emanated from the Saudi King and that this was collected monthly by Ricky May on behalf of Ken Flower. The Israelis did not contribute in any manner to the Selous Scouts war effort nor were they privy to any clandestine operation'. In McGuinness' interview with the FBI, he stated: '... [w]hile working with the Special Branch in Rhodesia, McGuinness received $800,000 US per month from (redacted) who obtained the money from the Saudi Government. This money was used by McGuinness for wages and stipends of Selous Scouts and SAS, supplies for the Selous Scouts and SAS, clothing, food, and kill bonuses. It was out of this money that McGuinness paid (redacted) and (redacted). McGuinness suspected that the Saudi's [*sic*] actually gave (redacted) $1 million US per month but that some of the money was skimmed off before it reached him'. See FBI interview with Michael McGuinness (Case 279A-WF-222396), London, UK, dated 19 October 2002; redacted version released under FOIA, dated 5 December 2011.

106   McGuinness, personal communication, dated 24 April 2006.

107   One simplistic rationale put forward is that the Saudis did it because they wished to contribute to the fight against communism. See McGuinness, personal communication, dated 23 April 2006.

108   McGuinness, personal communication, dated 25 April 2006.

109   FBI interview with undisclosed informant (Case 279A-WF-222936, serial 508), dated 19 November 2002; redacted version released under FOIA, dated 5 December 2011.

110   Ellert, p.90.

111   BSAP/2, personal communication (nd).

112   McAleese, pp.166-172.

113   Private communication (1998). One self-admitted participant in the Special Branch program suggested that they may have adopted a trial-and-error approach to determining lethality and effectiveness of the dissemination method. The participant stated that the first attempts to kill insurgents by poisoning their clothing resulted in illnesses, but few (if any) deaths. Only after the introduction of DMSO to the formula did the poisoning of clothing result in fatalities. He also claimed to possess a document – originally on Selous Scout letterhead – that listed the LD_{50} for several chemical agents. He stated the LD_{50} data was derived from

human experimentation on captured guerrillas. Several program participants have countered this claim – stating that no CBW-related documents would have ever been produced on Selous Scout letterhead; all documents related to the CBW project were exclusively on Special Branch stationery. Indications are that the Rhodesians almost certainly did experiment on captured guerrillas who could not be turned, and that these experiments were conducted at the Mount Darwin 'fort' after it ceased to be operational. Some evidence suggests that Winston Hart, Victor Noble and possibly Jan Coetzee used the Mount Darwin 'fort' without McGuinness' knowledge.

114 Doc/2, dated 21 September 2006.

115 Document/5 in the author's collection.

116 Ellert, p.110. BSAP/12 refutes Ellert's assertion that prisoners were captured in Salisbury, but he does not deny the fact that captured terrorists who could not be turned may have been used in CBW-related experiments.

117 Tsitsi Matope, '5,000 Bodies Found in War Mass Graves', *The Herald* (Zimbabwe), Wednesday, 7 July 2004: 'However, large areas were declared 'closed' to all but the Selous Scouts, especially in the final years of the liberation war, and during these special operations villagers and suspected war collaborators were abducted, interrogated and killed and their bodies dumped down mineshafts and in hidden mass graves. It is likely that many of the graves now coming to light are the result of these special operations rather than from the operations of the Rhodesian police, army and drafted units. Almost all Selous Scouts and others in special intelligence units fled to South Africa at Independence in 1980. Some villagers know the sites where war veterans and collaborators were dumped after they were poisoned, shot or beaten to death by these special units'.

118 Mangold, pp.222-223, citing Brickhill.

119 Burger and Gould (2002), p.16. According to Gould, she relied on Coetzee's trial testimony for the material found in the book and did not interview him separately (email from Gould to the author, dated 31 January 2005). Also see 'Trial Report Number 34'; online at <ccrweb. ccr.uct.ac.za/archive/cbw/34.html> (accessed on 10 August 2005): 'Coetzee founder and first managing director of EMLC said he was never involved in the killing of anyone by means of chemical substances. Coetzee did not know about the poisoned clothing found by van der Spuy. Coetzee said he was aware of experiments carried out with organophosphates on clothing in Rhodesia. In re-examination, Pretorius asked Coetzee to expand on his knowledge of organophosphates used in Rhodesia. He said he was approached on one occasion (prior to his departure from EMLC at the end of August, 1980) by a courier for Rhodesian Special Forces, who gave him a typed report, in point form, of toxic substances – including organophosphates, applied to various parts of the body, and outlining the exact results/ effects'. In his testimony, van der Spuy stated that when he assumed control of the EMLC in November 1980, he toured the facility and found a room containing a large amount of bulk chemicals and a carton of underwear. On going to inspect the clothing, an EMLC employee warned him not to touch the garments because they were poisoned.

120 To date, Coetzee has been less than forthcoming about the nature and extent of his involvement (and by extension, South Africa's involvement) in the Rhodesian CBW effort. A regular liaison mechanism existed – linking the Rhodesian CBW team with Coetzee and the EMLC. With at least one colleague, Coetzee visited the team at Bindura on multiple occasions, and the members of the Rhodesian team also visited the EMLC. The SB courier stated that he observed Professor Symington on several occasions in Pretoria with Coetzee and SAP Forensic Laboratory head Lothar Neethling. A Rhodesian SB courier also frequently picked up materials from the EMLC and the SAP Forensic Laboratory (and on one occasion, from the Onderstepoort Veterinary Laboratory) for delivery to Bindura; the same courier also

delivered reports to Coetzee. My assumption is that Professor Symington authored those reports. See Doc/3, dated 19 October 2006.

121   BSAP/4 conversation with the author, dated circa April 1998.

122   Rough translation of an anonymous, hand-written Afrikaans-language document (probably by Eugene de Kock) in file 14, 'Allegations/documents pertaining to chemical and biological warfare in Rhodesia' in AL2922, 'The Chemical and Biological Warfare (CBW) Project Collection', South African History Archive. Thanks to Dr Gary Ackerman for his translation.

123   ibid.

124   FBI interview with Michael McGuinness (Case 279A-WF-222936), London, UK, dated 19 October 2002; redacted version released under FOIA, dated 5 December 2011.

125   Doc/1, private communication in the author's hands, dated 19 July 2006.

126   FBI interview with Michael McGuinness (Case 279A-WF-222936), London, UK, dated 19 October 2002; redacted version released under FOIA, dated 5 December 2011.

127   Having spent considerable time in Rhodesia – and with ongoing contact with ex-Rhodesian mercenary circles – war correspondent A.J. Venter has written: 'From his own contacts during the Rhodesian war, the author is aware that cans of tinned food (corned beef, in particular) were systematically contaminated and, in a number of instances, bottles of liquor had tiny holes drilled into them and the contents laced with poison'. Al J. Venter, 'Biological warfare: the Poor Man's Atomic Bomb', *Jane's Intelligence Review*, 11/3 (11 March 1999).

128   John Cronin, *The Bleed* (Amazon Digital Services, 2014).

129   Private communication (1998). According to an admitted participant in the Rhodesian program, the initial attempts to cause insurgent deaths by impregnating underwear with pesticides failed. Although the pesticide was in contact with the groin area – an area of potential absorption into the body – reports indicated that insurgents were falling ill, but not dying. This participant admittedly suggested mixing dimethyl sulfoxide (DMSO) with the pesticide to act as a skin transfer agent. Easily absorbed by the body through the skin, DMSO would transport the pesticide through the thin skin of the groin into the soft tissues of the body – and the addition of DMSO to the pesticide resulted in a much greater number of insurgent deaths. The description of chemical processing described by McGuinness to Gould contradicts any use of DMSO. For DMSO to be effective, it is added to the liquid without drying – and reducing the DMSO-pesticide mixture to a powder negates any added advantage of DMSO.

130   McGuinness, personal communication, dated 24 April 2006. According to Doc/1, '… all clothing was purchased from Madziwa Trading, Bindura…' In Parker's book, he states that the 'required clothing was bought from a store in Bindura'. See Parker, p.159. According to Selous Scout/2, Rhodesian Intelligence had identified the Zambian clothing manufacturer who produced the clothing sought in the contact men's list; a South African manufacturer was contracted to duplicate the clothing down to the same labels. Selous Scout/2, personal communication, dated 30 October 2005.

131   Chandré Gould and Peter Folb, *Project Coast: Apartheid's Chemical and Biological Warfare Programme* (Geneva: United Nations Institute for Disarmament Research, 2002), p.27.

132   McGuinness, personal communication, dated 24 April 2006. He claimed that the drying was to eliminate the odor, which was described as 'foul'; drying would not have been needed if the objective was to eliminate an offensive, alerting odor or color. The more commonly distributed forms of parathion take the form of a brown liquid that smells of rotting eggs or garlic; online at <en.wikipedia.org/wiki/Parathion> (accessed on 18 November 2006).

133   Doc/2, Annex, p.1.

134   Doc/2.

135   BSAP/2, personal communication, dated 16 February 2005.

136 Ellert, p.110.

137 BSAP/2, personal communication (nd).

138 Stiff, *See You in November*, p.309. Sam Roberts was the *nom de guerre* given to Symington in the book. The former British SAS trooper then working for the CIO was 'Taffy' Bryce, now deceased.

139 McGuinness, personal communication, dated 16 November 2005. Also according to John Cronin, he saw a Special Branch member stacking clothing at the Mount Darwin 'fort'. When Cronin asked the man whether he was having a yard sale, the Special Branch member warned the officer not to touch the clothing because it had all been poisoned. (John Cronin, personal communication, dated 7 June 2005.)

140 Hayes et al., p.230.

141 op. cit., p.232.

142 ibid., p.231.

143 Richard O. Laing, 'Relapse in Organo Phosphate Poisoning', *The Central African Journal of Medicine* 25 (October 1979), pp.225-226. After the publication of his article, Dr Laing recalls that he was told the reason for the OP poisonings was that contaminated underpants were placed on the shelves of stores thought to be targets of guerrilla burglary. (Dr Richard O. Laing, personal communication, dated 16 February 2005.)

144 Private communication (1998). A self-admitted participant in the Rhodesian CBW program once claimed that the chemical used to poison the clothing destined for insurgent use was an Italian-manufactured pesticide that had been banned from agricultural use. The pesticide had been imported pre-economic sanctions and stored in Rhodesia.

145 Document/4.

146 White (2004), p.224.

147 Mangold, p.223.

148 White (2004), p.225.

149 Bird (2014), p.138.

150 ibid., p.139.

151 According to the Rhodesian CBW team, warfarin was never used because of its 'strong and vile taste'. See Doc /1, dated 19 July 2006, p.4.

152 In an email dated 28 April 2005, Dr Epstein recounted that he saw 36 Zimbabweans die of bleeding before his eyes. Also see Paul Epstein and Dan Ferber, *Changing Planet, Changing Health: How the Climate Crisis Threatens Our Health and What We Can Do about It* (Oakland, CA: University of California Press, 2011), pp.15-17.

153 Martin, p.3, quoting clinical notes prepared by Dr Paul Epstein.

154 ibid., pp.3-4.

155 White (2004), p.226. It did not dawn on Dr Epstein until the publication of Ken Flower's memoirs in 1987 that the introduction of warfarin into the insurgents' diet was an intentional act by the Rhodesian Government. Warfarin was such a ubiquitous compound – available in many stores – that anyone from a disgruntled insurgent, rival nationalist group, angry villager or Rhodesian agent could have poisoned the food.

156 Doc/2, dated 18 September 2006.

157 The EMLC, (*Elektroniks, Meganies, Landbou en Chemies*, or 'Electronics, Mechanical, Agricultural and Chemical' in English) under Dr Jan Coetzee, was responsible for supporting South African Special Forces. The EMLC grew out of the Chemical Defence Unit (CDU) of the Council for Scientific and Industrial Research (CSIR). From its creation in the early 1960s, the CDU was responsible for monitoring worldwide CBW developments and the CBW threat to South Africa. Originally, the CDU consisted of three principal members: J. de Villiers, Vernon Joynt and Jan Coetzee. Of the three, Coetzee was closely involved

in the Rhodesian CBW effort – supplying materials for testing and learning the results of Rhodesian CBW experimentation and testing. To support South African Special Forces, South African Defence Minister Magnus Malan – in the early 1970s – directed the establishment of the Defence Research Institute within the Armament Corporation (ARMSCOR), which was headed by Coetzee. Obstacles in the procurement process (probably due to international sanctions placed on ARMSCOR) led to the creation of the Department of Special Equipment (later known as EMLC) – working directly for Special Forces and later located at Special Forces HQ (Speskop) in Pretoria. In mid-to-late 1980, Coetzee was removed from the EMLC, with Sybie van der Spuy replacing him as the EMLC head. At the same time, the CBW component of the EMLC was transferred to Delta G Scientific – a component of the South African CBW program 'Project Coast'. (See Jeffrey M. Bale, 'South Africa's Project Coast: 'Death Squads,' Covert State-Sponsored Poisonings, and the Dangers of CBW Proliferation', *Democracy and Security*, 2 (2006), pp.28-29.

158 ibid.
159 RhMC/1, personal communication.
160 BSAP/15, personal communication, dated 23 May 2006.
161 We have no published account claiming that the Bindura 'fort' was used to produce biological pathogens.
162 The Rhodesian Light Infantry was responsible for the dissemination of the cholera bacterium into Mozambican water sources. See Parker.
163 McGuinness confirmed with a former RLI – and later Selous Scout – operator that he had used cholera against targeted wells and watering points in Mozambique, and close to ZANLA camps. (McGuinness interview with the operator, 22 November 2006.)
164 Martin, p.7.
165 Mediel Hove, 'War legacy: A reflection on the effects of the Rhodesian Security Forces (RSF) in south eastern Zimbabwe during Zimbabwe's war of liberation 1976 – 1980', *Journal of African Studies and Development* 4 (October 2012), p.196.
166 'Rhodesia: Cholera Outbreaks Reported Among War Refugees', *Scientific Intelligence Weekly Review*, Washington: Central Intelligence Agency, 9 April 1979 (declassified, April 1998, MORI DocID: 218337).
167 Alexander Binda, *The Saints: The Rhodesian Light Infantry* (Durban, SA: 30° South Publishers, 2013), p.158.
168 ibid., p.242.
169 Ellert (1985), p.112. Also see Jim Parker's lengthy description of the Rhodesian use of cholera to deny water supplies to guerrillas and FRELIMO, p.170: 'Sergeant Simpson nom de guerre and a small Selous Scout Reconnaissance Troop team infiltrated Mozambique with several vials of cholera bacterium which they discharged into the water tank at Malvernia and into Madulo Pan. A week later information from B2 intercepts monitoring FRELIMO radio signals revealed that an outbreak of vomitting and dirrhoea had occurred amongst FRELIMO troops and ZANLA guerrillas at Malvernia, Madulo Pan and Jorge do Limpopo'.
170 Ellert (1985), pp.112-113.
171 Site of the reported *Vibrio cholerae* contamination was Cochemane Administrative Centre (Teté Province, Mozambique); online at <www.nti.org/e_research/profiles/safrica/biological/2435.html> (accessed on 26 May 2006).
172 Online at <selousscouts.tripod.com/external_operations.html> (accessed on 22 May 2006).
173 McGuinness' account contradicts an account published on the Nuclear Threat Initiative website, which states that in 1976: 'Selous Scouts introduce 'measured quantities of bacteriological cultures' at several points along the Ruya River in the wildlife area near the Mozambique border. This action corresponds with, and may have resulted in, a reported

epidemic of deaths among people living on the river's banks. However, the cause of the epidemic was officially attributed to cholera'; online at <www.nti.org/e_research/profiles/ SAfrica/Biological/ 2435_2436.html> (accessed on 22 May 2006).

174 FBI interview with an undisclosed informant (Case 279A-WF-222936, serial 508), dated 19 November 2002; redacted version released under FOIA, dated 5 December 2011.

175 Mangold, p.221.

176 Doc/2, dated 21 September 2006.

177 Bale (2006). According to Bale, the Selous Scouts also distributed some tainted alcohol; according to McGuinness, the Special Branch often tainted alcoholic beverages by adding pure alcohol to the bottles or cans. The resulting intoxication of guerrillas – on occasion – caused them to turn their guns on each other (personal communication, dated 24 April 2006).

178 As an example of how the product distribution system worked, a named Special Branch officer 'received his supply of clothes (blue jeans, socks, underpants etc.) that he channeled through sources and agents to CT Communist Terrorist groups in the field. The clothes were supplied in accordance with want lists issued by various CT groups to their own agents – many of whom were 'turned' and run as sources and agents'. (BSAP/15, personal communication, nd.)

    Chandré Gould quotes Chief Superintendent McGuinness as claiming 'McGuinness told me that 'the distribution of contaminated items, e.g. clothing and food, was not as a general rule carried out by the Scouts but by the Projects Section of the British South Africa Police (BSAP) Special Branch'. (Chandré Gould, 'South Africa's Chemical and Biological Warfare Program 1981-1995' (PhD dissertation, Rhodes University 2005), p.37.)

    In Jim Parker's book, he stated: '... at first, contaminated tinned meat and cool drinks were supplied only to Selous Scout pseudo call-signs working on internal operations. They would pass the stuff to ZANLA contact men who they had turned who would then hand it to unsuspecting guerrillas. Poisoned clothing was eventually removed from the pseudo call-sign lists as it proved to be bulky and difficult to carry because of the volumes deployed'. (Parker, p.159.)

179 Only once did materials ever escape from this rigid accountability – and that was in the Liebig's beef case. See McGuinness, personal communication, dated 24 April 2006.

180 Doc/1, private communication in the author's hands, dated 19 July 2006, p.4.

181 Gould and Folb (2002), p.27.

182 ibid.

183 Ed Bird, *Special Branch War: Slaughter in the Rhodesian Bush Southern Matabeleland, 1976-1980* (Solihull, UK: Helion & Company, Ltd., 2014), pp.91-94.

184 BSAP/2, personal communication, dated 16 February 2005.

185 BSAP File No. XYP 9339/5/5; XYP 9339/10/100, dated 22 May 1978, p.18.

186 John Cronin, personal communication, 25 April 2006.

187 Cronin, *The Bleed* (Amazon Digital Services, 2014).

188 ibid.

189 BSAP/2, personal communication, dated 6 February 2005.

190 Eugene de Kock manuscript.

191 Jeremy Brickhill, email to the author, dated 13 August 2009.

192 Stiff, *See You in November*, p.106.

193 See BSAP document 'Statistics Requested by Combined Operations', dated 28 June 1977; see Appendix D (from Peter Stiff Collection).

194 Parker, p.166.

195 Moorcraft and McLaughlin (2008), p.106.

196 Flower, p.137.

197 McGuinness, personal communication, dated 24 April 2006. He offered to provide an explanation to support his statement. In the context of his other statements, he almost certainly
meant that more deaths could be attributed to poisoned clothing than to contaminated
foods, beverages or medicines.

198 Doc/1, private communication in the author's hands, dated 19 July 2006, p.5.

199 John Cronin, personal communication, dated 30 October 2005.

200 According to McGregor, et al.: 'ZIPRA commanders claimed that the 'Rhodesian poisoning
was the most effective' strategy used against them: Nicolas Nkomo claimed that more guerrillas died in NF2 Northern Front 2 through poisoning than in battle'. Nkomo also asserted
that the poisoning program also led to a complete cessation of guerrilla operations in NF2.
BSAP/12 discounts ZIPRA claims that the Rhodesian Security Forces targeted them as part
of the CBW program; the former senior BSAP officer has stated repeatedly that ZANLA –
and not ZIPRA – was the target of the CBW effort, and that ZIPRA was seen as insignificant.
(Conversations with the author.)

201 Christopher A. Marquardt, 'The Literature of the Zimbabwean Guerrilla War: Themes and
Conditions of Production' (M Lit thesis, St Anthony's College, the University of Oxford,
1989), pp.123-124. According to Marquardt, post-war disappointment and feelings of rejection disillusioned many ZIPRA and ZANLA veterans about their wartime experiences. They
also believe the public is uninterested in books on the war.

202 Jocelyn Alexander, JoAnn McGregor and Terence Ranger, *Violence & Memory: One Hundred
Years in the 'Dark Forests' of Matabeleland* (Oxford: James Currey Ltd., 2000).

203 ibid., p.144, quoting interview with Nicholas Nkomo and Richard Dube, Bulawayo, 4
September 1996. Nkomo estimated that between 50 to 70 guerrillas died as a direct result of
poisoning within a few months.

204 ibid. Brickhill also quotes Nkomo as claiming that the Rhodesian poisonings led to a halt in
guerrilla operations. (See Brickhill (1992-1993), p.9.)

205 JoAnn McGregor, 'Containing Violence: Poisoning and Guerrilla/Civilian Relations in the
Memories of Zimbabwe's Liberation War' in K.L. Rogers, S. Leysesdorff and G. Dawson
(eds.), *Trauma and Life Stories: An International Perspective* (London: Routledge, 1999),
pp.131-159.

206 ibid., p.131.

207 ibid.

208 Doc/1, private communication, dated 19 July 2006, p.2.

209 Beit Bridge is the border crossing area between Rhodesia and South Africa. It was one of the
areas targeted for dissemination of poisoned items. See BSAP bi-weekly report in Appendix
D.

210 Report to Officer Commanding Special Branch and Director-General CIO, dated 25 August
1977; reproduced in Parker, p.164.

211 John Cronin. *The Bleed* (Amazon Digital Services, 2014).

212 N.J. Brendon, *The Man – and His Ways: An Introduction to the Customs and Beliefs of Rhodesia's
African People* (Salisbury, Rhodesia: Ministry of Information, Immigration and Tourism,
nd), p.7.

213 David Lan, *Guns & Rain: Guerrillas & Spirit Mediums in Zimbabwe* (London: James Currey,
1985), p.32.

214 ibid., p.35.

215 op. cit., p.36.

216 BSAP publication, 'The African Way of Life', dated September 1974, p.11.

217 Kalister Christine Manyame-Tazarurwa, *Health Implications of Participation in the Liberation Struggle of Zimbabwe by ZANLA Women Ex-Combatants in the ZANLA Operational Areas* (Bloomington, Indiana: AuthorHouse, 2011), p.88.

218 Presentation by Dr Kevin A. Lee, 'The Role of the Forensic Pathologist in the Rhodesian War' at a conference entitled: 'From Hobart to Harare: Tropical Medicine in Times of Conflict and Natural Disasters', *Proceedings of the Regional Scientific Meeting of the Australasian College of Tropical Medicine*, University of Tasmania, 11-13 November 2005.

219 BSAP File Number XYS 9339/5/1, nd, p.10.

220 McGuinness, personal communication, dated 25 April 2006.

221 Hove (2012), p.195.

222 John Goldsmid, communication dated 29 September 2005.

223 Stockholm International Peace Research Institute, *The Problem of Chemical and Biological Warfare: The Rise of CB Weapons, Volume 1* (New York: Humanities Press, 1971), p.211-212.

224 Wessels, p.195.

225 'Zambian Accuses Rhodesian Leader of Poisoning', *Washington Post*, 3 July 1975, p.A16 (byline: Agence France-Press, 2 July 1975).

226 Wessels, p.196.

227 Jeremy Brickhill, communication dated 13 August 2009.

228 Clapperton Chakanetsa Mayhunga, 'The Mobile Workshop: Mobility, Technology and Human-Animal Interaction in Gonarezhou (National Park), 1850-Present' (PhD dissertation, the University of Michigan, 2008), p. 384-385, citing *Facts and Reports*, 8th vol., no.1, 11 January 1978, p.63. Marcelino Komba, 'Maputo', *Daily News* (Tanz), 30 December 1977.

229 Mavhunga (2008), p.388, citing *Facts and Reports*, 8th vol., no.14, 14 July 1978, p.1,339; 'The Grim Reality of War', *Africa News* (US), 26 June 1978.

230 ibid.

231 James Watt MD, communication dated 25 August 2009.

232 James Watt MD, communication dated 7 September 2009.

233 ibid.

234 James Watt MD, communication dated 25 August 2009.

235 Alan Mills MD, communication dated 5 November 2005. Also see Mills' recent autobiography, *A Pathologist Remembers: Memoirs of Childhood and Later Life* (Bloomington, IN: AuthorHouse, 2013), pp.169-170.

236 Bird (2014), p.136.

237 Julie Frederikse, *None But Ourselves: Masses vs. Media in the Making of Zimbabwe* (New York: Penguin Books, 1984), p.219.

238 Anti-Apartheid Movement, *Fireforce Exposed* (London: Anti-Apartheid Movement, 1979).

239 ibid., p.39.

240 ibid.

241 ibid., citing BBC Monitoring Service Report – dated 5 May 1978 – reporting Maputo in English for Rhodesia.

242 Shamva is a village in the province of Mashonaland Central, Zimbabwe. Shamva is located in the Mazowe Valley, about 80km north-east of Harare and approximately 30km due east of Bindura. According to the 1982 population census, the village had a population of 4,617; online at <en.wikipedia.org/wiki/Shamva> (accessed on 2 June 2006).

243 Anti-Apartheid Movement, *Fireforce Exposed* (London: Anti-Apartheid Movement, 1979), p.39.

244 ibid., citing *Zimbabwe People's Voice*, dated 7 October 1978.

245 ibid., p.40.

246 ibid., citing *Zimbabwe People's Voice*, dated 3 February 1979.

247 ibid., citing *Zimbabwe People's Voice*, dated 7 April 1979.

248 See Doc/1 and Doc/3.

249 Ellert, p.112. Also see Chandré Gould and Peter Folb, *Project Coast: Apartheid's Chemical and Biological Warfare Programme* (Geneva: United Nations Institute for Disarmament Research, 2002), p.28. In Gould's PhD dissertation, she cites an interview between Peta Thornycroft and P.K. Allum, in which Allum recounted that 'in late 1977 when Commissioner of Police Peter Allum was told by a Medical Officer of Health (probably from Manicaland Province) that there were indications that there were mysterious deaths of Black people, he suspected chemical poisoning. He immediately ordered it be stopped. Allum was known to have tried hard to limit the Rhodesian security force atrocities against the civilian population. His role in stopping the chemical warfare project is confirmed by himself and several key sources'. See Chandré Gould, 'South Africa's Chemical and Biological Warfare Programme' (PhD dissertation, Rhodes University, 2005), p.40.

250 Doc/1, private communication in the author's hands, dated 19 July 2006, p.5: 'The Liebig's controversy was a very minor event, which received an insignificant amount of publicity and was never proven or admitted to being the work of the CBW unit'.

251 Parker, p.167.

252 McGuinness, personal communication, dated October 2006.

3

South Africa's Role in Rhodesian CBW

This chapter will explore the question of South African involvement in the Rhodesian CBW effort, and to what extent lessons from the Rhodesian CBW influenced South Africa's CBW program – commonly known as 'Project Coast'. Given the paucity of contemporaneous documents – and the questionable veracity of most participants in both the Rhodesian and South African efforts – this exploration cannot aim to provide incontrovertible proof; the only reasonable and achievable goal would be to establish a preponderance of evidence. Critics of this chapter's stance almost certainly will not be persuaded by the evidence presented, given the limited and fragmentary information available, as well as the dubious credibility of the sources.

Here, the limited available information about the South African involvement in the Rhodesian CBW effort is presented, and has been substantiated in at least one contemporaneous Rhodesian document; in the later statements of several Rhodesian participants in their CBW effort; in the accounts of two former senior Selous Scout officers; and some fragmentary hints from Dr Wouter Basson's trial. From those sources, South African support for the Rhodesian CBW effort had three major components: (1) raw materials and agents/pathogens for testing; (2) scientific expertise; and (3) financial contributions.[*][1]

The more contentious question is whether this involvement played a part in the development of South Africa's later 'Project Coast'; none of the publicly available records of South Africa's CBW program hint at events in South Africa. The Truth and Reconciliation Commission – and other investigations into apartheid-era wrongdoing – do not provide details of South African involvement in Rhodesia's CBW effort. Evidence of a Rhodesian connection to South Africa's 'Project Coast' comes from Rhodesian Security Force members who migrated south after Zimbabwean Independence in 1980. Hints of a connection also arose during Wouter Basson's trial. As will be discussed later, several South African officials linked to 'Project Coast' had ties with Rhodesian CBW participants – and the former 'Project Coast' head,

---

*   Several published sources have stated that South African Intelligence helped to fund the CIO's budget and provided funds for use by the Selous Scouts. Almost certainly, a portion of the South African funds was allocated to support the Rhodesian CBW program.

Wouter Basson himself, mentioned his involvement in 'joint operations' during the Rhodesian counterinsurgency.

Given the criticism of some skeptics, complete transparency regarding information sources is needed. The sources of our information largely are former members of the Rhodesian Security Forces – notably BSAP Chief Superintendent Michael McGuinness. McGuinness' information comes in several forms – including audio-recorded interviews with the author, lengthy statements made to FBI Special Agents investigating AMERITHRAX, and comments made to others. At the author's urging, McGuinness also reached out to the remaining members of his 'Z' Branch and participants in the Rhodesian CBW effort. He had one meeting with several key players in Cape Town and phone calls with others – keeping records of all those interactions and, on several occasions, using questions developed by the author to elicit information from his former colleagues and subordinates. All of McGuinness' notes and records now are in the author's possession. Through the US Government's Freedom of Information program, the author also has obtained redacted copies of all the FBI records relating to the Rhodesian and South African CBW programs. These files largely are of interviews with McGuinness, but others were interviewed as well. The FBI interviews and the information provided by McGuinness to the author are consistent[2] – and several Selous Scout officers were interviewed, and their statements also support McGuinness' information. All of this material is further bolstered by information uncovered by investigative journalist Peta Thorycroft. At least some of her materials are available at the South African History Archive (SAHA), as are materials on 'Project Coast' deposited there by Chandré Gould.

Sources on the South African use of Rhodesian CBW information and materials are sketchier, but their information can be said to support a reasonable belief that Rhodesian information and materials were not only transferred to South Africa, but used. That Rhodesian information was transferred to South Africa is reasonably established by the fact that Rhodesian documents were wholesale transferred to South Africa prior to Zimbabwean Independence. South Africa's Directorate of Military Intelligence (DMI), the Directorate of Covert Collection (DCC) and the Civil Cooperation Bureau (CCB) all employed former Rhodesian Security Force members – and the DMI, in particular, received truckloads of sensitive Rhodesian documents. Rhodesian CBW materials were transferred to South Africa, according to McGuinness – and testimony at Wouter Basson's trial also asserts that Rhodesian CBW materials were transferred and stored at South Africa's EMLC. How the Rhodesian information and materials were used by South Africa rests on thinner reeds – notably statements by McGuinness.

South African interest in CBW

South African sources on 'Project Coast' date the government's interest in CBW to two events roughly contemporaneous: (a) the 1976 Soweto Uprising, in which South African police used overwhelming force to quell large-scale protests in the Soweto township outside Johannesburg;[3] and (b) the escalating involvement against Cuban forces in Angola. Prior to 1976, the South African entity monitoring CBW development was a small three-man team referred to as the Chemical Defense Unit (CDU) in South Africa's government-funded scientific research and development (R&D) corporation, the Council for Scientific and Industrial Research (CSIR). The CDU – sometimes referred to as the Applied Chemistry Unit (ACU) – was contracted solely to the South African military and later was renamed Mechem.

A South African scientist named Jean de Villiers headed the CDU for most of its existence. Several of de Villiers' papers exist that demonstrate an ambiguity, if not an evolution, in South African thinking on the CBW topic. In de Villiers' first paper – dated 12 February 1971 and classified 'Secret' – he argues that lethal chemical warfare agents are unlikely to be important, but suggests that a potential exists for the use of non-lethal irritants. He went on to dismiss biological warfare in the South African context as very unlikely.[4] De Villiers did admit a possible role for monofluoroacetate in poisoning water supplies. We find that fluoroacetates feature prominently in the presumably Rhodesian 'founding' document from a slightly later time, and know that South Africa provided Rhodesia with monofluoroacetate. In a May 1977 paper, de Villiers wrote: '... the major possibility of biological warfare is that it can be used in a covert operation...'[5] In a 12 July 1977 paper, he noted that the 'treatment of terrorist bases with a non-persistent, non-lethal agent just before a security force attack can affect both the terrorists' ability to defend themselves and their ability to escape'. In the same paper, on the question of BW use, de Villiers stated: 'Due to the nature of South Africa's enemies and their spon-

sors, the tactical application of these agents against South Africa is not a real option. Therefore, it can be said that biological warfare poses no threat and is also of no advantage to South Africa'.[6]

De Villiers' writings, as captured in the Mechem archive, focus on CBW in a military inter-State context. Here, he is highly skeptical about the utility of CBW in Southern Africa. Although initially dismissive of CBW use in a Southern African context, de Villiers seems to have become more receptive to the idea of CBW utility. He pointed out that many of the difficulties in filling chemical munitions had been solved in the pesticide and nuclear industries.[7] De Villiers believed that CW held an allure for chemists,[8] but pointed out that a chief obstacle to CW use was the disinterest in military commanders in unproven weapons systems. He claimed that the ban on CBW was effective not because of any moral revulsion to CBW use, but because the weapons were unproven and believed to be unreliable.

Figure 3.1 Dr Jean de Villiers – head of South Africa's Applied Chemistry Unit. (Source: <www.nixt.co.za> with permission of the National Institute of Explosives Technology (NIXT) South Africa)[9]

The only utility of either chemical or biological warfare agents was de Villiers' suggestion that BW could be used in covert operations – probably meaning small-scale special operations (i.e. assassinations). De Villiers also displays a focused interest in the potential of monofluoroacetates – especially in water contamination – and his other writings focus on the use of non-lethal chemical agents in crowd and riot control. In none of the available papers, which often include historical surveys of CBW use, does de Villiers mention the Rhodesian CBW example.

Support to the Rhodesian CBW effort

The Rhodesia CBW participants and knowledgeable Special Branch officers seem in steadfast agreement that the Rhodesian effort was Rhodesian from its birth. The South Africans had no hand in the Rhodesian program inception or design, and the effort focused on serving Rhodesian interests. Although the South Africans were very knowledgeable about – if not involved in – the Rhodesian CBW effort, no concrete evidence exists to suggest when their CBW cooperation may have begun. The originator of the Rhodesian CBW effort – Robert Symington – maintained close ties with South African EMLC head Dr Jan Coetzee, SAPS Forensic Laboratory chief Lothar Neethling and Dr Wouter Basson, who would go on to head South Africa's own CBW program.[10] Although the idea of a CBW effort originated in Rhodesia with Professor Symington, we cannot discount the possibility that South African scientists may have influenced Symington's choice of agents, as well as providing agents for testing in Rhodesia.[11]

According to Parker, the Rhodesian CBW program also depended on South African supplies of raw materials.[12] Parker asserts that a Special Branch liaison officer regularly couriered materials from South Africa to Rhodesia. One of McGuinness' fortnightly reports stated that the decline in guerrilla casualties during the reporting period was due to delays in getting needed materials from South Africa;[13] another observer also stated that the Rhodesian CBW program obtained its raw materials from South African suppliers.[14] In early 1979, Noble visited EMLC and returned to Bindura with Coetzee, a vial of *Clostridium botulinum* and an anthrax sample.[15] With the approval of the South African Security Police, the Rhodesians visited Onderstepoort Veterinary Laboratories – then producing anthrax vaccine. At one point, the dedicated SB courier picked up an unidentified material at Onderstepoort for delivery to Bindura. Other materials provided by the South Africans included colchicine, ricin, amanita extract, 2,4-D,* compound 1080†, cyanide, arsenic and warfarin. Rhodesian participants have stated that the South African-provided chemicals were ineffective.[16]

---

*   2,4-dichlorophenoxyacetic acid is a common herbicide and one of the major ingredients in Agent Orange.

†   As mentioned in chapter 2, compound 1080 is sodium fluoroacetate – an extremely lethal chemical identified in both the 1977 South African study by de Villiers and in the presumably Rhodesian 'founding' document.

As discussed earlier, the South Africans provided some materials, as mentioned in the one McGuinness fortnightly report to Ken Flower – and another Rhodesian CBW participant identified several chemical agents and toxins provided by the South Africans. McGuinness' Special Branch courier also delivered cans of liquids wrapped in plastic addressed to Symington.[17] The funding for the program lay almost entirely came from South African largesse.[18]

One Rhodesian planning document from 1973 strongly suggests that the Rhodesian military relied on South African scientific expertise regarding CBW issues. The JPS document was exploring innovative solutions to incorporate into the *cordon sanitaire* – including a proposal to salt the ground in the *cordon sanitaire* with dichloroethyl sulphide (sulfur mustard – the chemical used in mustard gas, which is a lethal CW agent used in World War I). The proposal claimed that this chemical would penetrate through the boots of guerrillas transiting through the cordon and result in chemical burns on their feet. The Rhodesians tasked a South African scientific panel from CSIR to evaluate the proposal; the panel recommended against adoption of the proposal – stating that it was not a practical proposition. To support their position, the South Africans pointed to the scientific uncertainties surrounding the use of the chemical as a solid in the cordon, as well as the serious international political repercussions when the use of the chemical was inevitably discovered.[19]

Given the earlier South African review of the proposal examined by the JPS, the Rhodesians (i.e. Symington) almost certainly consulted with South African colleagues (i.e. the CDU) on later plans for CBW development and use. Of the three-man CSIR team that reviewed the JPS proposal, apart from Jan Coetzee, no additional mention can be found indicating that they played any later role in the Rhodesian CBW effort.[20]

One member of the team (Coetzee) did provide substantial support to the Rhodesian CBW team and technical assistance to a variety of Selous Scout special operations tasks, as Ron Reid-Daly described Coetzee:

> I now began to get an insight into the thoroughness of the South African Army, for amongst the contingent was a doctor. This, in itself, is a normal practice in any army, but Doctor Jan Coetzee was not a medical doctor. He was a scientist. His function was to see what scientific input would be required to incorporate our methods into the South African Army. And what a star he turned out to be! He had his own machine shop in Pretoria and produced some magical goodies, which went bang in the night for us.[21]

The implication is that Coetzee (and EMLC) were involved in designing mines and other explosives for the Rhodesian Special Forces.[22] Although EMLC was responsible for producing devices for South African Special Forces, as well as for the Selous Scouts and RhSAS, Coetzee – with his years in the CDU – almost certainly addressed on CBW issues as well. Also, Coetzee almost certainly was part of a two-man team (described as 'professors' – possibly from the CSIR) that questioned Selous Scout officers about characteristics (e.g. lethality, time to effect) and possible dissemination methods of chemical agents.[23] According to information from a Rhodesian CBW participant, '... we learned nothing from the South Africans, they learned from us and two of their number (unidentified) visited our primitive laboratory several times in Bindura while we visited them on two or three occasions in Pretoria at Special Forces headquarters...'[24]

According to the former Zimbabwean Intelligence operative Jeremy Brickhill, South African scientists and intelligence officers was directly involved in the Rhodesian CBW program and may have aided in the development of CBW agents – including warfarin, thallium and bacteriological agents such as anthrax.[25] Brickhill also stated that the human and other assets involved in this CBW program were transferred to South Africa in early 1980;[26] the popular media – and on the internet – often describes Rhodesia as South Africa's 'testing ground'. Former Zimbabwe Health Minister Dr Timothy Stamps would argue that epidemics plaguing Rhodesia resulted from the intentional dissemination of disease, and that at least some pathogens originated in South Africa.[27] Although erring in some details, Brickhill's account is consistent broadly with statements from Rhodesian Security Force sources. Dr Stamps' statements cannot be substantiated based on publicly available information, however; Zimbabwean Government plans for an investigation came to nothing. Based on the 1973 JPS document citing the CDU team, Symington's close ties to CDU members – and the similarity between South African and Rhodesian interests in fluoroacetates – that a relationship between the Rhodesian and South African CBW efforts was apparent.

CBW information exchanges

The exchange of scientific information on the effectiveness of CBW agents and pathogens was intense, with the Rhodesians making frequent trips to several South African sites. Sites visited included the SAPS Forensic Laboratory, EMLC at South African Special Forces Headquarters and the CSIR. South African scientists from these institutions visited Bindura and the Selous Scout Headquarters on multiple occasions. McGuinness' Special Branch courier made to trip to Pretoria once every 10 days during the course of the CBW effort, and became well acquainted with Jan Coetzee and SAPS Forensic Laboratory head Dr Lothar Neethling. The courier remarked that on at least four separate occasions, he met Symington in the company of either Coetzee or Neethling. The courier added that Symington flew to Pretoria for these exchanges on either South African police or military aircraft, and that it became a running joke for Symington that he got to fly while the courier was forced to drive. In all, the courier may have made as many as 100 trips to South Africa – largely to Special Forces Headquarters (Speskop) and the SAPS Forensics Laboratory – and to the Onderstepoort Veterinary Laboratories. The South African contacts were Dr Jan Coetzee (Special Forces/EMLC), Dr Lothar Neethling and SAPS Security Branch Colonel J.J. Viktor.[28] One Rhodesian CBW participant stated that he knew Coetzee and that CSIR chemists had visited the CBW effort at Bindura. According to the participant, the purpose of the South African visits was to gather information for use in creating their own CBW program.[29]

As described earlier, Coetzee also was the recipient of CBW test data from the Rhodesians – involving application of the chemicals to different human body parts and through different types of contaminated clothing.[30] When Coetzee asked McGuinness about the source of the report, he was told that it came from a professor at the University of Rhodesia. Coetzee shared the report with Special Forces commander Fritz Loots and SAMS Surgeon-General Nicolaas Nieuwoudt. Loots reportedly reacted with revulsion, and refused to have anything to do with the document.

Among the South African officers most involved in collecting data on the Rhodesian CBW effort – and with the greatest access to Rhodesian information – were senior SAPS officers J.J. Viktor and Hans Dreyer. Both had been attached to McGuinness' unit at Bindura at times, and were both very aware of the Rhodesian CBW effort. The South Africans were keen students of the CBW lessons learned in Rhodesia – and McGuinness singled out Dreyer especially. Those lessons almost certainly would have been useful to South Africa when it formally established its own CBW efforts; some elements of the South African program suggest it adopted tactics developed by the Rhodesians (i.e. the use of parathion-poisoned underwear, poisoned food and beverages etc.).

Figure 3.2 Dr Lothar Neethling – former chief of the SAPS Forensics Laboratory. (Source: courtesy of the Hennie Heymans collection)

Figure 3.3 Lieutenant General Nicolaas Nieuwoudt – former SAMS Surgeon-General. (Source: official SADF portrait (*SA Government Gazette*, accessed at <http://www.sadf.info/InCommandMecicalServices.html>))

Figure 3.4 South African Police General
Hans Dreyer. (Source: the University of
Cape Town Library, with permission of
John Liebenberg)

Dr Wouter Basson – later the head
of South Africa's 'Project Coast' –
reportedly traveled to Rhodesia on
several occasions and visited the Selous
Scout HQ. During Basson's trial, a (former Selous Scout) witness said he 'first met
Basson 'in passing' in then Rhodesia in the late 1970s. This meeting took place in the
communal mess at the Selous Scouts Headquarters (i.e. Inkomo Barracks) outside
Salisbury. Basson was in a group of South African security force members who had
gone to Rhodesia to take part in joint operations with the Selous Scouts'.[31]

According to an observer in the court:

> In answering questions relating to the testimony of an earlier witness that
> Basson had been in Zimbabwe before the independence of that country, Basson
> said he was aware of allegations that chemical and biological weapons had been
> used in Rhodesia because in 1981, he was summoned by the then chief director
> counter-intelligence and told that a container of poisons had been uncovered
> as part of an ANC arms cache. It was a green metal trunk and Basson had to
> examine the contents. Being still a novice, he landed up in hospital as a result.
> He was told that the ANC had captured the trunk of toxins from the Selous
> Scouts. It contained mainly insecticides, which were analysed at the University
> of Pretoria.[32]

In an email, Dr Basson denied any knowledge of – or involvement in – the Rhodesian
CBW effort. Asked about his role in Rhodesia, he replied that he attended many
joint operational meetings and was not aware of any discussion taking place in this
regard (i.e. on CBW). No feedback (regarding Rhodesian CBW) was ever brought to
Basson's attention, and given that no information on the Rhodesian CBW effort was
available, it had no impact on 'Project Coast'. Basson was aware of extensive cooperation between the Rhodesian armed forces and the CSIR – and, more specifically, the
CDU of the CSIR. According to Basson, this latter nomenclature was, however, a
misnomer, as the so-called 'CDU' was not conducting any chemical work; this had
been stopped by their head (probably de Villiers), who considered CBW as largely
impractical. Their deputy head, Dr Vernon Joynt, was the main advisor to the SADF
and the Rhodesian Army in the field of mine-protected vehicles. This was, to the best
of Basson's knowledge, the only cooperation at that time. Basson admitted he met
Professor Symington in Symington's capacity as an external examiner in anatomy at
the University of Cape Town after he had left Rhodesia, and had contact with him
on academic matters while he was lecturing in Salisbury.[33]

Figure 3.5 Former 'Project Coast' head Dr Wouter Basson. (Source: <http://www.vice.com/read/wouter-basson-dr-death-south-africa-ecstasy-957>)[34]

Regarding the possible involvement of the SAPS Forensic Laboratory and Dr Lothar Neethling, Dr Basson recounted that Neethling and the staff of the forensic laboratory were involved in the solving of crimes in Southern Africa. To this end, they amassed a mountain of knowledge on the subject of toxicology. According to Basson, this would have been of tremendous benefit to any CBW program. As mentioned earlier in the chapter, Dr Basson denies having any knowledge of Rhodesia's CBW program, but admits having worked in Rhodesia on 'joint operations'.[35] Knowing the ethics of that unit, Basson stated that he will be veritably surprised if any such cooperation existed! The labs at forensics were not suitable for storing anthrax, and it is impossible that any anthrax could have been supplied from there.[36]

Contrary to Dr Basson's statements, South African researchers have uncovered evidence of information-sharing between the Rhodesians and the South Africans – including periodic reports on the Rhodesian program sent to South Africa and liaison meetings. One published paper mentions that the South Africans provided support to one rudimentary Rhodesian chemical and biological warfare plant;[37] lastly, according to Ellert, both Bindura and Andre Rabie Barracks were open to select members of the SADF and the SP, who were regularly briefed on developments. As Ellert puts it, given that the South Africans were bankrolling the operations, they had a right to be kept informed.[38] Brickhill claims that '… Former CIO sources who spoke to me confirmed that the South Africans played a role in the poisons war, providing technical help and anxiously monitoring the 'results in the field.' South African 'specialists' were present in all secret Rhodesian bases, including top secret Selous Scout forts from where the poison war was developed…'[39]

South African military officers and CSIR researchers visited Selous Scout Headquarters (Inkomo Barracks). Jan Coetzee – and possibly others – visited Bindura and met with Symington and Noble. As stated earlier, Symington was a frequent visitor to EMLC and the SAPS Forensic Laboratory, with Symington maintaining close contact with Coetzee and Neethling. Noble also visited EMLC and had a close working relationship with Coetzee.[40] Comments by Noble indicate that the South Africans sought as much information about the Rhodesian CBW effort as possible.[41]

The South African presence at Bindura was headed by SAPS Security Police Colonel Johannes Jacobus Viktor (aka J.J.Viktor), who was Chief Superintendent McGuinness' South African liaison. Colonel Viktor spent 18 months assigned to Bindura in the late 1970s and was fully informed about details of the Rhodesian CBW effort:[42]

> Colonel Viktor of the South African Security Branch [sic] who was based in Bindura had unlimited access to the fort and provided any materials that Symington or Noble required from South Africa. Harvey Richter,* who was in Bindura to study Selous Scout tactics before he formed the South African covert unit, showed great interest in our use of poisons.[43]

Ellert recounts that the South Africans maintained a teletype communications capability linking Bindura with Pretoria;[44] however, McGuinness claims that Viktor never reported his privileged information on the CBW effort to his superiors in Pretoria.[45]

Several Rhodesians central to the CBW effort later emigrated to South Africa – including Robert Symington, Michael McGuinness and Victor Noble. Symington could have shared a great deal with the South Africans before his death in 1982, and his animosity toward black nationalists would have allied him to South Africa – especially as the apartheid regime grew entrenched in its *laager* mentality and developed the strategy to combat 'Total Onslaught'. McGuinness went on to work for South African Intelligence in a variety of roles and clearly was in a position to share details about the Rhodesian CBW program, if he was ever asked. Others tangential to the Rhodesian CBW program also moved to South Africa – namely BSAP members Henry Wolhuter[†] and George Mitchell, who both joined SAPS. Wolhuter went on to join the SAPS Brixton Murder and Robbery Squad, from which several members of the CCB were recruited; Mitchell rose to a senior position in the Durban Narcotics Squad. Former Selous Scouts Charlie Krause, Neil Kriel and Peter Stanton were to be involved in aspects of Project 'Barnacle' and later with the CCB.

Based on all the material relayed above, the diagram attempts to chart the ties and associations among the Rhodesian CBW effort and the South African link to CBW development and use. The diagram illustrates several points: first, that the key South African point of contact for the Rhodesian CBW effort was Dr Jan Coetzee at EMLC. Coetzee has the greatest number of contacts with the Rhodesian CBW team, and most of his contacts are strong ties; secondly, Dr Lothar Neethling had the next greatest number of ties to the Rhodesians, but still only half the number

---

* Almost certainly a pseudonym for SAPS Colonel Hans 'Sterk' Dreyer – the founder and commander of Koevoet, which was a special SAPS paramilitary unit deployed to Namibia to counter an insurgency led by the South West African Peoples' Organization (SWAPO). Koevoet was modeled after the Selous Scouts and made up mostly of Ovambo tribesmen, as well as a small number of white South African Police.

† As mentioned in chapter 2, Wolhuter and his wife died of cancer in the mid-1980s – a cancer that he believes was caused by their work with poisoned clothes.

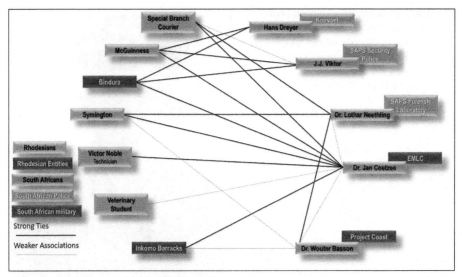

Figure 3.6 South African ties to the Rhodesian CBW effort. (Source: the author's collection)

Coetzee had. Dr Basson's significant ties are not with Rhodesians, but with South Africans – notably Neethling. Testimony at South Africa's Truth and Reconciliation Commission (TRC) hearings dates Basson's association with Neethling to after 1980, when the two became close. Based on his own description of his association, Basson's links to Symington probably were weak; lastly, Hans Dreyer and J.J. Viktor had strong ties to operational Rhodesian CBW elements, but not to the scientific or technical aspect of the CBW effort. In addition, neither Dreyer nor Viktor had clear ties to Neethling, Coetzee or Basson.

Impact of the Rhodesian CBW effort on South Africa's 'Project Coast'

Clearly a robust information exchange on Rhodesian CBW developments and experiences existed between the Rhodesian team and certain South Africans – that point is undeniable – yet the question that remains unresolved is whether the Rhodesian information was retained or used by the South Africans in any meaningful way. The official record is unclear: the Rhodesians certainly believed that their information was useful and needed, but South African recollections claim the contrary. Both 'Project Coast' head Wouter Basson and his commanding officer – Surgeon-General Daniel Knobel – both emphatically deny any knowledge of the Rhodesian CBW program, and thus any Rhodesian influence on 'Project Coast'.[46] The possibility that the Rhodesian CBW lessons were transmitted and retained through an informal network inside the South African securitocracy is plausible. Especially under Minister of Defense Magnus Malan, the informal power structure on security issues rivaled – if not exceeded – the formal bureaucracy in influence. If tracing how Rhodesian lessons learned might have traveled through this informal network on its way to

Figure 3.7 Lieutenant General Daniel
Knobel – former SAMS Surgeon-
General. (Source: official SADF
portrait (*SA Government Gazette*,
accessed at <http://www.sadf.info/
InCommandMecicalServices.html>))

'Project Coast', the likely point of entry to the South African securitocracy would
have been through either Neethling or Jan Coetzee.

In the TRC hearings and Wouter Basson's trial record, no meaningful mention is
made of the Rhodesian CBW effort apart from van der Spuy's testimony of poisoned
clothing in EMLC's warehouse, and Coetzee's recollection of a Rhodesian CBW
document. Given the limitations on the TRC and the focus of Basson's trial, the
absence of any mention of the Rhodesian CBW effort is not proof that no link exists
between the Rhodesian and South African CBW efforts. In the available records of
'Project Coast', its subprogram 'Project Black',* or Mechem, no mention is ever made
about the Rhodesian experience – and no other records of Rhodesia's CBW program
exist in publicly available South African archives. Likely, if any records did exist, they
were destroyed in the massive document purges following the Harms and Goldstone
Commissions preceding Nelson Mandela's 1994 election to the South African presidency. Similarly, van der Spuy probably destroyed or transferred CBW-related documents from EMLC after he succeeded Coetzee in 1980.

Evidence of clothing contaminated with poison also surfaced at the trial of Dr
Wouter Basson. At the trial, prosecutor Dr Torie Pretorius called to the stand Sybie
van der Spuy† – managing director of EMLC for 12 years from 1 November 1980,

---

*   'Project Black' was a subproject within 'Project Coast' and was designed to study the history
     of CBW programs and CBW use; the legal context; international norms etc.
†   Commandant (Lieutenant Colonel equivalent) Danie 'Sybie' van der Spuy was an SADF Special
     Forces officer when he assumed leadership of EMLC in November 1980 – and he retained
     that post at EMLC until it was abolished in 1992. A former commander of 2 Reconnaissance

according to a summary of the court proceedings compiled by Chandré Gould and Marlene Burger. In their account:

> van der Spuy said no chemical work was ever carried out by the company. He said that when he first joined EMLC he found a room containing a large amount of bulk chemicals and a carton of what appeared to be clothing. As he moved across the room to examine the clothing, one of his new employees warned him not to touch it. Asked why not, the employee told van der Spuy: "Because those clothes are poisoned and if you put those underpants on, you'll be dead by tonight." Van der Spuy offered no further explanation, but says he immediately ordered the contents of this room to be destroyed. In cross-examination, Cilliers put it to van der Spuy that prior to him joining EMLC in November 1980, the company obviously was involved in the manufacture/supply of toxins, and, as illustrated by his encounter with the underpants, clearly had the ability to apply toxins to items of clothing. Van der Spuy says this may or may not have been the case, but he put an end to the practice immediately, in terms of his agreement with Loots that no chemical work would be done.[47]

Although the materials van der Spuy uncovered at the EMLC warehouse may have been produced there, a more likely explanation is that the underwear were remnants of the Rhodesian CBW efforts and delivered to EMLC following that country's transition to majority rule – and Independence – earlier in 1980. According to one knowledgeable Rhodesian official, all of the CBW materials – including a warehouse of contaminated items – were shipped to South Africa just prior to Independence.[48] The question is whether these Rhodesian materials were destined for 'Project Coast', or other South African operations. Given that the beginning of 'Project Coast' is dated at May 1981, these materials probably were not stored with 'Project Coast' in mind. Given that Jan Coetzee's tenure at EMLC ended in November 1980, he was no longer in an official position to retain or transmit lessons of the Rhodesian experience to 'Project Coast' – and given that Coetzee's ouster from EMLC came about after Defense Minister Malan had lost confidence in Coetzee's abilities, he probably was removed from any informal role as well.

Interestingly – and yet unexplained – the Rhodesian and South African CBW efforts were remarkably similar in most of the agent choices and some of the dissemination means despite the lack of concrete evidence that South Africa's 'Project Coast' adopted the lessons of the Rhodesian CBW effort. Although greatly expanded by the South Africans – and lavished with more personnel, equipment and facilities than afforded the Rhodesians – the South African program essentially adopted agents and dissemination techniques similar to those developed in Rhodesia. The similarity in CBW agents and dissemination methods is a circumstantial indication of an information transfer between CBW efforts. To simply deny the similarities is

Regiment ('2 Recce'), van der Spuy – along with Colonel Jan Breytenbach – had founded Bravo Group, which later became 32 Battalion. Van der Spuy died in July 2013, aged 81.

problematic – especially when the Rhodesian program shut down in late 1979, most all of the materials associated with the program almost certainly were handed over to the South Africans.[49]

The Rhodesian impact on other South African CBW operations

'Project Coast' aside, in 1979 (as the Rhodesian War drew to a close), some in the South African security establishment sought to duplicate the Rhodesian unconventional capabilities – including 'chemical operations'. The Rhodesian Special Branch supported the creation of the SAPS Unit at Vlakplaas[50] and Koevoet, and the South African Special Forces established a unit (3 Recce) modeled after the Selous Scouts. The SAPS Security Police Unit – headed by J.J. Viktor – went on to form the Counterterrorism Unit 1 (or C1) at Vlakplaas. Viktor's successor as C1 commander, Dirk Coetzee, commented at his hearing in response to a question about who taught him about the use of poisons that '... who taught me to kill with poison? That story comes from the Rhodesian war in the [sic], while Rhodesian [sic] was still independent, where clothes of so-called recruited terrorists were poisoned and they were dished out with these clothes and they died on their way out...'[51] Coetzee added that a storeroom at Vlakplaas was filled with goods obtained by J. J. Viktor from McGuinness.

According to Coetzee:

> They [Vlakplaas] basically functioned out of a lot of ... Colonel J J Viktor had a close relationship with the Rhodesian special branches and had a storeroom full of clothes and shoes and beds and boxes of canned food out of the security fund as such. So I got them onto the official quartermaster record so that we can order meat, milk, vegetables, fruit, proper diet for the Askaris.[52]

According to the testimony of former Selous Scout officer 'Mr K' at Dr Wouter Basson's trial:

> ... he ['Mr K'] had been one of the founder members of the Selous Scouts in Rhodesia. He left Rhodesia in 1978 and joined the South African Defence Force as a member of Special Forces in 1979. In the same year, he was approached by the Commander of Special Forces, Gen Loots and the Minister of Defence, General Magnus Malan and instructed to establish a covert unit within Special Forces that would adopt the modus operandi of the Selous Scouts. The unit was known as Operation Barnacle. The chief objective of the unit was elimination of identified state enemies and the carrying out of "super-sensitive" covert operations, which could include eliminations. Other objectives of the unit included:
> • The elimination of members of own forces who threatened to expose covert operations;
> • Intelligence gathering;
> • Ambushes;
> • Combat intelligence and,
> • Conducting of chemical operations...[53]

Interestingly, the creation of this Special Forces unit* to carry out 'chemical operations' occurred two years before the acknowledged establishment of South Africa's 'Project Coast' in 1981.

Rhodesian CBW materials also made their way to the SAPS counterinsurgency unit in Namibia, Koevoet, which was commanded by Hans Dreyer. Dreyer – an ardent student of the Rhodesian CBW effort and the Selous Scouts – established Koevoet and modeled it initially after the Selous Scouts. Both McGuinness and Eugene de Kock describe the transfer of Rhodesian stocks of contaminated foods to Koevoet.

De Kock, in his autobiography, stated:

> In about 1980, canned food contaminated with thallium arrived at Koevoet from the former Rhodesia. I don't know if anyone was ever poisoned with the food, but I do know that a large amount of these canned goods had to be destroyed when Koevoet closed down in 1989. I also know that a large amount of the canned food and especially canned meat that was supposed to be destroyed fell into the hands of members of the Ovambo Home Guard who ate it. Some became seriously ill and a number were treated at 1 Military Hospital. I heard that Captain Chris Geldenhuys, previously attached to the Murder and Robbery Unit, and who would end up being the first witness at my trial in 1996, was treated at 1 Military Hospital after he ate some of this food. Several people and also children in the Okatana township in Oshakati became seriously ill or died as a result of thallium poisoning.[54]

Despite these accidental poisonings, no evidence exists that Koevoet ever made operational use of its poisoned Rhodesian food; histories of the unit contain no references to poisons or the intentional use of poisons against SWAPO. 'Project Coast' reportedly used CBW agents against SWAPO prisoners in Namibia, but those activities likely are separate from Koevoet operations.

Those that would argue against a significant Rhodesian influence on South Africa's chemical and biological weapons might point to the fact that the South African liaison at the Bindura 'fort' consisted of South African police officers – and not members of the SADF. The conclusion is that the South Africans most keenly aware of the Rhodesian poisons program did not come from the South African elements directly involved in the creation of 'Project Coast'.

Conclusion

Although South African pressure to end the war was one of the factors leading to the Lancaster House Agreement, the South African Government had been Rhodesia's staunchest supporter – supplying equipment, men, materiel, money and every other conceivable means to sustain the Rhodesian war effort. Cooperation also included

---

*   Initially known as 'D40', 'Barnacle' was a forerunner to the notorious CCB.

a very close intelligence network; support for Rhodesian sanctions-busting efforts; SIGINT collection and analysis; and joint military operations and training. As the war drew to a close, the South Africans were providing sophisticated, specialized operational equipment to the Rhodesian Special Forces – both the Selous Scouts and the SAS – such as mine-laying and de-mining technology, letter bombs, CBW materials etc. The South Africans also had given almost complete *carte blanche* with the Selous Scouts. South African Special Forces (the 'Recces') – in Selous Scout uniforms – operated alongside the Rhodesians and, almost certainly, also conducted unilateral operations inside Rhodesia. Recce members formed most of, if not all, of the Rhodesian SAS's 'D' Squadron – wearing Rhodesian uniforms and kit during their assignment. The SAPS Security Police also worked hand in glove with the BSAP Special Branch – especially those Special Branch liaison officers assigned to the Selous Scouts. The SAPS Security Police took the lessons learned from their Special Branch colleagues and used those lessons when forming the C1 Squad at Vlakplaas and the Koevoet.

The South African military's interest in the Rhodesian CBW effort at the time is manifest. Although many are skeptical about any suggestion that lessons from the Rhodesian CBW program were incorporated in South Africa's CBW program, the preponderance of evidence demonstrates that the South Africans were very actively involved in the Rhodesian CBW effort at the time. The South Africans sent teams of observers to Bindura; hosted Rhodesian CBW team members on visits to Pretoria; provided materials for use in CBW production and testing; received written reports from the Rhodesians on CBW agents; and accepted all of the remaining records, materials and equipment when the Rhodesian effort ceased operations. Testimony at Dr Wouter Basson's trial indicated that Basson and Dr Daniel Knobel were seen at least once at the Selous Scouts' Inkomo Barracks.* Other information suggests that South Africans, almost certainly, from CSIR – and possibly including Basson – were frequent visitors to Inkomo, and that Basson may have visited other Selous Scout facilities in Rhodesia. South African involvement in the Rhodesian CBW program may have included sharing information on agent toxicity, applicability to use in various specified scenarios, vetting Rhodesian CBW-related proposals and test results.

The *prima facie* conclusion is that the Rhodesian CBW effort originated entirely within Rhodesia to serve Rhodesian needs, yet the South Africans contributed to the effort – supplying materials, money and scientific and technical resources. The documentary evidence demonstrates that the Rhodesians were dependent at one point on South African supplies of critical materials – and South Africans involved in supporting the Rhodesian CBW operations were keen students, with a robust exchange on CBW matters in existence. After Rhodesia transitioned to Zimbabwe, the legacy of the Rhodesian CBW effort disappeared into obscurity, however. Records were lost or destroyed, and a key South African link to the Rhodesian effort – Jan Coetzee – was dismissed before 'Project Coast' began. The

---

*   These statements are denied by both Basson and Knobel.

extant documentary record relating to 'Project Coast' is entirely ignorant of the Rhodesian experience, and the major 'Project Coast' players all claim no knowledge then of the Rhodesian effort.

Some South Africans brought knowledge of the Rhodesian poisons effort back. These men – Hans Dreyer and J.J. Viktor – had witnessed the Rhodesians produce and use CBW agents. Dreyer, in particular, was keenly interested in the CBW aspect, and Koevoet almost certainly 'inherited' much of the contaminated stocks left at the end of the Rhodesian conflict; however, no information exists to suggest that Koevoet made any operational use of its stocks of old Rhodesian poisoned food. Other remnants of the Rhodesian CBW warehouses were destroyed at Sybie van der Spuy's order in late 1980. The archive of Rhodesia's CBW activities was transferred in its entirety to South Africa, but almost certainly was destroyed either in van der Spuy's purge of EMLC documents, or in the general SADF's 1994 purge of sensitive documents. If South African Surgeon-General Nicolaas Nieuwoudt* had retained any of the documents he reportedly received on Rhodesian CBW activities, those papers may have been left for his successor, Daniel Knobel – yet Knobel claims absolutely no knowledge of the Rhodesian CBW effort.[55]

With the wholesale destruction of Rhodesian and apartheid-era South African Intelligence files, the question of whether knowledge derived from the Rhodesian experience was transmitted to South Africa may never be conclusively answered – yet the issue of how secret knowledge is developed, transmitted and retained remains an interesting and relevant topic for CBW analysts. In the Rhodesian case, knowledge was developed by trial and error; the approach to the science was amateurish. Tinkering was the rule of the day, and lessons were learned incrementally. As for knowledge retention, information on agents, processes, production and dissemination, very few records remain – and most of the key players are now dead. Most records are assumed destroyed, but the likelihood is that few records probably were ever produced. Knowledge – especially tacit knowledge (related to the processing of the agents) – remained with a very, very small group of people. To access that knowledge today would require the cooperation of the one or two surviving members of the Rhodesian CBW team and a probably equal number of South Africans involved in the knowledge transmission. This knowledge was transmitted person to person, much as the art of cooking is learned through experience in the kitchen; although recipes exist, chefs learn more from doing than reading cookbooks. Unfortunately, the key South Africans – Surgeon-General Nicolaas Nieuwoudt, General Lothar Neethling, General Fritz Loots and General Magnus Malan now are deceased; others – Jan Coetzee and Hans Dreyer – are too ill or incapacitated to address these topics; one – J.J. Viktor – refuses to discuss any of his experiences in Rhodesia. Here the story ends, unless miraculously, records appear to resolve any of the many unanswered questions.

---

* Nieuwoudt was Surgeon-General from 1977 to 1988. Jan Coetzee claimed that he provided a copy of the Rhodesian LD50 document to Nieuwoudt.

Unanswered questions

The key unanswered questions remain: first, what was the extent of the South African involvement in the Rhodesian CBW activities? Which South African entities and individuals were involved? What prompted their involvement and what was the purpose and intended goals behind their involvement?

Second, what was the South African contribution to the Rhodesian effort? What supplies, materials and scientific/technology knowledge was provided to Rhodesia? When did the cooperation begin? What specific materials and supplies were provided in what quantities and over what time period? What was the frequency of supply? Who and how often did South Africans visit Bindura and/or Inkomo Barracks? What was the purpose of those visits, what was discussed and who were the Rhodesian participants?

Third, what documents or records were exchanged? What topics were addressed? What did the documents or records contain? Do any remain in South African archives (particularly those of the SAPS, MoD or South African Intelligence services), or in the private collections of former Rhodesians – notably the Rhodesian Army archive, which was formerly housed in the British Empire and Commonwealth Museum? Given that the Rhodesian CBW archive was sent to South Africa in February/March 1980, to whom was it sent and what became of it?

Fourth, how did the Rhodesian CBW effort contribute to South Africa's CBW efforts? Was there an informal transmission of Rhodesian CBW lessons to 'Project Coast'? If one existed, it probably operated through Lothar Neethling via his personal connections to Wouter Basson and/or Daan Goosen. Did that channel exist?

Fifth, the question remains about the similarities between the Rhodesian and South African CBW efforts in their choice of agents and dissemination methods. If the legacy of the Rhodesian CBW effort did not pass to 'Project Coast' via official or informal channels, how are these similarities explained? The answer to that hotly-debated question remains unexplored. Interestingly, 'Project Coast' seems to have adopted many of the Rhodesian failures (anthrax-tainted cigarettes), as well as their successes (poisoned clothing).

Sixth, a time gap exists between the end of the Rhodesian CBW effort in early 1980 and the official beginning of 'Project Coast' in May 1981. Vernon Joynt has suggested that South African interest in CBW may have begun as early as 1977 – coincidentally, the time when Rhodesia's CBW effort was gathering momentum. When did South Africa begin to seriously look at a CBW capability post-World War II?

Seventh, the liaison at Bindura was a SAPS officer – not a military officer – and 'Project Coast' was a military program, with the implication being that information flowing through SAPS channels was not/would not be shared with the SADF. Did formal or informal mechanisms exist in the late 1970s by which information on the Rhodesian CBW effort would have been shared among different South African Government departments – notably between military intelligence, SAMS and SAPS?

Eighth, how do we weigh the credibility of vehement denials that the Rhodesian CBW effort and 'Project Coast' were ever connected? Every single South African officer linked to 'Project Coast' available to comment has denied any link between the

Rhodesian CBW effort and 'Project Coast'. Also, all have disclaimed any knowledge of the Rhodesian CBW effort – and these officers include former Surgeon-General Dr Daniel Knobel and Dr Wouter Basson. For the most part, an objective observer might be skeptical about these South African denials, but the question remains.

Notes

1   McGuinness told his FBI investigators in 2002 that the poison used in the clothes at JOC Bindura came from South Africa. The Rhodesians collaborated occasionally with the South Africans during the war. The barracks at Nkomo had an airfield on which the South Africans landed, and the South Africans would collaborate with Symington. See FBI interview with McGuinness (Case 279A-WF-222936), London, UK, dated 19 October 2002; redacted version released under FOIA, dated 5 December 2011.

2   McGuinness has critics and detractors. James Parker, author of *Assignment Selous Scout*, interviewed McGuinness at length and claims that he was far more revealing and unguarded in his interviews than with me. (Communication between James Parker and the author.)

3   Chandré Gould & Peter Folb, *Project Coast: Apartheid's Chemical and Biological Warfare Programme* (Geneva, Switzerland: United Nations Institute for Disarmament Research, 2002), p.17.

4   Jean de Villiers, 'Chemical and Biological Warfare in a South African Context in the Seventies', CBW151, dated 12 February 1971; Mechem archives in AL2922, 'The Chemical and Biological Warfare (CBW) Project Collection', South African History Archive.

5   Jean de Villiers, 'Strategic Implications of Chemical Warfare', CBW149, dated May 1977; Mechem archives in AL2922, 'The Chemical and Biological Warfare (CBW) Project Collection', South African History Archive.

6   Jean de Villiers, 'Handbook for the SADF Command System, Vol 1 National Security and Total War, Chapter 12: Application of Chemical and Biological Aspects of Total War', CBW145, dated July 1977; Mechem archives in AL2922, 'The Chemical and Biological Warfare (CBW) Project Collection', South African History Archive.

7   Jean de Villiers, 'Perspectives in Chemical Warfare' – lecture to be given to a joint meeting of the Northern Transvaal Branch of the SA Chemical Institute and the Institute for Strategic Studies, the University of Pretoria, CBW147, dated August 1982; Mechem archives in AL2922, 'The Chemical and Biological Warfare (CBW) Project Collection', South African History Archive.

8   ibid. In this paper, de Villiers waxes almost poetically about the allure of CBW: 'It is illuminating to sum up briefly how these various groups see chemical warfare. Many research scientists may initially have moral reservations about working on chemical warfare agents. But they will find chemical warfare a fascinating subject, full of intellectual stimulation and obscure byways, and these will, like any other intellectual problem, rapidly intrigue them and seduce them from practical judgements'.

9   See <http://www.nixt.co.za/viewpage.php?page_id=6>.

10   Doc/2, dated 21 September 2006. Basson and Daniel Knobel also recounted their association with Symington, when Symington was an external examiner to the University of Pretoria. (See emails to the author.)

11   As stated in previous chapters, a distinguished Selous Scout officer recalled discussions with South African scientists about deployable chemical agents. One of the few extant Special Branch documents also reported their dependence on South African supplies; lastly, one of McGuinness' lieutenants transported CBW-related materials to and from South Africa.

12   Parker, p.132.
13   Parker, p.164 for a reproduction of Special Branch report, File Number XYS 8777/7, dated 25 August 1977 from M.J.P. McGuinness to Officer Commanding Special Branch Headquarters and the Director-General CIO.
14   Selous Scout/2, personal communication, dated 30 October 2005.
15   Doc/2, dated 21 September 2006.
16   ibid.
17   Document/3 in the author's possession.
18   As described in previous chapters, McGuinness' operations – including the CBW effort – were funded almost exclusively from South African-provided funds.
19   JPS 700, Annex D, dated 20 August 1973 (see Appendix D).
20   According to SA/1 (who was a member of the CSIR team), he and Dr Jan Coetzee (who later joined EMLC) were part of the Applied Chemistry Unit (ACU) at the CSIR. CSIR's ACU was one of the earliest South African entities to become involved in CBW until the team decided to abandon CBW-related work. One member of the team had been asked to head the effort that became 'Project Coast', but declined. Dr Wouter Basson was the individual who made the offer and went on himself to lead 'Project Coast'. (See SA/1, personal communication, 7 January 2006.)
      Dr Jean de Villiers was responsible for South Africa's post-WWII research into chemical weapons. His research largely consisted of a literature review of possible CW agents and studies of their battlefield effectiveness based on historical case studies. SA/1 stated that when he took charge of the ACU, he turned all the CBW-related files to the South African military. De Villiers – founder of the former Unit for Applied Chemistry at the CSIR – led this very successful research group for 17 years. During this phase of his life, he received many medals and awards for his contributions to combating terrorism; the Order of the Star of South Africa (Commander) and the South African Police Medal for Combating Terrorism are among these. On Friday, 2 March 1984, de Villiers died of a heart attack while attending a Strategic Studies Symposium. He was 54 years old. (See <www.nixt.co.za/content/whoswho.html> (accessed on 21 May 2006.))
21   Reid-Daly (1999), p.474.
22   'When Dr Jan Coetzee left the ACU (CDU) at CSIR to go to EMLC he had gone to a rival organization that had absolutely no co-operation with ACU and later on with Mechem. On the contrary, they had used their official position to exclude us from Rhodesia and probably for security reasons had succeeded in doing so. The countermine, demolition involvement, and mine were getting good feedback from their hot war involvement and Coetzee's EMLC cut that off for at least a three-year period. To fill the vacuum left by the removal of CDU/Mechem in the explosive requirements of the Rhodesian Special Groups and for that matter the South African Special Forces EMLC also started doing explosives and mines. The latter also became one of the official responsibilities of EMLC'. (See SA/1, personal communication.)
23   Selous Scout/2, personal communication, dated 30 October 2005.
24   Doc/1, private communication in the author's hands, dated 19 July 2006, p.4.
25   Jeremy Brickhill, 'Zimbabwe's Poisoned Legacy: Secret War in Southern Africa', *Covert Action Quarterly* 43 (Winter 1992-1993), pp.7-10. Also see Mangold, p.220, citing then-Zimbabwean Health Minister Timothy Stamps' allegation that South Africa provided Rhodesia with anthrax for use in its counterinsurgency efforts.
26   Email to the author, dated 13 August 2009.
27   PBS interview with Timothy Stamps for program *Plague Wars* <http://www.pbs.org/wgbh/pages/frontline/shows/plague/sa/stamps.html> (accessed on 7 September 2015).

28   Document/3 in the author's possession.

29   Document/5 in the author's possession.

30   Burger and Gould (2002), p.16. According to Gould, she relied on Coetzee's trial testimony for the material found in the book and did not interview him separately. (Email from Gould to the author, dated 31 January 2005.) Also see 'Trial Report Number 34'; online at <http://ccrweb.ccr.uct.ac.za/archive/cbw/34.html> accessed on 10 August 2005: 'Coetzee founder and first managing director of EMLC said he was never involved in the killing of anyone by means of chemical substances. Coetzee did not know about the poisoned clothing found by van der Spuy. Coetzee said he was aware of experiments carried out with organophosphates on clothing in Rhodesia. In re-examination, Pretorius asked Coetzee to expand on his knowledge of organophosphates used in Rhodesia. He said he was approached on one occasion (prior to his departure from EMLC at the end of August, 1980) by a courier for Rhodesian Special Forces, who gave him a typed report, in point form, of toxic substances, including organophosphates, applied to various parts of the body, and outlining the exact results/effects'. In his testimony, van der Spuy stated that when he assumed control of EMLC in November 1980, he toured the facility and found a room containing a large amount of bulk chemicals and a carton of underwear. On going to inspect the clothing, an EMLC employee warned him not to touch the garments because they were poisoned. (See <http://ccrweb.ccr.uct.ac.za/archive/cbw/34.html>.)

31   Centre for Conflict Resolution, the University of Cape Town: published reports summarizing events during the course of Basson's trial. See Trial Report: 20b, Wednesday, 31 May 2000 (http://ccrweb.ccr.uct.ac.za/archive/cbw/cbw_index.html).

32   South African Chemical and Biological Warfare Programme, Trial Report: Fifty-Four. See <http://ccrweb.ccr.uct.ac.za/archive/cbw/54.html> (accessed on 29 May 2006).

33   Email from Dr Wouter Basson, dated 17 November 2011.

34   Photograph of Dr Wouter Basson; online at <http://www.vice.com/read/wouter-basson-dr-death-south-africa-ecstasy-957> (accessed on 18 September 2015).

35   Email with the author.

36   Email from Dr Wouter Basson to the author, dated 17 November 2011.

37   Stephen F. Burgess and Helen E. Purkitt, 'The Rollback of South Africa's Chemical and Biological Warfare Program' (USAF Counterproliferation Center: Air War College, Maxwell Air Force Base, April 2001), p.8.

38   Ellert, p.102.

39   Jeremy Brickhill, 'Doctors of Death', *Horizons* (Harare), March 1992, p.15.

40   'Vic Noble worked closely with Jan Coetzee and other unnamed South African personnel'. See Doc/2, dated 21 September 2006. Selous Scout/4 confirms that Jan Coetzee and Joe Visteer – then a major in the South African Special Forces and involved in the 'dirty tricks' side of operations – had both liaised with Bob Symington at Inkomo Barracks and at Special Forces Headquarters outside Pretoria, South Africa. See Selous Scout/4, personal communication, dated 9 August 2006.

41   Doc/1, dated 19 July 2006.

42   BSAP/12, personal communication, dated 24 April 2006. Viktor was technically assigned to SAP Security Branch Headquarters in Pretoria from 1976 to 1981. He retired in 1989 with the rank of Major General.

43   Doc/2, dated 21 September 2006. Dreyer's secret counterinsurgency unit was codenamed 'Koevoet' ('Crowbar'), which used Selous Scout-type tactics against insurgents in Namibia until 1989.

44   Ellert, p.101.

45   For his part, Viktor has stated that while in Bindura, he commanded a South African police element of approximately 60 men assigned to support BSAP 'Ground Coverage' efforts. He asserts he was not involved in the Rhodesian CBW effort, but was aware of it because McGuinness frequently mentioned it during social occasions. Viktor surmises that McGuinness used these revelations about the CBW effort to ingratiate himself with the South African.

46   Emails to the author from Dr Knobel and Dr Basson.

47   Trial Report 34 (Monday, 6 November 2000). See <http://ccrweb.ccr.uct.ac.za/archive/cbw/34.html> (accessed on 21 February 2011).

48   McGuinness. We also know from multiple sources that CIO and SB records were transferred *en masse* to South Africa – including the formulae and description of the processes used to produce the Rhodesian chemical agents. By February/March 1980, all of the Rhodesian CBW materials and records had been transferred to EMLC; the non-CBW-related equipment (cots, blankets, communist weapons) was delivered to Vlakplaas. Once in South Africa, some Special Branch records were destroyed; some were transferred to the South African Intelligence service BOSS (Bureau of State Security); and some were marked for eventual return to Zimbabwe. Having reviewed the index of SB documents retained for return to Zimbabwe, XYS-8777/7 is not among those files – leading me to conclude that the files on the Rhodesian CBW effort were either destroyed or turned over to the South African Defense Force CSI, or EMLC.

49   Doc/3, dated 19 October 2006.

50   '.. A storeroom in the farmhouse at Vlakplaas was stocked with supplies that Johan Viktor, in charge of Vlakplaas until the end of 1980, had received from his Rhodesian police friends after the bush war had ended … The rations for the askaris came out of a secret security fund and from Viktor's connections in the Rhodesian Special Branch … Coetzee was present at various conversations where former members of the Rhodesian Special Branch told how they had booby-trapped arms caches by removing the delay fuses of hand grenades, and poisoned food supplies, clothes and water holes used by guerrillas…' See Jacques Pauw, *In the Heart of the Whore: The Story of Apartheid's Death Squads* (Halfway House, South Africa: Southern Book Publishers, 1991), pp.47-48.

51   Hearing of Dirk Coetzee: <www.historicalpapers.wits.ac.za/inventories/inv_pdfo/AK2300/AK2300-A2-01-jpeg.pdf>, p.541 (accessed on 16 September 2015).

52   op cit., p.287.

53   'The Continuing Trial of Wouter Basson', *The CBW Conventions Bulletin*, Issue No.49 – Supplement (September 2000), p.1: <http://fas-www.harvard.edu/~hsp/bulletin/supp49.pdf> (accessed on 1 June 2006).

54   Eugene de Kock, *A Long Night's Damage: Working for the Apartheid State*, as told to Jeremy Gordin (Saxonwold, RSA: Contra Press, 1998), p.83.

55   Email communication with the author.

4

Rhodesian Anthrax Outbreak

Beginning in November 1978, Rhodesia experienced one of the largest epizootic outbreaks of anthrax in recorded human history. Coming as the Rhodesian War intensified – and coinciding with the Rhodesian use of chemical and biological weapons – some claim that the outbreak resulted from the deliberate spread of *Bacillus anthracis* spores by either Rhodesian or South African agents.[*] This chapter will describe the Rhodesian anthrax epizootic and discuss its likely causes. Given the suggestions by some that the Rhodesian anthrax outbreak was a deliberate act by the Rhodesian Security Forces, this chapter will demonstrate that the outbreak was a naturally occurring event exacerbated by the collapse of the nation's veterinary services due to the worsening security situation – chiefly in the rural areas.

Anthrax: background

As the causative agent of the zoonotic disease anthrax, *Bacillus anthracis* is a large (1-1.5 μm x 3-10 μm) gram-positive, spore-forming, nonmotile bacillus largely affecting domesticated and non-domesticated herbivores, but *anthracis* can infect a wide range of species. Found in the soils of endemic regions, *Bacillus anthracis* spores can survive in the environment for many decades. The disease has two known virulence factors: a tripartite protein exotoxin (lethal factor, edema factor and protective antigen) and an antiphagocytic capsule. The presence of the capsule is a key virulence factor; strains without a capsule exhibit a reduced virulence.[1] *Bacillus anthracis* is endemic to many parts of the world – including most of Southern Africa. Human cases of anthrax in the developed world are usually rare, but from 2000 to 2015, Turkey saw between 532 and 135 human cases per year, and only lately has Spain's annual total fallen below 30. Human outbreaks are not uncommon in Africa, Central Asia and China, and Latin America.

Disease characteristics

Clinical presentations of anthrax include cutaneous (95 percent of cases), inhalational, oropharyngeal and gastrointestinal forms; in addition, clinics lately have observed injection anthrax (largely due to recent incidents involving heroin

---

[*] Chief among the claimants are Jeremy Brickhill, David Martin and Meryl Nass.

addicts).[2] Anthrax is non-contagious, with only very rare person-to-person transmission.[3] Inoculation occurs when *Bacillus anthracis* spores enter the body through the skin or mucosa, where they are ingested by macrophages. The anaerobic conditions within the macrophages allow the spore to germinate into vegetative cells capable of producing the capsule and toxins. The bacteria proliferate inside the body and produce increasing amounts of toxins that attack leukocyte function. Impaired leukocyte function results in the pathological findings associated with anthrax – including edema, hemorrhage, tissue necrosis and leukocyte depletion.[4] Anthrax normally has a relatively short incubation period, though latent infections are known,[5] and the course of the disease progresses rapidly. Mortality rates vary depending on the type of clinical presentation, from 1 percent associated with cutaneous anthrax to 50 percent for oropharyngeal and gastrointestinal anthrax, to nearly 100 percent for inhalational anthrax. Death usually results from acute respiratory distress and shock. Cutaneous anthrax presents a limited differential diagnosis and is easily treated with any of several antibiotics – resulting in its low mortality rate.

According to the US Center for Disease Control's description:

> Cutaneous anthrax begins as a pruritic papule or vesicle that enlarges and erodes (1-2 days), leaving a necrotic ulcer with subsequent formation of a central black eschar; inhalation anthrax may begin as a prodrome of fever, chills, nonproductive cough, chest pain, headache, myalgias, and malaise, with more distinctive clinical hallmarks of hemorrhagic mediastinal lymphadenitis, hemorrhagic pleural effusions, bacteremia, and toxemia resulting in severe dyspnea, hypoxia, and septic shock; gastrointestinal anthrax may result in pharyngeal lesions with sore throat, dysphagia marked neck swelling and regional lymphadenopathy, or intestinal infection characterized by fever, severe abdominal pain, massive ascites, hematemesis, and bloody diarrhea. As with any form of anthrax, hemorrhagic meningitis can result from hematogenous spread of the organism from the primary site.[6]

Epidemiology of anthrax

Bacillus anthracis is found worldwide – and anthrax occurs naturally as a disease infecting herbivores grazing on grasses containing *Bacillus anthracis* spores. Mechanical spread of the disease can occur through biting flies, vultures and ravens (*Corvus corax*) feeding on contaminated carcasses. Vultures and ravens reportedly can mechanically contaminate water sources and pastures with *anthracis* spores over significant distances.[7] Blood-covered vultures subsequently bathing in cattle water troughs – sometimes at a significant distance from where the vultures had fed – can contaminate these water sources with *B. anthracis*. Bacterial amplification occurs when vegetative cells in a diseased animal multiply, the animal dies of the disease and the multiplied vegetative cells sporulate when the carcass is opened – exposing the cells to the environment. Certain alkaline soil conditions (pH > 6.0) and rainfall patterns combine to create 'anthrax zones' in areas with high herbivore populations;

for example, anthrax is endemic in regions in the United States associated with cattle drives and historical grazing areas.

Although cases of naturally occurring anthrax among humans in the developed world are rare, cases are found – chiefly in Asia and Africa – among individuals handling infected carcasses or hides (sources of cutaneous infection) and those persons consuming infected meat (gastrointestinal anthrax); as an aerosol, anthrax also is a possible biological weapon. In 2001, letters containing an anthrax powder killed five individuals and infected another 17 persons. The death toll almost certainly would have been higher if victims had not received intensive medical intervention – including broad-spectrum antibiotics and aggressive removal of toxic fluids from the thoracic cavity.

In humans, 95 percent of anthrax cases are cutaneous and occur when abraded skin is exposed to contaminated blood, hides, hair, wool, bone or meal; anthrax spores are unable to penetrate intact skin. In the United States, most cases of inhalational anthrax took place in an occupational context (textile mills – hence the name 'Woolsorter's disease') before the advent of an effective anthrax vaccine and improved hygiene and ventilation. Contaminated goat hair or wool was the primary vehicle of infection for cases in the modern United States; in those cases, workers handling raw, unprocessed (albeit dried) skin and hides were at the greatest risk of infection. Workers processing contaminated wool or hides in enclosed spaces were vulnerable to contracting anthrax if the processing machinery created an aerosol containing a sufficient quantity of *Bacillus anthracis* spores. No cases of gastrointestinal anthrax have been reported in developed nations because of the precautions preventing anthrax-contaminated meat from reaching market, though there have been some close calls.

Rhodesian anthrax epidemic

Anthrax is endemic to Rhodesia (now Zimbabwe) – affecting livestock and wildlife – but the occurrence of the disease in humans was confined to limited, sporadic outbreaks. Until the 1978 pandemic, anthrax occurred sporadically in Rhodesia and on a relatively small-scale, but the disease definitely was not unheard of. The total reported number of human anthrax cases from 1926 until the 1978-1980 epidemic probably did not amount to more than 500 (see Figure 4.1). The average mortality resulting from these cases was estimated at between 6 and 7 percent;[8] however, the historical record of anthrax outbreaks in Rhodesia is incomplete. According to a team of researchers at the University of Zimbabwe, '... during the pre-independence era (before 1980), the incidence of anthrax (in animal populations) could not be accurately determined as data on anthrax and other diseases could not be collected systematically, especially in rural areas ... In most instances, many anthrax outbreaks, particularly in rural areas, were unlikely to have been diagnosed...'

A minor outbreak affecting humans did occur in April 1974 in the Mondoro Tribal Trust Land – first affecting cattle before spreading to humans.[9] According to Roberts and Chambers, the anthrax outbreak occurred at the end of an exceptionally heavy rainy season. Rains are associated with anthrax outbreaks because periods of heavy rains lead to the hatching of tabanids, which are often thought to contribute to the

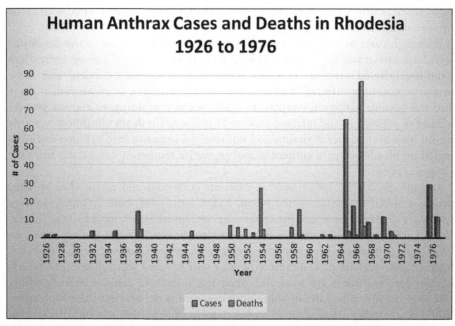

Figure 4.1 Reported human anthrax cases (and deaths) in Rhodesia, 1926-1976. (Source: the author's work, based on statistical data taken from J.C.A. Davies, 'A Major Epidemic of Anthrax in Zimbabwe', *The Central African Journal of Medicine* 28 (December 1982), p.291)

spread of the disease.[10] The chief veterinary officer at Gatooma received reports of a large number of sudden cattle deaths; anthrax was suspected and later confirmed. Six human cases (including two deaths) of cutaneous anthrax were reported – and of these six cases, three involved lesions on the hand, one had a lesion on the head, one had a lesion on the chest and one had a lesion on the neck. Case One had slaughtered an infected cow, and two of the other cases lived in the same compound (*kraal*).[11] In all cases, the transmission of anthrax was attributed to handling raw, contaminated meat; handling contaminated butchering knives; having contact with contaminated cattle hides; or being bitten by insects.

The 1978-1980 anthrax epidemic began with an unknown number of bovine deaths in the Nkayi District of the Matabeleland North Province, probably in mid-1978. Calculating the total number of cattle deaths due to the anthrax outbreak is difficult, but the figure possibly amounted to hundreds of thousands of cattle.[*] Given that only 11 cattle in the commercial farming areas reportedly were affected, the communal herd[†] in the TTLs suffered the greatest losses.

---

[*]   According to Dr Stuart Hargreaves, the Rhodesian rule of thumb was that four cattle cases occurred for every one human case.

[†]   In Rhodesia at the time, the cattle population was divided into two categories: the first was the commercial herd, which was made up of cattle from largely European stock on modern

As of 31 December 1977, the communal herd size had peaked at 3,388,000 head; a year later, the herd size had fallen by 430,000 head (13 percent decrease) after more than a decade of continual growth. According to Dr Stuart Hargreaves – the former chief government veterinary scientist in Rhodesia: '… It is estimated that 1,000,000 head of communal cattle died during the war from disease … mainly tick borne, but also anthrax and trypanosmiasis in Tsetse-infested areas'.[12] Quantifying how much of this loss was attributable to the anthrax epidemic – and how much was due to wartime uncertainties (including cattle thefts and other types of loss) – is impossible, but, the epidemic almost certainly was a significant contributor to livestock losses in the communal herd. [13] According to the *Chronicle* (Bulawayo newspaper), as of 1 August 1979, approximately 750,000 head of cattle were dead of anthrax – and more than 90 percent of cattle in the Honde Valley had perished from the disease.[14] The graph in Figure 4.2 below demonstrates the steep decline in the communal herd from 1977 to 1978. Although this decline is due to all causes (disease, theft etc.), the loss coincides with the onset of the anthrax epizootic.

The human cases appeared after the initial bovine deaths – and the exact time between the initial cattle deaths and the first human cases of anthrax remains unknown. Cattle deaths in the communal herd were not often reported, given that the worsening security situation hampered the ability of government workers to operate in rural areas late in the war. Government efforts to persuade villagers to produce their cattle for vaccination failed[16] – and villagers also feared reporting dead or diseased animals to veterinary workers out of a real fear of being labeled government collaborators, or 'sell-outs'.[17] Even in peacetime, veterinary workers rarely found dead livestock; the common practice was to scavenge dead animals.* All these factors contribute to uncertainty over the exact number of livestock deaths due to anthrax during this period.

The outbreak first occurred in the Ndebele TTLs, where the bulk of Rhodesia's communal herd grazed. The epidemic quickly spread – infecting cattle and humans from the Matabeleland North Province through the Midlands Province to Mashonaland. Eventually, cases were reported in five of Rhodesia's six provinces. Rapid and extensive spread of anthrax outbreaks is not uncommon: similar events were reported in West Texas in 2006 and in Italy in 2004.[18]

---

commercial beef or dairy farms that were owned and operated by white Rhodesians. According to World Bank statistics, the approximate size of the Rhodesian commercial herd was 3,128,000 head of cattle. Ninety-eight percent of the commercial herd were beef cattle, and the remainder were dairy cows. The communal herd consisted of cattle – often hybrid African breeds – belonging to African villagers engaged in subsistence agriculture. The communal herd was used as draught animals and as a symbol of status and wealth – and for milk, meat and manure. Cattle in the communal herd were seen as substitutes for bank accounts and insurance policies, and were exchanged as bridal dowries.

* Unlike the San tribe, the Matabele and Shona peoples have no cultural taboos or restrictions preventing them from consuming livestock that died of disease.

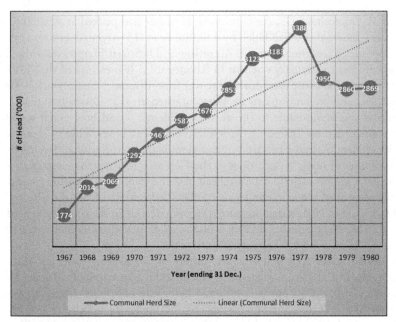

Figure 4.2 Size of the Rhodesian communal herd. (Source: the author's work, based on statistical data taken from John C. Barrett, 'The Economic Role of Cattle in Communal Farming Systems in Zimbabwe', <http://www.odi.org.uk/pdn/papers/32b.pdf>)[15]

Figure 4.3 Scavenging carrion meat. (Source: from the collection of the late Professor Margaretha Isaacson, with permission. © reserved by the South African National Institute for Communicable Diseases, part of the National Health Laboratory Service (NICD/NHLS))

Matabeleland North Province

The anthrax epidemic first manifested as a localized outbreak in the Nkayi District of Matabeleland North Province. On 24 November 1978, the first reported human anthrax case presented to Nkayi Rural Hospital with a cutaneous anthrax lesion – the result of butchering and skinning a diseased animal.[19] From 1978 to June 1979, human cases of anthrax were confined to the Nkayi region; in October 1979, the disease was reported in Lupane, west of Nkayi. At the Christian Care Field Hospital at St Paul's Mission – a settlement in the Eastern Lupane District – 913 human cases of cutaneous anthrax were seen between March 1980 and October 1980.

Anthrax cases were reported in all the cattle-grazing areas in and around St Paul's Mission. According to Dr Davies, the population in the area relied on meat (even if contaminated) as their major food source, given a shortage of all alternative food supplies.[20] The total number of human anthrax cases reported in Matabeleland Province was 2,065 – of which 1,769 (86 percent) originated in the Nkayi District. Davies also claimed that he heard reports that many people had died without seeking medical treatment.[21] If so, the unreported death toll would push the total disease mortality to much higher levels.

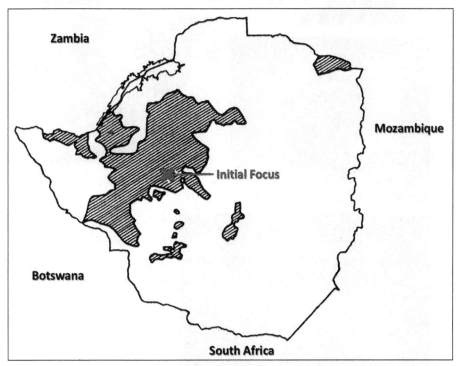

Figure 4.4 Areas of anthrax infection in Rhodesia in 1979. (Source: derived from J.A. Lawrence, C.M. Foggin and R.A.I. Norval, 'The Effects of War on the Control of Diseases of Livestock in Rhodesia (Zimbabwe)', *The Veterinary Record* 107 (26 July 1980), p.84)

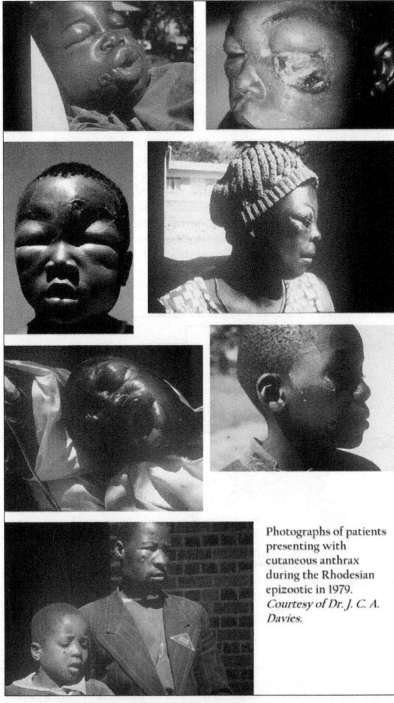

Photographs of patients presenting with cutaneous anthrax during the Rhodesian epizootic in 1979. *Courtesy of Dr. J. C. A. Davies.*

Figure 4.5 Anthrax patients. (Source: Dr. J.C.A. Davies, with permission)

Midlands Province

Until mid-1979, human cases of anthrax seemed confined to Nkayi and Lupane, but by June 1979, the disease was identified in the bordering region of the Que Que (now Kwekwe) District, Midlands Province. According to Davies, the Que Que and Nkayi Districts were similar in that each had economies dominated by cattle production and associated livestock industries. Once anthrax was present in Que Que, the disease did not spread to adjacent districts in the Midlands Province. Que Que reported 6,491 of the human cases in the Midlands Province (98 percent) and 99 fatalities (99 percent of those dying in Midlands); all reported cases were cutaneous.[22] Curiously, in Gwelo (Midlands Province) – west of Que Que – the Bata shoe factory, which processed 130,000 cattle hides a year, experienced no cases of anthrax among its workers.[23] The assumption here is that the Bata shoe factory purchased its hides from commercial herd suppliers – thus minimizing (if not eliminating) the anthrax risk from those hides.

By October 1979, the Zimbabwe-Rhodesian Department of Veterinary Services had issued a health warning regarding the anthrax epizootic advising that people should avoid eating meat from sick animals, or from animals that had died inexplicably. According to the report, 21 people by then had died, and 500 people had been treated for anthrax. The disease reportedly had broken out in the tribal areas of Lupane, Umzingwant, Gwelo, Que Que, Gatooma and Lomagundi.[24]

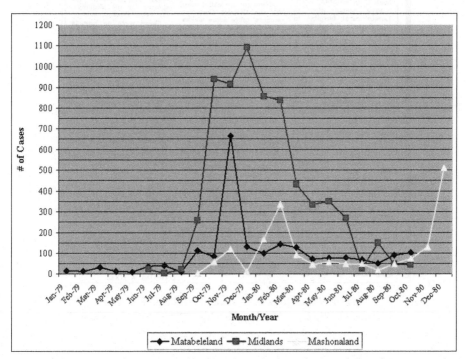

Figure 4.6 Human anthrax cases in Rhodesia. (Source: the author's work, based on statistics in Table 5 found in Davies (1982), p.296)

As the disease spread,* the incidence of anthrax in humans seems to have 'hopped' over bordering regions in November 1979, when it was identified in districts south and east of Bulawayo (135km south of the original epicenter). As Dr Davies points out, the disease in humans very unusually 'hopped' over areas that were disease-free; diseases usually spread contiguously – and geographic 'hops' are unusual.

Anthrax toll is now 13

THE known human death toll from anthrax in Matabeleland and, the Midlands is now 13. More than 370 people with the disease have been given treatment in rural hospitals.

Herald Correspondent: BULAWAYO

A reliable source said yesterday: "There is no doubt that many more people have died in the bush from anthrax."

Five people died in Loreto rural hospital in the Silobela Tribal Trust Land: four in Que Que hospital; and four, one of them yesterday morning in Nkai rural hospital.

Anthrax broke out in the Nkai Tribal Trust area of Matabeleland in January. Because of security problems in the area the exact number of stock deaths is not known.

"We think many more than 1 000 cattle have died, and many goats and sheep," a Department of Veterinary Services spokesman said.

"We believe the Matabeleland outbreak is moving towards the Lupane area."

Despite problems in mounting vaccination campaigns in security sensitive areas, 13 233 cattle were vaccinated by the Department's teams in January

and July this year. The vaccinations were carried out in Nkai village and areas close to it.

Through a leaflet-drop by the District Commissioners' office some weeks ago, tribesmen have been urged to bring more cattle to collection points, for vaccinating.

"When we hear that tribesmen are willing to bring their cattle along, we will arrange vaccinations in other parts of Nkai," the spokesman said.

2 000 DOSES

In the past six weeks, 2 000 doses of the vaccine have been bought by Nkai tribesmen who came into the department's offices in Bulawayo, the spokesman said.

"The vaccine is very cheap and gives immunity for at least one year, probably much longer," he said.

Anthrax spread from the Nkai district into

Lower Gwelo, Silobela and Zhombe Tribal Trust lands, and many cattle in those areas have died, the senior animal health inspector for the Midlands, Mr Peter Benzon, said.

There were no reports of the disease in the Gokwe district north of Nkai, but the department of veterinary services cannot get into the area to check animals.

It is tracing the spread of the disease by the human cases, he said.

The contamination can last for years, the spokesman said. Any warm-blooded animal can contract anthrax. Any person or other animal that eats anthrax-infested flesh will get the disease. It is also spread to humans by breathing in the anthrax spores, he said.

The Provincial Medical Officer of Health for the Midlands, Dr I. M. Campbell, said that by the end of September there were 260 recorded cases of anthrax among people in his province.

Another source said that up to the end of July, 116 people with anthrax were being treated in Nkai.

eaders are

Figure 4.7 *Rhodesian Herald* (Rhodesia) on the anthrax outbreak. (Source: 'Anthrax Toll Now is 13', *Rhodesian Herald* (9 October 1979), permission requested)

---

*   Note that the spread of anthrax in Rhodesia for this time period was observed though recorded human cases; no means exists to chart the anthrax spread through the animal populations.

Of the 39 human cases admitted to hospitals in Bulawayo, 20 deaths were reported. Of those 20 deaths, five were due to gastrointestinal anthrax; one was due to anthrax-related meningitis; and two were cases of septicemic anthrax.[25] These 'hops' relate only to human cases and may have resulted from the smuggling and black market butchering of diseased cattle. The deaths attributed to gastrointestinal anthrax point to consumption of spore-contaminated meat; aso, as Rhodesia's second largest city, Bulawayo would have drawn anthrax patients from a wide area. That these patients presented to hospitals in Bulawayo does not indicate that the disease had spread to Bulawayo itself.

Mashonaland Province

During this epidemic, the first recorded human case of anthrax in Mashonaland was identified in the Sanyati communal areas north of Gatooma in September 1979 (Gatooma was the site of the 1974 outbreak).[26] The disease reportedly spread throughout most of Eastern Mashonaland – prevented possibly from reaching Rhodesia's north-western border with Zambia by the tsetse fly infestation zone.*

The explosive growth and epidemiological curve associated with this anthrax epidemic in Mashonaland can be seen in the statistics from Mrewa District Hospital.

Environmental factors supporting naturally occurring anthrax outbreaks

Our current understanding of anthrax ecology in Southern Africa – particularly in the Rhodesia of the 1970s – raises unanswered questions about the life cycle of anthrax in that environment and the conditions necessary for an anthrax outbreak to occur. According to the World Health Organization paper on anthrax: 'Much has been written and hypothesized about the effects of season, rainfall, temperature, soil, vegetation, host condition, and population density on the epidemiology of anthrax, but little agreement exists on the roles played by these factors in the incidence of the disease'.[27]

Able to remain viable after decades in the soil, *B. anthracis* spores are highly resistant to environmental factors – including heat, dehydration, microbial competitors or soil conditions. *B. anthracis* spores do not propagate in soil, despite earlier work to the contrary, however.[28] According to Pepper and Gentry, '... spores probably do not germinate under normal soil conditions, but instead require a host for germination and infection with proliferation via an animal-soil-animal cycle...'[29]

---

*   Tsetse flies infest the north-western regions of Rhodesia along the Zambezi River – making those areas unsuitable for cattle grazing. The tsetse fly is the principal insect vector for trypanosomiasis ('African sleeping sickness') – a devastating disease in cattle, horses and humans caused by protozoa (*Trypanosoma brucei* var. *gambiense* and *rhodesiense*). The tsetse fly infestation belt is thought to have limited the spread of Islam and European settlement into much of Africa's interior until the mid-to-late 19th century.

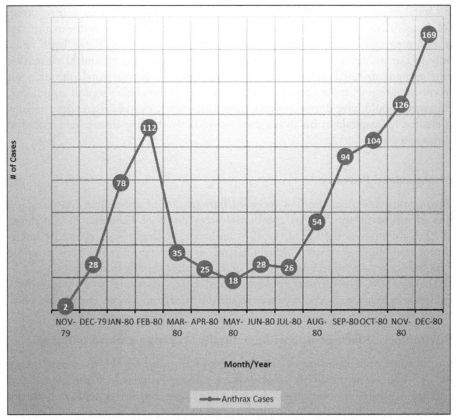

Figure 4.8 Anthrax cases seen at Mrewa District Hospital, Mashonaland. (Source: the author's work, based on statistics derived from J.C.A. Davies (1982), p.297)

The more accepted theory is that once deposited in the soil, *anthracis* spores remain dormant until suitable environmental conditions exist for an outbreak. Work by Kellogg, Prestwood and Noble on anthrax among white-tailed deer stated:

> The idea that anthrax outbreaks often "develop" in an area, rather than "spread" to it, is strongly suggested by this epizootic. Conditions favouring anthrax were: previous occurrence of anthrax in the area, high deer population, low food supply, bottomland soils, presence of large numbers of biting flies, high summer temperatures, drought conditions, and utilization of stagnant lakes for water supply.[30]

The most research seems to indicate that the disease course associated with anthrax limits the geographic spread of anthrax and the duration of the outbreak. Anthrax is not contagious, with little evidence of animal-to-animal transmission, except in cases in which cattle lick the cutaneous anthrax lesions on others in the herd ('salty-split'). Human-to-human transmission is extremely rare and is limited to direct contact with infectious fluids seeping from a cutaneous anthrax lesion.[31] *B. anthracis* is infectious only in its spore form; the vegetative cells are not themselves infectious. The vegetative cells sporulate when environmentally stressed (e.g. dehydration conditions, oxygen exposure, nutrient shortage, temperature increases, microbial competition etc.). The *B. anthracis* spores are deposited in the soil and water when infected animals die and exude contaminated bodily fluids from their orifices; contamination also occurs when scavengers open the carcasses. Once the vegetative *B. anthracis* cells are exposed to the atmosphere, they begin to sporulate; if the carcasses are not opened, the cells have a limited viability. Scavengers potentially can transport *anthracis* spores over significant distances. Research has indicated that carrion vultures will carry *anthracis* spores from carcass sites to distant watering holes where they bathe.[32] Seasonal climatic variations may lead to other conditions that would support an anthrax outbreak – chiefly environmental stresses that limit the food/water supplies, immunosuppress animal health and promote large vector populations.

Peter Turnbull wrote:

> The examination of associations between climatic conditions and peak anthrax periods around the world has resulted in a number of other theories. Some contribute to the hypothesis that an animal can harbour the spores for long periods, only manifesting the disease when stressed or compromised immunologically; seasonal stress may play a role in this regard. Others believe that acquisition of the disease by inhalation of spore-laden dust is not infrequent. The extent to which this might occur would vary with season. It is widely accepted that, in some regions, certain types of flies transmit anthrax; again, this would be associated with season.[33]

The role of the flood-drought cycle is frequently cited in relation to the occurrence of anthrax outbreaks,[34] but whether drought conditions are necessary for an anthrax epidemic remains undetermined. The secondary literature indicates that anthrax outbreaks occur during drought periods following prolonged rainy seasons with flooding. The argument is that the rains wash the *B. anthracis* spores to low-lying areas, where the higher concentrations are more likely to infect cattle. The same type of argument posits that as anthrax-contaminated waterholes shrink during droughts, concentrations of spores are left on vegetation at the edge of the waterhole. Droughts also force animals to congregate and to travel longer distances as they search for water. Canadian researchers found in their study of bison affected by anthrax that: '... The flood-drought meteorological cycle preceding an outbreak results in diminished food and water resources, crowding around the remaining resources, sweltering weather, and high concentrations of biting insects. All these factors could contribute to an overall immunosuppression of the bison...'[35]

Droughts also force cattle to graze on shorter grasses – causing them to feed closer to the ground – thereby making their inhalation of spore-laden dust more likely. In one interpretation, the "incubator theory' suggests that spores are concentrated in low-lying areas during rainfall events and animals are subsequently exposed to contaminated soil during foraging in dry periods'.[36]

Naturally occurring anthrax outbreaks in endemic regions exhibit a seasonality – typically occurring during periods of droughts following heavy rainfall. Estimating the onset of the Rhodesian anthrax outbreak from the first reported human case, the outbreak probably began shortly before or during November 1978 after a period of below-average rainfall that followed a dry winter. In the preceding years, Rhodesia had experienced a multi-year drought – stretching from roughly 1964 to 1974. Rainfall in 1975 was slightly above the national mean, with rainfall totals for 1976 through to 1982 significantly above the national mean. Rainfall is an important factor, in that rains can wash *anthracis* spores from the soil to low-lying collection pools. Once the rainwater evaporates, the soil there contains a higher concentration of spores.[37] In the classic anthrax outbreak scenario, drought limits the forage available to cattle, so they resort to less desirable woody materials that abrade their mouths. The higher summer temperatures then reduce their innate immunity – making them susceptible to even a small number of *anthracis* spores.[38] The higher-than-average rains preceding a hot-dry season also create ideal conditions for a large hatch of possible insect vectors – including blowflies and biting flies.

The precipitation data shown below in Figures 4.9 and 4.10[39] demonstrates that November 1978 rainfall in the selected Rhodesian regions was above average in three out of four selected towns. The decreased annual rainfall for these years followed an above-average rainfall, and the dry season in the Rhodesian winter of 1978 also seems to have been shorter than preceding years. A prolonged period of hot and dry weather followed a heavy rain season.

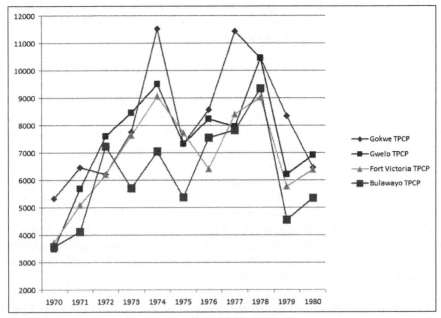

Figure 4.9 Annual precipitation totals for four Rhodesian towns. (Source: the author's work, using data derived from the US National Oceanographic author's work and the atmospheric administration database)

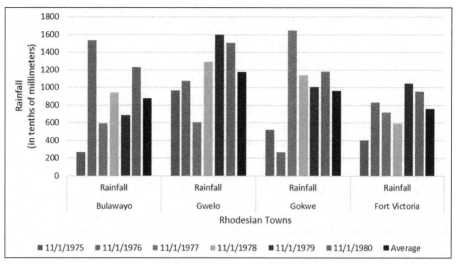

Figure 4.10 November rainfall for four Rhodesian sites, 1975-1979. (Source: the author's work, using data derived from the US National Oceanographic author's work and the atmospheric administration database)

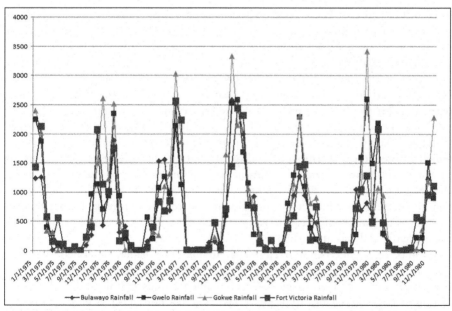

Figure 4.11 Rhodesian monthly rainfall totals for four locations. (Source: the author's work, using data derived from the US National Oceanographic author's work and the atmospheric administration database)

Some evidence suggests that anthrax can be contracted when cattle drink contaminated water; *B. anthracis* spores in water remain in their spore form and should remain infective. According to Pepper and Gentry: '... no tendency of *B. anthracis* spores to germinate in natural waters without the addition of heart infusion broth. The authors also found that, unlike spores, vegetative *B. anthracis* cells introduced into water samples rapidly died, dropping from the approximately 106 CFU ml inoculum to undetectable levels within 24 h...'[40] The major obstacle to anthrax infectivity from contaminated water is the dilution factor. Depending on the size of the body of water – and whether it is stagnant or flowing – *B. anthracis* contamination of water sufficient to cause infection probably would be difficult: cattle water troughs are the exception – and pores have been recovered from sediment in cattle watering troughs.[41]

Possible transmission paths

Several possible transmission paths have been posited to explain the Rhodesian epidemic of the late 1970s. Most of these theories take into account the wartime conditions (i.e. the collapse of veterinary and healthcare services, food shortages in the TTLs, disruption of transportation in rural areas, guerrilla activity and Security Force reactions) to explain the severity and extent of the epidemic. According to Dr Stuart Hargreaves – a seasoned veterinarian in Rhodesia at the time: 'In the years before the pandemic, vaccination was carried out immediately in any area where anthrax occurred, and the disease was effectively controlled. Quarantine and movement controls were also enforced. Large-scale vaccinations were not done as it was not necessary. Almost every commercial farmer vaccinated his cattle during the pandemic, and this prevented commercially owned cattle contracting the disease'.[42]

Undoubtedly, the Rhodesian conflict exacerbated the epidemic. Guerrillas targeted veterinary workers and cattle dip tanks – and many dip tanks were destroyed during the war; preventative veterinary health measures in the TTLs were halted out of concern for the safety of veterinary workers. As the war intensified, guerrilla operations caused the rural veterinary and health services to collapse, which limited the government's ability to contain the disease. Disease control measures that were routine in peacetime became impractical by the late 1970s. At the epidemic's start, veterinary workers could not check the health of much of the communal herd, or conduct vaccinations to control the outbreak. Davies reports that one veterinary health team was dispatched to a TTL to vaccinate cattle during the epidemic and was ambushed.[43]

Anthrax researcher Antonio Fasanella, in his 2014 paper, described epidemic anthrax outbreaks as evolutions from the classic outbreak pattern that became epidemic because of hemorrhagic insects (notably tabanids, gadflies etc.).[44] The association of large biting flies (typically tabanids – aka horseflies) to anthrax cases is often noted in the scientific literature. Female tabanids are hematophagous (consume mammalian blood); the males feed solely on plant nectar. The female tabanids have large mouthparts (maxillae) that tear open the skin in a scissor-like fashion. The wound often is deep and painful, and results in a significant blood pool. The amount of blood on the fly's mouthparts can be considerable, as is the pain to the mammal. When disturbed, the fly will travel a short distance and resume feeding – often on a neighboring animal or nearby herd. The female tabanid moving from animal to animal in a short period of time can result in the transmission of pathogens from one animal to another. The tabanid's high mobility; its large mouth/feeding parts; its behavior following disrupted feeding; and the size of the potential blood meal characterize this species as an excellent potential vector for anthrax transmission.[45] Research into an anthrax outbreak that affected a white-tailed deer population in the United States correlated the disease outbreak with tabanids.[46, 47, 48] The scientific literature also reports human anthrax infection resulting from a tabanid bite.

Tabanids were present in significant numbers during the Rhodesian anthrax epidemic, and the first anthrax cases coincided with the start of seasonal tabanid activity. The published literature of the Rhodesian epidemic contains reports of individuals who stated that they had been bitten by flies and, subsequently, developed cutaneous anthrax lesions.[49]

According to Peter Turnbull, the human subcutaneous ID_{50}:

> probably is in the order of tens of spores rather than thousands. If one tabanid fails to deliver that, then if you are bitten by several flies, the chances of one or more of the bites resulting in infection increases. The same goes for the cattle, for which, again, there are very few data, none especially reliable, on transcutaneous infectious doses.[50]

The tabanid role in human anthrax cases seems highly probable based on the reported tabanid involvement in transmitting anthrax in Rhodesia, other accounts of tabanid transmission and the experimental data.

According to Turrell and Knudson's research:

> Various forms of evidence strongly suggest that flies play a role in the transmission of B. anthracis to humans and domestic animals during an anthrax outbreak. This evidence includes the cutaneous anthrax cases associated with insect bites in both Zimbabwe and India, the demonstrated ability of several species of hematophagous diptera to transmit B. anthracis mechanically for at least 4 h after contact with an infected animal; and the ability of other diptera to contaminate surfaces with B. anthracis, either with spores in their feces or by direct contamination with spores or vegetative forms on their body surfaces.[51]

Turrell and Knudson's research was designed to optimize conditions for anthracis transmission, however. They chose the rodent species most susceptible to contracting anthrax, shaved the animals' fur to expose skin to the insect vector and held the insect vector in a cage next to the exposed portion of the animals. The experiment demonstrated that tabanids and stable flies can mechanically transmit anthrax, but questions remain as to whether these experimental conditions help explain anthrax epidemics.

According to Arnold Kaufmann:

> If the bacteremia level is 107/ml and the amount of blood on fly mouth parts post-feeding is 0.01 ml, the number of B. *anthracis* bacilli on the mouth parts would be about 10^5. If efficiency of mechanical transfer from the mouth parts to a second host is 1%, the number of B. *anthracis* bacilli transferred would be about 1,000. This dose would certainly be within the range of susceptibility of the mouse and guinea pig.[52]

The evidence from the Rhodesian anthrax epidemic – and other documented cases of anthrax in humans – points to tabanids as a likely anthrax vector for transmission to humans.[53] Anthrax transmission via tabanids also is seasonally dependent: in Rhodesia, tabanids are most active during the spring and summer months, or during its rainy season (from November through to April).

The pattern of highest tabanid activity correlates with the Rhodesian anthrax outbreak in humans – supporting the recorded observations that tabanids are linked to the occurrence of human anthrax cases. Figure 4.12 above demonstrates that tabanid activity in Rhodesia corresponds strongly with the warmer, wetter Rhodesian summer beginning in November and lasting until about March. This seasonal increase in insect activity also correlates with the first human case of anthrax reported in the 1978 Rhodesian anthrax epidemic (November 1978).

Other insect vectors associated with anthrax include blowflies (family *Calliphoridae*), stable flies (*Stomoxys calcitrans*) and mosquitoes (family *Culicidae*). Blowflies often are

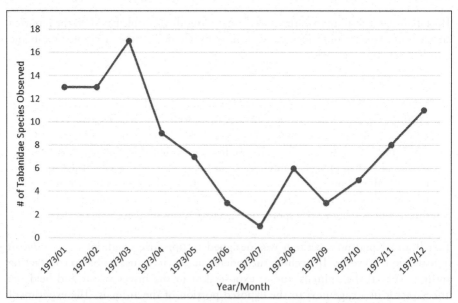

Figure 4.12 Annual tabanid activity in Rhodesia by month. (Source: the author's work, based on statistics found in J.C.A. Davies, 'A Major Epidemic of Anthrax in Rhodesia', *Central African Journal of Medicine* 29 (January 1983), p.10)

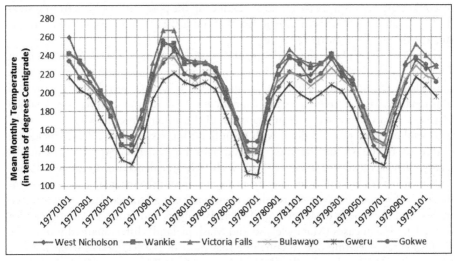

Figure 4.13 Temperatures for selected Rhodesian towns. (Source: the author's work, using data derived from the US National Oceanographic author's work and the atmospheric administration database)

carrion feeders – ingesting anthrax spores as part of a carrion meal – but the flies will not bite living animals (therefore, the blowflies' role in anthrax transmission is limited to depositing spores on vegetation through vomitus or feces). Blowflies deposit their anthrax-contaminated vomitus and feces on vegetation at a height of 1 to 3 meters close to the carcass on which they had fed. Browsing herbivores consuming the contaminated vegetation then become infected with anthrax. This observation explains the possible transmission from carrion to deer, antelope, kudu and other browsers.

Prevalent in Rhodesia, stable flies are biting flies that can mechanically transmit anthrax spores from an infected animal under ideal conditions:[54]

> The minimal transmission rate was five of 24 (21%) for flies held for 4 h or less after their initial exposure. None of the five flies transmitted *B. anthracis* 24 h after their initial exposure. Transmission to mice, although slightly lower, with 1 of 8 mice for 1 of 12 flies (minimal transmission rate, 8%), was not significantly different from transmission to guinea pigs … Although transmission rates were relatively low in this study, 17% for stable flies and 12% for mosquitoes, the high population densities of many hematophagous diptera and the numerous bites they inflict on humans and domestic animals imply that mechanical transmission may play a role in the dissemination of this agent … In addition to the species tested in our study, *B. anthracis* has also been mechanically transmitted by *Tabanus striatus*, *Haematobia irritans*, and various species of mosquitoes.[55]

The blood meal associated with stable flies is significantly smaller than the meal associated with tabanids. The smaller blood meal size reduces the likelihood that a stable fly could transmit anthrax to humans – excluding the possibility of bites from several flies – and almost excludes the possibility that stable flies are responsible for transmitting the disease from cattle to cattle.

In trying to explain the widespread transmission of anthrax to humans in Rhodesia, insect bites and the butchering and handling of contaminated meat are the most plausible causes. By comparing cutaneous anthrax cases from Matabeleland and Mashonaland (Rhodesia) with cases from a cutaneous anthrax outbreak in Anatolia (Turkey), the evidence seems clear that most of the human cases in Rhodesia[56] probably resulted from tabanid bites, with meat-handling resulting in a lower incidence of disease. In the Rhodesian cases, tabanid bites most likely occurred on the heads, faces and necks (exposed areas of skin), with fewer incidence on the fingers, hands and forearms (likely infection sites from meat handling). According to the patient histories, the cases in Anatolia resulted from butchering and handling raw infected meat – and the lesions developed on the hands, fingers and arms. The lesion pattern in the Rhodesian cases (Matabeleland and Mashonaland) differs markedly from the Turkish cases – leading one to conclude that most of the Rhodesian cases resulted from insect bites, whereas the Turkish cases resulted from contaminated meat handling. Although the two Rhodesian lesion patterns are remarkably similar, they differ in that the Mashonaland cases exhibited a greater percentage of lesions on the arms (and a small increase in the percentage of lesions found on the legs and thighs) than did the Matabeleland cases. The percentage increase of cases involving the arms may be due to insect bites or handling infected meat, and the increased incidence of lesions on the legs and thighs probably is due to bites from anthrax-carrying insects. Anthrax lesions also may result from scratching and abrading skin by using fingernails contaminated with spore-laden blood or soil. In cases where an individual has multiple cutaneous anthrax lesions, the victim may have scratched the lesion and transferred spores to other abraded skin sites. This may explain the incidence of cutaneous anthrax eschars near eyes and on the faces of patients.

Transmission via contaminated meat should not be dismissed as a contributing factor in the spread of cutaneous anthrax. The Rhodesian anthrax cases involving hand lesions suggest that almost 30 percent of cases at St Luke's Mission may have become infected due to butchering or handling anthrax-contaminated meat.

According to Dr Stuart Hargreaves:

> Dead animals are also most commonly eaten by people ... Anthrax carcasses in the communal areas are almost never observed by veterinarians, and anthrax is almost exclusively diagnosed in the clinic or hospital due to infected human cases who have consumed or handled infected meat. Animals that die acutely are almost always cut up and eaten by people before the predators have a chance, and this habit occurs no matter how much extension work is done in order to sensitise [sic] people to the dangers of eating dead animals before veterinary clearance is given. The other issue is that communal families on average number about 7 or more people. Large families are common, unlike in developed countries. Thus when a bovine animal dies, the local community is called and large numbers of families may purchase the meat, thus exposing large numbers of

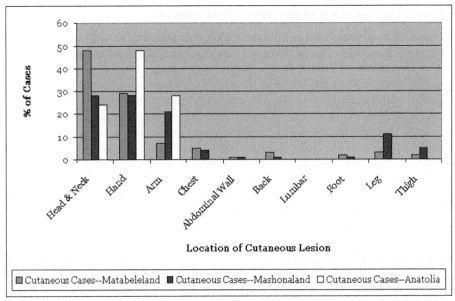

Figure 4.14 Comparison of cutaneous anthrax lesion sites. (Source: the author's work, based on data for the Rhodesian cases derived from J.C.A. Davies (1982), p.293. Data for the Turkish cases was derived from K. Demirdag, M. Ozden, Y. Saral, A. Kalkan, S.S. Kilic and A. Ozdarendeli, 'Cutaneous Anthrax in Adults: A Review of 25 Cases in the Eastern Anatolian Region of Turkey', *Infection* 31 (2003), p.328)[57]

people to the disease. Perhaps 20 to 30 families may purchase or receive meat from one carcass, thus exposing over 100 people to the disease. This may be a conservative estimate, and many more people could become exposed from one bovine carcass. One only has to get several hundred animals dying from anthrax to see that a large number of people could become infected.[58]

The widespread distribution of contaminated meat has been implicated in the spread of the disease. Meat was transported by scotch cart and by passengers on rural buses[59] over significant distances, despite Security Force efforts to control the movement of food and to limit food surpluses (e.g. Operation 'Turkey', as discussed previously). Multiple Rhodesian press accounts from that time point out that given the food shortages in rural areas, villagers relied heavily on black market meat to make up their calorie deficit, as Dr Davies stated: 'One contributing factor was the meat of carcasses infected by anthrax being sold around to the public as meat slaughtered at home. So the disease spread rapidly as the meat was carried on scotch carts to distant places in the TTL'.[60] Government food controls – and a burgeoning black market in beef – accounts for the anthrax 'hops' (incidents in which human anthrax cases in regions of Rhodesia were not contiguous to areas with earlier cases). In these 'hops', the disease pops up in one area and months later, pops up in another area possibly hundreds of kilometers away.

Unusual features of the Rhodesian anthrax epidemic

Some academics, journalists and commentators have stated that the scale (case count) and extent (geographic spread over time) of the Rhodesian anthrax epizootic were due to an intentional dissemination of anthrax by combatants in the conflict, with possible South African involvement. Meryl Nass has been a proponent of that argument[61] – and she also asserts that the alleged Rhodesian dissemination of anthrax was targeted against the country's rural black population. Dr Nass based her allegation on the fact that the anthrax epidemic was unique in its size and scope, and possessed some unusual characteristics. Irrefutable evidence supporting claims that the Rhodesians were culpable for intentionally causing the epidemic is lacking, however; yet the 1978-1980 Rhodesian anthrax epidemic remains one of the largest in recorded human history – and the epidemic does bear some unusual hallmarks, with the suspicions of intentional human origins for the anthrax epizootic based upon several observations:

Rare occurrence in Rhodesia: One argument is that despite being endemic to Rhodesia, human cases of anthrax were relatively rare, with an average of only 13 cases a year reported before the epidemic.[62] Few physicians in the country had experience treating patients with anthrax – and according to Dr Davies, the attitude of most medical professionals in Rhodesia regarding anthrax was perhaps 'cavalier'.[63] Anthrax was largely viewed as a veterinary disease and was routinely controlled through cattle vaccinations administered during an outbreak. Rhodesian veterinarians were very familiar with the disease, which among cattle was neither rare, nor unusual. On average, Rhodesia saw 20 cases of anthrax in livestock each year; in fact, most Rhodesian ranchers – and many of the medical staffs – easily recognized the cutaneous anthrax eschar for what it was. Recall that the male nurse who attended to the first human case in Nkayi Rural Hospital in November 1978 recognized the eschar – having treated similar cases during the 1963 outbreak. When Dr Davies described physicians' attitude as 'cavalier', he was not implying that their attitudes stemmed from ignorance, but rather from complacency. The disease was not penicillin-resistant, nor did it exhibit a greater than expected mortality rate. Also, given that the vast majority of human anthrax cases during this epidemic were cutaneous presentations, the disease transmission almost certainly was via expected routes (insect bites and the slaughtering and butchering of diseased animals). In all, this epizootic was not an unusual event, but a naturally occurring disease outbreak exacerbated by the collapse of veterinary services to a population in dire need of help.

Unprecedented scale: The anthrax epidemic – and the magnitude of reported human cases (10,738 individuals and 182 deaths) – are historically unprecedented,[64] but an unknown number of cases (and deaths) went unreported.
    According to Wilson:

> substantial underreporting of human cases by as much as 50 percent can be
> inferred given the number of district hospitals and medical facilities who

responded to Davies' survey and the likelihood that many patients either chose not to be evaluated by a medical facility or did not survive long enough for evaluation, as was observed in prior anthrax outbreaks in Zimbabwe.[65]

Although the scale of the Rhodesian anthrax epidemic was large, it was not unprecedented. The 1770 Saint-Domingue (Haiti) epidemic was much larger, perhaps by two orders of magnitude with an estimated 15,000 deaths.[*][66] In addition, the *anthracis* involved in the Rhodesian epizootic did not exhibit unusual characteristics such as drug resistance or an abnormal mortality rate.

Not repeated since 1982: No country – including Zimbabwe – has experienced an anthrax epidemic on the scale of the 1978 outbreak. The absence of any subsequent anthrax epidemics makes the 1978 outbreak an anomaly, with no known prior or subsequent pattern of outbreaks on this scale. The most plausible explanation is that the 1978 epidemic was a naturally occurring outbreak exacerbated by wartime conditions – namely the collapse of veterinary care. Prior to 1978 and the collapse of rural veterinary services, Rhodesia possessed an effective system of measures to control anthrax outbreaks. Those measures were vigorously implemented once an outbreak focus was identified – including the burning or burial of carcasses, vaccination of all livestock in the surrounding area and the prohibition on movement of all livestock and livestock products (quarantine). These measures were seen as effective in reducing the average annual number of anthrax cases in animals to about 20 per year;[67] however, Zimbabwe's veterinary services have suffered from considerable neglect during the past two decades, and no anthrax epidemic to compare with the 1978 occurrence has been reported yet. This observation hinges on a faulty assumption: that the only tool needed to deal with an anthrax outbreak is vaccination, and that veterinary services are ineffective without vaccines. Although Zimbabwe's veterinary services have been under considerable financial strain – limiting their ability to access vaccines – they still have other tools (e.g. quarantine, early detection, carcass disposal and public awareness campaigns). Even absent vaccines, while perhaps not as effective, can still reduce the scale and extent of an outbreak so that the epizootic of 1978-1980 is not repeated.

Another feature that distinguished the epizootic from all others is the Rhodesian Government's imposition of food restrictions and the resultant widespread hunger and malnutrition. These controls – and a reliance on meat as a critical calorie source – led to widespread smuggling of diseased meat throughout the country. This feature alone probably is responsible for the extent, if not the scale, of the human anthrax cases in Rhodesia from 1978 to 1982.

---

[*]   Although the Saint-Domingue epidemic likely was anthrax, no modern means of confirmation existed. The disease presentation and its epidemiological characteristics are consistent with a presumptive assessment of anthrax.

Rapid spread: Although the initial outbreak was confined to Matabeleland for several months, the disease spread rapidly once outside the confines of its original focus, with the spread of anthrax cases being remarkably rapid in the Mashonaland provinces. In districts in Mashonaland, the onset of the epidemic was explosive, as witnessed by the statistics on human cases at Mrewa District Hospital. Two points undercut the argument that rapid anthrax spread is unusual: first, as Dr David Morens points out, anthrax's natural potential for rapid and widespread infection among humans is not widely understood[68] – and making claims for a rapid disease spread based on reported human cases is mistaken. The record of human anthrax cases in Rhodesia probably only represents a fraction of the true total of cases – and even if the assumption that the reported numbers are accurate, two Rhodesian provinces are missing from the count; lastly, humans are highly mobile animals. Because a case is recorded at a hospital in location X should not imply that the case infection occurred near X. The infection could have occurred tens of kilometers away in any direction from X. This fact also undercuts the argument for the geospatial 'hops' and raises doubts about the infection's large geographic area.

Large geographic area: Typically, human and animal cases of anthrax are confined to a limited geographic area. Animals become infected after consuming spores from contaminated food or soil, and local humans fall ill after butchering, handling or eating anthrax-contaminated meat from infected cattle or game animals. Previous anthrax cases in Rhodesia emanated from a point source and were limited to a specific *kraal*, village or district. In the 1978-1980 outbreaks, however, the anthrax cases were widespread through much of the country (approximately 17 percent)[69] and occurred over a nearly four-year period.

Before the late 1970s, Rhodesia had effective procedures in place to contain anthrax outbreaks as they occurred,[*] but wartime conditions prevented the implementation of those procedures; for example, the lack of veterinary controls to contain the disease during the war would have contributed to the spread. Also, the security situation made timely identification of a point source or human index case impossible, and doubts remain as to whether the man who presented to the Nkayi Rural Hospital in November 1978 was truly the index case.

To further discount that the disease's spread of a large geographic area could be attributed to the Rhodesian Security Forces, intentional contamination of that large an area with *B. anthracis* spores would have required a very large amount of spores spread over a wide area.[70] Spore production and the manufacture of contaminated cattle cakes on an industrial scale would have been required – and clearly, that scale was far beyond Rhodesia's capability. No such cattle cakes were ever found, despite

---

[*]   In Rhodesia, veterinary officials used quarantines and cattle vaccinations to prevent the spread of anthrax. With frequent guerrilla ambushes and mine-laying commonplace in the TTLs in the late 1970s, veterinary officials were unable to enforce their disease control policies. At no time in Rhodesia's history did veterinary services routinely vaccinate cattle before an outbreak occurred.

the large quantity that would be needed to cause such a widespread epidemic. Even if a facility with such a large footprint had existed, it would have operated in secret and been contaminated with spores. Hiding such a facility would have been nearly impossible, yet no candidate site has ever been suggested, let alone identified.

Non-involvement of cattle on commercial ranches: Only 11 cases of bovine anthrax were reported on white-owned commercial farms in Rhodesia during the 1978-1980 epidemic. Given the extent of the epidemic, some commentators have found the absence of anthrax on the white-owned farms as evidence that the disease outbreak was intentional and targeted against the rural black population; however, the commercial ranches still had access to excellent veterinary care and vaccinated their cattle when outbreaks occurred. The communal herd remained largely unvaccinated and vulnerable to anthrax infection throughout the entire time the epidemic was taking place. Apart from the bovine anthrax cases, this epidemic infected more than 10,000 people – all of whom were rural blacks; no anthrax cases among the European population in Rhodesia were reported. The absence of such cases is not unusual, given that the European-origin population did not scavenge meat from dead animals, and likely had only limited exposure to tabanids.

Cases of inhalational anthrax: Of the 17 fatalities due to anthrax reported in the Nkayi District, eight were due to inhalational anthrax. Inhalational anthrax is a very rare form of the disease – with an incidence in humans of <5 percent – and is an occupational health hazard most commonly associated with individuals handling and/or processing animal hides, wool or hair. Rhodesia had a very large industry processing animal hides, and likely no case of inhalational anthrax was reported in the 1978 to 1982 timeframe. Given that inhalational anthrax has a very high mortality rate – and is more difficult to diagnose than cutaneous anthrax, which presents with a visible lesion – the unreported number of inhalational anthrax cases might be significantly higher.

Non-involvement of bordering countries: While Rhodesia was experiencing the largest recorded anthrax (bovine and human) epidemic, no anthrax cases in either livestock or people was reported in the bordering countries of Zambia, Botswana, South Africa, Malawi or Mozambique. Anthrax cases in livestock and/or people outside Rhodesia would presuppose contact with wildlife or people in neighboring countries. Again, wildlife cases of anthrax in Rhodesia or Zimbabwe are very rare: the wartime wildlife population in the affected TTLs was negligible, so wildlife contact with spore-carrying tabanids or blowfly-deposited vomitus or feces would have been limited, if not existent. Wildlife disease surveillance in these regions also was hampered by the same security concerns as affected veterinary workers, so any disease likely would have gone unreported. Human movement across borders also was limited by the security situation, with armed patrols searching for guerrillas crossing the border and extensive minefields creating a *cordon sanitaire*. These conditions explain the lack of anthrax cases in neighboring countries.

Claims of possible intentional anthrax use: Ever since Zimbabwe's transition to Independence, unsubstantiated claims have surfaced that the Rhodesian Security Forces intentionally disseminated anthrax near the end of the conflict – and some of these claims include possible South African involvement as well. Whether the Rhodesian Security Forces actually ever used anthrax on a wide scale is highly debatable; some indications in the oral history mention that the use of anthrax was discussed by the political leadership. The Rhodesian National Joint Operations Center (NATJOC) reportedly debated the use of anthrax, but rejected the idea out of concern that the disease would spread to the national cattle herd (i.e. the white-owned commercial herd).

Widespread rumors also exist that at one time or another, the RhSAS and/or the Selous Scouts were tasked with anthrax dissemination. McGuinness reported that the then-commanding officer of the Selous Scouts – Lieutenant Colonel Ron Reid-Daly – was adamant that the subject of deploying anthrax was raised only once, and that time by the army commander. Reid-Daly reportedly went on that he had never seen anthrax in any form, and had never given orders for its use. Regarding the published incident in which Reid-Daly had been ordered to disseminate anthrax spores, he reportedly refused to carry out his instructions – citing concerns that the task was too dangerous for his men.[*] The mission reportedly was reassigned to the Rhodesian SAS, which inserted anthrax on Botswana's side of the border with Rhodesia, near Plumtree.[71][72] The reported goal was to kill cattle as a means of discouraging local herders from supporting guerrillas.

Former RhSAS commanders Lieutenant Colonel Garth Barrett and Lieutenant Colonel Brian Robinson have adamantly repudiated any suggestion that the RhSAS was involved in the use of anthrax. If the proposal had reached them, they too would have rejected it – citing concerns about the safety of their men. Barrett recalls that he had heard the mission went to the Selous Scouts; lastly, former RIC Major Ian King – military assistant to Prime Minister Ian Smith and military liaison to the CIO – told McGuinness that the topic of anthrax was never even raised. [73] McGuinness recalled that he was shocked to hear that the topic of anthrax came up at the NATJOC, but that the NATJOC dismissed the use of anthrax largely out of concern that the disease would infect the commercial herd. With beef being a major Rhodesian export and hard currency earner, the possible threat to the commercial herd outweighed the benefits in the minds of Rhodesian policy-makers.

As a footnote, 'Mac' also asked the former quartermaster of the Selous Scouts – V. Myers – about anthrax. Myers reportedly replied that no anthrax was ever stored at the Scouts' Inkomo Barracks. Despite having confirmed that the dissemination of anthrax was discussed at the highest levels of the Rhodesian Government, all the

---

[*]   Several attempts were made to contact Reid-Daly directly in the years before his death, and he refused any communication. A number of intermediaries have contacted him regarding this research, and he has 'angrily' rejected any suggestion that he or the Selous Scouts had any role or knowledge of any intentional anthrax dissemination.

parties to those discussions are steadfast in their denial of any subsequent anthrax use by the Rhodesians to attack cattle.

In writing about the Rhodesian use of anthrax, Jim Parker stated that:

> in 1979 the late Doctor Sandy Kirk was based at the fort. He told me that Selous Scouts teams had recently deployed anthrax spores to infect cattle of Black tribesmen in the Nkayi and Lupane areas of Matabeleland. He said the strain of anthrax deployed was not contagious to humans, but they probably would become ill and die if they ate infected meat. The purpose of the exercise, he said, was to limit the availability of food that troops could forage if a large ZIPRA force invaded the country. Outbreaks of anthrax in cattle in the Lupane and Plumtree areas had occurred in the past, so it wouldn't appear unusual if similar outbreaks happened in those adjoining areas.[74]

In statements by McGuinness, he jokingly discounted that Sandy Kirk – a gynecologist by training – had the wherewithal to be involved in the use of anthrax.[75]

The Rhodesian CBW effort reportedly did experiment with the use of anthrax. Symington believed that contaminating the tobacco in cigarettes with anthrax would have been an effective tool to kill Rhodesia's opponents – far more effective than parathion-poisoned cigarettes. Reportedly limited to contaminating cigarettes and foodstuffs, the Rhodesians' alleged experimental use of anthrax allegedly took place late in the war after Victor Noble and Jan Coetzee brought an anthrax sample from Onderstepoort Veterinary Research Institute, the University of Pretoria in early 1979. According to McGuinness, Noble reported that the anthrax was effective on animals, but not on humans;[76] according to this information, the experiment failed when no human deaths attributed to anthrax were reported.[77]

According to some, the Rhodesians used *B. anthracis* targeted against cattle in Rhodesia, Mozambique and Botswana to eliminate was to eliminate cattle as a food source for guerrillas based in those countries, and the disease spread to Rhodesia because of the collapse of veterinary services there.[78] One hypothesis is that the Rhodesians introduced *Bacillus anthracis* to the Ndebele-inhabited Rhodesian provinces to eliminate a food source for ZIPRA's anticipated 'zero-zero' offensive. According to Parker, the Rhodesians anticipated that the ZIPRA forces would rely on the cattle herds in the Ndebele TTLs for food. A second hypothesis is that the South Africans introduced *Bacillus anthracis* into Matabeleland to counter ANC infiltration through that region to South Africa; the argument that the anthrax use was designed to counter ZIPRA's 'zero-zero' is not supported. According to several senior BSAP officers and Selous Scout officers, ZIPRA was not perceived as a serious threat; in fact, the Rhodesians focused little attention on the threat from Matabeleland – and certainly would have had little-to-no reason to infect cattle in that region with anthrax. As a conventional military – or even guerrilla – threat to Rhodesia, ZIPRA was largely irrelevant; as a guerrilla force, ZIPRA was smaller and less active inside Rhodesia than ZANLA. The ZIPRA focus was on developing a conventional military capability able of fighting toe to toe against the Rhodesian Army. The alleged plans for a conventional invasion almost certainly were a face-saving gesture by ZIPRA to diffuse ZANU criticism that ZIPRA was not shouldering its share of the struggle, while ZANLA was experiencing all the costs, hardships and losses in the Liberation War. The result was that ZIPRA constituted a much less serious guerrilla threat than did ZANLA, and therefore any accusations of Rhodesian use of anthracis against ZIPRA are untenable.

David Martin, an author based in Zimbabwe (with good contacts with ruling ZANU-PF officials), has written that the Rhodesian Army's Psychological Operations (PsyOps) Unit was responsible for the use of anthrax in a field test: "'It is true that anthrax spoor was used in an experimental role in the Gutu, Chilimanzi, Masvingo, and Mberengwa areas, and the anthrax idea came from army PsyOps (Psychological Operations)," the former Rhodesian officer says'.[79] The map below depicts the regions cited in Martin's article – and none of the regions cited corresponds with areas of significant anthrax incidence, which cast doubt on the veracity of Martin's source. Rhodesian PsyOps lacked the means to disseminate *B. anthracis* spores – making this story implausible. Martin, now deceased, never revealed the identity of his source, so confirmation is impossible.

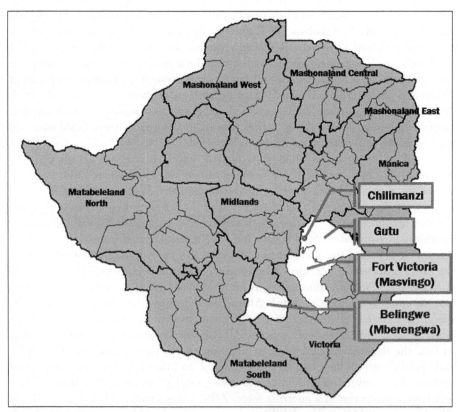

Figure 4.15 Anthrax laydown, as described by Martin. (Source: the author's work, based on data from David Martin, 'Ex-officer claims Ian Smith used chemical weapons in Rhodesian war', *New York Amsterdam News* (New York, NY: 31 July 1993), p.2)

Although based on questionable information, published accounts report that anthrax use – possibly very late in the conflict – was the brainchild of the Rhodesian Army's Psychological Warfare Unit rather than the Special Branch. The army plan called for the introduction of anthrax to the Gutu, Chilimanzi, Masvingo and Mberengwa areas of Rhodesia.[80] In this context, the intentional release of anthrax targeted against the cattle in the TTLs would have been consistent with the goals of Operation 'Turkey', which was designed to control access to food in rural areas of Rhodesia; lastly, statements by Zimbabwean government officials – notably by former Health Minister Dr Timothy Stamps – support the contention that the Rhodesian anthrax epidemic of 1978-1980 resulted from a deliberate South African effort to spread the disease.

In an interview for a US Public Broadcasting Service (PBS) documentary, entitled 'Plague Wars', the interviewer asked Stamps: "Who do you believe could have been responsible for the introduction of these biological agents?" Stamps replied:

> That is really outside my capacity to conjecture. But we know that it could not have been the Rhodesian forces acting on their own, they didn't have the logistics ... We know that there was a tremendous amount of support from the apartheid regime because they were intensely concerned that if this country became independent and democratized, it wouldn't be long before apartheid fell apart ... I think this was introduced by foreign agencies probably through South Africa and probably by the South Africans in order to use Zimbabwe as a mechanism for protecting their apartheid regime against the overwhelming freedom movement which was threatening the structure of apartheid ... In my own mind there is no doubt that there were deliberate attempts to inoculate our country with those organisms. It's a deliberate attempt at destroying a population. I would put it on the same level as ethnic cleansing.

When asked: "Anthrax is not readily available; where do you think the original spores came from?" Stamps replied:

> I'm sure it was a laboratory-devised virulent type because there are some anthrax bacilli which are not particularly virulent, and I suspect that they were responsible for the sporadic cases we had in the thirty years before the major epidemic, and one suspects that these were specifically developed as a weapon against an overwhelming number of people who were regarded as enemies to those who occupied power at the time. If you can destroy a person's cattle, you can destroy his livelihood; if you can kill a few people in the process, then you can subjugate a large number of people. That is the evil of biological warfare.[81]

Stamps offered no evidence to support his assertions – indicating that the proof could come only from participants (presumably from South Africa) who were involved in the deliberate dissemination of anthrax spores.

In trying to track down the claims of South African involvement in the Rhodesian anthrax epidemic, McGuinness contacted several of his associates. One of these associates – a South Africa Secret Service (SASS) officer who reportedly had extensive personal involvement in South Africa's 'Project Coast' – stated categorically that during the early 1980s (and not before), SADF laboratories had done little to no research on anthrax as an offensive weapon. McGuinness also asked a former senior officer in South Africa's Special Forces whether anthrax had ever been used. That friend stated that neither he, nor his men, had ever been called on to deploy *B. anthracis*.[82] A former officer in the Selous Scouts recruited by the South Africans during the Rhodesian counterinsurgency – and who later went on to serve in South African covert units – rejected rumors that he had dropped *B. anthracis*-contaminated materials for either the Rhodesians or South Africans;[83] lastly, when 'Project Coast' chief veterinarian Daan Goosen was asked about the Rhodesian anthrax epidemic, he rejected the notion of any South African involvement – stating that if the epidemic had been intentional, it probably was the handiwork of Bob Symington.[84]

Attribution

Attribution of a State or non-State actors' use of naturally occurring pathogens to cause harm is complex – and the challenge is daunting. In the midst of a conflict, obtaining documents, testimony, pathogen samples and clinical data from patients may be nearly impossible – and retrospective attribution efforts are increasingly difficult with the passage of time. In the Rhodesian case, 37 years now separate any investigator from the actual events. In that time, documents have been destroyed or lost; memories have faded or have been distorted; and clinical records and samples are gone. Rumors of intent swirl and seem amplified by the passage of time, but are never proven. Sample collection probably would have been feckless – assuming that all the collected samples contained native strains. No known samples of contaminated feed exist, and no candidate spore production facility has been named, or even suggested. No means exist to recreate the events – and attribution efforts should be held accountable to a very high standard of evidence. In the Rhodesian case, this standard cannot be met; all that can be reasonably concluded is that the epidemic is consistent with a natural occurrence exacerbated by a deteriorating security environment.

The Rhodesian case highlights the challenges of bioattribution – the attribution of a disease event to human actors as opposed to a natural outbreak. Disease is a natural and all-too-common occurrence, with outbreaks typically falling into the bailiwick or in-basket of public health officials. Until the October 2001 anthrax letter attacks in the United States, public health officials – and security officials in general – gave only passing nods to the possibility of the intentional use of disease by terrorists. Military preparedness efforts and the capabilities of the Western Intelligence communities focused on the CBW programs of major Nation-States – notably that of the Soviet Union; meaningful bioattribution just did not exist. If anyone doubts that statement, just recall the 1984 intentional use of *Salmonella enterica* by the Rajneeshees in The Dalles, Oregon.

Successful bioattribution hinges on possessing two crucial capabilities: (a) a presence on the ground in the outbreak zone to collect environmental and clinical samples; and (b) intelligence collection focused on obtaining clandestine human intelligence and signals intelligence about the suspected actor(s)'s intentions, capabilities, plans, preparations and actions. Without these capabilities, a bioattribution effort is meaningless – largely because of policy-makers and the public demand for convincing evidence of absolute guilt. Science and intelligence deal with probabilities and uncertainties; high degrees of confidence in information or certainty in judgment (i.e. the proverbial 'slam-dunk') very rarely, if ever, exist in the real world. Those analysts promising a definitive attribution of a bioevent to a specific human actor should be met with an extraordinary amount of skepticism.

Conclusion

In looking at the available clinical and epidemiological data, the Rhodesian anthrax epidemic of 1978-1980 seems to be a propagated epidemic. The data is highly consistent with a naturally occurring epidemic, and its propagation almost certainly was due to wartime conditions. From what is known about the ecology of anthrax in Zimbabwe, the life-cycle of anthrax in the soil; its seasonality; the role of insect vectors; the factors affecting human susceptibility to anthrax infection; the role of water contamination etc. – all these point to the explanation that the Rhodesian case was a natural occurrence exacerbated by the collapse of veterinary services to the communal herd in the TTLs. The epidemiology of this outbreak conforms to our understanding of how a natural anthrax outbreak would begin, both in terms of seasonality of the outbreak, location and the role of the insect vector. The human clinical presentation is consistent with the butchering and scavenging of diseased animals, and tabanids as insect vectors. The unusual spread of the disease in the human population – giving the false impression of multiple foci and geographic/temporal 'hops' – can be explained by the widespread smuggling of contaminated meat, given Rhodesian Government attempts to limit the food supply in rural areas available to guerrillas; widespread cattle rustling also may have played a role in these 'hops'.

The collapse of the veterinary and public health system in rural Rhodesia explains the unprecedented scale and spread of the disease in terms of both human and animal infections. By 1978, the veterinary services to the TTLs had virtually collapsed – and the guerrillas targeted Rhodesian veterinary workers, animal clinics and livestock dips. The Rhodesian ability to prevent, detect and treat any animal disease outbreak was non-existent. At the same time, the Rhodesian rural public health system had similarly collapsed; rural clinics and hospitals had shuttered, and several diseases had become epidemic. These conditions left both livestock and humans in the TTLs vulnerable to epidemic disease.

Intentional human involvement in initiating or furthering the spread of the disease cannot be determined based on the currently available data. Without some corroborated statement by a direct participant who can state the facts about the use of anthrax in the conflict, the epidemic's unique characteristics can only suggest – not prove – human involvement. In the end, determining if the epidemic was intentional or attributing it to a specific actor is impossible without claims or proof of responsibility, either in the form of documents or testimony. In this case, both are wholly lacking. No witnesses among the black African population or the guerrillas have come forward to claim they witnessed the dissemination of anthrax by either Rhodesian or South African Security Forces – and no one has ever brought forward a spore-laden cattle cake or sample of feed as evidence of intentional spore dissemination.

Notes

1   Arthur M. Friedlander, chapter 22: 'Anthrax' in F.R. Sidel, E.T. Takafuji and D.F. Franz (eds.), *Medical Aspects of Chemical and Biological Warfare*, pp.467-478; office of the Surgeon-General, Department of the Army. Brigadier General R. Zajtchuk (editor-in-chief) and R.F. Bellamy (managing editor); office of the Surgeon-General, Department of the Army; online at <www.vnh.org/MedAspChemBioWar> (accessed on 3 July 2007).

2   Norah E. Palmateer, Vivian D. Hope, Kirsty Roy, Andrea Marongiu, Joanne M. White, Kathie A. Grant, Colin N. Ramsay, David J. Goldberg and Fortune Ncube, 'Infections with Spore-forming Bacteria in Persons Who Inject Drugs, 2000–2009', *Emerg Infect Dis* 19 (1), pp.29-34.

3   T.J. Cieslak and E.M. Eitzen, 'Clinical and Epidemiologic Principles of Anthrax', *Emerg Infect Dis* serial online July-August 1999, cited 2005 – September 2005; online at < www.cdc.gov/ncidod/ EID/vol5no4/cieslak.html> (accessed on 3 October 2005). Rare human-to-human transmission of anthrax has been known to occur in cases where a person has had direct contact with fluids from a cutaneous anthrax lesion.

4   Friedlander (1997).

5   Margaret E. Coleman, Brandolyn Thran, Stephen S. Morse, Martin Hugh-Jones and Stacy Massulik, 'Inhalation anthrax: Dose response and risk analysis', *Biosecurity & Bioterrorism: Biodefense Strategy, Practice, and Science* 6(2), pp.147-159.

6   Division of Bacterial and Mycotic Diseases, US Centers for Disease Control (CDC), 'Anthrax' (22 February 2006); online at <www.cdc.gov/ncidod/dbmd/diseaseinfo/cholera_g.htm#What%20is%20anthrax> (accessed on 24 May 2006).

7   Antonio Fasanella, Domenico Galante, Giuliano Garofolo and Martin Hugh-Jones, 'Anthrax undervalued zoonosis', *Veterinary Microbiology* 140 (3-4), p.318.

8   J.C.A. Davies, 'A Major Epidemic of Anthrax in Zimbabwe', *The Central African Journal of Medicine* 28 (December 1982), p.291.

9   C.J. Roberts and P.J. Chambers, 'An Outbreak of Anthrax in the Mondoro Tribal Trust Lands', *The Central African Journal of Medicine* 21 (April 1975), p.73.

10 Martin Hugh-Jones and Jason Blackburn, 'The Ecology of Bacillus anthracis', *Molecular Aspects of Medicine* 30 (2009), pp.356–367.

11 op. cit., p.74.

12 Hargreaves, personal communication, dated 2 January 2006.

13 According to one estimate, roughly 180,000 head of cattle in the communal herd reportedly contracted anthrax in 1980. (Document in the author's possession.)

14 'Death of 750000 Cattle Feared', *Chronicle* (Bulawayo), 1 August 1979, p.5.

15 John C. Barrett, 'The Economic Role of Cattle in Communal Farming Systems in Zimbabwe': this paper was originally presented at a workshop on 'The socio-economic impact of improved tick and tick-borne disease control in Zimbabwe', which was held at the Veterinary Research Laboratory, Harare on 9 May 1991. The full proceedings of this workshop are expected to be published as a special issue of the *Zimbabwe Veterinary Journal*; online at <www.odi.org.uk/pdn/papers/32b.pdf> (accessed on 21 July 2006).

16 J.A. Lawrence, C.M. Foggin and R.A.I. Norval, 'The Effects of War on the Control of Diseases of Livestock in Rhodesia (Zimbabwe)', *Veterinary Record* (1980) 107, p.84.

17 Notes of discussion with Stuart Hargreaves, dated 21 July 2006.

18 Antonio Fasanella, Giuliano Garofolo, Domenico Galante, Vincenzo Quaranta, Lucia Palazzo, Romano Lista, Rosanna Adone and Martin Hugh-Jones, 'Anthrax outbreaks in Italy in 2004: genetic analysis of isolates and evaluation of risk factors associated with outbreaks', *New Microbiologica* 33 (1), pp.83-86.

19 A.O. Pugh and J.C.A. Davies, 'Human Anthrax in Zimbabwe', *Salisbury Med Bull* (1990) 68 (special supplement), p.32.

20 ibid., p.294.

21 ibid.

22 Davies (1982), p.295.

23 ibid.

24 Unclassified Defence Intelligence IIR 6 880 0558 79, dated 19 October 1979, citing press report in *Pretoria News,* dated 17 October 1979; information acquired through FOIA request.

25 Davies (1982), p.292.

26 ibid., p.296.

27 P.C.B. Turnbull, *Guidelines for the Surveillance and Control of Anthrax in Humans and Animals,* 3rd ed., WHO/EMC/ZDI/98/6 (Geneva: World Health Organization, 1998), p.3; online at <www.who.int/csr/resources/publications/anthrax/whoemczdi986text.pdf> (accessed on 20 November 2006).

28 Glenn B. van Ness, 'Ecology of Anthrax', *Science,* vol.172, no.3990 (25 June 1971), p.1,303. Akula et al., 'Anthrax: An Overview', *Int. J. Risk Assessment and Management,* vol.5, no.1 (2005), p.4. See the issue of soil propagation of *B. anthracis* as an open question. They wrote: '… the question remains unsettled as to whether its persistence in the soil is due to significant multiplication of the organism in the soil, or if it is due solely to cycles of bacterial amplification in infected animals whose carcasses then contaminate the soil…' Also see Martin Hugh-Jones and Jason Blackburn, 'The Ecology of Bacillus Anthracis', *Molecular Aspects of Medicine* 30 (2009), pp.356-367 for a discussion of both soil propagation of *Bacillus anthracis* and the role of climatic conditions in the promoting of disease outbreaks.

29 Ian L. Pepper and Terry J. Gentry, 'Incidence of Bacillus Anthracis in Soil', *Soil Science* 167 (2002), p.620.

30 Forest E. Kellogg, Annie K. Prestwood and Robert E. Noble, 'Anthrax Epizootic in White-Tailed Deer', *Journal of Wildlife Diseases* 6 (October 1970), p.228.

31 'Person-to-person transmission is extremely unlikely and only reported with cutaneous anthrax where discharges from cutaneous lesions are potentially infectious'; online at <www.cdc.gov/ncidod/dbmd/diseaseinfo/anthrax_t.html> (accessed on 20 July 2006).

32 Ude V. Pienaar, 'Epidemiology of anthrax in wild animals and the control of anthrax epidemics in the Kruger National Park, South Africa', *Federation Proceedings* 26 (1967), pp.1,496-1,502.

33 Turnbull (1998), p.6.

34 Widespread deaths in wildlife have also been witnessed during periods of sudden severe drops in environmental temperature and droughts (Hugh-Jones, p.373).

35 D.C. Dragon, B.T. Elkin, J.S. Nishi and T.R. Ellsworth, 'A Review of Anthrax in Canada and Implications for Research on the Disease in Northern Bison', *Journal of Applied Microbiology* 87 (1999), pp.208-213.

36 Pepper and Gentry, p.107.

37 D.C. Dragon and R.P. Rennie, 'The ecology of anthrax spores: Tough but not invincible', *Canadian Veterinary Journal* 36 (1995), pp.295-301.

38   Antonio Fasanella, Rosanna Adone and Martin Hugh-Jones, 'Classification and management of animal anthrax outbreaks based on the source of infection', *Ann Ist Super Sanità* 50, 2 (2014), pp.192-195.

39   See US National Oceanographic and Atmospheric Administration (NOAA) weather data (www.noaa.gov). Also see 'Climate Change in Zimbabwe'; online at <maps.grida.no/go/download/mode/attachment/f/   climate_change_in_zimbabwe_trends_in_temperature_and_rainfall.jpg&imgrefurl=http://maps.grida.no/go/graphic/climate_change_in_zimbabwe_trends_in_temperature_and_rainfall&h=745&w=550&sz=54&hl=en&start=2&tbnid=g5WgEIKWf4HdkM:&tbnh=141&tbnw=104&prev=/images%3Fq%3Dzimbabwe%2Brainfall%26svnum%3D10%26hl%3Den%26lr%3D%26sa%3DG> (accessed on 3 September 2006).

40   Pepper and Gentry, p.106.

41   Hugh-Jones, personal communication, dated 26 August 2015.

42   Hargreaves, personal communication, dated 15 January 2006.

43   A.O. Pugh and J.C.A. Davies (1990), p.32.

44   Antonio Fasanella, Rosanna Adone and Martin Hugh-Jones, 'Classification and management of animal anthrax outbreaks based on the source of infection', *Ann Ist Super Sanità* 50, 2 (2014), p.194.

45   'Because tabanids have intermittent feeding habits and attack a wide range of vertebrate host types, they are excellent candidates for mechanical transmission of the disease agents that cause anthrax and tularemia'. See Donald R. Barnard, 'Control of Fly-Borne Diseases', *Pesticide Outlook* (October 2003), p.222.

46   'For two months prior to deer mortality, drought conditions prevailed throughout the area. During that period heavy concentrations of biting flies (*Tabanidae*) were prevalent and reached peak populations in early June'. See Forest E. Kellogg, Annie K. Prestwood and Robert E. Noble, 'Anthrax Epizootic in White-Tailed Deer', *Journal of Wildlife Diseases*, vol.6 (October 1970), p.228.

47   Jason K. Blackburn, Ted L. Hadfield, Andrew Curtis and Martin E. Hugh-Jones, 'Spatial and temporal patterns of anthrax in White-Tailed Deer, *Odocoileus virginianus*, and hematophagous flies in West Texas during the Summertime Anthrax Risk Period', *Annals of the Association of American Geographers* 104 (5), pp.939-958.

48   Jason K. Blackburn, Andrew Curtis, Ted L. Hadfield, Bob O'Shea, Mark A. Mitchell and Martin E. Hugh-Jones, 'Confirmation of Bacillus anthracis from Flesh-eating Flies Collected during a West Texas Anthrax Season', *Journal of Wildlife Diseases* 46 (3), pp.918–922.

49   Hugh-Jones, personal communication, dated 26 August 2015.

50   Turnbull, personal communication, dated 15 June 2006.

51   Turrell, p.1,860.

52   Kaufmann, personal communication, dated 15 June 2006.

53   Nikola Bradaric and Volga Punda-Polic, 'Cutaneous Anthrax due to Penicillin-Resistant Bacillus Anthrax', *The Lancet* 340 (1 August 1992), pp.360-361.

54   See Turrell and Knudson, p.1,860.

55   ibid.

56   The Matabeleland statistics were based on 107 human cases of cutaneous anthrax at St Luke's Mission, the Lupane District, Rhodesia; the Mashonaland statistics came from Gatooma General Hospital. See J.C.A. Davies (1982).

57   According to the researchers reporting on the Turkish cases, '... most of our cases (88%) had a history of contact; 16 cases (64%) had a history of direct contact with animals...' (p.329).

58   Dr Stuart Hargreaves, personal communication, dated 2 January 2006.

59   A physician working in the district where the original focus of the epidemic was located indicated that he attended to victims of a bus crash in 1979. The victims were inhabitants of a remote rural area and many of them were carrying meat that was possibly contaminated. See personal communication, dated 16 February 2005.

60   Davies (1982), p.293.

61   Meryl Nass, 'Anthrax Epizootic in Zimbabwe, 1978-1980: Due to Deliberate Spread?' *Physicians for Social Responsibility Quarterly* 2 (1992); online at <www.ippnw.org/MGS/PSRQV2N4Nass.html> (accessed on 21 November 2006). Interestingly, Dr Hargreaves claims that he tried to dissuade Dr Nass from her stance on the Rhodesian epizootic. (See notes of discussion with Stuart Hargreaves, dated 21 July 2006.)

62   Meryl Nass, 'Zimbabwe's Anthrax Epizootic', *Covert Action* 3 (Winter 1993-1994), p.13.

63   Davies (1982), p.291.

64   Reports of the Secretary of Health (Harare, Zimbabwe) quoted in Meryl Nass, 'Zimbabwe's Anthrax Epizootic', *Covert Action* 3 (Winter 1993-1994), p.13.

65   James M. Wilson, Marat G. Polyak, Morgan C. Baker, Guilan Huang, Richard C. Doyle, Stephen Burgess and David M. Hartley, 'Anthrax in Zimbabwe, 1978–80: A Case Study in the Problem of Assessing Attribution for a Bioevent' (unpublished paper).

66   David M. Morens, 'Epidemic Anthrax in the Eighteenth Century, the Americas', *Emerging Infectious Diseases* 8 (October 2002), pp.1,160-1,161.

67   Lawrence, Foggin and Norval (1980), p.84.

68   Morens (2002), p.1,160.

69   Parker, p.173.

70   Mark Wheelis, 'A Short History of Biological Warfare and Weapons' in M.I. Chevrier, K. Chomiczewski, M.R. Dando, H. Garrigue, G. Granasztoi and G.S. Pearson (eds.), *The Implementation of Legally Binding Measures to Strengthen the Biological and Toxin Weapons Convention* (ISO Press Amsterdam).

71   In his 2002 FBI interview, McGuinness recounted that the first time he ever heard about using anthrax as a weapon was in 1978. Symington asked him about using anthrax in the ground as a weapon against the terrorists, but McGuinness did not think using anthrax was a good idea. The majority of the Selous Scouts knew about the dangers of anthrax and its effects on cattle – and, as a result, McGuinness believes the idea to use anthrax was initially turned down. (redacted) later told McGuinness not to worry about the idea of using anthrax as a weapon. The responsibility for that operation was given to the SAS instead of the Selous Scouts. McGuiness knew of one instance where anthrax was used as a biological weapon: 'In Plum Tree [*sic*], Rhodesia, which is on the border with Botswana, the SAS placed anthrax in the ground just inside Botswana who [*sic*] was supporting the terrorists. At no time was anthrax brought to JOC Bindura. McGuinness was not familiar with an outbreak of anthrax at Mount Darwin, Rhodesia'. See FBI interview of Michael McGuinness (Case 271A-WF-222396), London, UK, dated 19 October 2002; redacted version released under FOIA, dated 5 December 2011.

72   Gould and Folb (2002), p.27.

73   McGuiness meeting with Ian King, 22 November 2006.

74   Parker, pp.171-172. Unfortunately, Dr Kirk is deceased, so his side of the story is obviously lost to us. Residing and practicing obstetrics and gynecology in Bulawayo, Dr Kirk was a reservist assigned to the Selous Scouts. Ostensibly, his chief duty was caring for the OB/GYN needs of women married to Selous Scout operators, and their daughters. As such, he would have had little-to-no access to information on a sensitive Selous Scout operation.

75   According to McGuinness, Kirk was not involved in the Special Branch CBW efforts. (The author's interview with McGuinness.)

76   Statement by Victor Noble, according to McGuinness, in a document dated 16 July 2006.

77   Doc/1, dated 19 July 2006, p.4.

78   According to an unidentified FBI informant, (redacted) said that he heard that (redacted) and Symington worked with anthrax and talked about getting anthrax into the ground in Zambia in order to kill the enemy's cattle. (redacted) said that the theory behind killing the enemy's cattle with anthrax was to eliminate the enemy's food supply. (redacted) believed that Symington was the 'Medical Brains' of the 'Dirty Trick Squad', because Symington spent so much time at Fort Bindura. (redacted) states that Symington is the overall 'Poison Guy' of the 'Dirty Trick Squad'. (redacted) stated it may have been (redacted) who knew first hand and advised (redacted) about the deployment of anthrax. One of them told (redacted) that the anthrax was deployed along the areas of the Zambezi and Lusaka Rivers. The anthrax was deployed in those areas three to four separate times. (redacted) believes that the anthrax may have been created at the 'fort' at Mount Darwin. (See FBI interview with undisclosed informant (Case 279A-WF-222936, serial 508), dated 19 November 2002; redacted version released under FOIA, dated 5 December 2011.)

79   David Martin, 'Ex-officer claims Ian Smith used chemical weapons in Rhodesian war', *New York Amsterdam News* (New York, NY: 31 July1993) p.2. ProQuest (accessed on 31 May 2006) available via the George Mason Library.

80   Martin, p.7, based on a confidential communication from a former Special Branch officer with direct access to the information.

81   Online at <www.pbs.org/wgbh/pages/frontline/shows/plague/sa/stamps.html> (accessed on 20 November 2006).

82   McGuinness, written communication, dated 20 April 2006.

83   Email from Selous Scout/4, dated 10 August 2015.

84   Interview report in the author's collection, dated 31 October 2007.

5

Lessons and Legacy

'Silent enim leges inter arma'.
Cicero, *Pro Milone*

The lessons of the Rhodesian CBW program and its legacy are perhaps more relevant to the issues of today than is commonly realized. The history of the program has been long lost or ignored, yet it can help lead scholars and policy-makers to understand better some aspects of CBW development and use. Rhodesia's relevance touches on the incentives behind CBW development in the context of regime survival; the circumstances leading to the erosion of widely-held norms; the effectiveness of CBW in counterinsurgencies and the challenges confronting WMD-related intelligence collection and analysis; and the difficulties in attempting bioattribution of a suspicious, but native, disease epidemic. Grasping the factors that led Rhodesia to begin its CBW effort contributes significantly to our understanding of why and how small resource-constrained States and non-State actors develop, test and disseminate chemical agents, biological pathogens and toxins against their enemies.

This study also demonstrates the comparative ease by which a small, rudimentary and relatively unsophisticated CBW effort can develop deadly materials from readily available, toxic agricultural and industrial materials and use them to devastating effect. The relative simplicity – along with the resulting low cost and effort required for such a CBW effort – provides us with an insight into how nations and non-State actors today (and for the foreseeable future) could resort to simple CBW agents and low-cost, technically unsophisticated dissemination methods to effect a disproportionate impact on their adversaries. An important corollary is that intelligence agencies likely would be hard pressed to detect CBW efforts similar to Rhodesia's today. Lastly, attributing the use of BW usage to a specific actor even today is extremely difficult – and the results likely would be hotly debated. Accurately attributing CW use may be easier, but it is highly dependent on the circumstances, as the recent Syrian CW attack on civilians demonstrates.

The legacy: assessing the Rhodesian CBW program

The origins of the Rhodesian CBW effort are found in the historical context of the Rhodesian counterinsurgency. This conflict was an increasingly desperate struggle to ensure regime survival by a very small minority population against a disenfranchised, marginalized majority. The divide separating these groups was immense, but it was based largely on differences in race, cultures, ethnic origins, socioeconomic status and opportunities, and legal standing. The white minority not only held a firm monopoly on political and military power, but also reaped all the social and economic advantages their dominant position allowed. Although the white minority cast the conflict as a clash of civilizations – notably a battle to preserve Western civilization and democratic values – the insurgents' battle was for a place in the sun. The vision of the insurgents was not truly revolutionary; their goal was to shift political, social and economic power into other hands – replacing the ruling white elite with a new elite from the insurgent ranks. In effect, they sought to replace one regime with another while maintaining the same political, economic and security apparatus.

In this historical context, the white elite fought to maintain their regime and they saw the conflict in terms of preserving a way of life. In the struggle, several fundamental factors key for the adoption of a CBW effort emerged, which included: scarce national resources (especially manpower); a numerically superior opponent operating from safe havens in neighboring countries; an asymmetrical threat or significant change in the strategic balance, pariah or rogue-State status – outside international law, conventions and regimes – and international political, diplomatic and economic isolation. In Rhodesia, the conflict contained characteristics that created a permissive environment for CBW use, such as intrastate insurgency or civil war; regime survival in jeopardy (e.g. race, values, religion and political/economic power at risk); a demonized/dehumanized adversary; available materials; know-how; infrastructure; and a foreign sponsor (e.g. South Africa). These conflict traits could be useful in identifying potential CBW use in modern conflicts.

In Rhodesia, these factors combined to lead decision-makers to adopt an unconventional response to the perceived shift in the strategic balance, and to the realization within the security structure that the counterinsurgency could not be won solely through use of the conventional military; this realization followed the collapse of Portuguese colonial power in Mozambique, the dramatic increase in guerrilla recruitments and the escalating violence. The limitations of the conventional Rhodesian military were further demonstrated by Rhodesia's increasing reliance throughout the war on unconventional warfare units and tactics – notably the use of the Selous Scouts and the RhSAS, which played dramatic roles in external raids late in the war. If some of the Rhodesian sources are credible, the CBW effort at times inflicted greater numbers of guerrilla casualties than the conventional Rhodesian military. This comparative success largely was due to guerrilla hit-and-run tactics that emphasized avoiding contact with Rhodesian forces and a preference for attacking softer civilian targets. In other words, the CBW effort sought to kill the guerrillas in their camps and bases, and also among their village supporters, where the Rhodesian military struggled to locate and engage an elusive foe. These attributes of CBW made it well suited to counterinsurgency, where the government aim was regime survival. In the limited history of modern CBW use, Rhodesia perhaps is the best, if not the only, case study for CBW use in a regime survival scenario. The only other example that comes readily to mind is the current Syrian CW use against its own insurgents. Most other closely related cases are those of colonial governments using CW in native insurrections. The Spanish and Italian uses of CW in the interwar years – and the Egyptian CW use in the 1960s against Yemeni rebels[1] – are all examples of external actors' use of CW, where the Rhodesian example illustrates a regime's use against insurgents.

Early in the conflict, the Rhodesian Security Forces had successfully confronted guerrilla incursions and eliminated most of the guerrilla presence in the country. With the Portuguese withdrawal from Mozambique in 1974, ZANLA was able to establish base camps, training facilities and infiltration routes along Mozambique's long border with Rhodesia. With a growing guerrilla force and new camps in Mozambique, ZANLA opened a second front that further stretched scant Rhodesian resources. Crippled by chronic manpower and materiel shortages, the Rhodesian Army and Air Force struggled to cope with a deteriorating security situation. Although the Rhodesian Security Forces could decimate guerrilla forces wherever found, the guerrillas enjoyed significant advantages in manpower, an often-passive local population and mobility. The guerrilla strategy instructed insurgents to avoid direct combat with the Security Forces and focus instead on ambushes, hit-and-run attacks and the placement of landmines.

By 1975, informed Rhodesian Intelligence officials and Army Special Forces officers were concerned about the significant increase in guerrilla recruitment and the threat of escalating guerrilla violence posed by these new recruits. Complacent following the country's earlier successes in thwarting guerrilla offensives, Rhodesia's political and military leadership seemingly remained lulled into relative ill-preparedness. The Rhodesian war effort and intelligence collection continued to be dominated by the BSAP, with its emphasis on maintaining law and order and prosecuting terrorists for criminal offenses.

In Rhodesia's rudderless bureaucratic environment – dominated by informal hierarchies and personal networks – the Rhodesian Government's acceptance of a proposed CBW project is easy to see. Obsessed with the prospect of a seriously deteriorating security situation posed by the growing guerrilla threat, one of the many personal networks began to consider innovative solutions to the overwhelming imbalance between the large-scale influx of guerrilla recruits and manpower-poor Rhodesia. This network – centered on P.K. van der Byl and Professor Robert Symington – conceived of using chemical and biological agents against the guerrillas by inserting contaminated clothing, food, beverages, cigarettes and medicines. Rhodesian Prime Minister Ian Smith almost certainly was briefed on the proposed program and approved its creation – and he may have been briefed subsequently despite his public denials.

Largely the product of wartime improvisation, the Rhodesian CBW effort was clandestine, small-scale and basic. Located at a Selous Scout 'fort' – and run by the Special Branch – a small team of laboratory technicians and students set out in a single room to process readily available agricultural pesticides and rodenticides into poisons for use against guerrillas. Although the funds were available for more sophisticated facilities, equipment and materials, the limited available materials and equipment met the program's needs. The focus of the program was on eliminating guerrilla recruits in transit from points inside Rhodesia to their training camps in Mozambique and Zambia – and the selection of specific chemical agents was tailored to kill specific targeted groups. 'Turned' contact men known – trusted by the guerrilla group – delivered the contaminated items.

The selected chemical agents were all readily available agricultural pesticides or rodenticides. The Rhodesian use of *V. cholerae* as a BW agent was very successful in eliminating water supplies for guerrillas transiting from training camps in Mozambique to operational areas in Rhodesia. Cholera also is believed to have caused the death of hundreds of guerrillas at camps in Mozambique.[2]

The cause of the Rhodesian anthrax epidemic from 1978 to 1980 is still debated. The weight of scientific evidence explains that the epidemic was due to natural causes exacerbated by the worsening security environment – and no reliable evidence exists to support the contention that the epidemic was caused by either Rhodesian or South African deliberate dissemination of anthrax spores. A non-contagious disease, this anthrax epidemic spread rapidly until it was reported in five out of Rhodesia's six provinces. As described in the previous chapter, the epidemic erupted in November 1978 in Western Rhodesia, in the Nkayi/Lupane region – largely a Ndebele-dominated rural area with little European settlement. Despite the rate of disease spread, almost all (96 percent) of the known human cases of anthrax were limited to Que Que (the Midlands Province). By some estimates, 25 to 50 percent of the communal cattle herds in the TTLs were lost to anthrax and tick-borne diseases during the last years of the war.

The number of human and livestock cases probably grossly underestimates the true extent of the disease. The epidemic generally is believed to have resulted in nearly 11,000 recorded human cases of anthrax (almost all cutaneous cases), with 182 deaths and untold cattle deaths. An epizootic disease – affecting animals and humans – anthrax almost certainly infected humans through insect bites (anthrax-contaminated tabanids) and the handling of anthrax-contaminated meat, as discussed in the previous chapter. Furthermore, we have no evidence that either the Rhodesians or the South Africans attempted to infect human community with anthrax on a large scale during the Rhodesian War; the Rhodesians, however, did experiment with anthrax-contaminated cigarettes as a dissemination method.

Aimed at exploiting known guerrilla vulnerabilities, the Rhodesian CBW effort was successful in killing several hundred, if not thousands, of guerrillas, but it was not – nor ever could be – decisive in forcing an end to the conflict that was favorable to the European Rhodesians. As long as the Rhodesian Government continued to deny the black population fair opportunities for education, employment and land ownership, African nationalism would remain appealing to the majority of the aggrieved population. The escalating Rhodesian external raids aimed at Mozambican and Zambian road and rail infrastructure were far more successful in pressuring the frontline African nations to force ZANU and ZAPU to Lancaster House than any of the CIO or Special Branch tactics. Although the CIO and Special Branch operations did succeed in causing division and dissension in the guerrilla ranks, both ZANLA and ZIPRA – like most non-State actors – were resilient enough organizations to bounce back from temporary setbacks.

Did the Rhodesian CBW program contribute to a 'hurting stalemate', or provide pressure for a negotiated war cessation? Without access to ZANU or ZAPU documents, or insight into internal discussions, no conclusive answer can be reached – and available information describing factors leading to the war's end contains no reference to Rhodesia's CBW efforts. From the limited perspective allowed by the available information, the CBW operations probably had no effect on moving the adversaries to a negotiated settlement. The Rhodesian and insurgent sides were both incapable of sustaining combat operations without continual and substantial support from their respective external supporters, and the Rhodesian and insurgent efforts would have each collapsed – weakening arguments for a 'hurting stalemate' in Rhodesia.[3] The only question would have been which side collapsed first. Concern within the Rhodesian leadership about the fragility of their military position, economic weakness and growing net white Rhodesian emigration almost certainly resulted in an anxiety that led to their adoption of CBW.

The major impetus behind the talks to end the war was pressure from external supporters (South Africa in the case of Rhodesia, and Zambia and Mozambique in the case of ZAPU and ZANU respectively). The United States and Great Britain induced Pretoria to strong-arm Salisbury to the negotiations. International diplomatic activities – and Rhodesian external raids on Zambia and Mozambique – led those governments to pressure their clients (ZAPU and ZANU) to Lancaster House as well. The dependency of all fighting parties on foreign support was the essential condition that brought all parties to the table. The willingness of the adversaries to participate in the Lancaster House talks was reinforced by the politicians' belief on each side that they would dominate the political process and subsequent elections; each adversary's military and intelligence elements were less sanguine.

As an interesting footnote, interest in CBW did not die in Zimbabwe with the transition to majority rule and Independence in 1980. In 1986, Edson Shirihuru, who was then-Assistant Deputy Director-General for Operations in the Zimbabwean CIO, asked a senior CIO colleague to acquire poisons and the formula from a source in South Africa with ties to the Rhodesian CBW program. The source in South Africa reportedly turned over the formula used in the Rhodesian CBW effort for use by the Zimbabwean CIO. We have no information that Shirihuru ever produced any of the poisons, and he died several years later while still serving as a senior Zimbabwean CIO official.[4]

The lessons

Incentives promoting CBW development and use: The academic literature on the pursuit of WMD and its proliferation largely focuses on incentives and disincentives behind States and non-State actors' (i.e. terrorists') adoption of WMD and less on the rationales behind WMD use. In looking at States' interest in WMD, these weapons can be categorized as substitutionary or complementary.[5] The term 'WMD' erroneously conflates chemical and biological weapons with nuclear arms. Given that nuclear weapons have no practical military utility on the modern battlefield – and function today as a deterrent and political tool (to convey great power status) – CBW are no more complementary or substitutionary than other weapons systems. As a deterrent, modern conventional weapons have the potential to devastate an adversary in retaliation for CBW use. The basic premise is that nations seek chemical and/or biological weapons because those weapons either complement a nuclear arsenal, or can substitute for nuclear weapons. These categories are less meaningful when addressing the rationale behind CBW use in situations when regime survival is threatened. In those cases, the realist principle of self-help in maximizing security might be most applicable in discussing incentives underpinning the adoption and use of CBW.

The perceived utility of CW lay in (1) its psychological and political effects as a deterrent; (2) it ability to intimidate and terrorize; and (3) its ability to serve as a weapon against ill-equipped, untrained and unprepared adversaries. As the 1991 Gulf War demonstrated, CW's psychological effects and military utility have rapidly diminishing returns against a well-trained, properly equipped modern military. CBW are the weapons of the weak; those facing otherwise larger (or better trained and equipped) adversaries; or those whose conventional armies lack effective means to target elusive enemies. CBW use against larger or better-equipped and trained adversaries is feckless; at best, such asymmetrical use, as the Iran-Iraq War demonstrates, results in only tactical gains. Despite the international moratorium on CW use in interstate conflict, CW use is effective in suppressing internal violence.[6] The post-World War II examples of CW use show its greatest practical utility is in intrastate counterinsurgency operations – including Egypt in Yemen (1960s), Rhodesia (1970s), South Africa in Namibia (1980s), Iraq against the Kurds (1980s) and Syria (2013-ongoing).

What are the explanatory conditions – posited in the academic literature – behind a State's decision to adopt BW? According to Jeanne Guillemin, four factors are necessary (but not sufficient) for States to develop biological weapons: a dire national security threat; lobbying by scientists to persuade political and military leaders to invest in these weapons; a substantial military-industrial complex to support such a program; and the adoption of a 'total war' doctrine that justifies indiscriminate attacks on civilian targets. Jonathan Tucker argues that the proliferation of biological weapons is driven by 'the perception of an acute security threat accompanied by a deficit in the ability of the state to counter that threat by alternative means'. Marie Chevrier states that the most likely candidates for developing biological weapons 'are small, nonnuclear nations under relatively constant security threats from a militarily stronger country'. According to Susan Martin, '… It is the ability of biological weapons to serve as a strategic deterrent that provides an incentive for states to acquire them…'[7]

Each of these 'requirements' for State adoption of a BW program is faulty: first, nations have BW programs to develop BW absent a 'dire national security threat'. Evidence of this is Bulgaria's use of Soviet-supplied ricin in the assassination of Georgii Markov. Secondly, as Raymond Zilinkas pointed out, BW can be produced absent a substantial military-industrial complex – and the Rhodesian CBW experience further reinforces this point. To nitpick Jonathan Tucker's assertion, BW acquisition is driven by a lack of conventional means, not alternative means. To contrast Dr Chevrier's comment, nations seeking BW are neither necessarily small, nor nonnuclear – and their adversaries are not necessarily militarily stronger. Again, for example, the Soviet BW program belonged to a nation that was large, nuclear and possessed a strong conventional military; lastly, as demonstrated earlier, BW possesses no strategic deterrent value. Given the international abhorrence of BW, State BW programs most likely are small, covert operations that are well-hidden and disguised. Surrounded by such stringent secrecy, possession of BW is no deterrent at all.

Adoption of BW persists because BW has utility – namely in small-scale covert operations where other means are not possible, or would become public. Unlike other forms of WMD, BW can be used covertly – typically in assassinations – because BW agents can mimic natural disease. Advances in the life sciences will continue to lower the bar for States and non-State actors to acquire and use BW agents (pathogens and toxins) – and the perplexing question is why have not more examples of BW use been observed. One possible answer to that question is that the widely-held abhorrence of BW has severely limited its use and largely restricted its use to covert – thus largely undetected – occurrences. Again, the most well-known BW incident (mentioned earlier) involved the use of ricin to assassinate Bulgarian dissident Georgii Markov in 1979, although other BW uses in assassinations are well documented.[8]

CBW utility in counterinsurgency: The utility of CBW in a counterforce role against a well-prepared, well-equipped military is doubtful at present. CBW defenses available to most military forces negate CBW's advantages, and most military doctrines emphasize maneuver over static warfare – further reducing the utility of CBW as a counterforce option. The examples of actual force-on-force CW use come from the static warfare, such as the stalemate of trench warfare on World War I's Western Front; German use against ill-prepared Russian troops in 1915; and the Iran-Iraq War. Military CBW attacks against 'soft' targets in interstate conflicts – such as civilian populations – risk an escalatory response; however, as seen with the Iraqi and Syrian CW attacks on their own civilian inhabitants, that international response never materialized.

States such as Iraq and Syria, initially, may have adopted CBW as a means to deter Israeli nuclear attacks, but the weapons were used for much different purposes. The deterrent potential of CBW also is questionable: nuclear-armed nations often retained CBW weapons not to deter CBW use, but to retaliate if ever faced with a CBW attack; meeting like with like was believed to limit possible escalation to a nuclear exchange. Deterrence ultimately always rested with nuclear weapons – and doubts remain as to whether an Iraqi CBW attack on Israeli civilians would have deterred Jerusalem from nuclear use. Nations such as Saddam Hussein's Iraq (pre-1991) may have sought chemical and biological weapons to deter nuclear use by more powerful neighbors only because nuclear weapons were beyond their grasp (i.e. as a substitute for nuclear weapons – assuming some non-existent equivalence between nuclear weapons and CBW). Other than as a deterrent, Iraq reserved CBW use for *in extremis* situations, where the survival of the Baathist regime was seriously threatened.

According to a declassified CIA intelligence assessment from 1990:

> Apparently, Iraq believes it needs chemical weapons for deterrent purposes – primarily against Israel's nuclear option – and as a key weapon supporting its professed role as military "protector" of the Arab world ... The high priority enjoyed by the CW program probably also reflects Iraq's pleasure with the results of massive nerve agent strikes against Iranian forces in 1988 and subsequent

CW use against Kurdish insurgents. However, Iraqi willingness to initiate use of chemical weapons in any future conflict undoubtedly will be tempered if its opponents possess credible CW capabilities.[9]

The CIA assessment asserts that the Iraqi CW program had two roles: one as a deterrent and a second as an effective weapon. The use of CW as a weapon reportedly was reserved only for extreme situations. According to Scott Sagan, Hussein reportedly stated: '...WMD was for the defense of Iraq's sovereignty. Iraq demonstrated this with the use of WMD during the Iraq and Iran War, as Iran had threatened the sovereignty of Iraq. Yet, Iraq did not use WMD during the 1991 Gulf War as its sovereignty was not threatened...'[10]

Not only has CW proven to be a weak deterrent, it may be a negative deterrent (i.e. an incentive – encouraging an adversary's use of WMD). First, as outlawed weapons, CBW – especially BW – are pursued in secret; no nations thought to have active CBW programs do so openly, as any State openly acknowledging that it develops CBW would damage that nation's international standing. Given that the deterrent value of CBW lays in adversaries' knowledge of the opponent's capability, secrecy surrounding CBW undermines the power of deterrence. A secret weapon is no deterrent absent some signaling.

Nations that have obtained CW capabilities ostensibly for deterrent purposes have seen little benefit from their deterrent – and both Iraq and Syria probably sought CW capabilities to substitute for their lack of nuclear arsenals. In Syria's case, its CW capability probably was intended to deter an Israeli nuclear attack. The effectiveness of Syria's CW deterrent is untested, and Damascus – perceiving the weakness of its CW deterrent – began its nuclear weapons program. Syria's nascent nuclear reactor at al-Kibar (destroyed in a 2007 Israeli airstrike) probably was designed to produce enough plutonium for one to two nuclear weapons a year – assuming the reactor design was similar to North Korea's Yongbyon nuclear reactor facility. As with most national CW programs, CW is seen as an intermediate step to developing a nuclear deterrent, or a means for retaliating in kind. More colloquially, CBW is the 'poor man's nuclear bomb'.

The impetus behind the adoption of CW in both Iraq and Syria stemmed from the Egyptian experience in Yemen during the 1960s. Following an Egyptian-inspired military coup in Yemen to replace the monarchy with a republican form of government, a royalist insurgency formed. Egyptian President Gamal Abdul Nasser dispatched troops to Yemen to quell the rebellion. After an initial – perhaps experimental[11] – use of CW against royalists, Egypt's CW attacks halted in 1963 and resumed in 1966 only after Egyptian conventional aerial bombings failed to neutralize the insurgents operating in a mountainous and cavernous region. Beginning with Egypt's brief CW use in 1963, Egypt intensified its CW attacks from fall 1966 to July 1967. CW use in Yemen only ended when Egypt's defeat in the 1967 war against Israel forced Cairo to withdraw from Yemen. The Egyptian rationale for its CW use in Yemen may have been to intimidate Yemeni tribesmen, but more likely, the result was a second-order effect. More probable, the Egyptian military saw the utility of CW in counterinsurgency operations against an inaccessible foe. In the end, Cairo's withdrawal from Yemen ended CW use there before its full utility could be exploited.

Iraqi leaders watched Egypt's CW use in Yemen with interest, and Baghdad's own CW efforts date from the early-to-mid-1970s. A National Intelligence Council (NIC) intelligence assessment from 1988 argues that the utility of CW to the Iraqi leadership was as a means to offset Iran's numerical superiority in manpower. The effectiveness of Iraqi CW was due to the Iranian troops' inadequate protective equipment and poor training:

> President Saddam Husayn's [sic] initial political and military decision to use chemical weapons against Iran seems to have been made in an effort to compensate for Iraq's limited military manpower pool. Iraq was able to use CW to minimize personnel and territorial losses by stalling or preventing Iranian human wave attacks and because Iran had only limited CW protective capabilities and could not retaliate in kind. Although Iraq has not achieved its strategic military and political goal of ending the war, CW has been a significant element in helping Iraq achieve its tactical battlefield objectives. In our judgment, the Iraqis perceive chemical weapons to be an effective complement to their conventional arsenal.[12]

In the face of advanced military forces – such as the international coalition confronting Saddam during the 1991 Gulf War – CBW has little battlefield utility, and perhaps its only role then is as a deterrent to WMD use or regime collapse. In audio recordings and internal Iraqi documents released after Operation 'Iraqi Freedom', Saddam's thinking on the role of CBW is stated:

> A month before he invaded Kuwait, Saddam said, "According to our technical, scientific, and military calculations, [Iraq's chemical and biological weapons are] a sufficient deterrent to confront the Israeli nuclear weapon." He also, however, told military advisors to prepare options for WMD retaliation, as a revenge strike, if necessary: "I know if the going gets hard, then the Americans or the British will use the atomic weapons against me, and so will Israel. The only things I have are chemical and biological weapons, and I shall have to use them. I have no alternative."[13]

The experiences of the Iran-Iraq War demonstrate the effectiveness of CW in modern warfare – albeit against an adversary with little-to no CW defensive equipment. The same lessons are more transparently evident in counterinsurgency examples – including Rhodesia, South Africa and Iraq against the Kurds. (The utility of CBW in the Rhodesian and South African counterinsurgencies should be obvious from the preceding chapters.)

Regarding the Iraqi use of CW against its Kurdish population, the declassified 1988 National Intelligence Council assessment stated:

Iraqi use of chemical weapons to subdue the Kurdish population inside Iraq, along the triborder area with Iran and Turkey, is qualitatively different from the use of chemicals against another country. The Iraqis have primarily used riot control agents and possibly, in some cases, chemical weapons against the Kurds to minimize the diversion of troops from more critical fronts and the losses that might occur in inaccessible areas that favour guerrilla forces. It is very difficult to determine the type of agents and the exact circumstances under which any of the agents may have been used.[14]

The Iraqi aerial CW bombardment of the predominantly Kurdish town of Halabja in March 1988 perhaps is the most infamous of Baghdad's attacks on its own citizens. The Iraqi airstrikes – delivering mustard and sarin on targets in and around the town – occurred 48 hours after Halabja fell to Iranian and Kurdish fighters. The NIC assessment judged that the unintended civilian casualties had been caught in the 'crossfire' between the combatants: 'In mid-March 1988 Iraq and possibly Iran used lethal agents during counterattacks near Halabjah, with casualty figures among the Kurds caught in the crossfire estimated to be in the hundreds. We do not believe the prospect of further civilian casualties would dissuade either side from using chemical weapons'.[15]

Despite the early assessment that the Iraqi attack targeted Iranian and Kurdish fighters in a bid to retake the town, later reporting indicates that most of the 3,200 to 5,000 casualties were civilians. Rather than being part of Iraqi operations against Iran, some see the attack on Halabja as part of Iraq's al-Anfal campaign – a systematic genocide of Kurds and other minority populations in Northern and North-Eastern Iraq. Chemical weapons played a major role in the al-Anfal campaign, as described by Iraqi General Ali Hassan Abd al-Majid al-Tikriti (aka 'Chemical Ali'):

[Human Rights Watch: Response to a question about the success of the deportation campaign.] … Jalal Talabani asked me to open a special channel of communication with him. That evening I went to Suleimaniyeh and hit them with the special ammunition. [Human Rights Watch: This presumably refers to the April 1987 chemical attack on the PUK [Patriotic Union of Kurdistan] headquarters in the Jafati Valley.] That was my answer. We continued the deportations. I told the mustashars that they might say that they like their villages and that they won't leave. I said I cannot let your village stay because I will attack it with chemical weapons. Then you and your family will die. You must leave right now. Because I cannot tell you the same day that I am going to attack with chemical weapons. I will kill them all with chemical weapons! Who is going to say anything? The international community? Fuck them! The international community and those who listen to them.[16]

The genocidal comments of 'Chemical Ali' reveal the value and import the Iraqi leadership placed on the international norms regarding CW. In the case of CW use against Kurdish civilians, the utility was in terror and intimidation; the goal was to force the Kurds from their villages and their homeland.

Like the Iraqi CW program, Syria's interest in CW began following the Egyptian use in Yemen – and probably was intended to defend the Asad regime from 'strategic surrender' in the face of an overwhelming Israeli attack, although initial Syrian interest in CW began in 1973 with receipt of Egyptian CW munitions.[17] Damascus did not adopt a full-fledged CW program until Syria's military inferiority was unmasked by the 1982 Israeli invasion of Lebanon.[18] The sense of military inferiority – and the perceived unwillingness of Arab neighbors to rise to Syria's aid – resulted in Damascus' adoption of CW by the mid-1980s.[19] In the Syrian context, CW was the most expedient means of self-help available to guarantee the survival of the Asad regime from catastrophic defeat at Israeli hands. Despite a conscious focus on deterring Israel, Damascus has used CW against civilians in the current civil war. Syrian decision-making behind its CW use remains obscure: one possible conclusion is that Syrian authorities used CW indiscriminately to clear an urban environment of insurgents – and the reckless disregard for civilian casualties may have stemmed from an assumption of civilian support for the rebel combatants.

Reports alleging Syrian CW use began in early 2013[20] after warnings of 'enormous consequences' from President Obama in comments he made in August 2012.[21] Obama reiterated his warning in a December 2012 speech – adding that Asad and his commanders would be held accountable if CW was used (the use of which was totally unacceptable).[22] Reports of Syrian CW use gained currency after videos and photographs of gas attack victims became public following a large-scale assault using sarin-loaded rockets against the rebel-held Damascus suburb of Ghouta on 21 August 2013. Estimates of deaths from the attack range from 355 to 1,729 – making the Ghouta attack the largest use of CW since the Iran-Iraq War.* This attack sparked widespread international outrage – and responsibility was clearly laid at the foot of the Asad regime, despite Russian and Syrian efforts to blame rebel factions. The motive behind the attack remains unclear, but most likely it was intended to terrorize the civilian populations supporting the rebels. Bashir al-Asad's personal involvement in authorizing the attack was thrown into question by an article in *Der Bild*, which claimed that Asad had no role in ordering the CW use.[23]

The international outrage failed to galvanize national governments into a consensus as to how to respond. Allied unwillingness to respond with military force to the Syrian CW attacks undercut Obama's statements of 'enormous consequences' and his promise to hold the attackers accountable. The compromise reached – facilitated largely by the Russians – was for Syria to accede to the CWC; make full declarations of CW facilities, materials and munitions; and turn materials and munitions over for

---

*   Estimates of deaths include: 355 killed (*Médecins Sans Frontières*); 494 killed (Damascus Media Office); 502 killed (Syrian Observatory for Human Rights); 635 killed (Syrian Revolution General Commission); 924 killed (Center for Documentation of Violations in Syria); 1,300 killed (National Coalition of Syrian Revolutionary and Opposition Forces); 1,338 killed (Local Coordination Committees of Syria); 1,429 killed (United States); 1,729 killed (Free Syrian Army)

destruction. Allegations of Syrian and rebel CW use persist (chlorine and mustard) – highlighting the perceived utility of CW by both sides.[24]

Unlike CW, biological weapons have little-to-no battlefield utility – except perhaps as anti-material agents. Even in an anti-material role, BW agents can take weeks to months before any equipment or POL (petroleum, oils and lubricants) degradation takes place. BW's utility is in the realm of small-scale, covert attacks (including assassinations) by intelligence services and Special Forces units. In such scenarios, small teams of technicians can prepare small amounts of agent (pathogens and/or toxins) secretly; for small-scale, covert use, BW agent production and weaponization does not require industrial scale facilities, state-of-the-art laboratories or teams of PhD scientists.

With apologies to Raymond Zilinkas, who stated:

> Efforts to develop biological weapons using low technology, such as the mass propagation of common water or food borne pathogens or the "bath tub" production of crude, toxin-containing solutions (which could be done by well-trained technicians with no more than the usual equipment available in a clinical microbiology laboratory) that would at first glance seem to hold little interest for governments.[25]

These low-technology approaches have interested governments such as Rhodesia and South Africa, and probably remain of interest to some governments today, as well as to terrorist groups. Non-State actors – including terrorist groups – have demonstrated a greater propensity for CBW use than States, but on a far more limited scale than national programs. The most noteworthy non-State CBW use has included the Rajneeshee use of *Salmonella enterica* against restaurants in The Dalles, Oregon in 1984 (referenced in the previous chapter); the Aum Shinrikyo's development of *C. botulinum* and *B. anthracis* and use of sarin against Tokyo subways in March 1995; and the 2001 anthrax letter attacks against politicians and news outlets. Of concern has been al-Qaeda's interest in CBW and Islamic State in the Levant's (ISIL) possible access to materials, facilities and expertise to produce and deploy CW agents (most likely mustard and chlorine) for use against adversaries and non-Muslim minority populations in Syria and Iraq.

Effect of CBW norms and nonproliferation regimes: Chemical and biological weapons such as disease epidemics conjure up dreadful imagery and have featured as the backdrop for films, television shows, graphic novels and other expressions of the public imagination. Arguably, this sense of dread has contributed to the generally accepted moratorium on the development and use of chemical and biological weapons, as embodied in the three major international agreements: the 1925 Geneva Protocol; the 1972 Biological Weapons Convention (BWC); and the 1997 Convention on the Prohibition of Chemical Weapons (CWC). These agreements also enshrine ('institutionalize') a set of international norms that generally are held to be universally accepted – chiefly that the production and use of chemical or biological weapons violates basic tenets of humanity, and thus are inhumane. Jessica Stern has posited that biological weapons in particular induce dread. Dread can be defined as a disproportionate fear characterized by involuntary exposure, unpredictability, unfamiliarity, delayed or unpredictable effects, or events in which the mechanism of harm is poorly understood.[26] Hand in hand with the concept of dread is the characterization of CBW use as taboo. In a taboo, moral revulsion rises to its heights; taboos typically prohibit an action based on the belief that such behavior is either too sacred and consecrated, or too dangerous and accursed for ordinary individuals to undertake.[27]

The concept of dread – and its connection to BW – might be useful for governments as they plan their biodefense strategies and develop communication plans for informing their citizens in the event of a bioterror attack. The concept of dread has little applicability in the calculus of States deciding whether to adopt chemical or biological weapons; some nations may see dread as an incentive to adopt CBW – and the Rhodesian case is illustrative of a second-order effect of dread that could be seen as an incentive. As the Rhodesians spread poisoned food, beverages and clothing through the insurgents' supply chain, affected guerrilla groups often turned on their village supporters, who may have been innocent or unwitting of any wrongdoing – and the result was a witch hunt and the deaths of villagers. The Shona culture, in particular, emphasizes witches as a source of illness, and death is noteworthy: sudden or unexplained deaths typically are attributed to witches, with all the dread that entails. The incentive from the Rhodesian perspective was that this dread and the resulting reaction (witch hunts) would sever the guerrillas from the local supporters on whom they were dependent.

The norms constraining chemical weapons – and possibly on biological weapons as well – have been said to stem from societal and cultural aversions to poisons in general.[28] Poisons work in secrecy, and poisoners are portrayed as weak and cowardly – requiring treachery and subterfuge to accomplish their villainous harm. More importantly is how military organizations institutionalize – or fail to institutionalize – these norms, as Jeffrey Legro stated: 'The dominant beliefs in military organizations about the appropriate ways to fight wars shaped how soldiers thought about and prepared for war, which in turn shaped the vary impact of norms on state aims'.[29] The portrait of the poisoner runs contrary to the military ethos of the hero warrior vanquishing his foe with honor and dignity following a fair fight. This description of a military ethos helps explain the general aversion for chemical (and biological weapons) in the military writ large, but that ethos is not necessarily shared by all intelligence services which could use CBW. In many, if not most cases, special units have controlled CBW assets in State programs. In Rhodesia, the Special Branch unit assigned to the Selous Scouts – and overseen by the CIO – controlled CBW activities; in South Africa, CBW belonged to a medical unit attached to Special Forces, and a covert unit – the Civil Cooperation Bureau – conducted operations; in Iraq, the Chemical Corps controlled CW assets, and BW assets fell under the Special Security Office (SSO); Syrian CW was managed by the Scientific Studies and Research Center (SSRC), and Unit 450 controlled CW munitions and logistics.[30] A Congressional Research Service report stated: '... President Asad is 'the ultimate decision maker for the chemical weapons program and members of the program are carefully vetted to ensure security and loyalty'...'[31] In all these examples, the units controlling or overseeing CBW assets were highly secretive specialized units with demonstrated loyalty to the regime.

The bottom line is that while the taboo has a general cultural relevance embraced by militaries, the taboo may be less relevant or applicable to covert units or intelligence agencies. The Rhodesian experience highlights how different elements within the Security Forces viewed CBW use. The conventional Rhodesian Army – many of whose officers graduated from Sandhurst – probably would have recoiled from the thought of CBW use. Similarly, BSAP elements – apart from the Special Branch – clearly opposed CBW use, as demonstrated by BSAP Commissioner Allum's effort to halt CBW operations while the CIO embraced CBW use.

Normative constraints must evolve to remain relevant, whether it is through reaffirmation and reinforcement, or stigmatization, as Jean Pascal Zanders stated: 'In order to retain its prohibitory quality, a rule will require reaffirmation and indeed reinforcement with the passage of time'.[32] The suffering experienced during World War I stigmatized poison gas for generations – thus reinforcing the taboo; however, the CW taboo may have had greater significance for earlier generations than now. As time now greatly separates the current generation from the generation of the Great War, the horrors –including the experiences of poison gas – fade. Poison gases may now not hold the same stigma as they did for earlier generations. In many ways, modern Western societies are as much removed from the experiences of the Great War as they are from life in the 19th century.

The stigma of CBW probably was weakened in the Rhodesian example because the adversaries were not seen as equals. The Rhodesian Government worked to demonize and dehumanize the insurgents – and this propaganda was more or less successful among the white population, but much less successful among the black Africans. Assuming that the CBW norms are most effectively observed among adversaries of equal strength and international standing,[33] the logical corollary is that the norms and constraints are less effective when at least one adversary is not a State (i.e. insurgents, terrorists or criminals). In the Rhodesian case, the insurgents were labeled as terrorists, communists and criminals. That the Rhodesian legal system tried captured insurgents as criminals – and executed many – is witness to the insurgents' legal status. The secrecy of the Rhodesian CBW efforts further lessened the likelihood that the stigma would be attached to the regime – and similar dehumanization of adversaries in the content of threats to the regime extends to the South African use against domestic opponents; the Iraqi use against the Kurds; and Syria's CW use.

Despite the international agreements, the State use of CBW has never been effectively punished (one exception may be the trial of some, but not all, Japanese individuals involved in CBW experimentation and use during World War II), regardless of international outrage. As evident in the case of Syrian use of chemical weapons against its own population, international protests and 'red lines' have done little to punish the transgressor; the normative constraint on CW use was breached with impunity. Yes, Syria was forced to declare its CW production facilities and stockpiles to the Organization for the Prohibition of Chemical Weapons (OPCW) for destruction, but the Syrian leadership has not been held accountable for the deaths that resulted from CW use. The breach of the norm does not mean the destruction or invalidation of the constraint: the constraint remains, but is weakened so that other States struggling for regime survival might be emboldened to use chemical or biological weapons without fear of international consequences.

In the Rhodesian case, the normative prohibition on CBW was weak for two reasons: first, Rhodesia already was a pariah State – and the international community denied its very existence as an independent State. Outside the international system – and already under crushing sanctions – Salisbury had very little to lose in adopting CBW, and international opprobrium would have had little effect on Rhodesian decision-making; second, little world attention was focused on events inside Rhodesia – and what international attention was devoted to Rhodesia myopically monitored Soviet and Chinese support for the insurgent parties widely seen as Marxist proxies. The covert nature of the Rhodesian CBW effort compounded the lack of attention. Western diplomatic, intelligence or journalistic channels did not report the Rhodesian production and use of CBW agents, despite ineffective insurgent efforts to raise awareness of the issue.

The power of the norm to dissuade CBW development, production or use has contextual (not universal) applicability. Probably unintentionally, the CBW norm has its greatest force in condemning the development, production and use of CBW in an interstate military conflict (e.g. the use of CBW against conventional military forces to kill or incapacitate personnel, or degrade equipment). As demonstrated in Rhodesia, the CBW norm is weakest in low-intensity counterinsurgencies involving rogue/pariah regimes, and when used in the context of special operations and assassinations. The law enforcement exemption in the CWC might also serve to weaken the CW taboo in those cases in which States argue internal use by law enforcement units. An example of this argument could be police use of incapacitating or behavior-modifying agents in riot control – basically, the use of non-lethal agents with a greater effect than the use of traditional tear gases (e.g. CN, CS or CR); the CWC prohibits use of tear gases as 'a method of warfare'.[34]

The Biological Weapons Convention (BWC) Article 1 states:

> Each State Party to this Convention undertakes never in any circumstances to develop, produce, stockpile, or otherwise acquire or retain:
> 1 Microbial or other biological agents, or toxins whatever their origin or method of production, of types and in quantities that have no justification for prophylactic, protective, or other peaceful purposes;
> 2 Weapons, equipment or means of delivery designed to use such agents or toxins for hostile purposes or in armed conflict.[35]

Article 1 constrains activities not defined as being for prophylactic, protective or other peaceful purposes; Article 1 does not prohibit production of the agents and toxins themselves and allows development, production and use for the defined purposes. The interpretation of the purposes is left to the actor – and given the dual-use nature of most life sciences research, the research purpose could serve both peaceful and non-peaceful aims simultaneously. The intended application of the research, or how it may be used or misused by others, is not readily apparent from its public purpose. The oft-discussed weakness of the BWC is that it lacks a verification provision; the Convention holds forth lofty goals, but it has no means beyond moral suasion to enforce its provisions. That weakness was never more manifest than when then-Russian President Boris Yeltsin, in 1992, publicly terminated the Russian BW program (20 years after his country had acceded to the BWC).

Through the prism of Realist theory ('realpolitik'), the potential erosion of the international norms and cultural taboos against CBW use are apparent – especially where regime survival is in jeopardy. Again, the norms are context-dependent – and if the elite's interests in preserving its monopoly over power, and the instruments of government are paramount, all else falls away. Cicero's classic dictum pertains: '*Silent enim leges inter arma*';[36] a more modern version of this thought is embodied in the 19th century German concept of *Kriegsraison*.[37] Although the breach does not abrogate the constraint, the breach reinforces that the constraint is context-dependent. The Iraqi use of nerve gas against its Kurdish population – and the Syrian use of chlorine gas in 2013 against civilian targets – demonstrate the point.

One argument against the power of the CBW prohibitory norms and taboos is that these constraints are reinforced by the common perception that chemical and biological weapons do not have military utility and that they are ineffective, uncontrollable, unproven or supplanted by advanced conventional weapons. Prohibiting weapons seen as useless would be easy, and the Rhodesian case supports this argument in that once CBW is seen as effective (in fact, more effective than conventional weapons), the normative prohibitions and taboo constraints fall away. Ultimately, for CBW norms and taboos to be effective in constraining the adoption of CBW agents, verification and enforcement tools must be available. If the international community wills the end (the abolition of CBW), it also must will the means. In the absence of effective means, the norms and taboos merely are moral suasion.

If we accept the premise that CBW prohibitions are context-dependent, how will the demonstrated utility of CBW in specific cases affect the international norm? Will repeated CBW use erode the response of the international community? Will other nations become emboldened to adopt and use CBW because of perceptions of weak or ineffectual international responses? Will scientific advances further erode the norms as science improves the potential utility of CBW? The revolution in the life sciences offers up both wondrous and terrifying possibilities – and the same revolution threatens to undermine the existing BW convention and regimes.

National acceptance of any set of normative constraints depends on where the nation sits in the international community. Those nations – rogue or marginalized; failed or nearly failed – have little invested in abiding by the norms, if self-preservation is threatened. Richard Price has argued that the normative prohibitions on CW – and probably, by extension, on BW – have evolved over time to become taboos.[38] Counterintuitively, Price has claimed that the repeated violations have strengthened the taboos. He stated:

> The Iran-Iraq War proved the resilience of the taboo. When Iraq first used chemical weapons against Iran in 1982 -- a desperate measure to try to turn the tide

of a seemingly lost war – the international reaction was muted. Emboldened, Saddam turned his chemical arsenal against the Kurds. It is noteworthy, however, that Saddam initiated Iraq's use of chemical weapons incrementally – gradually moving from nonlethal tear gas to mustard gas, and only after repeated warnings – indicating a keen appreciation for the possibility of international reaction. Further, even as Saddam proceeded to use chemical weapons, he refused to admit it; such behavior actually reinforced the notion that chemical weapons were politically sensitive.

Although Saddam was able to get away with using chemical weapons in the short term, this last significant episode of chemical warfare wound up strengthening the taboo in the long term. Eventually, the international community responded to Saddam's actions by crafting the CWC, which was signed in 1993 and extended the ban from the use of chemical weapons to possession, production, and transfer. Throughout the 1990s, UN enforcement of the intrusive weapons inspection regime in Iraq further cemented the reputation of chemical agents as "weapons of mass destruction."[39]

The argument that cases of CBW use have eroded the prohibitory norms misses the point that CBW use or non-use is context-dependent, not norm-dependent. Even one BWC State-Party (South Africa) developed and used BW agents for over a decade – and the well-known example of Yeltsin's 1992 termination of the former Soviet BW program further illustrates the point. Syria's recent use of CW itself has not strengthened or diminished the CBW prohibition, but the failure of the international community to act more decisively may have emboldened other marginal nations to explore CBW adoption and use to counter threats to their own internal security.

Challenges facing CBW-related intelligence: Intelligence collection and analysis of CBW topics remains difficult for many reasons, and intelligence agencies often are strongly criticized for their poor performance when addressing CBW-related issues. The debacle over the CIA's assessment of Iraq's WMD programs in the run-up to the 2003 invasion of Iraq is only one in a long list of intelligence failures. Although true that intelligence agencies often blunder when dealing with collection and analysis on CBW issues, those failures often stemmed from the inherent challenges surrounding CBW. The Rhodesian example illustrates many of those challenges and highlights how agencies can fail to identify, target, collect and analyze intelligence related to CBW.

Intelligence agencies are tasked with the mission of collecting and analyzing intelligence for decision-makers.* Intelligence is a tool and must have a purpose if it is to be useful – and the term 'actionable' is often used to describe valuable intelligence.

---

* An exhaustive literature on intelligence already exists, and the intention here is not to provide a lengthy or detailed description of the intelligence profession, or of any one intelligence service. The objective here is to highlight some of the key challenges facing CBW intelligence collection and analysis, with the Rhodesian case study as an illustration.

To be actionable means that the information enables the 'customer' to make a decision regarding a course of action. Information for information's sake is less useful; generally, that purpose comes in the form of intelligence requirements. Requirements are statements of an intelligence need and are generally prioritized by importance to national policy, audience (e.g. the President, Department etc.), urgency etc. Intelligence agencies receive intelligence requirements and vet them as to whether resources are available to address the particular intelligence need. If the requirement has a high priority, or responds to the needs of a senior-level decision-maker(s), resources could be developed or redirected. Resources are finite and expensive, and intelligence agencies typically receive far more intelligence requirements than they have resources to cover adequately. In the end, many intelligence requirements receive little-to-no attention because more pressing issues trumped their priority, or because resources could not be developed or allocated to the topic. This truth is especially evident for CBW-related collection and analysis.

The President's WMD Commission reported in 2005 that:

> For many years, the U.S. intelligence and policy communities did not take the biological weapons threat as seriously as the dangers posed by nuclear weapons. Many felt that states might experiment with biological weapons, but would not use them against the United States for fear of nuclear retaliation. Similarly, terrorists who promised to bring "plagues" upon the United States were thought to be merely indulging in grandiose threats; they lacked the technical expertise to actually develop and deploy a biological weapon.[40]

Intelligence collection takes several forms – including clandestinely acquired human intelligence (HUMINT), electronically acquired signals intelligence (SIGINT), imagery intelligence (IMINT) and measurement and signature intelligence (MASINT). Open-source 'intelligence' (OSINT) has gained recognition with the explosion of information available over the internet.* Each of these collection types has its own sub-disciplines – and each of these intelligence fields provides insights from different perspectives. Very generally, HUMINT sources are best at revealing foreign government intentions, plans and activities; SIGINT provides insight into activities; IMINT allows intelligence agencies to observe activities; MASINT, from a CBW perspective, informs intelligence agencies about activities that have occurred.

Analysis assembles intelligence from all these sources – including open-source information – and attempts to provide the customers with a reasonably accurate, coherent

---

* Open-source monitoring has a long and distinguished history of supporting intelligence stretching back to World War II and the UK's BBC Monitoring (founded in 1939) and the US' Foreign Broadcast Information Service (founded in 1941 and now known as the Open Source Center). To purists, intelligence involves the clandestine collection of secret information (information hidden or protected by another party); for this reason, open-source should be referred to as information, and not intelligence. The motto on the Open Source Center's web portal is 'Information to Intelligence'.

description of foreign activities and some predictive insights. The goal is not to describe past events, except to perhaps briefly provide some context; instead, the objective focuses on providing customers with insights that allow them to shape their decisions to best further the national interest.* Intelligence analysis also has a warning function: that is to warn of emerging developments or trends that could affect national policy or welfare. Most obviously, this function is to warn of impending danger or threats to national security, but warning also can mean the responsibility to alert decision-makers to significant developments of which they were unaware. In all, intelligence analysis is the handmaiden to decision-making. Ideally, intelligence is a support function; it does not act on its own, except to inform and execute policy-makers' decisions. The relative autonomy of different intelligence agencies will vary from country to country, however. The intelligence culture found in Russia differs from that in China, or Germany, or Canada, or Britain, or the US, or South Africa *ad nauseam.*

The secrecy surrounding offensive CBW research, development and production – as well as related doctrine, planning, training, deployment and preparations for use – remains one of the key challenges for CBW intelligence collection and analysis. In the pantheon of national secrets, few are as closely and jealously guarded as those touching on WMD – including CBW. The rationale behind the tight security surrounding CBW is that virtually all of the nations assessed to have active offensive CBW efforts have signed and/or ratified the BWC and CWC – making CBW development and use illegal. Nations also want to avoid the international stigma and opprobrium of being linked to the possession or use of CBW, along with the resulting possibility of international isolation and sanctions. For these reasons, offensive CBW work is done in extreme secrecy. Scientists working on CBW programs are carefully vetted for loyalty and absence of foreign ties or allegiances; CBW facilities are disguised and may operate as legitimate laboratories or production facilities until mobilized. In his April 1999 Congressional testimony on the WMD threat, Nonproliferation Center chief John Lauder stated that: 'Even supposedly 'legitimate' facilities can readily conduct clandestine CBW research and can convert rapidly to agent production, providing a mobilization or 'breakout' capability. As a result, large stockpiles of CBW munitions simply may not be required in today's CBW arena';[41] for example, the Soviet Union at the height of its CBW effort could turn production from an innocuous good to produce agents on demand during wartime ('mobilization').

Jonathan Tucker and Kathleen Vogel described the Soviet mobilization capability as:

> The Soviet BW complex also included several mobilization plants for large-scale production and weaponization of BW agents in wartime. For example, a major production facility at Stepnogorsk, Kazakhstan, had sufficient capacity

---

* This is the idealized goal. Realistically (and cynically speaking), many internal and external factors separate from purely the national interest influence the actions of decision-makers and how they use intelligence.

to cultivate, process, and load into munitions a total of 300 tons of dry anthrax during a 220-day wartime mobilization period.[42]

Efforts to collect against and analyze possible CBW activities also face the dual-use problem. Virtually all research that could be labeled as offensive CBW work also has legitimate scientific and commercial applications. Similarly, CBW defensive research into prophylaxis, treatments or therapeutics can be applied to offensive CBW programs. Nefarious actors could even disguise offensive CBW research within a defensive research program, with the offensive purpose only revealed at the point of weaponization, as the President's WMD Commission pointed out in 2005:

> The same technology that is used for good today, can, if it falls into the wrong hands, be used for evil tomorrow. The overlap between BW agents and vaccines and between nerve agents and pesticides is, as you know, considerable. The technologies used to prolong our lives and improve our standard of living can quite easily be used to cause mass casualties. BW technology is, in part, widely available because all societies have a legitimate need for the biotechnology on which it is based.[43]

Exactly because of the dual-use conundrum, intelligence agencies should prioritize their efforts on intent. Although more difficult to collect on the intent of foreign decision-makers, intent is far more 'diagnostic' as to whether an offensive CBW program exists; its rationale; the underlying threat perceptions; the doctrine defining use etc. The problem with collecting against foreign intent is that intent can vary over time and may not be acted on, or may be implemented imperfectly by subordinates, as John Lauder stated:

> I would offer one footnote on the difficulty of assessing the threat from biological and chemical weapons today: Intelligence is all about ascertaining not only the capabilities, but also the intentions of one's adversaries. Because of the dual utility of the technology and expertise involved, the actual CBW threat is in fact tied directly to intentions. Getting at this intent is the hardest thing for intelligence to do, but it is essential if we are to determine with certainty the scope and nature of the global biological and chemical warfare threat.[44]

Foreign leaders also compartmentalize decisions related to offensive CBW programs, as well as restricting involvement in the decision-making process and information sharing to an absolute minimum. This compartmentalization of decision-making reduces the possibility that HUMINT collectors will have access to information on leadership intent and planning, as the WMD Commission stated in its final report:

> There are several reasons for the lack of quality human sources reporting on Iraqi weapons programs. At the outset, and as noted above, Iraq was an uncommonly challenging target for human intelligence. And given the highly compartmented nature of Saddam Hussein's regime, it is unclear whether even a source

at the highest levels of the Iraqi government would have been able to provide true insight into Saddam's decisionmaking. The challenges revealed by the Iraq case study suggest some inherent limitations of human intelligence collection.[45]

Analysis of CBW programs constitutes a hard intelligence problem. The lack of reliable, credible HUMINT intelligence confounds the ability of intelligence analysts to come to meaningful conclusions about even some of the most basic questions, such as: 'Does country X have a chemical or biological weapons program?' What information is available to intelligence analysts often is dated, fragmentary or from less than reliable sources. As the Curveball fiasco demonstrated, sources lie – especially if they hope to gain.* In Curveball's case, he was looking for refugee status for himself and his pregnant wife[46] – and to achieve his goal, he concocted tales that reinforced the assumptions (and prejudices) of US Intelligence analysts. Even sources credible on some specific topics will exaggerate their knowledge or access regarding other issues in a struggle to remain relevant to their handlers; others will fabricate information based on trolling the internet, or will pass off rumors as fact so they will keep being paid.

Although massively expensive and technologically complex, SIGINT collection probably contributes the most information to CBW analysis. The overwhelming amount and array of information SIGINT gathers was illustrated by Edward Snowden's revelations. Despite the bewildering capabilities of SIGINT, it cannot match HUMINT for insight into intent and, as was mentioned, intent should be the gold standard for CBW intelligence analysis. SIGINT instead captures the flood of information related to dual-use scientific and commercial activities related to chemical research and production, and life sciences research. Also, SIGINT is useful in understanding the potential CBW capabilities of nations, but lacks the intent portion of the equation.

For all the intelligence collection disciplines (INTs), IMINT perhaps is the least relevant, in that most CBW activities take place indoors – away from prying eyes in the sky. IMINT can determine if a facility is active, but it cannot describe the activity in detail. IMINT also can determine when supplies are delivered and when shipments are made, but it typically lacks the ability to identify the specific contents. Also, IMINT can corroborate information from other 'INTs', such as the location of facilities etc.

MASINT – in the CBW context – generally is the collection and analysis of samples (air, water, soil etc.) and testing for chemicals, metabolites, organisms, toxins, remnants or other signs of CBW activities. MASINT perhaps is most useful for CBW analysts for the information it can provide for attribution; detecting possible CBW use; determining whether the event was naturally occurring or intentional; and identifying possible perpetrators. In the Rhodesian case, MASINT could have been useful in understanding the causes of the 1978-1980 anthrax epidemic.

---

*   The story of Curveball now is exhaustively documented in publicly available official documents, and by journalists in both print and television.

One of the challenges facing CBW collectors and analysts throughout the Cold War was the almost single-minded collection focus on the Soviet Union and its proxies, as the WMD Commission described:

> Throughout the Cold War, the United States focused its collection efforts against monolithic Communist powers – the Soviet Union and China – and their proxy states. These targets had sizeable military and industrial complexes that our satellites could observe, and they had hierarchical institutions, predictable communications procedures, and reporting behavior that we could selectively target for eavesdropping. As a result, although penetration took time and was far from perfect, on the whole the Intelligence Community gained an impressive understanding of our main adversaries. During this period, a number of intelligence agencies – the National Security Agency, the National Reconnaissance Office, and others – developed around the various technologies and disciplines used to collect against these targets.[47]

Given these priorities – and the focus of collection platforms to address specific Cold War requirements – CBW outside that group of adversarial nations was marginalized, and the available tool set was not optimized to efficiently collect CBW information elsewhere. The resource and requirements focus results in an observational bias – described by the oft-used analogy of the drunk looking for his keys under the streetlight – and this observational bias pertains to the Rhodesian case. Intelligence agencies tended to look where they already had collection resources and capabilities; during the Cold War, no emphasis was placed on CBW developments outside the Soviet Bloc (including Cuba), China and North Korea. One result was that Western Intelligence probably missed all the signs of Rhodesian CBW activities; the extent of reporting on the Rhodesian CBW effort in Russian, Cuban or Chinese archives is unknown. If reporting in the archives of the old Soviet KGB existed, such reporting likely would have surfaced by now. The Mitrokhin archive – perhaps the most comprehensive collection of Soviet Intelligence documents now publicly available – contains no reference at all to Rhodesian CBW activities. The irresistible question then is why, given all the insurgent claims at the time, did no intelligence agency act?

In the mid-to-late 1970s, the focus of US Intelligence in Southern Africa was on the Cuban presence in Angola and the activities of other perceived Soviet and Chinese proxies elsewhere (i.e. ZAPU, ZANU, ANC etc.). A review of declassified CIA assessments reveals that most of the focus was on Soviet-Bloc and Chinese support for ZAPU and ZANU respectively. Likely, the feeling among Africa hands in US Intelligence agencies was that resources needed to be devoted to stemming the tide of Marxist influence in Africa, rather than examining allegations of Rhodesian wrongdoing. Rhodesia's internationally recognized legal status as a British colony also hampered US Intelligence activities involving Rhodesia. In the intelligence partnership enshrined in the 'special relationship', the US was constrained from intelligence activities in Britain or British territories without London's prior consent. Britain's intelligence agencies – the Secret Intelligence Service (SIS) and the General

Communications Headquarters (GCHQ) – were responsible for collection of intelligence on Rhodesia. Lord Owen (then-Foreign Secretary, with oversight of SIS) and Lord Renwick (head of the Foreign and Commonwealth Office's Rhodesia Office) both stated that London had no intelligence about Rhodesian CBW efforts; however, Foreign Office documents discussing the UK's reservation to the BWC regarding Rhodesia suggest that London had reporting on the topic as early as February 1975.[48]

To this day, the ranks of the former Rhodesian Security Forces continue to rumor and speculate about Britain's very thorough penetration of Rhodesia's security elements. No doubt, British Intelligence used both HUMINT and SIGINT, and had very significant capabilities focused on Rhodesia. These capabilities almost certainly produced excellent intelligence on developments there, but still, despite all these resources, no evidence exists that London ever caught more than a glimmer of Rhodesia's CBW effort. Several explanations are plausible: first, Rhodesia so effectively compartmented the CBW program inside the CIO and Special Branch – restricting access to essentially Ken Flower and McGuinness – that only a very determined effort directed at the CBW operations might have successfully learned the truth. Given that Flower most often is suspected as being 'the mole' – and he maintained a decent working relationship with foreign intelligence services throughout the war – how then could the CBW effort have remained secret? The answer is that even if Flower were a mole, he may have retained either enough loyalty to the cause to keep the CBW secrets hidden, or he hid the CBW secrets for fear of self-recrimination.

Second, successful security hid the Rhodesian CBW effort. A corollary here is that the Rhodesian CBW effort had a very small footprint – using only materials that were commonly used in agricultural and industrial chemicals. The small footprints – few workers in a rudimentary facility with no specialized equipment or materials – are intrinsically harder to detect. A mirror-imaging bias is that because the US and Soviet programs developed CBW munitions in large, industrial-scale, highly specialized facilities, analysts assumed other countries would do the same. Consequently, intelligence collectors and analysts typically would miss indications of CBW cobbled together by half a dozen 'call-ups' in a 'fort' made of corrugated tin sheets out in the middle of nowhere. Today, the fear that al-Qaeda, ISIS or whoever is producing CBW in a cave, garage or mother's basement may nullify that bias.

Third, British Intelligence probably knew about the CBW effort; whether or not London focused collection and analytical resources to assess the activities remains unclear. However, any files that may have existed now are moldering in Vauxhall's impenetrable archives – and none of this information is publicly known or available to researchers. An equally plausible alternate scenario is that London was aware of the Rhodesian CBW activities and turned a blind eye.

US Intelligence channels first became aware of a Rhodesian CBW effort in 1990 – a decade after Rhodesia's transition; nine years after Johnson and Martin made mention of it in their book; and three years after Ken Flower wrote about it in his autobiography. Even a classified US Defense Department Intelligence Information Report (IIR)[49] – disseminated in 1990 – was dismissed in CBW intelligence circles. A brief, fleeting awareness of the Rhodesian CBW effort flickered following the revelations of South Africa's 'Project Coast' in 1993[50] – and some press coverage of the TRC hearings and Wouter Basson's trial mentioned the CBW activities in Rhodesia, as did Chandré Gould's books. The South African briefings to the US/UK Intelligence teams almost certainly did not reference Rhodesia, however. The neglect of those briefings to touch on the Rhodesian case probably was because of the irrelevance to 'Project Coast'; the passage of time; and the emergence of an Independent Zimbabwe.

The relative indifference to Rhodesia's CBW efforts contrasts sharply with the mobilization of the US and UK Intelligence communities to address South Africa's then-defunct 'Project Coast'. On 11 April 1994, the US and UK sent a joint *demarche* regarding 'Project Coast' to South African President F.J. de Klerk. The *demarche* asked that South Africa brief a bilateral team on all aspects of 'Project Coast'; destroy all records related to CBW; punish those accountable for CBW use; and brief Mandela:[51]

> According to Dr. Knobel, then South African Surgeon General, President de Klerk and the South Africans cooperated with the Americans and British. However, Knobel and other South African officials believed that the Americans and British were acting on the basis of questionable and uncorroborated evidence, some of which came from press reports. According to Knobel, he and Basson were given responsibility for briefing the US and British experts and Mandela. After the *demarche* and the inauguration of President Mandela in May 1994, American and British delegations arrived for the first of several visits to South Africa. Knobel, Basson, and others extensively briefed the delegations over a three-day period … The SADF compiled a large file on Project Coast and gave it to the Americans and British.[52]

Attribution: Attribution refers to the detection, characterization and identification of suspicious events (whether chemical releases or disease outbreaks) to determine if the event was natural, accidental or deliberate. Natural chemical releases are unlikely to occur, but distinguishing accidental from deliberate is important in characterizing an event as terrorist-related or not. Bioattribution is the process of determining if a disease outbreak is naturally occurring, or if an intentional release of a pathogen or toxin occurred. The ultimate goal of any attribution process is to identify those responsible for a deliberate release of a toxin, chemical or lethal pathogen and hold them accountable for their misdeeds.

Chemical attribution is somewhat straightforward, because most toxic chemicals are not naturally occurring. Typical chemical agents – such as chlorine, mustard, phosgene, lewisite and the nerve agents sarin, soman, tabun, VX etc. – are synthesized (manufactured). Release of these chemicals therefore is either accidental or intentional. Toxic industrial chemicals are those with industrial uses, such as chlorine, phosgene, cyanide and arsenic. Accidental releases typically occur at production or storage facilities, or while chemicals are in transit (tanker truck or railcar). Characteristics of accidental chemical releases include a point source (e.g. a leak at a chemical facility, or a spill from a tanker truck or rail car). Leaks can be due to poor facility maintenance or an operator error; spills in transit typically result when the chemical container (e.g. a tanker or rail car) is ruptured. Again, the location likely will be at a single point source and easily identified. Most cases involving the release of toxic industrial chemicals are treated as hazardous materials (HAZMAT) incidents.

Intentional chemical releases probably will involve either a kinetic attack (e.g. the use of explosives or firearms against a facility, pipeline or tanker truck or rail car); a chemical release by an insider with access to facility control systems (e.g. opening values, tampering with safety equipment, disabling sensors, venting gases to the atmosphere etc.); or the theft and release of chemicals. Attacks involving toxic industrial chemicals (TICs) usually are categorized as terrorist attacks. Unlike accidental releases occurring at single point sources, terrorists may attempt multiple attacks inside a short timeframe, or at line-source attack depending on the terrorist(s) access to materials and capabilities. This distinction should help investigators distinguish an accident from an intentional release; obviously, the use of explosives or firearms in a kinetic attack points to a deliberate release.

Differentiating a malicious insider's deliberate sabotage from an accident may prove slightly more challenging in the short term. An example of this challenge is the December 1984 Bhopal (India) disaster, in which a release of a pesticide precursor – methyl isocyanate (MIC) – was released from a Union Carbide India facility. Several investigations took place in the aftermath of the incident, which resulted in 3,787 deaths. The investigations reached different conclusions – and two concluded that the event resulted from deliberate sabotage:

> We believe that it was at this point – during the shift change – that a disgruntled operator entered the storage area and hooked up one of the readily available rubber water hoses to Tank 610 with the intention of contaminating and spoiling the tank's contents. It was well known among the plant's operators that water and MIC should not be mixed. He unscrewed the local pressure indicator, which can be easily accomplished by hand, and connected the hose to the tank. The entire operation could be completed within five minutes. Minor incidents of process sabotage by employees had occurred previously at the Bhopal plant, and, indeed, occur from time to time in industrial plants all over the world.[53]

A separate investigation by India's CSIR implicated lax management, poor worker training, inadequate maintenance and system design flaws in the accident. The CSIR report stated that the disaster resulted when a maintenance worker cleaning other equipment in the facility failed to follow standard operating procedures – and that oversight allowed water to enter a MIC storage tank; design and construction flaws failed to provide proper fail-safes. The water reacted exothermically with the MIC, and the resulting gas vented to the atmosphere.[54]

The difficulties almost certainly will be greater in attributing biological events (bioattribution), because bioattribution involves naturally occurring organisms or toxins produced by such organisms. Since the 2001 anthrax letter mailings, bioattribution has become a topic *du jour* among some scientists interested in promoting the study and advancement of microbial forensics. The thinking goes that syndromic surveillance[55] will detect a disease occurrence with unusual or suspect epidemiological characteristics. Unusual disease characteristics could include occurrence out of typical season; increased virulence and/or pathogencity; multi-foci outbreak (initial cases occurring simultaneously at different locations); antibiotic resistance; an unusual rate of morbidity or mortality; atypical disease vectors or transmission paths etc. All of these factors raise suspicions, but not are conclusive even when combined;[56] suspicion is heightened if the outbreak involves a reportable disease, and is heightened further if the disease is a Select Agent.'[57] Once the syndromic surveillance tools report an unusual occurrence, local or national public health agencies may monitor the event and investigate its cause.

Once the pathogen is isolated, microbial forensic scientists would hope to determine the organism's origins and any man-made modifications. Randy Murch, in his 2003 paper calling for the creation of microbial forensics stated: '… The new discipline of microbial forensics is in the process of being founded from an array of established and emerging fields, such as classical microbiology, microbial genetics, phylogenetics, and informatics, and it should embrace lessons learned from human DNA forensics and forensic informatics…'[58] Importantly, microbial forensics is a new and largely untested sub-discipline of traditional forensic science. Although the field holds promise – especially as the science and capabilities advance – microbial forensics is experiencing growing pains.

The outcome of the scientific work in the AMERITHRAX investigation is noteworthy for illustrating the challenges, as well as the advances made, in microbial forensics. As part of the investigation, the FBI collected samples of *B. anthracis* from collections in the US and around the world for comparison to the material recovered from the letters. Even with this massive sample library of nearly 1,100 samples, a match was difficult to make. Ultimately, the FBI scientists identified four morphological types in the material from the letters. They then concluded that only material from RMR-1029 – a flask of *B. anthracis* spores housed at the US Army Medical Institute of Infectious Diseases (USAMIIRD) – contained the same four morphological types.[59] The scientific community reacted to the FBI conclusion with skepticism – and a National Academies of Science panel reviewed the FBI findings and concluded: 'It is not possible to reach a definitive conclusion about the origins of the *B. anthracis* in the mailings based on the available scientific evidence alone'.[60] Their conclusion reinforces the point that science – especially a new scientific sub-discipline – cannot and may never be able to provide definitive answers to bioattribution questions. This runs contrary to the popular misconception promoted on television dramas such as '*CSI*' and its spin-offs that laboratory technicians crack cases.

The AMERITHRAX case is a best-case example in that the investigators had virtually *carte blanche*. They had access to leading experts, funding, large spore collections for reference, victim samples etc. – and they also were operating largely on their home turf. The team seemed to have all the advantages they would need, and yet critics continue to insist that the government fingered the wrong individual or overlooked

---

*   'Select Agent' is the US Federal Government's term for pathogens (including viruses and bacteria) and toxins with the potential to be used as bioweapons, or as posing a significant risk to agriculture or public health.

key exculpatory evidence, or was guilty of shoddy science.* The challenges facing foreign bioattribution efforts (except in advanced industrialized countries) likely will be compounded by a host of problems ranging from political, legal and jurisdiction hurdles; to operating in conflict zones; to uncooperative host governments; to unreliable witness testimony; to inability to access victims; to destruction of evidence; to chain of custody issues *ad infinitum*.

The Rhodesian anthrax epidemic illustrates many of the challenges confronting bioattribution overseas. As a case study for bioattribution, the Rhodesian example importantly mirrors the type of environment most likely to see possible BW use (i.e. a developing nation in a prolonged violent conflict – likely an insurgency or civil war involving differing racial, ethnic or religious groups). In Rhodesia, syndromic – or even clinical – surveillance of rural areas would have been difficult to impossible. Health infrastructure, where it existed, likely had been destroyed or seriously degraded due to lack of staff, supplies and equipment – and initial anthrax cases likely did not reach clinics. If they did, staff probably misdiagnosed them. Recall that the initial case at Nkayi's clinic was only identified because the chief healthcare worker there, a male nurse, recognized the cutaneous anthrax lesion from his experience treating anthrax cases 15 years before.

Cases of anthrax in animals almost certainly occurred for some time prior to the first reported human case. The information gaps in true location and timing of the initial animal and human anthrax cases – and the delays in reporting – produced anomalous results (including the appearance of a multi-foci outbreak, an unusual speed of transmission and geographic 'hops'). These features, which are otherwise explainable, appear suspicious, given the lack of accurate and timely reporting. Clinical case reviews would have found that case mortality was in the expected range (approximately 1.9 percent) and that the disease responded to antibiotics.

Clinical samples could have been collected for analysis, probably in South Africa or a Western country. Some environmental samples probably could have been collected, but only in areas free of suspected insurgent activity – and then only when under the protection of the Rhodesian Security Forces. That constraint would have affected how, when and where sample collection took place. Although subject to negotiation, Rhodesian authorities may have imposed conditions on the bioattribution exercise, if they permitted it at all; for example, the Rhodesian authorities would have had to approve all sample collection and may have insisted that Rhodesian scientists in Rhodesian facilities conduct all testing and analysis. If imposed, these conditions would have introduced issues of bias and chain of custody.

Critics could point to a lack of objectivity and impartiality on the part of Rhodesians involved in the bioattribution effort – and the issue of Rhodesia's legal status could have been another impediment to bioattribution. In the eyes of the international community, Rhodesia remained a British colony under London's jurisdiction *de jure*;

---

* Lacking in scientific credentials, the critics – like most conspiratorialists – are most vocal on internet blogs. None have published their views in peer-reviewed, academic journals, nor have they garnered any large or influential following.

yet Salisbury exercised *de facto* control; however, this distinction did not seem to hinder a World Health Organization (WHO) investigation of a 1975 Marburg virus outbreak in Rhodesia.

Although unavailable at the time, genomic analysis of the collected samples could determine the native ecology of the *B. anthracis* strains. Two strains of *B. anthracis* would have been identified: one was native to Rhodesia, and a second was native to neighboring South Africa. Because *B. anthracis* is a genetically conservative organism (i.e. genetic change occurs slowly), the South African strain could have been introduced to Rhodesia decades before and established itself in the ecological niche there. Testing almost certainly would have determined that neither strain was engineered or modified to increase virulence, pathogenicity or antibiotic resistance.

Lastly, witness testimony from black African patients would have pointed to infection due to butchering and preparing meat from anthrax-infected animals, or through insect bites. Witness testimony of intentional human dissemination of *B. anthracis* spores is unlikely, given that none was ever received during the epidemic. The Rhodesian foreign Government probably would not have allowed unfettered access to government officials or military personnel – and any such interviews would have been with individuals previously coached by the government so as to make them unreliable. No interviews with Selous Scout or Special Branch members would be permitted; no access to documents would be granted, and the Rhodesian press was censored – limiting its usefulness. Meetings with insurgents probably would have been limited to talks with headquarters personnel for each of the insurgent groups – and meetings with operational guerrillas inside Rhodesia would have been very difficult, if not impossible. As with Rhodesian officials, the likelihood of bias and propaganda would be very high in guerrilla interviews, and perhaps even higher when speaking with insurgent officials at headquarters.

In the end, a bioattribution exercise to determine the cause of the 1978-1980 anthrax epidemic in Rhodesia probably would have raised as many questions as it answered. The likely consensus would have been that the epidemic resulted from a natural occurrence that was exacerbated by the wartime conditions – and an objective post-mortem bioattribution examination of the epidemic today most certainly would come to the same conclusion.

The purpose of bioattribution is to hold those responsible accountable. In a domestic legal sense, this means, as in the AMERITHRAX case, identifying suspects and bringing them to trial. In cases of suspected CBW use overseas, the goal of attribution falls into the realm of international politics and diplomacy; for example, witness the 2013 instance of the Syrian Government's use of CW against its own civilian population. Even with strong evidence on videotape – from attending physicians, and from several intelligence agencies – the international community waffled on taking concrete action, while loudly condemning the Assad regime. Although the available evidence seemed incontrovertible that CW was used in an attack, the medical evidence alone was insufficient to identify the attackers definitively.[*] Diplomatic pres-

---

[*]   Little doubt remains that the Syrian regime of Bashar al-Assad was responsible for the CW attacks. Moscow had claimed that the Syrian Government's culpability was unproven; the

sure forced the Syrian Government to accede to the CWC, and it decommissioned its CW facilities and allowed the destruction of its declared CW stockpiles and munitions; yet allegations of CW use in Syria persist[61] and the media has reported evidence of sarin at previous undeclared Syrian facilities[62] – all pointing to the likelihood that diplomatic pressure to end Syria's CW program was less than completely successful.

In either case, attribution is a difficult endeavor. BW is more challenging because it deals with naturally occurring organisms, which may be hard to differentiate from organisms introduced by man. Microbial forensics as a science shows great potential, but as demonstrated in the AMERITHAX and Rhodesian examples, science alone cannot meet the bar of evidence needed by decision-makers. CW use may be easier to detect and identify scientifically, but hurdles remain in ascribing CW use to specific actors. As with bioattribution, CW attribution requires scientific analysis of collected materials, as well as an intelligence or investigative component. The international response to CBW use also is directly proportional to the weight of evidence and the confidence in the findings of any attribution effort.

Conclusion

Although knowledge of the Rhodesian CBW effort has been lost, the techniques and materials were basic, readily available and inexpensive. Recreation of Rhodesian CBW agents is within the grasp of nations' intent on a CBW capability and within the reach of most determined non-State actors' intent on causing harm. What differentiates a State-run Rhodesian-style CBW effort from a similar non-State effort is that non-States lack the means of disseminating the materials to consumers. Rhodesia and other nations can control a food supply network. Terrorist groups do not control the mechanics of the food supply chain; their reach is limited to product tampering. Product tampering likely would produce limited results, and the sad fact is that many more people fall ill annually from naturally occurring food poisoning than are likely to be affected by terrorist poisoning of food or water.

The Rhodesian CBW effort demonstrated the ease and low cost of creating and operating a CBW effort that resulted in the deaths of nearly 1,000 people during three years; the exact number will never be known. The team that processed the chemicals consisted of a laboratory technician and a veterinary student – and their technical expertise was limited. The chemicals themselves were readily available agricultural pesticides that were not further processed, and the facility used was little more than a corrugated sheet-metal hut with no sophisticated laboratory equipment or personal protective gear. Using crude techniques with common materials in a basic facility, the Rhodesians were able to process and disseminate enough poisoned material to kill, at least, hundreds of guerrilla recruits. Given the scale of the guerrilla recruitment successes, the impact of the Rhodesian CBW effort was significant, but hardly the decisive war-winning tactic that some believed it could be.

evidence presented was insufficient for an assertion of guilt. The Russians instead placed blame for the attack on the rebels.

The most enduring and relevant legacy of the Rhodesian CBW effort is that similar small-scale CBW efforts drawing on limited scientific knowhow, primitive equipment and crude materials can be effective for State and non-State actors today. Advances in the life sciences will lower the bar for the development, production and dissemination of CBW, but CBW capabilities are within the reach of most, if not all, nations (and within the reach of many, if not most, non-State actors). The difficulty is not in the production of the poisoned materials; the problem lay in how to get the materials inserted for use/consumption by the target. Rhodesia, like most nations, had the means to introduce agents into insurgents' food supplies. The Rhodesians and South Africans overcame the latter difficulty through use of their extensive informer/agent networks that penetrated the targeted organizations and delivered the poisoned materials. Other nations with similar intelligence or police capabilities could conduct similar operations against their internal adversaries. These capabilities remain viable three decades later and could be used by State and non-State actors to assassinate targeted individuals or small groups of people. The cost to acquire and process the materials would be negligible, and detection of CBW programs with limited-to-small footprints remains difficult. Intelligence agencies will continue to face obstacles (dual-use dilemma and the invisibility of intent) that limit their ability to identify State programs and, to some extent, non-State efforts.

The contextual nature of the international CBW norms weakens the norms' effectiveness in preventing CBW use – especially in intrastate conflict such as counterinsurgencies, where regime survival is at stake. Having no effective enforcement tools, the international norms have only political or moral value. The CWC and BWC possess the weight of law, but these conventions and related norms lack enforcement mechanisms. In cases of suspected CBW use, the recourse remains the UN Security Council. Efforts to extend international law to govern CBW use in intrastate conflict (e.g. the Rome Statute 2010 Review Conference in Kampala, Uganda and the Responsibility to Protect (R2P)) are maturing, but their impact is debatable; problems abound. Many nations are non-State parties, or have signed, but not ratified, the Rome Statute. R2P is a proposed international norm that would allow intervention in internal conflicts under specific conditions, but military intervention is allowed only as a last resort.

The difficulty surrounding attribution – especially bioattribution – also undermines the power of the international norm. If the international community can reach no agreement on the perpetrators' identity, efforts to hold the guilty accountable and punish them through diplomatic or legal action (such as sanctions), or through military action, is feckless. In almost all CBW incidents since World War II, questions persist about who conducted the CBW attack; who authorized it; how it was conducted; what agents were used; how targets were selected; and the outcome of the attack. The secrecy of the Rhodesian (and South African) CBW efforts ensured that public attention never focused on their activities until well after the fact.

The bottom line is that history has demonstrated that for nations entangled in intractable insurgencies or civil wars, expediency makes CBW highly attractive – especially if the survival of the regime is jeopardized. Those States could find CBW to be an effective means to defeat an unprepared adversary, or attack an elusive foe.

The application of current international law and norms prohibiting CBW will remain context-dependent, rather than universal. Casting CBW as abhorrent likely will not only prove unable to prevent CBW use, but may not be able to bring the guilty to justice. In the eyes of regime leaders, even the most repugnant in the eyes of the international community, CBW may be acceptable when those leaders are facing their destruction. Unless the international community wills the means to achieve its ends, the threat of CBW remains.

Notes

1   Dany Shoham, 'The Evolution of Chemical and Biological Weapons in Egypt, ACPR Policy Paper No.46', (1998); online at <http://www.acpr.org.il/pp/pp046-shohamE.pdf> (accessed on 17 September 2015).

2   The best documented example of the use of cholera (or suspected cholera) was in the second half of 1973 in the Mozambique provinces of Manica e Sofala and Teté. According to UN investigators, FRELIMO health officials received information of a large-scale cholera epidemic in those provinces. One of the physicians at a FRELIMO hospital, Dr Slavcho Slavov, reported to the UN commissioners that the incident was not typical of a cholera outbreak. The epidemic 'exploded' suddenly and ended abruptly, which is unusual for a natural cholera outbreak. Although the patients experienced vomiting and diarrhea, Slavov opined the diarrhea was atypical of cholera. According to UN documents, over 1,000 FRELIMO combatants died in this outbreak. Slavov suggested that the deaths were due to poisoning of water wells, but no testing had been done. Slavov went on to state that FRELIMO had captured supplies of water from Portuguese troops in the area – and he believed the capture of water supplies was indicative of the contamination of water sources. In the end, the UN Commission was inconclusive on claims of an intentional use of cholera, or on water poisoning. See 'Report of the Commission of Inquiry on the Reported Massacres in Mozambique, UN General Assembly, 29th Session, Supplement No.21' (A/9621) and 'Provisional Record of Testimony Taken at the Twentieth Meeting, UN Commission of Inquiry on the Reported Massacres in Mozambique' (A/AC.165/PV.20, dated 14 August 1974).

3   Matthew Preston, *Ending Civil War: Rhodesia and Lebanon in Perspective* (London: Tauris Academic Studies, 2004), pp.53-54.

4   CIO/3, communication dated 23 June 2007.

5   See Susan B. Martin, 'The Role of Biological Weapons in International Politics: The Real Military Revolution', *Journal of Strategic Studies* 25 (1) (2002), pp.63-98.

6   Michael C. Horowitz and Neil Narang, 'Poor Man's Atomic Bomb: Exploring the Relationship between 'Weapons of Mass Destruction'', *Journal of Conflict Resolution* 58 (3), p.513.

7   Gregory Koblentz, 'Regime Security: A New Theory for Understanding the Proliferation of Chemical and Biological Weapons', *Contemporary Security Policy* 34 (3), p.503.

8   Timothy V. McCarthy and Jonathan B. Tucker, 'Saddam's Toxic Arsenal: Chemical and Biological Weapons in the Gulf War' in Peter R. Lavoy, Scott D. Sagan and James J. Wirtz (eds.), *Planning the Unthinkable: How New Powers Will Use Nuclear, Biological, and Chemical Weapons* (New York: Cornell University Press, 2000), pp.47-78. Shlomo Shpiro, 'Poisoned Chalice: Intelligence Use of Chemical and Biological Weapons', *International Journal of Intelligence and CounterIntelligence* 22 (1), pp.1-30.

9   Central Intelligence Agency, 'Iraq's Chemical Warfare Program: More Self-Reliant, More Deadly', Research Paper (SW-90-10053JX), dated August 1990 (declassified as of 21 June 2011), p.iii.

10   Scott D. Sagan, 'Explaining Saddam's Non-Use of Chemical Weapons in the Gulf War', PASCC Workshop (6 June 2014), quoting FBI Summary of March 2004 Conversation between Saddam and Piro.

11   Robert Mandel, 'Chemical Warfare: Act of Intimidation or Desperation?', *Armed Forces and Society* 19 (2), p.199.

12   National Intelligence Council, 'Impact and Implications of Chemical Weapons Use in the Iran-Iraq War', Interagency Intelligence Memorandum (NI-IIM-88-1004C), dated April 1988 (declassified as of 8 October 2010), p.3.

13   Benjamin Buch and Scott D. Sagan, 'Our Red Lines and Theirs: New information reveals why Saddam Hussein never used chemical weapons in the Gulf War', *Foreign Policy*, dated 13 December 2013; online at <http://foreignpolicy.com/2013/12/13/our-red-lines-and-theirs/> (accessed on 10 September 2015).

14   National Intelligence Council (1988), p.6.

15   ibid.

16   Human Rights Watch, 'Appendix A: The Ali Hassan Al-Majid Tapes'; online at <http://www.hrw.org/legacy/campaigns/iraq/chemicalali.html> (accessed on 1 October 2015).

17   M. Zuhair Diab, 'Syria's Chemical and Biological Weapons: Assess Capabilities and Motivations', *The Nonproliferation Review* (Fall 1997), p.104.

18   ibid., p.107.

19   Mary Beth D. Nikitin, Paul K. Kerr and Andrew Feickert, *Syria's Chemical Weapons: Issues for Congress*, CRS Report for Congress 7-500 (Washington, DC: Congressional Research Service, 2013), p.4.

20   Julian Perry Robinson, 'Alleged Use of Chemical Weapons in Syria', Harvard-Sussex Program Occasional Paper Issue 04, dated 26 June 2013, pp.7-8.

21   Mark Lander, 'Obama Threatens Force Against Syria', *New York Times* (21 August 2012), p.A.7.

22   '"Today I want to make it absolutely clear to Assad and those under his command: The world is watching," Mr. Obama said in a speech at the National Defense University in Washington. "The use of chemical weapons is and would be totally unacceptable. If you make the tragic mistake of using these weapons, there will be consequences and you will be held accountable."' Peter Baker and Michael R. Gordon, 'U.S. Warns Syria on Chemical Weapons', *New York Times* (4 December 2012), p.A.8.

23   Simon Tisdall and Josie Le Blond, 'Assad did not order chemical attacks, claims Bild', *The Guardian* (9 September 2013), p.26.

24   C.J. Chivers and Eric Schmidt, 'Islamic State Ordnance Shows Traces of Chemical Agents, U.S. Says', *New York Times* (12 September 2015), p.A.4. Kareem Shaheen and Ian Black, 'Mustard gas 'likely used' in suspected Islamic State attack in Syria', *The Guardian* (1 September 2015), p.20.

25   Raymond A. Zilinkas, 'Biological Warfare and the Third World', *Politics and the Life Sciences* 1 (August 1990), p.61.

26   Jessica Stern, 'Dreaded Risks and the Control of Biological Weapons', *International Security* 27, p.3 (Winter 2002/2003); quoting Slovic, Fischoff and Lichtenstein, 'Facts and Fears', pp.89-123; and Slovic, 'Perception of Risk', pp.280–281.

27   'Taboo', *Encyclopedia Britanica*; online at < www.britannica.com/topic/taboo-sociology> (accessed on 8 October 2015).

28   See John Ellis van Courtland Moon, 'The development of the norm against the use of poison: What literature tells us', *Politics and the Life Sciences* 27 (1), pp.55-78 and Richard Price, 'A Genealogy of the Chemical Weapons Taboo', *International Organizations* 49 (1), pp.73-103.

29 Jeffrey W. Legro, 'Which Norms Matter? Revisiting the "Failure" of Internationalism', *International Organization* 51 (1), p.32.

30 Nikitin (2013), p.8.

31 ibid.

32 Jean Zanders, 'International Norms Against Chemical and Biological Warfare', *Journal of Conflict & Security Law* 8 (2) (2003), pp.401-402.

33 ibid., pp.403-405.

34 Article I (General Obligations), No.5 of the Chemical Weapons Convention states: 'Each State Party undertakes not to use riot control agents as a method of warfare'.

35 Biological Weapons Convention, Article 1.

36 Commonly rendered as 'in times of war, laws fall silent'; from Cicero's *Pro Milone*.

37 'Kriegsrasion' is a German legal concept that all means to achieving a legitimate military objective are permissible in war. See Zanders (2003), p.410.

38 Richard Price, *The Chemical Weapons Taboo* (New York: Cornell University Press, 1997). Richard Price, 'How Chemical Weapons Became Taboo And Why Syria Won't Overturn the Aversion', *Foreign Affairs* (23 January 2013); online at <https://www.foreignaffairs.com/articles/syria/2013-01-22/how-chemical-weapons-became-taboo> (accessed on 8 October 2015).

39 Price (2013).

40 WMD Commission (2005), p.503.

41 John Lauder, 'Unclassified Statement for the Record by Special Assistant to the DCI for Nonproliferation John A. Lauder on the Worldwide WMD Threat to the Commission to Assess the Organization of the Federal Government to Combat the Proliferation of Weapons of Mass Destruction'; online at <https://www.cia.gov/news-information/speeches-testimony/1999/lauder_speech_042999.html> (accessed on 23 September 2015).

42 Jonathan B. Tucker and Kathleen M. Vogel, 'Preventing the Proliferation of Chemical and Biological Weapon Material and Know-How', *The Nonproliferation Review* (Spring 2000), p.89.

43 Lauder (1999).

44 ibid.

45 The Commission on the Intelligence Capabilities of the United States Regarding Weapons of Mass Destruction, 'Final Report to the President' (31 March 2005), p.158.

46 Martin Chulov and Helen Pidd, 'Defector admits to WMD lies that triggered Iraq war', *The Guardian* (15 February 2011); online at <http://www.theguardian.com/world/2011/feb/15/defector-admits-wmd-lies-iraq-war> (accessed on 23 September 2015).

47 WMD Commission (2005), pp.353-354.

48 See FCO 66/794. Thanks for this information goes to Dr Caitriona McLeish at the University of Sussex.

49 DOD IIR 2 201 0952 90, 'Zimbabwe: Use of Basic Chemical and Biological Warfare During the Civil War'; partially declassified by USAINSCOM FOI/PA as of 29 May 2012.

50 In August 1993, South Africa's Office of Serious Economic Offenses (OSEO) informed the CIA and MI-6 of the misdeeds of Basson and 'Project Coast'. See Steven F. Burgess and Helen Purkitt, *The Rollback of South Africa's Chemical and Biological Warfare Program* (Air University: Maxwell, GA, 2001), p.60.

51 ibid.

52 Burgess and Purkitt (2001), p.58.

53 Ashok S. Kalelkar, 'Investigation of Large-Magnitude Incidents: Bhopal as a Case Study', presented at the Institution of Chemical Engineers Conference on Preventing Major Chemical Accidents, London, UK (1988), p.15.

54 Council for Scientific and Industrial Research, 'Report on Scientific Studies on the Factors Related to Bhopal Toxic Gas Leakage', (December 1985).

55 Defining syndromic surveillance, Kelly Henning stated: '… the fundamental objective of syndromic surveillance is to identify illness clusters early, before diagnoses are confirmed and reported to public health agencies, and to mobilize a rapid response, thereby reducing morbidity and mortality. Epidemic curves for persons with earliest symptom onset and those with severe illness can be depicted graphically. The time between symptom onset for an increasing number of cases caused by deliberate release of a biologic agent and subsequent patient visits to a health-care facility resulting in a definitive diagnosis is represented by t. Syndromic surveillance aims to identify a threshold number of early symptomatic cases, allowing detection of an outbreak t days earlier than would conventional reporting of confirmed cases. The ability of syndromic surveillance to detect outbreaks earlier than conventional surveillance methods depends on such factors as the size of the outbreak, the population dispersion of those affected, the data sources and syndrome definitions used, the criteria for investigating threshold alerts, and the health-care provider's ability to detect and report unusual cases…' (Kelly J. Henning, 'Overview of Syndromic Surveillance What is Syndromic Surveillance?', *Morbidity and Mortality Weekly Report* 53 (Suppl), pp.5-11.)

56 Julie A. Pavlin, 'Epidemiology of Bioterrorism', *Emerging Infectious Diseases* 5 (4), p.529.

57 Select Agents are those pathogens and toxins identified by the US Government as most often associated with biological weapons. Examples include *Bacillus anthracis, Yesinia pestis, Clostridium botulinum, Brucella suis, Rickettsia prowazekii, Coxiella burnetiid* and many others. For the complete list, see <http://www.selectagents.gov/SelectAgentsandToxinsList.html> (accessed on 24 September 2015).

58 Randall S. Murch, 'Microbial Forensics: Building a National Capability to Investigate Bioterrorism', *Biosecurity and Bioterrorism: Biodefense Strategy, Practice, and Science* 1 (2), p.2.

59 David A. Rasko, Patricia L. Worsham, Terry G. Abshire, Scott T. Stanley, Jason D. Bannand, Mark R. Wilson, Richard J. Langham, R. Scott Decker, Lingxia Jiang, Timothy D. Read, Adam M. Phillippy, Steven L. Salzberg, Mihai Pop, Matthew N. van Ert, Leo J. Kenefic, Paul S. Keim, Claire M. Fraser-Liggett and Jacques Ravel, 'Bacillus anthracis comparative genome analysis in support of the Amerithrax investigation', *Proceedings of the National Academies of Science* 108 (12).

60 'Committee on Review of the Scientific Approaches Used During the FBI's Investigation of the 2001 *Bacillus anthracis* Mailings', *Review of the Scientific Approaches Used During The FBI's Investigation of the 2001 Anthrax Letters* (Washington, DC: The National Academies Press, 2011) p.144.

61 Human Rights Watch, 'Syria: Chemicals Used in Idlib Attacks', 13 April 2015; online at <http://www.hrw.org/news/2015/04/13/syria-chemicals-used-idlib-attacks> (accessed on 25 September 2015); Anne Barnard and Somini Sengupta, 'Syria Is Using Chemical Weapons Again, Rescue Workers Say', *New York Times* (6 May 2015); online at <http://www.nytimes.com/2015/05/07/world/middleeast/syria-chemical-weapons.html> (accessed on 25 September 2015).

62 Louisa Loveluck, 'UN inspectors find undeclared sarin-linked chemicals at Syrian military site', *The Telegraph* (9 May 2015); online at <http://www.telegraph.co.uk/news/worldnews/middleeast/syria/11594763/UN-inspectors-find-undeclared-sarin-linked-chemicals-at-Syrian-military-site.html> (accessed on 25 September 2015).

Appendix I

Rhodesian CBW Agents

This appendix describes the general characteristics of the chemical and biological agents associated with the Rhodesian CBW effort – including each agent's toxicology and symptoms of intoxication.

Known CW agents

1 Parathion (Paraoxon): Parathion is a highly toxic organophosphate chemical used as a pesticide in many parts of the world. In its pure form, parathion consists of almost colorless, almost odorless crystals; in its technical form, it is a yellow-to-dark brown liquid with an odor of garlic, or rotten eggs. When exposed in highly concentrated doses, parathion breaks down to form paraoxon, which is the lethal metabolite. The action of parathion is similar to other anticholinesterese neurotoxins – and it is easily absorbed through the skin. Dermal absorption rates vary by regions of the human body, but comparative rates are: scrotum = 11.8, axilla (armpit) = 7.4, ear canal = 5.4, forehead = 4.2, scalp = 3.7, abdomen = 2.2, palm = 1.4 and forearm = 1.0.[1]

With these absorption rates, the underwear and T-shirts perhaps were the most effective choice of clothing to poison. Poisoned underwear and T-shirts would have contact with the scrotum and axilla respectively – allowing effective dermal absorption of parathion.

'Project Coast' investigated paraoxon as a possible CW agent. In a 'Project Coast' document – undated and unsigned, probably from Roodeplaat Research Laboratories – the following reasons were outlined to justify their investigation of paraoxon:

a. The substance can be manufactured with ease in the existing facilities.
b. The metabolite is highly toxic; information shows 1 mg/kg as a lethal dosage.
c. The substance is a highly lipid soluble and is rapidly absorbed by all routes, even through the skin.
d. If traces are found in the body of a patient, they can easily be explained as the available amount of parathion and can therefore have its origins in a number of places. Other, more specialized organophosphates will, however, immediately reveal the source.[2]

Symptoms of acute organophosphate poisoning develop during or after exposure and within minutes to hours, depending on the method of contact. Exposure by inhalation results in the fastest appearance of toxic symptoms, followed by the gastrointestinal route, and finally, the dermal route. All signs and symptoms are cholinergic in nature and affect muscarinic, nicotinic and central nervous system receptors. The critical symptoms in management are the respiratory symptoms. Sufficient muscular fasciculations and weakness are often observed as to require respiratory support; respiratory arrest can occur suddenly.

Loss of consciousness, incontinence, convulsions and respiratory depression indicate a life-threatening severity of poisoning. The primary cause of death is respiratory failure, with a secondary cardiovascular component. The classic cardiovascular sign is bradycardia, which can progress to sinus arrest; however, this symptom may be superseded by tachycardia and hypertension from nicotinic (sympathetic ganglia) stimulation. Toxic myocardiopathy has been a prominent feature of some severe organophosphate poisonings.[3]

2 Telodrin ($C_9H_4OCl_8$): Telodrin (also known as Isobenzan) is a chlorinated cyclodiene insecticide manufactured from 1958 to 1965 in the Netherlands by the Shell Corporation; existing stocks were used for several years thereafter. Telodrin is extremely toxic to mammals via both the oral and percutaneous routes, with the chemical easily penetrating the gastrointestinal lining and the skin. Like other cyclodienes, acute telodrin toxicity involves inhibition of the GABA receptors and prevents chlorine influx into the central nervous system. Toxicity is characterized by an over-stimulation of the central nervous system – resulting in agitation, confusion and convulsions. Telodrin typically is a whitish-to-light brown crystalline powder.[4]

According to a 1967 South African paper on vertebrate pest control:

> Laboratory tests of Telodrin established [LD_{50} values] for the Baboon (9 mg/kg.). Vervet Monkey (9 mg/kg.) and Dog (2 mg/kg.). This is appreciably lower for Baboon and Vervet Monkey than 1080 (in other words it is more toxic), whereas Telodrin is 12 and 18 times less toxic to the Dog ... Telodrin appears to be tasteless and odourless and has a rapid action causing death in a matter of hours as compared to three to five days in the case of thallium.[5]

With a lethality greater than sodium fluoroacetate (compound 1080) and a time-to-action faster than thallium, telodrin would have been an excellent replacement for parathion; however, available supplies of telodrin almost certainly were limited following Shell's decision to end production of the chemical in 1965.*

3 Thallium: Most commonly used as a rodenticide, thallium is an odorless, tasteless and water-soluble multi-system poison. Thallium also has been used as a food or beverage poison in a number of high-profile murders and assassination attempts. The lethal human dose of thallium is approximately 15-20mg/kg. Initial symptoms of thallium poisoning – including non-specific 'colicky' gastrointestinal discomfort,

---

* The question remains: could BSAP/4 have confused telodrin for the banned Italian pesticide referenced in a 1998 discussion?

nausea, vomiting and diarrhea – can be easily confused with influenza or diseases endemic to Rhodesia, such as malaria. Symptoms usually begin within 12 to 48 hours after ingestion – and after approximately five days, neurological symptoms (including intense pain in the lower extremities, headache, loss of sensation, ataxia, restlessness, delirium, dementia, hallucinations, semi-coma, blindness and psychosis) can manifest themselves.[6]

Because of a prolonged elimination phase (the body will try to eliminate the majority of the thallium through the intestine, where most is reabsorbed), thallium has a cumulative toxicity. In a paper on the pharmacology of rodenticides:

> Its mechanism of action is not completely understood but it apparently reacts with the free-SH groups in such essential proteins as enzymes thereby producing widespread damage in most organ systems. In acute poisoning, there is gastro-intestinal irritation, motor paralysis, and death from respiratory failure. If lower or repeated sublethal doses are taken, characteristic reddening of the skin of the face and abdomen with alopecia will develop. Pathological changes occur in most organs involving perivascular "cuffing" around blood vessels and degenerative changes in the brain, liver, and kidney.[7]

According to Clapperton Mavhunga in his PhD dissertation:

> In 1964, the Rhodesian Department of National Parks and Wildlife Management established the Vermin Control Unit (VCU) to carry out experiments on captured baboons treated in cages with two poisons: sodium-mono-fluoroace-tate (compound 1080) and thallium sulfate. It was decided that thallium sulfate was the most suitable poison to use … The toxicity of compound 1080 and thallium sulfate for baboons was tested on captive specimens and in a field trial at Victoria Falls. Compound 1080 was found to be much less toxic to baboons than rodents. The primates were willing to take thallium sulfate in bulk (when as little as 10 mg/kg bodyweight was sufficient to kill) because it was completely odorless and tasteless in nature. Its extreme insolubility meant that 2-3 days elapsed before animals fell sick. By then, the primates would have repeatedly ingested non-toxic doses that, as they accumulated in the organism, rose above lethal level. Death occurs after three to five days.[8]

4 Warfarin (Sodium Coumadin): An anticoagulant used as a blood thinner in treating some heart conditions in humans (in small doses, to prevent heart attack or strokes) – and as a rodenticide – warfarin almost certainly was used to poison insurgent food supplies. Warfarin works by interfering with the body's ability to manufacture Vitamin K – an essential ingredient in blood clotting. A related chemical, brodifacum, often is referred to as 'super warfarin' and was one of the chemicals used in South African experimentation as part of 'Project Coast'. Used to poison food and beverages, warfarin is a deadly anticoagulant – producing the hemorrhagic symptoms observed in Rhodesian insurgents at Beira General Hospital in 1979. Warfarin is a colorless crystal, non-water soluble, but moderately soluble in alcohol, and easily absorbed through the gastrointestinal tract. The probable human LD_{50} (oral) dose is between 50 to 500mg/kg.

According to an International Program on Chemical Safety (IPCS) fact sheet on warfarin, the initial symptoms of warfarin poisoning begin a few days or weeks after ingestion. Symptoms of warfarin poisoning include the following: nosebleeds, bleeding gums, bloody urine and feces, extensive bruising in the absence of injury (ecchymosis), fatigue, shortness of breath (dyspnea) on exertion, possible fluid in the lungs (pulmonary edema), pallor and, sometimes, hematomas around joints and on the buttocks. These symptoms are followed by paralysis due to cerebral hemorrhage and, finally, hemorrhagic shock and death may occur.[9]

Known BW agents

1 Cholera: According to the CDC, cholera is an acute, diarrheal illness caused by infection of the intestine with the bacterium *Vibrio cholerae*. The infection is often asymptomatic or with only mild symptoms, but sometimes it can be severe. Approximately 1 in 20 infected persons has severe disease (cholera gravis) characterized by profuse watery diarrhea, vomiting and leg cramps. In these persons, rapid loss of body fluids leads to dehydration and shock. Without treatment, death can occur within hours; mortality occurs in 25-50 percent of untreated cases.[10]

2 Botulinum Toxin: One of the most poisonous substances known to man, botulinum toxin is a neuroparalytic protein produced by *Clostridium botulinum*. Death from botulinum intoxication results from respiratory failure due to paralysis of the respiratory muscles.

According to the CDC:

> Incubation periods for foodborne botulism are reported to be as short as 6 hours or as long as 10 days, but generally the time between toxin ingestion and onset of symptoms ranges from 18 to 36 hours. The ingestion of other bacteria or their toxins in the improperly preserved food or changes in bowel motility are likely to account for the abdominal pain, nausea and vomiting, and diarrhea that often precede or accompany the neurologic symptoms of foodborne botulism. Dryness of the mouth, inability to focus to a near point (prompting the patient to complain of "blurred vision"), and diplopia are usually the earliest neurologic complaints. If the disease is mild, no other symptoms may develop and the initial symptoms will gradually resolve. The person with mild botulism may not come to medical attention. In more severe cases, however, these initial symptoms may be followed by dysphonia, dysarthria, dysphagia, and peripheral-muscle weakness. If illness is severe, respiratory muscles are involved, leading to ventilatory failure and death.[11]

The Rhodesian research proposal

Among the documents provided by Henry Wolhuter is a paper[12] describing several chemicals, toxins and venoms, as well as their potential applicability to a CBW effort. The document – referred to by both Peter Stiff and Jim Parker as the 'founding' document – is undated and unsigned, but Parker and Stiff both believe that Robert Symington was the probable author. In their opinion, the document was part of a CBW research proposal that Symington put together. From the references to 'I', an individual prepared the document – almost certainly referencing a Sigma-Aldrich catalogue – and was identifying promising chemicals for further research.* The chief criterion for inclusion on the list was toxicity. The document listed 12 chemicals that were 'commercially available, require small doses of administration, and have provable, reproducible lethality in contact with the solid, liquid, vapor, or dust form'.[13]

The paper also highlighted monofluoroacetic acid (MFAA, or FAA), diisopropyl flurophosphate (DFP) and alloxan as deserving special attention;[14] monofluoroacetic acid also was a chemical of interest to the South Africans.

In Chandré Gould's notes from a conversation with Dr Vernon Joynt, who had served with Drs de Villiers and Coetzee on the South African panel that reviewed the Rhodesian sulfur mustard proposal, he stated that:

> De Villiers used to monitor international scientific achievements and would always keep in touch with scientific developments internationally. At one stage he discovered that Soviet chemists were doing a lot of work on monofluoroacetic acid. MFAA is tasteless and odourless and highly toxic. De Villiers had a table, which indicated the rate at which advances were being made by the Russians, suddenly he noted that all publication stopped, which indicated to him that the research had been taken on for offensive purposes.
>
> Monofluoroacetic acid is constructed in such a way that if a string of carbons is attached to the compound, it acts as a timer so that it will delay symptoms and soldiers would therefore put on their protective clothing too late. This was an important issue for De Villiers who wanted something done about it, but nothing was done.[15]

Aflatoxin and the mushroom-derived toxins also were highlighted as 'extremely interesting', but their high cost was seen as prohibitive. A CBW expert who reviewed the document commented that the inclusion of the chemicals on the list probably reflected 'a lack of knowledge about nerve agents and an interest in assassinations or other uses where the target is close at hand – perhaps in custody';[16] few of these chemicals were ever used. The Rhodesian program seemed focused on adapting readily available (i.e. 'commercially available') agricultural pesticides and rodenticides to use in poisoning

---

* CIO/2 believes that an American may have authored it because the chemical catalogue lists prices in US dollars. I assess that this assumption almost certainly is incorrect, because the author of the document uses British spelling throughout.

clothing, beverages, medicines etc. The emphasis on 'commercially available' seems to highlight the fact that the Rhodesians were not proposing to produce chemical agents, but merely to process them from the agent's commercial form to a form more applicable to the covert CBW program.

Discussion of chemicals in the Rhodesian 'founding' document

1 1,5-bis-(4-Allyldimethyl-Ammoniumphenyl)   Pentane-3-One   Dibromide: The Rhodesian document refers to this chemical as 'an anticholinesterase and toxic doses inhibit respiration leading to respiratory paralysis'.[17] This chemical was one of the experimental cholinesterase inhibitors studied during World War II and shortly thereafter, as the nature of the nerve agents became of interest.[18]

2 N,N'-Dicyclohexyl Carbodiimide (DCC) ($C_{13}H_{22}N_2$): DCC is a known stabilizing agent for G- and V-series nerve agents. The Rhodesian document claimed that DCC was extremely toxic in small doses, but DCC primarily is a caustic material that affects the mucus membranes. Based on the DCC LD_{50} listed in the standard Material Safety Data Sheet (MSDS), DCC is not extremely toxic and would have been an unsuitable choice for a CW agent, given the readily available alternatives.[19]

3 DL-Fluorocitric Acid (FCA): Odorless, colorless and water-soluble, fluorocitric acid is a metabolite of monofluoroacetate (see below). An excellent choice for an assassination poison, the toxic dose is about 1/1000 – the dose one might detect on autopsy. According to the Rhodesian document, FCA 'is prepared as a pale yellow oily liquid and is extremely toxic. It appears fairly stable and is supplied in ampoules. Because of its toxicity, the distributor will not assay it to ensure its potency, and it is not made in the distributor's own laboratories'.[20]

4 Monofluoroacetic Acid (MFAA, or FAA): According to the Rhodesian document, MFAA is 'made as a sodium salt and its toxicity is emphasized in the chemical catalogues. Its potency is not assayed by the distributor due to its danger to lab personnel according to the catalogue'.[21]

Sodium monofluoroacetate (compound 1080) is an extremely toxic mammalian poison often used as a rodenticide. The material is a colourless, odourless, water-soluble salt that is readily absorbed by the gastrointestinal tract. Sodium monofluoroacetate acts by inhibiting energy production in most cells of the body.[22] According to the CDC case definition, '... clinical effects usually develop within 30 minutes to 2.5 hours of exposure but might be delayed as long as 20 hours. The predominant manifestations of sodium monofluoroacetate poisoning are metabolic, cardiovascular, and neurologic signs and symptoms...'[23] Serious symptoms may be broadly divided into neurological and cardiac effects: central nervous system (CNS) effects include tremulousness, hallucinations, convulsions and respiratory depression, whereas cardiac effects comprise arrhythmias, ventricular fibrillation and cardiac arrest.[24] Judging from fatal and near-fatal cases, the dangerous dose for man is 0.5-2.0mg/kg;[25] the lethal human dose is estimated to be approximately 5mg/kg.[26] Monofluoroacetate poisoning is rapidly fatal, and no known antidote exists.[27] The South Africans reportedly provided sodium monofluoroacetate to the Rhodesians for testing, but the Rhodesian CBW team found compound 1080 to be ineffective. Conditions of the testing are unknown.

5 Diethyl-P-Nitrophenyl Phosphate: Also known as methyl paraoxon, diethyl-p-nitrophenyl phosphate is extremely toxic and is the principal metabolite of the organophosphate pesticide parathion. Paraoxon is an odorless, colorless-to-pale yellow solid. According to the Rhodesian proposal, this chemical is 'prepared as a pale yellow oily liquid and is extremely toxic. It appears fairly stable and is supplied in ampoules'.[28] The Rhodesians adopted this chemical in its commercial form (the readily available pesticide parathion) for use in the country's CBW program.

6 Diisopropyl Flurophosphate (DFP): The Rhodesian document describes DFP as:

the most toxic substance I could find. It is stable at room temperature. The distributor states that they prefer not to handle the substance but offer it only as a convenience to customers. It is packaged and shipped in sealed ampoules which are in turn packed in individual canisters. It is an impressive inhibitor of several biological processes and inhibits acetylcholinesterase causing respiratory paralysis. The method of packing and shipping suggests it is absorbable through the skin.[29]

According to the Sigma-Aldrich data sheet, DFP is a powerful cholinesterase inhibitor and possesses powerful myotic action (constriction of the pupils of the eyes). A structural analog of the military-grade nerve agent sarin, DFP was the model compound selected by the US, the UK and Canada during World War II when the Allies suspected Germany was developing a novel chemical warfare agent. DFP is toxic, but GA (tabun), GB (sarin) and GD (soman) were found to be many times more toxic.[30] DFP is highly toxic by all routes of administration[31] – and symptoms of severe exposure include fever, cyanosis, pulmonary edema, areflexia, loss of sphincter control, convulsions, coma, heart block, shock and respiratory failure.[32] The onset of the clinical manifestation of organophosphate poisoning usually occurs within 12 hours of exposure.[33]

7 Methyl Fluorosulfonate: The Rhodesian study describes methyl fluorosulfonate as 'extremely toxic but has the requirement of having to be stored at cool temperatures'.[34] According to Hite (et al.):

methyl fluorosulfonate (magic methyl), an active methylating agent used by research chemists, was studied for acute oral toxicity, acute inhalation toxicity, ocular irritation, and dermal irritation. This compound is very hazardous and may have been responsible for at least one human death. The results of these studies confirmed that magic methyl is markedly toxic by all routes studied and particularly by the inhalation route since the LC_{50} value for rats was found to be between 5 and 6 parts per million (ppm).[35]

8 Aflatoxin: According to the Rhodesian proposal, these toxins:

> cause liver cancer in small doses (micrograms), and large doses would cause immediate results. Research by us should make it possible to find a variety of dosages causing a number of effects. It is, however, extremely expensive but can be ingested and would have no taste or odor. An impressive amount of literature is available on these substances, which would make research a much easier matter. There is no antidote and ingestion of even the smallest amounts appears to cause liver cancer and death in a matter of months. It is impossible to detect once in the body, and detection in contaminated foods is a difficult process, but can be done as all peanut crops are assayed prior to commercial use.

9 Phalloidin: Phalloidin is a toxin from the death cap mushroom *Amanita phalloides* that binds actin – preventing its depolymerisation and thus, poisoning the cell.[36]

10 Alpha-Amanitin, or α-amanitin: The Rhodesian document claims that:

> amanitins are natural-occurring products of the amanita mushrooms and are extremely lethal in small doses when ingested. They cause death in 2 to 3 days from massive destruction of liver and kidney tissue. This type of poisoning occurs in the States and ingestion of even one mushroom can cause death leading to the name 'Death Angel' given to the mushroom. An experimental antidote has been used but with poor results.

A careful reading of the Rhodesian document suggests a rather amateurish understanding of the poisons and toxins described. The paper describes amanita mushrooms as if they are a single species of mushroom; instead, over 600 species of mushrooms are classified in the *Amanita* genus, and these mushrooms account for over 95 percent of all mushroom poisonings. *Amanita phalloides* ('Death Cap'), in particular, are responsible for 50 percent of the poisonings attributed to *Amanita* genus poisoning cases. 'Death Angel' (*Amanita virosa, A. bisporigera, A. verna* and *A. ocreata)* also contains amatoxin, but 'Death Cap' is responsible for more poisoning cases. The oral LD_{50} of amanitin is approximately 0.1mg/kg.

The initial symptoms include diarrhea and abdominal cramps, but symptoms will cease – leaving the patient with a false sense of remission. On the fourth to fifth day, the toxin starts to have severe effects on the liver and kidneys – leading to total system failure in both. Death usually takes place around a week from ingestion; around 15 percent of those poisoned will die in approximately 10 days, after progressing through a comatose stage to renal failure, liver failure, hepatic coma, respiratory failure and death. [37]

Particularly dangerous about this toxin are its delayed effects. Amanitin poisoning is characterized by a long latent period (range 6-48 hours, average 6-15 hours), during which the patient shows no symptoms while the toxin slowly attacks a ribonucleic acid (RNA polymerase II) in the liver. Few effects are reported within 10 hours; it is not unusual for significant effects to take as much as 24 hours after ingestion – and this is far past the time when the stomach could be usefully pumped. Symptoms appear at the end of the latent period in the form of sudden, severe seizures of abdominal pain, persistent vomiting and watery diarrhea, extreme thirst and a lack of urine production. If this early phase is survived, the patient may appear to recover for a short time, but this period will generally be followed by a rapid and severe loss of strength, prostration and pain-caused restlessness. Death in 50-90 percent of the cases from progressive and irreversible liver, kidney, cardiac and skeletal muscle damage may follow within 48 hours (large dose), but the disease more typically lasts six to eight days in adults and four to six days in children. Two or three days after the onset of the later phase, jaundice, cyanosis and coldness of the skin occur; death usually follows a period of coma and occasionally convulsions – and autopsy will usually reveal fatty degeneration and necrosis of the liver and kidney.[38] If recovery occurs, it generally requires at least a month and is accompanied by enlargement of the liver.

11 Tetrodotoxin: Tetrodotoxin is a powerful neurotoxin produced by a bacteria found in the pufferfish, the porcupine fish and some other species of fish, toads and newts. Tetrodotoxin intoxication results in a gradual paralysis that eventually affects the diaphragm – resulting in respiratory distress. Because of its high cost and limited availability, tetrodotoxin would be useful only as an assassination poison;[39] however, given that tetrodotoxin synthesis was only developed in 1972 – and Rhodesia lacked natural sources of the toxin – tetrodotoxin would have been a highly impractical CW agent for the Rhodesian program.

The first symptom of intoxication is a slight numbness of the lips and tongue; the next symptom is increasing paresthesia in the face and extremities, which may be followed by sensations of lightness or floating. Headache, epigastric pain, nausea, diarrhea and/or vomiting may occur; occasionally, some reeling or difficulty in walking may occur. The second stage of the intoxication is increasing paralysis. Many victims are unable to move; even sitting may be difficult – and there is increasing respiratory distress. Speech is affected, and the victim usually exhibits dyspnea, cyanosis and hypotension. Paralysis increases and convulsions, mental impairment and cardiac arrhythmia may occur. The victim, although completely paralyzed, may be conscious and, in some cases, completely lucid until shortly before death. Death usually occurs within four to six hours, with a known range of about 20 minutes to eight hours.[40]

12 Alloxan ($C_4H_4N_2O_2$): Alloxan has a pale reddish color and is readily soluble in water or alcohol. An oxidation product of uric acid, alloxan is used to induce diabetes in animals used in laboratory experiments through necrosis of the insulin-producing pancreatic islet beta-cells. Alloxan's toxicity almost certainly is due to selective uptake of the compound because of its structural similarity to glucose.[41] According to an expert in CW agents, mention of alloxan in the 'founding' document is 'suggestive of a patient approach to having substances to use on a captive group where any diseases are likely to increase their possibilities for an early, nearly natural death owing to inadequate or primitive health care'.[42]

13 Venoms: The Rhodesian research plan discussed the use of venoms in a very general sense: '... a wide variety of snake, spider, and scorpion venoms are commercially available, some which cause death in seconds. All have to be injected. The venoms are from all types of snakes of the world. They are extremely labile and prices vary, the most toxic ones being the most expensive...'[43] The use of snake or insect venoms would only be practical in assassinations.

Comparison of victim symptomology with possible causative agents

Detailed descriptions of poisoning symptoms experienced by guerrillas are rare.[44] The notable excerpts are an account by Dr Paul Epstein of his experiences in Mozambique, and an article published in 1978 in the *South Africa Medical Journal*. Other accounts are extremely vague and anecdotal – and often the guerrillas seem to confuse possible poisoning cases with malaria. According to Jim Parker: 'On 9 January 1977 a report in the journal of a captured guerrilla named eight comrades in the Takawira Sector who had died mysterious deaths after bleeding from their noses and mouths and developing very high temperatures. The guerrillas suspected it was malaria'.[45]

According to Charles Melson's article on the Selous Scouts, '... victims reported becoming dizzy, with blurred vision and vomiting, and shortness of breath. Death followed without immediate medical intervention and hospitalization, not available to guerrillas in the bush...'[46] Researchers with extensive experience interviewing former guerrillas describe the symptoms as '... after exposure to the poison ... where prolonged contact could be achieved... After exposure to the poison ... the victim would experience symptoms which included bleeding from the nose and mouth and a rise in temperature...'[47] From these general symptoms, one can deduce that malarial symptoms are most consistent with exposure to OPs such as parathion.[48] Some of the symptoms also are consistent with thallium, and the hemorrhagic symptoms are most consistent with warfarin intoxication. Reported symptoms consistent with OP poisoning include abdominal pain, confusion, convulsions, diarrhea, headache and vomiting. In the reported cases, what is not described – but would be expected in OP poisonings and easily noticed by the guerrillas – are miosis, bronchorrhea, profuse sweating and excessive lacrimation. Reported symptoms consistent with thallium poisoning include abdominal pain, convulsions, diarrhea, fever and vomiting. Symptoms associated with thallium poisoning are alopecia (loss of hair), ataxia (loss of muscle coordination), 'burning feet', neuropathy, confusion and paresthesia (a sensation of prickling, tingling or creeping on the skin). A few sparse accounts mention bleeding gums and nosebleeds, which seem more indicative of warfarin poisoning.

None of the known or suspected CBW agents/pathogens associated with the Rhodesian CBW effort can explain the variety of reported symptoms – and bearing in mind that guerrilla descriptions of their symptoms are sparse, the available symptomology is vague and unreliable. Of the 17 clinical manifestations representing guerrilla symptoms, thallium intoxication was consistent with eight symptoms (47 percent) and parathion was consistent with eight symptoms (47 percent). This exercise demonstrates that parathion and thallium poisoning explain nearly all the symptoms reported by guerrillas. The admissions by the Rhodesian CBW team that parathion and thallium were their principal poisons also are consistent with the comparison of guerrilla symptomology.

Most guerrilla accounts are consistent with organophosphate poisoning (namely parathion) over the course of several days. As previously outlined, the parathion was converted to a powder and applied to clothing in contact with vulnerable areas of skin; reportedly, the parathion was absorbed by the wearer through hair follicles over a period of several days. The cumulative effect produced symptoms not unlike malaria – and the advantage of administering the lethal dose over several days was that it provided a measure of security. The delay in the poison's action reduced the guerrillas' ability to pinpoint which village, supporters or stores provided the tainted clothing or food – assuming that guerrillas received supplies from more than one source.

Notes

1   H.I. Maibach et al., *Arch. Environ. Health* 23 (1971), pp.208-211.

2   'The Uses of Paraoxon', ns, nd; English translation from the original Afrikaans, CBW90, the South African History Archive, the University of Witswatersrand.

3   J. Routt Reigart and James R. Roberts, *Recognition and Management of Pesticide Poisonings*, fifth edition (1999), p.38; online at <http://www.epa.gov/pesticides/safety/healthcare/handbook/Chap04.pdf> (accessed on 22 May 2006).

4   E.A.H. van Heemstra-Lequin and Dr G.J. van Esch, 'Isobenzan, Environmental Health Criteria 129', International Programme on Chemical Safety (Geneva: World Health Organization, 1992). See <http://www.inchem.org/documents/ehc/ehc/ehc129.html>.

5   Douglas Hey, 'Recent Developments in the Control of Vertebrate Problem Animals in the Province of the Cape of Good Hope, Republic of South Africa', Proceedings of the 3rd Vertebrate Pest Conference (1967). See <http://digitalcommons.unl.edu/cgi/view content. cgi?article=1029&context=vpc3>.

6   'Thallium Poisoning: An Epidemic of False Positives – Georgetown, Guyana', CDC *Mortality and Morbidity Weekly Review* (31 July1987) 36 (29), pp.481-482 and pp.487-488; online at <http://www.cdc.gov/mmwr/ preview/mmwrhtml/00000941.html> (accessed on 11 August 2005).

7   S.A. Peoples, 'The Pharmacology of Rodenticides', *Proceedings: Fourth Vertebrate Pest Conference* (1970). This paper is posted at DigitalCommons@University of Nebraska – Lincoln <http://digitalcommons.unl.edu/vpcfour/6>, p.17.

8   Clapperton Chakanetsa Mavhunga, 'The Mobile Workshop: Mobility, Technology and Human-Animal Interaction in Gonarezhou (National Park), 1850-Present' (PhD dissertation, the University of Michigan, 2008), pp.361-362, citing 'NAZ SRG/3 Report of the Director of National Parks and Wild Life Management Rhodesia' (1964), p.27.

9   '"Warfarin" Health and Safety Guide No.96', International Programme on Chemical Safety (Geneva: World Health Organization, 1995); online at <http://www.cepis.ops-oms.org/bvsapud/i/ fulltext/warfarin96/warfarin96.html> (accessed on 11 August 2005).

10   Division of Bacterial and Mycotic Diseases, US Centers for Disease Control (CDC), 'Cholera' (6 October 2005); online at <http://www.cdc.gov/ncidod/dbmd/diseaseinfo/cholera_g. htm#What%20is%20cholera> (accessed on 24 May 2006).

11   'Centers for Disease Control and Prevention: Botulism in the United States, 1899-1996', *Handbook for Epidemiologists, Clinicians, and Laboratory Workers* (Atlanta, GA: Centers for

Disease Control and Prevention, 1998); online at <http://www.cdc.gov/ncidod/dbmd/disea-seinfo/ files/botulism_manual.htm#II>.

12   The five-page document, now part of the Peter Stiff collection, is reproduced in Appendix D.

13   'Founding' document, ns, nd, p.1 (Peter Stiff collection).

14   The author of the document states: 'I suggest ordering the following items as soon as possible'. See 'founding' document, ns, nd, p.5 (Peter Stiff collection).

15   Chandré Gould, 'Notes from meeting with Dr Vernon Joynt at Mechem' (dated 6 October 1999); available from the South Africa History Archive, the University of Witswatersrand (file number AL2922 I2).

16   Science/1, personal communication, dated 2 March 2006.

17   'Founding' document, ns, nd, p.1 (Peter Stiff collection).

18   Science/1, personal communication, dated 7 March 2006.

19   'Material Safety Data Sheet, Selected LD LD50s: Oral Rat (LD50: 400mg/kg); Oral Mouse (LD50: > 800mg/kg); Dermal Guinea pig (LD50: 10ml/kg)'.

20   'Founding' document, ns, nd, p.2 (Peter Stiff collection).

21   'Founding' document, ns, nd, p.1 (Peter Stiff collection).

22   Poisons Information Monograph 494, International Programme on Chemical Safety (IPCS), November 2001; online at <http://www.intox.org/databank/documents/chemical/sodfluor/pim494.html> (accessed on 22 May 2006).

23   'Sodium Monofluroracetate', Centers for Disease Control. See <http://www.bt.cdc.gov/agent/sodiummonofluoro/pdf/sodiummonoflcasedef.pdf>.

24   Monograph 494, IPCS (2001).

25   "'Sodium Monofluoroacetate," Data Sheets on Pesticides No.16', June 1975; online at <http://www.inchem.org/documents/pds/pds/pest16_e.html> (accessed on 22 May 2006).

26   Online at <http://www.eeaa.gov.eg/cmuic/cmuic_pdfs/picdoc/Decision%20guidance%20document/ Decision%20Guidance%20Document%20pdf/Fluoroacetamide.pdf> (accessed on 20 November 2006).

27   Peoples (1970), p.16.

28   'Founding' document, ns, nd, p.1 (Peter Stiff collection).

29   ibid.

30   Science/1, personal communication, dated 7 March 2006.

31   "'Diisopropyl fluorophosphates," Sigma-Aldrich Technical Information Bulletin', AL-122, February 1993. The toxicity data for DFP is: oral-rat (LD50 6mg/kg); skin-mus (LD50 72mg/kg); ihl-rat (LD50 360mg/m3/10min); ivn-mus (LD50 3200µg/kg); ipr-rat (LD50 1280µg/kg); ims-rat (LD50 1800µg/kg); scu-dog (LD50 3mg/kg).

32   ibid.

33   C.D. Klaassen, M.O. Amdur and J. Doull (eds.), *Casarett and Doull's Toxicology: The Basic Science of Poisons*, fifth edition (New York, NY: McGraw-Hill, 1995), p.979.

34   'Founding' document, ns, nd, p.2 (Peter Stiff collection).

35   M. Hite, W. Rinehart, W. Braun and H. Peck, 'Acute Toxicity of Methyl Fluorosulfonate (Magic Methyl)', *Am Ind Hyg Assoc J*. 40 (July 1979), pp.600-603.

36   Online at <http://en.wikipedia.org/wiki/Phalloidin> (accessed on 30 July 2006).

37   Online at <http://en.wikipedia.org/wiki/Alpha-amanitin> (accessed on 30 July 2006).

38   Center for Food Safety and Applied Nutrition, US Food & Drug Administration, *Foodborne Pathogenic Microorganisms and Natural Toxins Handbook*; online at <http://www.cfsan.fda.gov/~mow/chap40.html#proto> (accessed on 22 May 2006).

39   Science/1, personal communication, dated 7 March 2006.

40   Online at <http://en.wikipedia.org/wiki/Tetrodotoxin> (accessed on 20 November 2006).

41   Online at <http://en.wikipedia.org/wiki/Alloxan> (accessed on 24 May 2006).

42   Science/1, personal communication, dated 7 March 2006.

43   'Founding' document, ns, nd, p.4 (Peter Stiff collection).

44   Rhodesian hospitals did report unusual clinical presentations that may reflect instances of intentional chemical poisoning; however, no evidence exists to link these cases to the Rhodesian Security Forces, or the victims to any guerrilla group. See M.M. Hayes, N.G. van der Westhuizen and M. Gelfand, 'Organophosphate Poisoning in Rhodesia: A Study of the Clinical Features and Management of 105 Patients', *South Africa Medical Journal* 55 (5 August 1978), pp.230-234. One of the authors of this article, Malcolm Hayes, is the brother of St Clair Hayes (one of the Rhodesian CBW team members).

45   Parker, p.160.

46   Charles D. Melson, 'Top Secret War: Rhodesian Special Operations', *Small Wars and Insurgencies* 16 (March 2005), pp.70-71.

47   Jocelyn Alexander, JoAnn McGregor and Terence Ranger, *Violence & Memory: One Hundred Years in the 'Dark Forests' of Matabeleland* (Oxford: James Currey Ltd., 2000), p.144.

48   According to a study conducted by the South Africa Police Service Forensic Science Laboratory, the symptoms of parathion poisoning may be misdiagnosed as malaria. Their study looked at the case of a nine-year-old girl admitted to the hospital and treated for malaria. The treatment was unsuccessful, and the patient died. The girl presented with headache, nausea, stomach cramps, fatigue, sore throat, coughing, fever, sweating, vomiting, loss of appetite, blurred vision and general weakness, which were consistent with parathion poisoning. See Alida Grove and Stephanie de Wet, 'Parathion Poisoning or Malaria? The Question Remains Unanswered', presentation to the 2nd World Conference of the ICC, Durban, South Africa (3-7 December 2001); online at <http://www.crimeinstitute.ac.za/2ndconf/papers/ grove_dewet.pdf> (accessed on 9 June 2006).

Appendix II

Rhodesian CBW Documents

The following Special Branch documents are reproduced from Jim Parker's book *Assignment Selous Scouts* (pp.162-165) from originals provided to Parker by Peter Stiff. As Parker's book explains:

> During the mid-1980s, several years after the end of the Rhodesian Bush War, ex-Detective Inspector Henry Wolhuter, formerly of the Special Branch Selous Scouts, called on South African author Peter Stiff – an ex-BSAP superintendent. They had been friends for many years having served together in the Force. He [Wolhuter] said that his wife Beryl had died of cancer a few months before and that he had been given only a short time left to live for the same reason. He was convinced that both he and his wife contracted cancer from handling goods impregnated with toxins and poisons at the Bindura Fort. He gave Stiff a file of top-secret documents relating to Rhodesia's biological and chemical program.[1]

Peter Stiff recounted the same version of events during a discussion I had with him at his home outside Johannesburg. Stiff still possesses the original documents, but slightly altered versions can be found in the South Africa History Archive (SAHA) at the University of Witswatersrand in Johannesburg. The following copy of the 'founding' document, which is thought to be Robert Symington's original proposal for a CBW effort, was obtained from SAHA; the top of page three is missing. I have compared all of these documents with the originals belonging to Mr Stiff and have found no significant substantive difference, save the missing portion of page three. Regarding the Special Branch reports to Officer Commanding Special Branch, Chief Superintendent McGuinness confirmed to me – and several other people – that the signature above his printed name on the Special Branch documents is his and that he authored those bi-weekly reports. Independently, I have compared McGuinness' signature with the signature on the documents and they are identical; the documents are undoubtedly genuine. Only this handful of bi-weekly reports covering a brief period of the program – preserved by Wolhuter and turned over to Peter Stiff – remain; all other reports on the subject are presumed destroyed.

Every indication is that McGuinness handed over whatever CBW-relevant Rhodesian documents he retained to the South Africans when he emigrated to that country in 1980. Despite repeated requests for any CBW documents he may have kept, he was unable or unwilling to provide any. My belief is that McGuinness, in the end, had not saved any documentary material related to the CBW program, given that he was not reticent about sharing documents on his other activities. If he did, we have no indication that any of those papers remain extant after the apartheid regime's own culling of potentially sensitive documents on the eve of ANC rule.

A possibility remains that Rhodesian CBW documents – or documents related to the Rhodesian CBW effort – remain in the South African military or police archives; my limited efforts have not detected any such papers. The Rhodesian Special Branch did transfer a large number of files to South Africa at the war's end, but none of those documents appear to have touched on the CBW activities. Given that the South African Police assigned a senior officer to liaise with McGuiness at Bindura, SAPS may have information on the CBW program. Records of the SAPS Forensic Laboratory also may have retained some information on Rhodesian CBW activities. South African military records on the Rhodesian CBW effort – especially any of those held by SADF/CSI and the DCC – almost certainly did not survive the mass culling of files in the transition to an ANC Government.

One sizable archive does remain at SAHA related to South Africa's 'Project Coast'. The archive – largely compiled by Chandré Gould – contains some CDU and Mechem files, as well as some files from the Truth and Reconciliation investigation of Dr Wouter Basson and 'Project Coast'. Having visited SAHA and combed through their CBW archive, I found nothing there relating to the Rhodesian CBW not already described here.

The Rhodesian Army Archive – a project of the Rhodesian Army Association – was a collection of documents from former members of the Rhodesian Security Forces; the result was perhaps the largest collection anywhere of Rhodesian documents detailing the war. Stored at one time in the now-defunct Museum of the British Empire and Commonwealth, the location of those papers is unknown, following the museum's closure. Although this archive may have contained documents relevant to the Rhodesian CBW effort, the Rhodesian collectors admittedly attempted to cull any documents that could have brought Rhodesia or its Security Forces into disrepute.

TOP SECRET

The Officer Commanding,
Special Branch Headquarters,
SALISBURY

24th June, 1977

COMBINED OPERATIONS

Statistics requested by Combined Operations

It will be appreciated that the full extent of our success may never be known but information gleaned from a variety of sources... both theirs and our own ... indicates the following:-

BINDI	347
MREWA/MTOKO	155
RUSHBA	60
MELONI	42
FORT VICTORIA	17
GWANDA	48
MOUNT DARWIN	77
BUHERA	48
CHIPEDZI	28
MASVINGRA	2
SHABANI/MHANGNI	70
SIPLIZA	42

727
809

A border store, two food caches and one hundred and fifty nine items are still to be reported upon and may be considered current in the field. In operations at Malvernia sixteen were accounted for and a further six at Mazi Kozo.

Our methods of operation are changing continually in order to keep the enemy guessing and new and improved methods have recently come to light which augur well for the future.

TOP SECRET

Figures B.1-B.10 The BSAP documents.
(Source: Peter Stiff collection, with permission of Peter Stiff)

OFFICIAL COMMUNICATIONS
SHOULD NOT BE ADDRESSED
TO INDIVIDUALS

TELEGRAMS: "POLSPEC" SALISBURY

TELEPHONE: 700501 Salisbury

IN REPLY PLEASE QUOTE
REF. NO.:

NYS 8777/1

TOP SECRET

TOP SECRET

SPECIAL BRANCH,
B.S.A. POLICE G.H.Q.,
P.O. Box 8538, Causeway,
RHODESIA.

Provincial Special Branch Officer
SALISBURY AND MASHONALAND PROVINCE,
MATABELELAND, MANICALAND, MIDLANDS
and VICTORIA PROVINCE

29 June 1977

cc   Chief Superintendent McGUINNESS
Selous Scouts
BINDURA   (For information)

CLANDESTINE ACTIVITY : SELOUS SCOUTS

      Recent references have been made to certain clandestine
activities of the Selous Scouts in secret reports and captured
documents which are forwarded to CID Headquarters. These
concern allegations of the use of poison allegedly introduced in
both food and clothing.

2.   Addressees are to ensure that this is no longer done
and that any captured documents containing allegations of this
nature are destroyed after being made the subject of a Top Secret
report to this Headquarters and Supt. McGUINNESS only.

A/Officer Commanding
SPECIAL BRANCH

TOP SECRET

Figure B.2.

TOP SECRET

Ref: XYS 8777/7

Selous Scouts,
P.O. Box 901,
BINDURA.

18th July, 1977.

Officer Commanding,
SPECIAL BRANCH HEADQUARTERS.

DELIVERY OF MATERIALS : 4TH TO 18TH JULY, 1977

During the period under review, the following items
have been distributed:-

12 Sets Clothing	Gwelo
10 Cases Beer/Minerals	Fort Victoria
12 Packets Tobacco	Chiredzi
15 Sets Clothing	Enkeldoorn
34 Sets Clothing	Mount Darwin
1 5kg Packet Mealie Meal	Sinoia
12 Sets Clothing	Buhera
20 Sets Clothing	Beit Bridge
2 5kg Packets Mealie Meal	Beit Bridge
16 Packets Biscuits	Beit Bridge
10 Tins Corned Beef	Beit Bridge
10 Packets Sweats	Beit Bridge

Little information of interest has been received,
but the murder of tribespeople in areas where materials
have been distributed is on the increase. Our confirmed
total for this period is six in Chiduku and a further twenty
in the Shabani/Selukwe area.

(M.J.P. McGUINNESS) Chief Superintendent,
Officer in Charge Operations,
SPECIAL BRANCH HEADQUARTERS.

Figure B.3.

TOP SECRET

479

25th August, 1977.

The Officer Commanding,
SPECIAL BRANCH HEADQUARTERS.

c.c. The Director-General,
CENTRAL INTELLIGENCE ORGANISATION.

ISSUE OF EQUIPMENT : 8.8.77 - 17.8.77.

During the period under review, the following have been
issued:-

59 Sets of Clothing.
2   Sets of Cigarettes.
1   Set of Medical Supplies.
2   Sets of Assorted Food and Drink.

Resultant terrorist deaths have been confirmed as follows:-

1 Killed   Sinoia
2 Killed   Beit Bridge.

One group of ten terrorists is believed to have been
seriously affected and is no longer operating in the Beit Bridge
area.

Nineteen African civilians in the Beit Bridge area have
been murdered by terrorists, who believed that they were responsible
for giving them poisoned food.

It will be noted that there is a considerable decrease in
the quantity of materials directed into the field during the
fortnight under review, this being due to

(a) staff shortage in the field and subsequent
     inability to recruit contact men,

                  and

(b) the shortage of necessary ingredients which
     are to be obtained from South Africa within
     the next two weeks.

The low kill rate reflected herein is again due to lack of
follow up and accurate reporting by stations to whom material has
been supplied.

(M.J.F. McGUINNESS) Chief Superintendent,
Officer in Charge Operations,
SPECIAL BRANCH HEADQUARTERS.

FOR SIGHT AND DESTRUCTION PLEASE

Figure B.4.

TOP SECRET

479

28th November, 1977.

The Officer Commanding,
SPECIAL BRANCH HEADQUARTERS.

c.c. The Director-General,
CENTRAL INTELLIGENCE ORGANISATION.

ISSUE OF EQUIPMENT : 14th TO 27th NOVEMBER, 1977

During the period under review, the following items have
been distributed:-

365 items of clothing to cover 201 terrorists
 86 tins meat
  5 medical packs
  6 cartons cigarettes
 10 tubes toothpaste
 12 pkts biscuits
  2 tins jam
 12 packets Mopani worms
 15 tins peas
  1 bottle Codein
  3 FFLM Ratpacks
  3 bottles Arsenic
  6 x 15g Strychnine
  3 pkts "dog" biscuits   External
  1 bottle Portuguese brandy
 32 bottles Penicillin
  2 bottles Vit. B Complex
  1 bottle Chloroquin
  1 bottle Milk of Magnesia
  5 ampoules Paraganal Injection)

Results have been confirmed as follows:-

15 terrorists dead at Bikita
14 terrorists dead at Belingwe
36 terrorists dead at Nyahunda
 1 terrorist dead at Chiredzi
12 terrorists dead at Gwelo

A total of 79 terrorists killed.

(W.J.P. McGUINNESS) Chief Superintendent,
Officer in Charge Operations,
SPECIAL BRANCH HEADQUARTERS.

FOR SIGHT AND DESTRUCTION PLEASE

Figure B.5.

PAGE ONE OF FIVE

The following substances are commercially available, require small doses of administration, and have provable, reproducable lethality in contact with the solid, liquid, vapor, or dust form. Classification is based on the most obtainable form of the material.

POWDERED SOLIDS

1,5-bis-(4-ALLYLDIMETHYL-AMMONIUMPHENYL)-
PENTANE-3-ONE DIBROMIDE
                    this is an anticholinesterase and toxic doses
  inhibit respiration leading to respiratory paralysis
                    PRICE: 32.00 US/ 250mg

N,N'-DICYCLOHEXYL CARBODIIMIDE-
                    this is extreamly toxic in small doses, is
  assayed by the manufacturers to assure potency
                    PRICE: 5.20US/25g
                           58.00/1kg

DL-FLUOROCITRIC ACID-
                    this is a barium salt and is most extreamly
  toxic in small doses
                    PRICE:4.30US/25mg
                          64.50/1g

MONOFLUORACETIC ACID-
                    this is made as a sodium salt and its toxicity is
  emphisised in the chemical catalogues. Its potency is not assayed by the
  distributor due to its danger to lab personel according to the catalogue
                    PRICE: 7.00US/can (about 25g).

Figure B.6.

PAGE TWO OF FIVE

LIQUIDS

DIETHYL-p-NITROPHENYL PHOSPHATE-

this is prepared as a pale yellow oily
liquid and is extreanly toxic. It appears fairly stable and is
supplied in ampules. Because of its toxicity, the distributor
will not assay it to ensure its potency and it is not made in the
distributors own laboratories.

PRICE: 30.00 US/ml.

•••• DIISOPROPYL FLUROPHOSPHATE-

this appears to be the most toxic substance
I could find. It is stable at room temperature. The distributor
states that they prefer not to handle the substance but offer it
only as a convenience to customers. It is packaged and shipped
in sealed ampules which are in turn packed in individual canisters.
It is an impressive inhibitor of several biological processes and
inhibits acetylcholinesterase causing respiratory paralysis. The
method of packing and shipping suggests it is absorbable through
the skin.

PRICE: 29.00US/g.

METHYL FLUOROSULFONATE-

extreanly toxic but has the requirement of
having to be stored at cool temperatures
PRICE: 31.00 US/ 100ml

Figure B.7.

produced by molds which grow on peanuts that are improperly stored.
They cause liver cancer in small doses(micrograms) and large doses
would cause immediant results. Research by us should make it possibl
to find a variety of dosages causing a number of effects. It is howe·
extreamly expensive but can be ingested and would have no taste or
odor. An impressive amount of literature is available on these
substances which would make research a much easier matter. There is
no antidote and injestion of even the smallest amounts appear to
cause liver cancer and death in a matter of months. It is impossible
to detect once in the body, and detection in contaminated foods is a
difficult process but can be done as all peanut crops are assayed
prior to commercial use.

AVERAGE PRICE: 70.00 US/.01mg.

PHALLOIDIN and ALPHA AMANITIN-

These are natural occuring products of the AMANITA MUSHROOMS
and are extreamly lethal in small doses when ingested. They cause deatl
in 2 to 3 days from massive destruction of liver and kidney tissue.
This type of poisioning occurs in the states and injestion of even
one mushroom can cause death leading to the name DEATH ANGEL given
to the mushroom. An experimental antidote has been used but with poor
results.

PRICE:both average about 45.50/1mg which would certainly be
enough for one toxic dose

Figure B.8.

PAGE FOUR OF FIVE

TETRODOXIN-
        this is isolated from the porcupine fish of Japan. It is
an extreamly dangerous substance and is completely water soluble but
must be buffered which parchibits its use in carbonated or fruit
beverages. Boiling destroys its potenny but it may have uses in cert-
patent medicines and drugs.
            PRICE: 39.00 US/1mg

ALLOXAN-
        this is an interesting drug and inexpensive which causes
irreversable diabetes upon a single administration and unless the
individual is brought under immediate medical care, undergoes death
in a matter of days. Larger doses destroy several other types of
tissue. It has the drawback of having to be injected although Im not
certain of this matter, and we may be able to get it in powder form.
        It could have applications in bringing selected individuals
under the domination of others by making them dependent upon daily
injections of insulin to survive.

            PRICE:19.00US/100g

VENOMS-
        a wide variety of snake, spider, scorpion venoms are commercia
available, some which cause death in seconds. All have to be injected.
The venoms are from all types of snakes of the world. They are extream
labile and prices vary the most toxic ones being the most expensive
usually averaging 30.00 US for 10mg.

Figure B.9.

PAGE FIVE OF FIVE

All of the mentioned substances are commercially available and easily obtained by institutions, from SIGMA CHEMICAL COMPANY. Wavers of liability must accompany each request for these materials which are provided in the sigma catalogue. This abstains the chemical company from any legal action brought on from handling the materials by purchasing reaserchers resulting in loss of life. The previous materials are all airmailed to any point in the world upon recipt of an order.

These materials can all be ordered through three distributors in three different countries;

SIGMA LONDON- DORSET ENGLAND
SIGMA MUNCHEN- WEST GERMANY
SIGMA CO- St LOUIS MO. USA (HOME OFFICE)

All of these materials must be ordered by letter.

I SUGGEST ORDERING THE FOLLOWING ITEMS AS SOON AS POSSIBLE

MONOFLUROACETIC ACID-solid-7.00 US/can
DIISOPROPYL FLUROPHOSPHATE- liquid- 29.00/gram

ALLOXAN-liquid-19.00 US/100grams

The AFLATOXINS or the extracts from the AMANITA mushroom should also be extreamly interesting, but run 70.00 and 45.50 respectively for only small amounts.

Figure B.10.

Facsimile of Rhodesian Joint Planning Staff – Annex D – on proposal to use dichloroethyl sulphide (sulfur mustard) in the *cordon sanitaire*

The following document is Annex D to a top-secret Rhodesian Joint Planning Staff document (JPS/700) dated 20 August 1973.[2] In what is the earliest indication of Rhodesian interest in CBW agents, the document notes that a Dr Barlow proposed using dichloroethyl sulphide in the *cordon sanitaire* as a means of causing skin burns on infiltrators. A South African panel from the Council for Scientific and Industrial Research reviewed the proposal and found it was not feasible. The JPS concluded that the use of dichloroethyl sulphide was not a practical option, but noted the 'somewhat conflicting evidence from experts'.

The South African panel consisted of the three members of the CSIR's Applied Chemistry Unit: Jean de Villiers, Jan Coetzee and Vernon Joynt. De Villiers was responsible for monitoring foreign CBW developments and reporting on those developments to the SADF; he also advised the SADF on the applicability of CBW use in Southern Africa. Coetzee went on to found EMLC and worked closely with the Selous Scouts – improvising weapons and other devices. Coetzee also had close ties with the Rhodesian CBW effort and admitted in court to receiving a Rhodesian report about the effects of chemical agents on humans. Vernon Joynt went on to head the CDU – later leaving CDU to specialize in mine warfare and de-mining technology.

Copy No. ..7.. of 7 Copies

ANNEX D TO
JPS/700
DATED 20 AUG 73

NOTES ON DICHLORETHYL SULPHIDE

1. The idea of using dichlorethyl sulphide was originally put forward by Dr C.V.L. Barlow, whose brother is a chemist in a large industrial chemical firm in the United Kingdom. According to Dr Barlow:

a. The chemical produces mustard gas which penetrates normal clothing and causes skin burns, which would necessitate medical attention.

b. The chemical should be sprayed at a density of 10 g/m^2 and its effects would last up to three weeks in bush country depending on temperature. Hence the more shade there is, the longer will the effects last.

c. Detector paper could be used by troops to detect it and bleaching powder as a neutralizing agent.

d. Although a form of chemical warfare and banned by the United Nations, it would be used in a non-aggressive manner.

e. The chemical is relatively cheap.

2. Dr Thompson of the Forensic Laboratory, however, stated that:

a. He thought that the chemical could be manufactured in South Africa.

b. If the chemical were encapsulated and sprayed on a strip of ground over which persons had to walk, it would burn through boots and cause burns to the feet, and that this was the dangerous aspect of the chemical, not the gas.

3. The CSIR team of Drs Coetzee, de Villiers and Joyce, on the other

Figure B.11 The Rhodesian military document.
(Source: Rhodesian Army Archive, courtesy of Charles D. Melton)

Notes

1 Parker, p.169.
2 This document was provided by Charles Melson, who uncovered it during his research in the Rhodesian Army Archive, which was then held at the Museum of the British Empire and Commonwealth.

a. The dangerous aspect of the chemical was the gas which would cause blindness for up to two weeks.

b. The harmful vapours of the gas could not be confined to the area and would move according to variations in climatic conditions.

c. There is no supply source of the chemical in Rhodesia or South Africa and production costs would be enormous.

d. Frequent re-sprays would be necessary particularly during the rainy season and even after heavy dews. This would be extremely expensive.

e. An encapsulation process to prolong the life of the chemical is not scientifically feasible at present and development costs would be high.

Comments

4. Based on the foregoing somewhat conflicting evidence from the experts, JPS has no option but to recommend that the use of the chemical should not be considered. Added to the scientific uncertainties about the use of the chemical, serious international political repercussions could be expected if its use became known, and this is bound to happen in time. Thus it is just not a practical proposition.

Figure B.11.

Bibliography

Published Works

Alexander, Jocelyn, McGregor, JoAnn and Ranger, Terence, *Violence & Memory: One Hundred Years in the "Dark Forests" of Ndebele land* (Oxford: James Currey Ltd., 2000).

Allison, Graham T., *Essence of Decision: Explaining the Cuban Missile Crisis* (Boston: Little, Brown and Company, 1971).

Anderson, David, *Histories of the Hanged: The Dirty War in Kenya and the End of Empire* (New York: W.W. Norton & Company Inc., 2005).

Bale, Jeffrey M., 'South Africa's Project Coast: 'Death Squads,' Covert State-Sponsored Poisonings, and the Dangers of CBW Proliferation', *Democracy and Security* 2 (2006), pp.27-59.

Beckett, Ian F.W., 'The Rhodesian Army: Counter-Insurgency, 1972-1979'; online at <http://members.tripod.com/selousscouts/rhodesian_army_coin_72_79_part1.htm>

Bendor, Jonathan and Hammond, Thomas H., 'Rethinking Allison's Models', *American Political Science Review* 86 (June 1992), pp.301-322.

Bird, Ed, *Special Branch War: Slaughter in the Rhodesian Bush Southern Ndebele land, 1976-1980* (Solihull, UK: Helion & Company, Ltd., 2014).

Bowyer Bell, J., 'The Frustration of Insurgency: The Rhodesian Example of the Sixties', *Military Affairs* (February 1971), pp.1-5.

Bhebe, Ngwabi and Ranger, Terence (eds.), *Soldiers in Zimbabwe's Liberation War* (London: James Currey Ltd., 1995).

Bowman, Larry W., 'Authoritarian Politics in Rhodesia' (PhD dissertation, Brandeis University, April 1971).

Brickhill, Jeremy, 'Making Peace with the Past: War Victims and the Work of the Mafela Trust' in Bhebe, Ngwabi and Ranger, Terence (eds.), *Soldiers in Zimbabwe's Liberation War* (London: James Currey Ltd., 1995), pp.163-173.

—— 'Zimbabwe's Poisoned Legacy: Secret War in Southern Africa', *Covert Action Quarterly* 43 (Winter 1992-1993).

—— 'Doctors of Death', *Horizon* (Harare, 1992), pp.14-17.

Brower, Ralph S. and Abolafia, Mitchel Y., 'Bureaucratic Politics: The View from Below', *Journal of Public Administration Research and Theory* 7 (April 1997), pp.305-331.

Bruton, James K., 'Counterinsurgency in Rhodesia', *Military Review* 59 (March 1979), pp.26-39.

Burger, Marlene and Gould, Chandré, *Secrets and Lies: Wouter Basson and South Africa's Chemical and Biological Warfare Programme* (Cape Town, South Africa: Zebra Press, 2002).

Burgess, Stephen F., and Purkitt, Helen E., 'The Rollback of South Africa's Chemical and Biological Warfare Program' (USAF Counterproliferation Center: Air War College, Maxwell Air Force Base, April 2001).

Burke, G.K., 'Insurgency in Rhodesia', *Assegai* (April 1979), pp.31-43.

Byron, T.J., *Elimination Theory: The Secret Covert Networks of Project Coast* (Baltimore: PublishAmerica, 2004).

Cary, Robert and Mitchell, Diana, 'African Nationalist Leaders – Who's Who', originally published in 1977; online at <www.colonialrelic.com> (accessed on 2 August 2015).

Catholic Commission for Justice and Peace, 'The Current Situation in Zimbabwe', *Issue: A Journal of Opinion* 9 (Spring/Summer 1979), pp.63-65.

Caute, David, *Under the Skin: The Death of White Rhodesia* (Evanston, Illinois: Northwestern University Press, 1983).

Center for Defense Information, 'Terrorism: The Problem of Definition'; online at <www.cdi.org>.

Chadwick, Elizabeth, 'It's War, Jim, But Not as We Know It: A 'Reality-Check' for International Laws of War', *Crime, Law, & Social Change* 39 (2003), pp.233-262.

Chan, Stephen, *Robert Mugabe: A Like in Power and Violence* (Ann Arbor, Michigan: University of Michigan Press, 2003).

Chingongo, Herbert, 'Revolutionary Warfare and the Zimbabwe War of Liberation: A Strategic Analysis', US National War College thesis paper (ASE-97-4 c.1); online at <http://www.ndu.edu/library/n1/99-ASE-04.pdf>.

Chung, Fay, *Re-Living the Second Chimurenga: Memories from Zimbabwe's Liberation Struggle* (Stockholm: The Nordic Africa Institute, 2006).

Cilliers, J.K., *Counter-Insurgency in Rhodesia* (London: Croom Helm, 1985).

Cline, Lawrence E., *Pseudo Operations and Counterinsurgency: Lessons from Other Countries* (Carlisle, PA: US Army War College, Strategic Studies Institute, June 2005).

Cooper, Simon, 'How One Man Lied His Way Into the Most Dangerous Lab in America', *SEED Magazine* (May/June 2003); online at <http://www.angelfire.com/ex/ projecthatfill/seed.html>.

Coyle, R.G. and Millar, C.J., 'A Methodology for Understanding Military Complexity: The Case of the Rhodesian Counter-Insurgency Campaign', *Small Wars and Insurgencies* 17 (Winter 1996), pp.360-378.

Crabtree, Bill, *Came the Fourth Flag* (Lancaster, UK: Scotforth Books, 2002).

Croukamp, Dennis, *Only My Friends Call Me "Crouks" – Rhodesian Reconnaissance Specialist* (Cape Town, South Africa: New Voices Publishing, 2006).

Danaher, Kevin, 'The Political Economy of Hunger in Rhodesia and Zimbabwe', *Issue: A Quarterly Journal of Africanist Opinion* 11 (Fall/Winter 1981), pp.33-35.

Davidow, Jeffrey, *A Peace in Southern Africa: The Lancaster House Conference on Rhodesia, 1979* (Boulder, Colorado: Westview Press, Inc., 1984).

Davies, J.C.A., 'A Major Epidemic of Anthrax in Rhodesia: The Experience at the Beatrice Road Infectious Diseases Hospital, Harare', *Central African Journal of Medicine* 31 (September 1985), pp.176-180.

—— 'A Major Epidemic of Anthrax in Rhodesia: Part II', *Central African Journal of Medicine* 29 (January 1983), pp.8-12.

—— 'Anthrax and Flies', *The Zimbabwe Science News* 17 (January 1983), pp.11-12.

—— 'A Major Epidemic of Anthrax in Rhodesia: Part I', *Central African Journal of Medicine* 28 (December 1982), pp.291-298.

DeRoche, Andrew J., 'Standing Firm for Principles: Jimmy Carter and Zimbabwe', *Diplomatic History* 23 (Fall 1999), pp.657-685.

Dobson, Christopher and Payne, Ronald, *The Dictionary of Espionage* (London: Grafton Books, 1986).

Ellert, Henrik, 'The Rhodesian Security and Intelligence Community, 1960-1980: A Brief Overview of the Structure and Operational Role of the Military, Civilian, and Police Security and Intelligence Organizations Which Served the Rhodesian Government During the Zimbabwean Liberation War' in Bhebe, N. and Ranger, T. (eds.), *Soldiers in Zimbabwe's Liberation War* (London: James Currey Ltd., 1995).

—— *The Rhodesian Front War: Counter-Insurgency and Guerilla War in Rhodesia, 1962-1980* (Gweru, Zimbabwe: Mambo Press, 1989).

Evans, Michael, 'Fighting Against Chimurenga: Analysis of Counter-Insurgency in Rhodesia, 1972-1979', *Local Series* 37 (Harare, Zimbabwe: The Historical Association of Zimbabwe, 1981).

Falk, Richard, *Revolutionaries and Functionaries: The Dual Face of Terrorism* (New York: E.P. Dutton, 1988).

Feaver, Paul D., 'Civil-Military Relations', *Annual Review of Political Science* 2 (1999), pp.211-241.

—— 'Crisis as Shirking: An Agency Theory Explanation of the Souring of American Civil-Military Relations', *Armed Forces & Society* 24 (Spring 1988), pp.407-434.

Feldman, Steven P., 'Secrecy, Information, and Politics: An Essay on Organization Decision Making', *Human Relations* 41 (1988), pp.73-90.

Foster, Don, Haupt, Paul and de Beer, Maresa, *The Theatre of Violence: Narratives of Protagonists in the South African Conflict* (Cape Town, South Africa: HSRC Press, 2005).

Flower, Ken, *Serving Secretly: An Intelligence Chief on the Record* (London: John Murray Ltd., 1987).

Frederikse, Julie, *None But Ourselves: Masses vs. Media in the Making of Zimbabwe* (New York: Penguin Books, 1984).

French, Paul, *Shadows of a Forgotten Past: To the Edge with the Rhodesian SAS and Selous Scouts* (Solihull, UK: Helion & Company Ltd., 2012).

Fuller, Alexandra, *Scribbling the Cat* (London: Penguin Press, 2004).

Galtung, Johan, 'On the Effects of International Economic Sanctions: With Examples from the Case of Rhodesia', *World Politics* 19 (April 1967), pp.378-416.

Gann, Lewis H. and Henriksen, Thomas H., *The Struggle for Zimbabwe: Battle in the Bush* (New York: Praeger Publishers, 1981).

Ganor, Boaz, 'Defining Terrorism: Is One Man's Terrorist Another Man's Freedom Fighter', *Police Practice and Research* 3 (2002), pp.27-304.

Geldenhuys, Deon, 'The Special Relationship Between South Africa and Zimbabwe', ad hoc publication no.41 (Pretoria: Institute for Strategic Studies, 2003).

Gerrans, G.C., 'Historical Overview of the South African Chemical Industry, 1896-1998', *Chemistry International* 21 (May 1999), pp.71-77.

Gershenson, Dmitriy, 'Sanctions and Civil Conflicts', *Economica* 69 (2002), pp.185-206.

Godwin, Peter and Hancock, Ian, *Rhodesians Never Die: The Impact of War and Political Change on White Rhodesia, c. 1970-1980* (Harare, Zimbabwe: Baobab Books, 1997).

Golder, Ben and Williams, George, 'What is Terrorism? Problems of Legal Definition', *University of New South Wales Law Journal* 27 (2004), pp.270-294.

Gould, Chandré, 'South Africa's Chemical and Biological Warfare Program, 1981-1995' (PhD dissertation, Rhodes University, May 2005).

Gould, Chandré and Folb, Peter, *Project Coast: Apartheid's Chemical and Biological Warfare Programme* (Geneva: United Nations Institute for Disarmament Research, 2002).

—— 'The Role of Professionals in the South African Chemical and Biological Warfare Programme', *Minerva* 40 (2002), pp.77-91.

—— 'The South African Chemical and Biological Warfare Program: An Overview', *The Nonproliferation Review* 7 (Fall/Winter 2000), pp.10-23.

Gregory, Martyn, 'The Zimbabwe Election: The Political and Military Implications', *The Journal of Southern African Studies* 7 (October 1980), pp.17-37.

Groenenduk, Nico, 'A Principal-Agent Model of Corruption', *Crime, Law, & Social Change* 27 (1997), pp.207-229.

Hills, Denis, *The Last Days of White Rhodesia* (London: Chatto & Windus, 1981).

Hoffman, Bruce, *Inside Terrorism* (London: Victor Gollancz, 1998).

Hoffman, Bruce, Taw, Jennifer M. and Arnold, David, *Lessons for Contemporary Counterinsugencies: The Rhodesian Experience* (Washington DC: The Rand Corporation, 1991).

Horne, Gerald, *From the Barrel of a Gun: The United States and the War Against Zimbabwe, 1965-1980* (Chapel Hill, North Carolina: University of North Carolina Press, 2001).

Hove, Mediel, 'War legacy: A reflection on the effects of the Rhodesian Security Forces (RSF) in south eastern Zimbabwe during Zimbabwe's war of liberation 1976 – 1980', *Journal of African Studies and Development* 4 (October 2012), pp.193-206.

Hugh-Jones, Martin and Blackburn, Jason, 'The Ecology of Bacillus Anthracis', *Molecular Aspects of Medicine* 30 (2009), pp.356-367.

Hutchinson, Martha Crenshaw, 'The Concept of Revolutionary Terrorism', *The Journal of Conflict Resolution* 16 (September 1972), pp.383-396.

Isaacman, Allen, Lalu, Premesh and Nygren, Thomas, 'Digitization, history, and the Making of a Postcolonial Archive of Southern African Liberation Struggles: the Aluka Project', *Africa Today* 52 (Winter 2005), pp.55-77.

Jervis, Robert L., *Perception and Misperception in International Politics* (Princeton: Princeton University Press, 1976).

Kirk, Tony, 'Politics and Violence in Rhodesia', *African Affairs* 74 (January 1975), pp.3-38.

Kriger, Norma, 'War Veterans: Continuities Between the Past and Present', *African Studies Quarterly: The Online Journal for African Studies*; online at <http://web.africa.ufl.edu/asq/v7/v7i2a7.htm> (accessed on 1 April 2005).

—— *Guerrilla Veterans in Post-War Zimbabwe: Symbolic and Violent Politics, 1980-1987* (Cambridge: Cambridge University Press, 2003).

—— *Zimbabwe's Guerrilla War: Peasant Voices* (Cambridge: Cambridge University Press, 1992).

—— 'The Zimbabwean War of Liberation: Struggles Within the Struggle', *Journal of Southern African Studies* 14 (January 1988), pp.304-322.

Lake, Anthony, *"The Tar Baby" Option: American Policy Toward Southern Rhodesia* (New York: Columbia University Press, 1976).

Laing, Robert O., 'Relapse in Organophosphate Poisoning', *The Central African Journal of Medicine* 25 (October 1979), pp.225-226.

Lan, David, *Guns & Rain: Guerrillas & Spirit Mediums in Zimbabwe* (London: James Currey Ltd., 1985).

Laqueur, Walter, *No End to War: Terrorism in the Twenty-First Century* (New York: Continuum, 2003).

—— *The New Terrorism: Fanaticism and the Arms of Mass Destruction* (London: Oxford University Press, 1999).

—— *Guerrilla: A Historical and Critical Study* (London: Weidenfield and Nicolson, 1977).

Lockley, R.E.H., 'A Brief Operational History of the Campaign in Rhodesia From 1964 to 1978'; online at <http:www.rhodesianforces.org/Pages/General/A_ Brief_ Operational_History.html> (accessed on 9 August 2005).

Lovett, John, *Contact* (Salisbury, Rhodesia: Galaxie Press, 1977).

Mangold, Tom and Goldberg, Jeff, *Plague Wars* (New York: St Martin's Griffin, 1999).

Manyame-Tazarurwa, Kalister Christine, *Health Implications of Participation in the Liberation Struggle of Zimbabwe by ZANLA Women Ex-Combatants in the ZANLA Operational Areas* (Bloomington, Indiana: AuthorHouse, 2011).

Maravanyika, Silvester Chikerema, Pfukenyi, D.M., Matope, Gift and Bhebhe, E., 'Temporal and spatial distribution of cattle anthrax outbreaks in Zimbabwe between 1967 and 2006', *Tropical Animal Health Prod* 44 (2012), pp.63-70.

Marquardt, Christopher A., 'The Literature of the Zimbabwean Guerrilla War: Themes and Conditions of Production' (M. Lit thesis, St Anthony's College, University of Oxford, 1989).

Marshall, H.H., 'The Legal Effects of U.D.I. (Based on Madzimbamuto v. Lardner-Burke)', *The International and Comparative Law Quarterly* 17 (October 1968), pp.1,022-1,034.

Marston, Roger, 'Not Ordinary White People: The Origins of Rhodesian COIN Theory and Practice', *RUSI* (December 1986), pp.25-32.

Martin, David, 'The Use of Poison and Biological Weapons in the Rhodesian War: Lecture for the University of Zimbabwe War and Strategic Studies Seminar Series' (University of Zimbabwe, 7 July 1993).

Martin, David and Johnson, Phyllis, *The Chitepo Assassination* (Harare, Zimbabwe: Zimbabwe Publishing House, 1985).

—— *The Struggle for Zimbabwe* (London: Faber & Faber Ltd., 1981).

Martinez, Ian, 'The History of the Use of Bacteriological and Chemical Agents During Zimbabwe's Liberation War of 1965-80 by Rhodesian Forces', *Third World Journal* 23 (6), pp.1,159-1,179.

Matope, Tsitsi, '5,000 Bodies Found in War Mass Graves', *The Herald* (Zimbabwe), Wednesday, 7 July 2004.

McAleese, Peter, *No Mean Soldier: The Story of the Ultimate Professional Soldier in the SAS and Other Forces* (London: Orion, 1993).

McCoy, James W., *Parade Grounds of the Dead* (self-published, 2003); online at <http://www.quikmaneuvers.com/parade_grounds_of_dead.html>.

McGregor, JoAnn, 'Containing Violence: Poisoning and Guerrilla/Civilian Relations in the Memories of Zimbabwe's Liberation War' in Rogers, K.L., Leysesdorff, S. and Dawson, G. (eds.), *Trauma and Life Stories: An International Perspective.* (London: Routledge, 1999), pp.131-159.

Merari, Ariel, 'Terrorism as a Strategy of Insurgency', *Terrorism and Political Violence* 5 (Winter 1993), pp.213-251.

Meredith, Martin, *The Past is Another Country: Rhodesia, 1890-1979* (London: Andre Deutsch, 1979).

Mills, Alan, *A Pathologist Remembers: Memoirs of Childhood and Later Life* (Bloomington, Indiana: AuthorHouse, 2013).

Mills, Greg and Wilson, Grahame, 'Who Dares Loses?: Assessing Rhodesia's Counter-Insurgency Experience', *RUSI* 152 (December 2007), pp.22-31.

Minter, William and Schmidt, Elizabeth, 'When Sanctions Worked: The Case of Rhodesia Reexamined', *African Affairs* 87 (April 1988), pp.207-237.

Moorcraft, Paul L., 'Rhodesia's War of Independence', *History Today* (September 1990).

Moorcraft, Paul L. and McLaughlin, Peter, *Chimurenga! The War in Rhodesia 1965-1980* (South Africa: Sygma/Collins, 1982).

—— *Contact II: Struggle for Peace* (Johannesburg, South Africa: Sygma Books, 1981).

—— *A Short Thousand Years: The End of Rhodesia's Rebellion* (Salisbury, Zimbabwe-Rhodesia: Galaxie Press Ltd., 1979).

Mothibe, T.H., 'Zimbabwe: African Working Class Nationalism, 1957-1963', *Zambezia* 23 (1996), pp.157-180.

Mozia, Timothy, 'International Economic Sanctions and Regime Policy Changes (South Africa, Zimbabwe, Iraq, China)' (PhD dissertation, University of Denver, 1998).

Munro, Gordon, *Bush Telegraph* (Johannesburg, South Africa: The Print Factory Ltd., 2002).

Murphy, Philip, 'Exporting a British Intelligence Culture: The British Intelligence Community and Decolonization, 1945-1960'; online at: <http://www.psa.ac.uk/cps/2004/ Murphy.pdf>.

—— 'Creating a Commonwealth Intelligence Culture: The View from Central Africa, 1945-1963', *Intelligence and National Security* 17 (Autumn 2002), pp.131-162.

—— 'Intelligence and Decolonization: The Life and Death of the Federal Intelligence and Security Bureau, 1954-1963', *Journal of Imperial and Commonwealth History* 29 (May 2001), pp.101-130.

Nass, Meryl, 'Anthrax Epizootic in Zimbabwe, 1978-1980: Due to Deliberate Spread?' *Physicians for Social Responsibility Quarterly* 2 (1992), pp.198-209.

Nelson, Harold D., *Area Handbook for Southern Rhodesia* (Washington DC: Government Printing Office, 1975).

Nesbit, Roy and Cowderoy, Dudley, *Britain's Rebel Air Force: The War from the Air in Rhodesia, 1965-1980* (London: Grub Street Publishing, 1998).

Novak, Andrew, 'Face-Saving Maneuvers and Strong Third-Party Mediation: The Lancaster House Conference on Zimbabwe-Rhodesia', *International Negotiation* 14 (2009), pp.149-174.

O'Brien, Kevin A., 'Counter-Intelligence for Counter-Revolutionary Warfare: The South African Police Security Branch, 1979-1990', *Intelligence and National Security* 16 (Autumn 2001), pp.27-59.

—— 'Special Forces for Counter-Revolutionary Warfare: The South African Case', *Small Wars and Insurgencies* 12 (Summer 2001), pp.79-109.

Olden, Mark, 'This Man Has Been Called Zimbabwe's Che Guevara: Did Mugabe Have Him Murdered?' *The New Statesman*, 12 April 2004.

Parker, Jim, *Assignment Selous Scouts: The Inside Story of a Rhodesian Special Branch Officer* (Johannesburg, South Africa: Galago Press, 2006).

Pauw, Jacques, *In the Heart of the Whore: The Story of Apartheid's Death Squads* (Halfway House, South Africa: Southern Book Publishing, 1991).

Petter-Bowyer, P.J.H., *Winds of Destruction* (Victoria, Canada: Trafford Publishing, 2003).

Preston, Matthew, *Ending Civil War: Rhodesia and Lebanon in Perspective* (London: Tauris Academic Studies, 2004).

Purkitt, Helen E. and Burgess, Stephen, 'South Africa's Chemical and Biological Warfare Programme: A Historical and International Perspective', *Journal of Southern African Studies* 28 (June 2002), pp.229-253.

Raeburn, Michael, *We Are Everywhere: Narratives from Rhodesian Guerrillas* (New York: Random House, 1979).

Ranger, Terence, 'Historiography, Patriotic History, and the History of the Nation: The Struggle Over the Past in Zimbabwe', *Journal of Southern African Studies* 30 (June 2004), pp.215-234.

—— 'Afterword: War, Violence, and Healing in Zimbabwe', *Journal of Southern African Studies* 18 (September 1992), pp.698-707.

—— *Peasant Consciousness and Guerrilla War in Zimbabwe* (London: John Currey Ltd., 1985).

—— 'Conflict in Rhodesia – A Question of Evidence', *African Affairs* 77 (January 1978), pp.3-5.

Reagan, Ronald, 'Message to the Senate Transmitting a Protocol to the 1949 Geneva Conventions' (29 January 1987); online at <http://www.reagan.utexas.edu/resource/speeches/1987/012987B.html>.

'Rhodesia – Mzilikaze to Smith', *Africa Institute Bulletin* 15 (1977); online at <http://home.wanadoo.nl/rhodesia/mztosm.html> (accessed on 9 August 2005).

Roberts, Adam, 'Counter-Terrorism, Armed Force, and the Laws of War', *Survival* 44 (Spring 2002), pp.7-32.

Roberts, C.J. and Chambers, P.J., 'An Outbreak of Anthrax in the Mondoro Tribal Trust Lands', *The Central African Journal of Medicine* 21 (April 1975), pp.73-76.

Rotberg, Robert I., 'Searching for a Common Idiom Among African Texts', *Journal of Interdisciplinary History* 24 (Spring 2004), pp.595-599.

Rothchild, Donald, *Managing Ethnic Conflict in Africa: Pressures and Incentives for Cooperation* (Washington DC: Brookings Institution Press, 1997).

Rubenstein, Richard E., *Alchemists of Revolution: Terrorism in the Modern World* (New York: Basic Books Inc., 1987).

Samii, Abbas William, 'The Iranian Nuclear Issue and Informal Networks', *Naval War College Review* 59 (Winter 2006); online at <http://www.nwc.navy.mil/press/Review/ 2006/winter/art3-w06.html> (accessed on 22 June 2006).

Sibanda, Eliakim M., *The Zimbabwe African People's Union, 1961-87: A Political History of the Insurgency in Southern Rhodesia* (Trenton, New Jersey: Africa World Press, Inc., 2005).

Smiley, Xan, 'Zimbabwe, Southern Africa, and the Rise of Robert Mugabe', *Foreign Affairs* 58 (1979-1980), pp.1,060-1,083.

Smith, Ian, *The Great Betrayal: The Memoirs of Africa's Most Controversial Leader* (London: Blake Publishing Ltd., 1997).

Smith, M.L.R., 'Guerrillas in the Mist: Reassessing Strategy and Low Intensity Conflict', *Review of International Studies* 29 (January 2003), pp.19-37.

Soames, Lord, 'From Rhodesia to Zimbabwe', *International Affairs* 56 (Summer 1980), pp.405-419.

Sofaer, Abraham, 'Terrorism and the Law', *Foreign Affairs* 64 (1985), pp.901-922.

Sowers, Thomas S., 'Beyond the Soldier and the State: Contemporary Operations and Variance in Principal-Agent Relationships', *Armed Forces & Society* 31 (Spring 2005), pp.385-409.

Stedman, Stephen John, *Peacemaking in Civil War: International Mediation in Zimbabwe, 1974-1980* (London: Lynne Rienner Publishers, 1991).

Stiff, Peter, *Warfare by Other Means: South Africa in the 1980s and 1990s* (Johannesburg, South Africa: Galago Publishing, 2001).

—— *The Silent War: South African Recce Operations, 1969-1994* (Johannesburg, South Africa: Galago Publishing, 1999).

—— *Selous Scouts Top Secret War – Ron Reid Daly as told to Peter Stiff* (Alberton, South Africa: Galago Publishing, 1982).

—— *See You in November* (Johannesburg, South Africa: Galago Publishing, 1985).

—— *Selous Scouts: A Pictorial Account* (Alberto, South Africa: Galago Publishing, 1984).

Stillman, Peter G., 'The Changing Meaning of Terrorism', *Perspectives on Evil and Human Wickedness* 1 (2). (See <http:www.wickedness.net>.)

Timmereck, Thomas C., *An Introduction to Epidemiology*, 2nd edition (Sudbury, MA: Jones and Bartlett Publishers, 1998).

Tucker, Jonathan B., *War of Nerves: Chemical Warfare From World War I to Al-Qaeda* (New York: Pantheon Books, 2006).

Ullman, Richard H., 'Salvaging America's Rhodesian Policy', *Foreign Affairs* 57 (1978-1979), pp.1,111-1,122.

Waldron, Jeremy, 'Terrorism and the Uses of Terror', *The Journal of Ethics* 8 (2004), pp.5-35.

Walzer, Michael, *Just and Unjust Wars: A Moral Argument with Historical Illustrations* (New York: Basic Books Inc., 1977).

Weinrich, A.K.H., Strategic Resettlement in Rhodesia', *Journal of Southern African Studies* 3 (April 1977), pp.207-229.

Weitzer, Ronald, *Transforming Settler States: Communal Conflict and Internal Security in Northern Ireland and Zimbabwe* (Berkeley: University of California Press, 1990); online at <http://ark.cdlib.org/ark:/13030/ft2199n7jp/> (accessed on 22 April 2012).

Wessels, Hannes, *PK van der Byl: African Statesman* (Johannesburg, South Africa: 30° South Publishers, 2010).

White, Luise, 'Precarious Conditions: A Note on Counter-Insurgency in Africa After 1945', *Gender & History* 16 (November 2004), pp.603-625.

—— 'Poisoned Food, Poisoned Uniforms, and Anthrax', *OSIRIS* 19 (2004), pp.220-233.

—— *The Assassination of Herbert Chitepo: Texts and Politics in Zimbabwe* (Bloomington, Indiana: Indiana University Press, 2003).

—— 'Telling More: Lies, Secrets, and History', *History and Theory* (December 2000), pp.11-22.

Wilkenson, A.R., 'The Impact of the War', *The Journal of Commonwealth and Comparative Politics* (March 1980), pp.110-123.

—— 'Insurgency in Rhodesia, 1957-1973', *Adelphi Paper No. 100* (London: International Institute for Strategic Studies, 1973); online at http://home.wanadoo.nl/rhodesia/wilkinson.html (accessed on 8 August 2005).

Wood, J.R.T., *The War Diaries of Andre Dennison* (Gibraltar: Ashanti Publishing Ltd., 1989).

—— 'Rhodesian Insurgency' (accessed at <http://home.wanadoo.nl/rhodesia/wood2.html on 20 November 2004>).

—— 'There Never Was Enough Intelligence: The Role of Intelligence in the Rhodesian Counter-Insurgency Campaign, 1962-1980' (nd).

Wylie, Dan, *Dead Leaves: Two Years in the Rhodesian War* (Pietermaritzburg, South Africa: University of Natal Press, 2002).

Zanders, Jean Pascal, 'A Verification and Transparency Concept for Technology Transfers under the BTWC', paper no.26 commissioned by the Weapons of Mass

Destruction Commission (Stockholm, Sweden), 17 December 2004; online at <http://www.wmdcommission.org/files/No26.pdf> (accessed on 22 June 2006).

—— 'Assessing the Risk of Chemical and Biological Weapons Proliferation to Terrorists', *The Nonproliferation Review* (Fall 1999), pp.17-34.

Audio/Visual Materials

Ken Flower interview: Ken Flower served as the head of the Rhodesian Central Intelligence Organisation (CIO) during the crucial war years of the late 1960s and 1970s. DVD format. Produced by Memories of Rhodesia Inc. Running time: 52 minutes.

The Warriors of Rhodesia: *'Rhodesia at War'*, Volume 1. It contains clips related to Rhodesian military and police units. DVD format. Produced by Memories of Rhodesia Inc. Running time: 100+ minutes.

The War Years: *'Rhodesia at War'*, Volume 2. It contains eight clips covering the Rhodesian War. DVD format. Produced by Memories of Rhodesia Inc. Running time: 100+ minutes.

Pamberi Ne Zimbabwe: *'The Winds of Change'*, Volume 1. DVD format. Produced by Memories of Rhodesia Inc. Running time: 129 minutes.

Chimurenga: *'The Winds of Change'*, Volume 2. DVD format. Produced by Memories of Rhodesia Inc. Running time: 100+ minutes.

From Rhodesia To Zimbabwe: *'The Winds of Change'*, Volume 3. DVD format. Produced by Memories of Rhodesia Inc. Running time: 100+ minutes.

'Rebellion!': A three-part television documentary series produced by the British Broadcasting Corporation (BBC). The series featured interviews with former Rhodesian Prime Minister Ian Smith; former members of the Rhodesian Cabinet; former Zimbabwe-Rhodesia Prime Minister Abel Muzorewa; General Peter Walls; General John Hickman; Colonel Ron Reid-Daly; Zimbabwean President Robert Mugabe; former ZANU head The Rev Ndabaningi Sithole; former ZAPU head Joshua Nkomo; senior ZANLA and ZIPRA military commanders and political commissars; former US Secretary of State Henry Kissinger; former South African Foreign Minister Pik Botha; former UK Foreign Secretary Lord Carrington; and British Foreign Office officials and diplomats.

Index

INDEX OF PEOPLE

INDEX OF PLACES

INDEX OF MILITARY, SECURITY AND PARA-MILITARY FORMATIONS AND TERMS

INDEX OF CHEMICAL AGENTS AND DISEASES

INDEX OF GENERAL AND MISCELLANEOUS TERMS

Lightning Source UK Ltd.
Milton Keynes UK
UKOW05f0741130417
299009UK00003B/60/P